JAVA 1.2

In Record Time

JAVA™ 1.2

In Record Time™

Steven Holzner

SYBEX®

San Francisco • Paris • Düsseldorf • Soest

Associate Publisher: Gary Masters
Contracts and Licensing Manager: Kristine Plachy
Acquisitions & Developmental Editors: Suzanne Rotondo and
Maureen Adams
Editors: Alison Moncrieff and Shelby Zimmerman
Technical Editor: Kirky Ringer
Book Designers: Franz Baumhackl, Patrick Dintino, Catalin Dulfu
Graphic Illustrator: Tony Jonick
Electronic Publishing Specialist: Robin Kibby
Production Coordinator: Susan Berge
Indexer: Ted Laux
Companion CD: Ginger Warner
Cover Designer: Design Site
Cover Photographer: Adri Berger/Tony Stone Images

Screen reproductions produced with Collage Complete.
Collage Complete is a trademark of Inner Media Inc.

SYBEX is a registered trademark of SYBEX Inc.

In Record Time is a trademark of SYBEX Inc.

TRADEMARKS: SYBEX has attempted throughout this book to
distinguish proprietary trademarks from descriptive terms by
following the capitalization style used by the manufacturer.

The author and publisher have made their best efforts to prepare
this book, and the content is based upon final release software
whenever possible. Portions of the manuscript may be based
upon pre-release versions supplied by software manufacturer(s).
The author and the publisher make no representation or war-
ranties of any kind with regard to the completeness or accuracy of
the contents herein and accept no liability of any kind including
but not limited to performance, merchantability, fitness for any
particular purpose, or any losses or damages of any kind caused
or alleged to be caused directly or indirectly from this book.

Library of Congress Card Number: 98-85539
ISBN: 0-7821-2171-3

Manufactured in the United States of America

10 9 8 7 6 5 4 3 2 1

To Tamsen Conner, future computer genius.
(You can just tell.)

Acknowledgments

Any book is a collaborative effort. Many people helped me along the way. Of course, there is not space to thank everyone who made contributions to this book. Certain people stand out as having made a difference.

In particular, I would like to thank Alison Moncrieff, Shelby Zimmerman, Kirky Ringer, Suzanne Rotondo, Maureen Adams, Tony Jonick, Susan Berge, Robin Kibby, and Ted Laux. These people made specific contributions to my book, from the concept to working through the physical pages. Many thanks for all the hours you've contributed—thanks to you all!

Contents at a Glance

Introduction   *xvii*

skills

  1 Building the First Java Examples   1
  2 Handling Java Text Fields   27
  3 Using Java Buttons   41
  4 Using Java Layouts and Check Boxes   73
  5 Working with Radio Buttons   107
  6 Adding Scroll Bars   139
  7 Using Choice Controls and Scrolling Lists   167
  8 Creating Windows and Menus   197
  9 Constructing Java Dialog Boxes   249
10 Java Graphics!   277
11 Displaying and Stretching Images   337
12 Swing and Java 2D   357
13 Setting and Modifying Text and Fonts   395
14 Understanding Graphics Animation   425
15 More Graphics Animation Power   453
16 Working with Multi-Threaded Programs and JAR Files   493
    Glossary   527

Index   *533*

Table of Contents

Introduction   *xvii*

Skill 1 Building the First Java Examples   **1**
    Building the Hello Example   2
      What's an Applet?   2
      Creating the Hello Example   3
    Setting Up the Java JDK   5
      What's New in 1.2?   5
      Compiling the Hello Applet   10
    Understanding Java   11
      Running the Hello Applet   11
      Understanding the Hello Example   13
    Object-Oriented Programming   14
      Understanding Java Objects   14
      What's a Java Class?   14
      Learning about Java Packages   16
      Understanding Java Inheritance   16
      What Are Java Access Modifiers?   18
      Understanding the Applet's Web Page   20
    Connecting Java and HTML   21
    Are You up to Speed?   25

Skill 2 Handling Java Text Fields   **27**
    Declaring a Text Field   29
    Initializing with the `init()` Method   33
    Handling Memory with the `new` Operator   34
    What Are Java Constructors?   35
    Overloading Java Methods   36
    Are You up to Speed?   40

Skill 3 Using Java Buttons   **41**
    Working with Buttons in Java   42
      Adding a Button to a Program   44
      What Are Java Events?   46

The this Keyword   48
Using Button Events   49
How to Handle Multiple Buttons   56
Creating clickers.java   57
Making clickers.java Work   59
Handling Java Text Areas   64
Creating txtarea.java   65
Making txtarea.java Work   67
Are You up to Speed?   71

Skill 4   Using Java Layouts and Check Boxes   73
What Is a Java Layout?   74
Building the Adder Applet   74
The Label Control   76
Adding a Java Label Control   78
Writing the Adder Applet   80
Reading Numeric Data from Text Fields   82
Putting Numeric Data into Text Fields   83
Working with the Java Grid Layout   87
Using the GridLayout Manager   88
Adding a GridLayout Manager   90
Building Programs with Check Boxes   94
Are You up to Speed?   105

Skill 5   Working with Radio Buttons   107
Building Programs with Radio Buttons   108
The Radios Applet   109
Connecting Check Boxes to a CheckBoxGroup   111
Building Programs with Panels   117
Creating a Panel   118
Putting Check Boxes and Radio Buttons Together   123
Creating the Menu Panel   126
Creating the Ingredients Panel   127
Adding Panels to the sandwich Class   128
Connecting the Buttons in Code   130
Are You up to Speed?   137

Skill 6   Adding Scroll Bars   139
Adding Scroll Bars to Programs   140
Installing Scroll Bars   143
Connecting Scroll Bars to Code   145

Using Scroll Bars and BorderLayouts 151
Working with the `ScrollPane` Class 161
Are You up to Speed? 165

Skill 7   Using Choice Controls and Scrolling Lists   167
Using `Choice` Controls 168
Using Scrolling Lists 177
Using the GridBagLayout Manager 185
Using GridBagConstraints 187
Are You up to Speed? 196

Skill 8   Creating Windows and Menus   197
Handling Java Windows 198
Using Menus 207
Building Full Menus 226
  Adding a Menu Separator 231
  Check Box Menu Items 232
  Incorporating Submenus 233
  Adding an Exit Item to a Menu 234
  Activating Our New Menu Items 235
Popup Menus 240
Are You up to Speed? 247

Skill 9   Constructing Java Dialog Boxes   249
Using Dialog Boxes 250
  Creating a Dialog Box 256
Building a Popup Calculator 263
Are You up to Speed? 276

Skill 10   Java Graphics!   277
Using the Mouse 278
  Using `MouseListener` 281
  Using `mousePressed()` 281
  Using `mouseClicked()` 285
  Using `mouseReleased()` 286
  Using `mouseEntered()` 288
  Using `mouseExited()` 290
The Dauber Applet 294
  Creating Dauber's Drawing Tools 295
  Creating Dauber's Boolean Flags 297

Drawing in the Dauber Applet   300
Using mousePressed() in Dauber   301
Adding MouseListener Support to Dauber   302
Using mouseReleased() in Dauber   304
Drawing Lines in Dauber   305
Creating Circles and Ovals in Dauber   310
Using Dauber to Draw Rectangles   316
Drawing 3D Rectangles in Dauber   318
Drawing Rounded Rectangles in Dauber   318
Dauber and Freehand Drawing   320
Printing from Java   332
Java Security   332
Java Applications   334
Are You up to Speed?   336

Skill 11 Displaying and Stretching Images   **337**
The Imagesizer Applet   338
Displaying Images in Java   344
Using Image Maps   348
Checking an Image Map's Hotspots   350
The Java URL Class   352
Are You up to Speed?   355

Skill 12 Swing and Java 2D   **357**
The Swing Package   358
Using Swing Buttons   358
Using Swing Combo Boxes   364
Using Swing Sliders   371
Using Swing Toolbars   377
Designing the Command Action Listener Class   380
Using Java 2D   384
Defining Shapes with GeneralPath   387
Moving and Rotating with Transforms   388
Are You up to Speed?   393

Skill 13 Setting and Modifying Text and Fonts   **395**
Creating the Scribbler Applet   396
Working with the Keyboard   403
Working with Fonts   405

Working with the FontMetrics Class   412
   Getting the Width of a Text String   414
   Centering Displayed Text   414
Using the Clipboard from Java   420
Are You up to Speed?   424

Skill 14 Understanding Graphics Animation   **425**
Creating Basic Animation   427
Your First True Animation   433
Working with Multi-Threading   435
   Handling the start() Method   436
   Handling the stop() Method   440
   Handling the run() Method   441
Eliminating Screen Flicker   445
   Stopping Java from Clearing an Applet's Display   445
   Restricting Drawing to a Section of the Applet   447
The Animator Class   449
Are You up to Speed?   451

Skill 15 More Graphics Animation Power   **453**
Working with Double Buffering   454
   Drawing in Images Stored in Memory   456
   Implementing the run() Method   458
Updating the Dauber Applet   463
   Updating the Dauber paint() Method   468
   Setting the XOR Mode   469
Using the Card Layout for Animation   479
   Showing a Card with the Card Layout Manager   483
   Animating Control Panels   484
Are You up to Speed?   491

Skill 16 Working with Multi-Threaded Programs and JAR Files **493**
Creating Thread Objects   494
   Using the Java Thread Class   495
Working with the Runnable Interface   498
Controlling Threads and Setting Priority   500
Suspending and Resuming Threads   501
Handling Multiple Threads   508
   Implementing the run() Method   511
   Naming Java Threads   511

Setting Up Thread Synchronization 515
Synchronizing Functions 518
Synchronizing Code Blocks 521
Fast Downloading: JAR Files 523
Are You up to Speed? 525

Glossary **527**

Index *533*

Introduction

Java is very, very popular right now, and no wonder: Java has transformed the Web and Web programming in many ways. Java makes your Web pages come alive, displaying buttons, menus, images, and animation. Because you can program for many different types of computers using Java, Java applications have also become very popular. And now that Java has arrived in its new 1.2 version, it's even more popular than before. As more and more Web browsers become Java-enabled, as more and more computers support Java, its popularity continues to spread.

Why Use Java?

Although it's possible to create Web pages without Java, they just can't compare to Java pages. Rather than have static images, why not have something that *moves*? Rather than have text that doesn't change, why not allow the user to enter their own text? There's nothing like an interactive Web page to get the attention of casual Web surfers.

Java is coming into its own as a programming language for non-Web applications as well. This is because it's a very powerful cross-platform language, allowing you to develop programs on one computer type and run them on many others. In today's world, that's a strong reason to use Java. Java 1.2 allows you many powerful options, from popup menus to using the clipboard to JAR files, from the Java Foundation Classes (JFC) to using the Java 2D graphics rendering system. We're going to explore them all in this book.

How This Book Is Organized

Our emphasis in this book will be seeing Java 1.2 at work and giving you the skills needed to use it effectively. If you want to get something from a programming book, there's nothing like seeing working code. Many programming books start off with abstractions, programming constructs, and theory; but here you will look at Java not as an end in itself but as a tool for creating programs you are interested in.

In this book, you'll see things from a different point of view—the getting things done point of view. Instead of chapters named "If Statements," "Java Modifiers," or "Abstract Java Classes," each unit in this book teaches a specific skill, such as "Check Boxes," "Radio Buttons," "Menus," and "Graphics Animation." You'll put Java to work creating the programs you want.

You'll work through plenty of bite-sized examples because trying to learn Java without running it is like trying to learn to fly by reading an airplane parts manual. These examples will be short and to the point, covering topics such as:

Text fields and text areas	JAR files
Popup calculators	Radio buttons and check boxes
The Java ScrollPane class	Printing
Popup menus	The system clipboard
Scroll bars and scrolling lists	The Java delegated event model
Employee databases	Image maps
Menus	Popup windows
Popup dialog boxes	Layouts
Java Swing (Java Foundation Classes)	Java 2D graphics system
Panels	Buttons
Navigating to other URLs	Multi-threading
Mouse-driven paint programming	Mouse-driven image resizing
Accessing the keyboard directly	Fonts
Graphics animation	The Sun Animator class

The plan, then, is to put Java to work for you, using all its power and classes in the process of creating working Java programs. Java has a great deal to offer, and you'll see just about all of it in this book, from creating Java applets to creating Java applications; from creating new dialog boxes to printing directly from a program. Java provides a great many tools, and you'll use them fully as you create the programs in this book.

Look What's on the CD and Beyond!

The code you'll use in this book will also appear on the CD-ROM, which means that you don't have to type anything in as you work through the examples. It's all there on the CD-ROM. You'll find the `.java` files, which hold the source code for the programs, and the `.class` files, which are ready to run. To install the files on your hard disk, see the `readme.txt` file in the CD-ROM's root directory.

This book also has a companion Web site. You can reach the site by clicking the hotlink on the CD, or you can point your Web browser to www.sybex.com. On the Web site, you'll find links to companies that provide shareware, demos, and other utilities you can use with Java 1.2.

Conventions Used in This Book

The examples in this book will be built incrementally; when you add a new line or lines of code, the new lines will be indicated with arrows, like this:

```
        drawbutton = new Button("Draw freehand");
        linebutton = new Button("Draw a line");
➜       ovalbutton = new Button("Draw an oval");
➜       rectbutton = new Button("Draw a rectangle");
➜       roundedbutton = new Button("Draw a rounded rectangle");
```

Some of the lines of code will be followed by continuation arrows (➡). This means that the entire line of code would not fit on one line in the text. The line of code after the continuation arrow should be written on the same line as the code preceding the continuation arrow when you write your code. For example, this should be written as one line of code:

```
        ptDrawTo = new Point(Math.max(ptAnchor.x, ptDrawTo.x), ➡
Math.max(ptAnchor.y, ptDrawTo.y));
```

You'll also find complete code listings for programs marked by code listing headings to let you know the code is available on the CD.

Throughout the book, Notes, Tips, and Warnings appear to give you extra insight.

 **NOTE**   Notes indicate points of special concern such as why working with the mouse one way instead of another is important at a particular time, or what you can do with one Web browser in Java that you can't with another.

TIP   Tips are written to save you time or to point out additional helpful information, such as a programming shortcut.

 **WARNING**   A Warning tells you about common programming errors or other potential mix-ups you should watch out for.

What You'll Need

Although Java is an object-oriented language, you don't need to have object-oriented programming experience to use this book. If you do have experience with an object-oriented programming language, there's still a lot to learn from this book.

You'll need an editor or word processor, such as Microsoft WordPad, to enter your Java programs into files you can compile and run. Your editor or word processor must be able to save files in simple text format.

And, of course, to use your completed Java programs on the Web, you should have a place to host your Web pages. Although Java can produce stand-alone applications, the majority of Java programmers target the Web in their Java development. In Skill 1, you'll learn how to embed Java applets in a Web page.

Your Internet service provider should be able to instruct you on how to upload your applets so you can use them in your Web pages. Usually you need to find out where to install your Web pages and applets (what directory in the ISP computer), and then you can use a File Transfer Protocol (FTP) program to upload your files to that directory.

You can find more information about Java on the Internet. Some resources include Sun's Java site, `http://www.javasoft.com` and `http://www.javasoft.com/doc`. You can also check out the Usenet group `comp.lang.java.programmer`. For updates to this book, visit the Sybex site, `http://www.sybex.com`.

SKILL 1

Building the First Java Examples

- Installing the JDK 1.2
- Using the Java applet viewer
- Creating Java applets
- Customizing applets
- Doing object-oriented programming
- Connecting Java and HTML

Welcome to Java 1.2! An ambitious agenda lies before you: You're going to get a firm grip on Java programming, creating both powerful Java programs and Web pages, and you will take a guided tour through Java 1.2. There is no more exciting programming package available. As you are probably aware, the popularity of Java has skyrocketed as more and more people have seen how versatile and powerful it is. Web programmers have found it an excellent tool because it allows them to write programs that will run on many different types of computers. They have started using it to make their Web pages actually *do* something.

With Java, you will be able to display animation and images, accept mouse clicks and text, use controls like scrollbars and check boxes, print graphics, support popup menus, and even support additional windows and menu bars.

Each of the skills in this book is specially set up to cover a Java skill, and you'll see plenty of bite-sized examples as you learn how to handle Java in depth. Other books might have only a few examples, partial examples, or examples that are too long to deal with comfortably; this book's examples will be plentiful and small enough to target a single skill.

You'll start working on your Java skills right away—no chapters full of abstractions to wade through first. We will concentrate on examples, on seeing things from the programmer's point of view—on seeing Java at *work*.

Java programs come two ways: as stand-alone applications and as small programs you can embed in Web pages, called *applets*. Of the two, applets are the most popular, and we'll concentrate primarily on them.

Building the Hello Example

The first example will be a simple one because right now we just want to get you started in Java without too many extra details to weigh you down. You will create a small Java applet, the type of Java program you can embed in a Web page, that will display the words, "Hello from Java!"

What's an Applet?

Just what do I mean by an applet? An applet is a special program that you can embed in a Web page such that the applet gains control over a certain part of the Web page. On that part of the page, the applet can display buttons, list boxes, images, and more. Applets make Web pages "come alive."

Each applet is given the amount of space (usually measured in pixels) that it requests in a Web page, such as the amount of space shown in Figure 1.1. (Soon I'll show you how an applet "requests" space.) This is the space that the applet will use for its display. We'll place the words "Hello from Java!" in the applet, as shown in Figure 1.2.

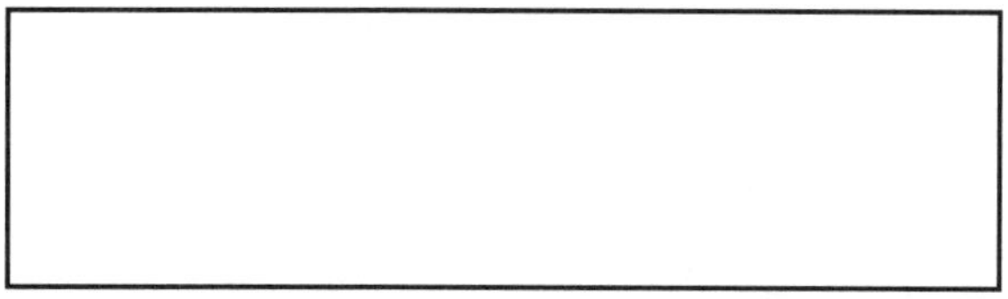

FIGURE 1.1:   An applet requests space in a Web page.

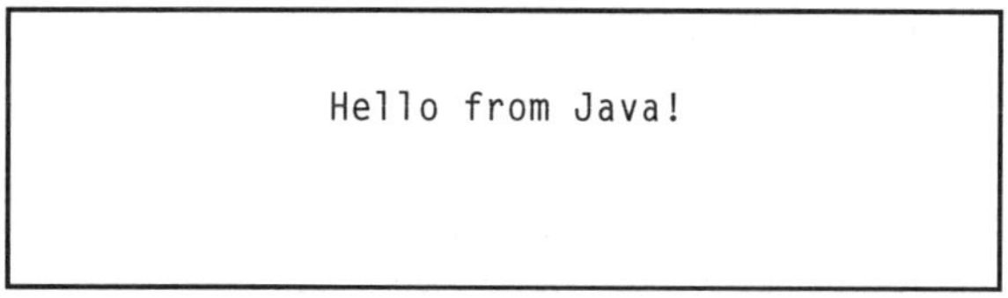

```
Hello from Java!
```

FIGURE 1.2:   Hello from Java!

That's how this applet will work; after you create it, you will be able to embed it in a Web page. Let's create and run the applet now.

Creating the Hello Example

Let's call this first applet *hello*. You will store the actual Java code (the lines of text that make up the program) for this applet in the file hello.java. You'll need an editor of some kind to create this file (such as Windows Wordpad or notepad). You will be creating .java files throughout the book, so use an editor you are comfortable with. Also notice that, if you are going to use a word processor like Microsoft Word, you'll have to save your .java files as straight text—something you can type out at the DOS prompt and read directly. Check your word processor's Save As menu item or your word processor's documentation to see how to do this. The Sun Java system won't be able to handle anything but straight text files. Now, type the following text into the file `hello.java` (this is the traditional first program in most java books):

```
import java.awt.Graphics;
public class hello extends java.applet.Applet
{
    public void paint(Graphics g)
    {
        g.drawString("Hello from Java!", 60, 30 );
    }
}
```

This is the text of your first Java program, and soon you'll see what each line means. Having typed in the text, save it to disk as `hello.java`.

NOTE   Note that case counts here—make sure you type hello.java, not Hello.java or hello.Java.

In general, the name of the file will match exactly (including case) the name given in the "class" statement in the file; in this case, that is `hello`:

```
import java.awt.Graphics;

→public class hello extends java.applet.Applet
{
    public void paint( Graphics g )
    {
        g.drawString("Hello from Java!", 60, 30 );
    }
}
```

In this book, you will place your programs into subdirectories of a new directory called `java1-2` (this is optional—you can choose any name). That means you'll save the `hello.java` file as `c:\java1-2\hello\hello.java`.

Now you have created `hello.java`. This is the source code for your applet, and it contains the Java code that you have written. The next step is to compile this Java code into a working applet and see your applet at work. Applets have the extension `.class`, making the name of your actual applet `hello.class`. I'll show you *why* applets have the extension `.class` shortly.

Setting Up the Java JDK

Now you'll use Java itself to create your applet, `hello.class`, from the code, `hello.java`. If you haven't already done so, you should install the Java Development Kit (JDK) 1.2. It's on the CD that came with this book.

With previous versions of Java, you used to have to go through a rather lengthy and involved installation process, but that's all changed now—you just have to run an `.EXE` file. You get this `.EXE` file online, from `http://developer.javasoft.com` —just download it and follow the instructions for installation.

The next step is to make sure you can run the JDK from any location in your computer (including the `c:\java1-2` directory and its subdirectories, which is where you'll put your Java programs). To do that, make sure the PATH statement in your AUTOEXEC.BAT file (found in the main directory of the c: drive) includes the JDK BIN and LIB directories (here I have installed the JDK in `c:\jdk12`—use whatever path is appropriate to the way you have installed the JDK):

```
PATH=C:\WINDOWS;C:\JDK12\JAVA\BIN;C:\JDK12\JAVA\LIB
```

The JDK 1.2 is ready to go.

TIP If you need more help installing the JDK, check out the Troubleshooting Web page at `http://www.javasoft.com`.

You can copy the Java documentation from JavaSoft to the same directory—for example, `c:\JDK12`. Unzip the documentation `.zip` file, creating a `docs` subdirectory (your unzipping program must be able to handle long filenames).

NOTE You'll need a Web browser to look at the Java documentation because it's formatted in HTML.

Now that you've installed Java 1.2, let's take a look at what's new in this version of Java.

What's New in 1.2?

If you're familiar with Java 1.0 or Java 1.1, then you'd probably expect there to be some changes in Java 1.2, and you'd be right. Let's get an overview of the changes in this new edition of Java. If you're not familiar with Java, you should probably skip to the next section and take a look at this material later—much of this won't make any sense unless you've programmed in Java before.

From Java 1.0 to Java 1.1

Many readers will be familiar with Java 1.0, not Java 1.1, so we will start by looking at the changes from Java 1.0 to Java 1.1,

Abstract Windowing Toolkit enhancements   Java 1.1 supports printing, faster scrolling, popup menus, the clipboard, a delegation-based event model, imaging and graphics enhancements, and more. In addition, it's faster than Java 1.0 (something Java programmers can definitely appreciate)!

.jar files   .jar (Java Archive) files were introduced in Java 1.1 and let you package a number of files together, zipping them to shrink them, so the user can download many files at once. You can put many applets and the data they need together into one .jar file, making downloading much faster. These files are analogous to .zip files except that your browser will download them and unzip them on-the-fly for you.

Internationalization   Java 1.1 lets you develop *locale-specific applets*, including using UNICODE characters, a locale mechanism, localized message support, locale-sensitive date, time, time zone, number handling, and more.

Signed applets and digital signatures   Java 1.1 can create digitally signed Java applications. A digital signature gives your users a "path" back to you in case something goes wrong. This is part of the new security precautions popular on the World Wide Web.

Remote method invocation   In Java 1.1 RMI lets Java objects have their methods invoked from Java code running in other Java sessions. This is sort of similar to Local Remote Procedure Calls (LRPCs).

Object serialization   Serialization was new in Java 1.1, and it lets you store objects and handle them with binary input/output streams. Besides allowing you to store copies of the objects you serialize, serialization is also the basis of communication between objects engaged in RMI. Object serialization is similar to MFC Serialization, for those who are familiar with Microsoft's Foundation Classes.

Reflection   In Java 1.1 reflection lets Java code examine information about the methods and constructors of loaded classes and make use of those reflected methods and constructors.

Inner classes   Java 1.1 makes it easier to create adapter classes. An adapter class is a class that implements an interface required by an API (Applications Programming Interface). An adapter class "delegates" control back to an enclosing main object.

New Java native method interface   Native code is code that is written specifically for a particular machine. In Java 1.1 this interface was introduced to provide a standard programming interface for writing Java native methods. The primary goal is binary compatibility of native method libraries across all Java virtual machine implementations on a given platform. Writing and calling native code can significantly improve execution speeds. Java 1.1 included a powerful new Java native method interface.

Byte, Short, and Void classes   In Java 1.1 Byte and short values can be handled as "wrapped" numbers when you use the new Java classes Byte and Short. The new Void class is a placeholder class that we can derive classes from, rather than use directly.

Deprecated methods   Quite a number of Java 1.0 methods were considered obsolete in Java 1.1, and they are marked as deprecated in the Java 1.1 documentation. (The Java compiler now displays a warning when it compiles code that uses a deprecated feature.)

Networking enhancements   Networking enhancements in Java 1.1 included support for selected BSD-style socket options in the java.net base classes. With Java 1.1, Socket and ServerSocket are non-final, extendable classes. New subclasses of SocketException were added for finer granularity in reporting and handling network errors.

I/O enhancements   In Java 1.1, the I/O package was extended with character streams, which are like byte streams except that they contain 16-bit Unicode characters rather than eight-bit bytes. Character streams make it easy to write programs that are independent of a specific character encoding and are therefore easier to internationalize. Nearly all of the functionality available for byte streams is also available for character streams.

That completes this overview of what's new in Java 1.1—if you have no idea what I'm talking about, don't worry, it'll become clear later.

From Java 1.1 to Java 1.2

Now let's have a look at what's new in Java 1.2.

Security Enhancements   Now when code is loaded, it is assigned permissions based on the security policy currently in effect. Each permission specifies a permitted access to a particular resource (such as "read" and "write" access to a specified file or directory, "connect" access to a given host and port, and so on). The policy, specifying which permissions are available for code from various signers/locations, can be initialized from an external configurable policy file. Unless a permission is explicitly granted to code, it cannot access the resource that is guarded by that permission.

Swing (JFC)   Swing is the part of the Java Foundation Classes (JFC) that implements a new set of GUI components with a "pluggable" look and feel. Swing is implemented in pure Java, and is based on the JDK 1.1 Lightweight UI Framework. The pluggable look and feel lets you design a single set of GUI components that can automatically have the look and feel of any platform (e.g., Windows, Solaris, Macintosh).

Java 2D (JFC)   The Java 2D API is a set of classes for advanced 2D graphics and imaging. It encompasses line art, text, and images in a single comprehensive model.

Accessibility (JFC)   Through the Java Accessibility API, developers will be able to create Java applications that can interact with assistive technologies such as screen readers, speech recognition systems, and Braille terminals.

Drag and Drop (JFC)   Drag and Drop enables data transfer across both Java and native applications, between Java applications, and within a single Java application.

Collections   The Java Collections API is a unified framework for representing and manipulating Java collections (I'll show you more about them later), allowing them to be manipulated independent of the details of their representation.

Java Extensions   Framework Extensions are packages of Java classes (and any associated native code) that application developers can use to extend the core platform. The extension mechanism allows the Java virtual machine (VM) to use the extension classes in much the same way it uses the system classes.

JavaBeans Enhancements Java 1.2 provides developers with standard means to create more sophisticated JavaBeans components and applications that offer their customers more seamless integration with the rest of their runtime environment, such as the desktop of the underlying operating system or the browser.

Input Method Framework The input method framework enables all text editing components to receive Japanese, Chinese, or Korean text input through standard input methods.

Package Version Identification "Versioning" introduces package level version control where applications and applets can identify (at runtime) the version of a specific Java Runtime Environment, VM, and class package.

RMI Enhancements Remote Method Invocation (RMI) has several new enhancements including Remote Object Activation, which introduces support for remote objects and automatic object activation, as well as Custom Socket Types that allow a remote object to specify the custom socket type that RMI will use for remote calls to that object. (RMI over a secure transport (such as SSL) can be supported using custom socket types.)

Serialization Enhancements Serialization now includes an API that allows the serialized data of an object to be specified independently of the fields of the class. This allows serialized data fields to be written to and read from the stream using the existing techniques (this ensures compatibility with the default writing and reading mechanisms).

Reference Objects A reference object encapsulates a reference to some other object so that the reference itself may be examined and manipulated like any other object. Reference objects allow a program to maintain a reference to an object that does not prevent the object from being reclaimed by the Java "garbage collector," which manages memory.

Audio Enhancements Audio enhancements include a new sound engine and support for audio in applications as well as applets.

Java IDL Java IDL adds CORBA (Common Object Request Broker Architecture) capability to Java, providing standards-based interoperability and connectivity. Java IDL enables distributed Web-enabled Java applications to invoke operations transparently on remote network services using the industry standard OMG IDL (Object Management Group Interface Definition Language) and IIOP (Internet Inter-ORB Protocol) defined by the Object Management Group.

JAR Enhancements   The enhancements include added functionality for the command-line JAR tool for creating and updating signed JAR files. There are also new standard APIs for reading and writing JAR files.

JNI Enhancements   The Java Native Interface is a standard programming interface for writing Java native methods and embedding the Java virtual machine into native applications. The primary goal is binary compatibility of native method libraries across all Java virtual machine implementations on a given platform. Java 1.2 extends the Java Native Interface (JNI) to incorporate new features in the Java platform.

JVMDI   A New Debugger Interface, the Java Virtual Machine, now provides low level services for debugging. The interface for these services is the Java Virtual Machine Debugger Interface (JVMDI).

JDBC Enhancements   Java Database Connectivity (JDBC) is a standard SQL database access interface, providing uniform access to a wide range of relational databases. JDBC also provides a common base on which higher level tools and interfaces can be built. The Java 1.2 software bundle includes JDBC and the JDBC-ODBC bridge.

These concepts will become clearer as we proceed. Now, you're ready to compile the hello applet and see it at work.

Compiling the Hello Applet

Now that you have installed the JDK and have your `hello.java` file ready to go, you can create the actual applet and see it run. To do this, move to the `c:\java1-2\hello` directory now (or wherever you have placed `hello.java`); this is how the DOS prompt should look:

```
c:\java1-2\hello>
```

Next, type this to create your applet:

```
c:\java1-2\hello>javac hello.java
```

The name of the Java program that takes your Java code and turns it into `.class` files ready to run in Web pages is called `javac.exe`, the Java *compiler* (i.e., it compiles `.java` files into `.class` files). If you type the DOS command `Dir` to look at the current directory contents, you should see both `hello.java` and `hello.class`. Because you've created `hello.class`, your applet is ready to go—but what does that mean? What have you really done?

Understanding Java

Let's take the time now to get an overview of Java. As in most programming languages, we write Java code using words and numbers that are then translated—that is, *compiled*—into binary files that computers can understand. The `hello.java` program is an example of this—you write it such that you can understand it, but when you want to actually run your program, you have to compile it into something a computer can use. In this case, that means using the Java *compiler* to produce the file named `hello.class`. `hello.class` is a binary file of *bytecodes* that Java-compatible Web browsers can run to produce the desired result. In this way, several lines of Java program code can be compiled neatly into a few bytes. Those bytes are what is actually downloaded when Web browsers read the Web page in which you have placed your Java applets—that is to say, the actual applet is a `.class` file, like `hello.class`, and those are the files you place on your Internet Service Provider's server so other people's Web browsers can download them, as you'll see very shortly.

TIP   Later, I'll show you how to use `.jar` files—Java Archive files—to zip up `.class` files even smaller, packing many of them into a single downloadable file.

Experienced programmers may wonder about these bytecodes—why isn't Java simply compiled into the normal machine code that each computer really runs? Because Java bytecodes were intentionally made machine-independent so that they could be run on a wide variety of machines, and that is what originally made them so popular on the Internet—it doesn't matter what type of machine you're downloading to, as long as the user's Web browser can run Java. The downloaded bytecodes are run by the *Java Virtual Machine*, or JVM, and it is the JVM's task to convert bytecodes into the machine language that users' individual computers can run.

The JVM is actually a hypothetical chip that runs Java—it is almost always software, not hardware, that runs Java. Each Web browser that supports Java has a JVM built right into it, and it loads the `.class` file that makes up your applet with JVM's *class loader* and then runs the applet.

Running the Hello Applet

To see `hello.class`, your first applet, running, you'll need a Web page to place it in. Use your editor again to create a new file, `hello.htm`, which will be your Web page, written in the language of Web pages, *HyperText Markup Language* (HTML). Enter the following text into `hello.htm` and save it (we'll review HTML in a minute):

```
<html>

<!- Web page written for the Sun Applet Viewer>

<head>
<title>hello</title>
</head>

<body>
<hr>

<applet
code=hello.class
width=200
height=200>

</applet>

<hr>
</body>
</html>
```

Now you can run the hello applet by simply viewing this new Web page, `hello.htm`. To do that, use the Applet Viewer that comes with the JDK 1.1. To use the Applet Viewer, go back to the `hello` subdirectory and type the following:

```
c:\java1-2\hello>appletviewer hello.htm
```

Again, capitalization is very important here—make sure your capitalization matches the exact spelling of the Web page name. When you've done this, the Applet Viewer runs, as shown below—and you see your message, "Hello from Java!" Your first applet is a success.

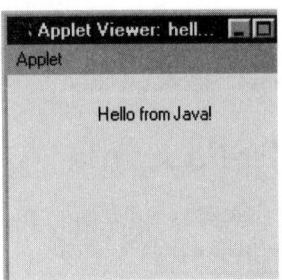

> **TIP**   You can use any Java-enabled Web browser to look at this Web page. For most of the applets in this book, however, you will have to use either a Web browser that supports Java 1.2 (not just Java 1.0 or Java 1.1) or the Sun Applet Viewer.

Your first applet, `hello.class`, runs—but what exactly did you do? Let's take a look now at the Java code that you entered for `hello.java`, examining it line by line to get a better idea of how Java programming works (even though Java will handle many of these details for you later).

Understanding the Hello Example

Let's take apart your first applet now. Begin with this line:

```
import java.awt.Graphics;
      .
      .
      .
```

What does this mean? This line actually points out one of the great advantages of Java programming. When you're adding menus and separate windows to your Java applets, you can imagine that it would be a great deal of work to create everything from scratch—that is, write the entire code for menu handling, separate window creation, and so forth. Instead of asking you to do so, Java comes complete with several pre-defined libraries, and much of this book will be an examination of the routines in these libraries. You'll learn more about this later, but what you're doing is adding support from the main Java graphics library of routines to your applet. In this way, we'll be able to draw the text string, "Hello from Java!", in the applet's window.

> **NOTE**   If you're a C/C++ programmer, you'll notice that the import statement works much like the C/C++ #include statement.

Next, add this line to `hello.java`:

```
import java.awt.Graphics;

→public class hello extends java.applet.Applet

→{
      .
      .
      .
```

You've just created a Java *class* named `hello`. What does this mean?

Object-Oriented Programming

Objects and *classes* are two fundamental concepts in object-oriented languages like Java. There's been a lot of hype about object-oriented programming (OOP), and that can make the whole topic seem mysterious and unapproachable. In fact, object-oriented programming was introduced to make longer programs *easier* to create. We'll start a mini-survey of object-oriented programming by looking at objects.

Understanding Java Objects

In long, involved programs, there can be a profusion of both variables and functions, sometimes hundreds of each. Creating and maintaining the program code can become a very cluttered task because you have to keep so many things in mind. There may also be unwanted interaction if various functions use variables of the same name. Object-oriented programming was invented to break up such large programs.

The idea behind objects is quite simple—you just break up your program into the various parts, each of which you can easily conceptualize as performing a discrete task, and those are your objects. For example, you may put all the screen-handling parts of a program together into an object named `screen`. Objects are more powerful than simple functions or sets of variables because an object can hold both functions and variables wrapped up together in a way that makes it easy to use. The `screen` object may hold not only all the data displayed on the screen, but also the functions needed to handle that data, like `drawString()` or `drawLine()`. This means that all the screen handling is hidden from the rest of the program in a convenient way, making the rest of the program easier to handle.

As another example, think of a refrigerator. A refrigerator would be far less useful if you had to regulate all the temperatures and pumps and so forth by hand at all times. Making all those functions internal and automatic to the refrigerator makes it into an easy object to deal with and a useful one: a *refrigerator*. Wrapping up code and data into objects this way is the basis of object-oriented programming.

What's a Java Class?

But how do you create objects? That's where *classes* come in. A class is to an object what a cookie cutter is to a cookie—a template or blueprint. In terms of programming, you might think of the relationship between a data type, like an integer, and the actual variable itself like this, where you set up an integer named the_data:

```
int the_data;
```

This is the actual way to create an integer variable in Java. Here, int is the type of variable you are declaring and the_data is the variable itself. This is the same relationship that a class has to an object, and informally you may think of a class as an object's *type*.

TIP   Java supports all the standard C and C++ primitive data types like int, double, long, float, and so forth.

For example, if you had set up a class named, say, graphicsClass, you can create an object of that class named screen this way:

```
graphicsClass screen;
```

You'll see how to actually create a class soon (creating a class like graphicsClass is not hard—when you create a class in code, you will just group all its functions and data inside the class definition), and then you'll see how to create objects of that class. What's important to remember is this: the object itself is what holds the data you want to work with; the class itself holds no data but just describes how the object should be set up.

Object-oriented programming at root is nothing more than a way of grouping functions and the data they work on together to make your program less cluttered. You'll see more about object-oriented programming throughout this book, including how to create a class, how to create an object of that class, and how to reach the functions and data in that object when you want to.

That completes the mini-overview of classes and objects. As you can see, a class is just a programming construct that groups together, or *encapsulates*, functions and data, and an object may be thought of as a variable of that class's type, as the object screen is to the class screenclass.

As it turns out, Java comes complete with several libraries of pre-defined classes, which save you a great deal of work. Throughout this book we will examine these pre-defined and very useful Java classes. Using these predefined classes, we'll create objects needed to handle buttons, text fields, scroll bars, and much more.

Learning about Java Packages

These class libraries are called *packages* in Java, and one such library is called java.awt (where awt stands for Abstract Window Toolkit). This library holds the Graphics class, which will handle the graphics work you undertake. So this line in the first applet:

```
import java.awt.Graphics;
```

actually means that you want to include the Java Graphics class and make use of it in your program. In a minute, you will use an object of the Graphics class for your graphics output.

You've added support for graphics handling by including the java.awt .Graphics class (and in Java, displaying the text string "Hello from Java!" is considered graphics handling). Next, it's time to set up your hello applet itself. To do so, define a new class named hello. This is the standard way of setting up an applet in Java, and in fact, the applet itself has the file extension .class. That's because each class defined in a .java file ends up being exported to a .class file, where you can make use of it. You'll learn more details about this soon.

It would be quite difficult to write all the code an applet class needs from scratch. For example, we'd need to interact with the Web browser, reserve a section of screen, initialize the appropriate Java packages, and much more. It turns out that all that functionality is already built into the Java Applet class, which is part of the java.applet package. But how do you make use of the Applet class? You want to customize the applet to display your text string, and the java.applet.Applet class itself knows nothing about that.

Understanding Java Inheritance

You can customize the java.applet.Applet class by *deriving* the hello class from the java.applet.Applet class. This makes java.applet.Applet the *base* class of the hello class, and it makes hello a class derived from java.applet .Applet. This gives you all the power of the java.applet.Applet class without the worries of writing it yourself, and you can add what you want to this class by adding code to your derived class hello.

This is an important part of object-oriented programming, and it's called *inheritance*. In this way, a derived class inherits the functionality of its base class and adds more on top of it. For example, you may have a base class called chassis. You can derive various classes from this base class called, say, car and truck. In this way, two derived classes can share the same base class, saving time and effort programmatically. Although the `car` and `truck` classes share the same base class, `chassis`, they added different items to the base class, ending up as two quite different classes, `car` and `truck`.

Using inheritance, then, you will *extend* the base class `java.applet.Applet` by creating your own class `hello` and adding onto the base class. Indicate that the `hello` class is derived from the `java.applet.Applet` class like this (note that you use the keyword *class* to indicate that you are defining a new class):

```
import java.awt.Graphics;

→public class hello extends java.applet.Applet
→{
     .
     .
     .
```

In starting to set up the new class, `hello`, you've given it all the power of the `java.applet.Applet` class (like the ability to request space from the Web browser and to respond to many browser-created commands). But how do you make additions and even alterations to the `java.applet.Applet` class to customize your own `hello` class? How do you display your text string? One way is by *overriding* the base class's built-in functions (overriding is an important part of object-oriented programming). When you re-define a base class's function in a derived class, the new version of the function is the one that takes over. In this way, you can customize the functions from the base class as you like them in the derived class.

For example, one function in the `java.applet.Applet` class is called `paint()`. This is a very important function that is called when the Web browser tells the applet to create its display on the screen. This happens when the applet first begins and every time it has to be re-displayed later (for example, if the Web browser was minimized and then maximized, or if some window was moved and the applet's display area was uncovered after having been covered).

Your goal in the `hello` class is to display the string "Hello from Java!" on the screen, and in fact, you will override the `java.applet.Applet` class's `paint()` function to do so. You override a base class's function simply by redefining it in the new class. Do that now for the `paint()` function, noting first that the built-in functions of a class are called that class's *methods*. In this case, then, you override (that is, re-define) the `paint()` method like this:

```
import java.awt.Graphics;

public class hello extends java.applet.Applet
{
```

➡
```
public void paint( Graphics g )[
{
        .
        .
        .
```

 **NOTE** The built-in functions of a class are called *methods*. Classes can also have built-in variables—called *data members*—and even constants. Collectively, all these parts are called a class's *members*.

What Are Java Access Modifiers?

The keyword *public* is called an *access modifier*. A class's methods can be declared public, private, or protected. If they are declared public, then you can call them from anywhere in the program, not just in the class in which they are defined. If they are private, they may be called from only the class in which they are defined. If they are protected, they may be called in only the class in which they are defined and the classes derived from that class.

Next, indicate the *return* type of the paint() method. When you call a method, you can pass parameters to it, and it can return data to you. In this case, paint() has no return value, which you indicate with the return type *void*. Other return types are int for an integer return value (this variable is usually 32 bits long), long for a long integer (this variable is usually 64 bits long), float for a floating point return, or double for a double-precision floating point value. You can also return arrays and objects in Java.

Finally, note that you indicate that the paint() method is automatically passed one parameter—an object of the Graphics class called g:

```
import java.awt.Graphics;

public class hello extends java.applet.Applet
{
➡    public void paint(Graphics g)
     {   .
         .
         .
```

This Graphics object represents the physical display of the applet. That is, you can use the built-in methods of this object—such as drawImage(), drawLine(), drawOval(), and others—to drawn on the screen. In this case, you want to place the string "Hello from Java!" on the screen, and you can do that with the drawString() method.

How do you reach the methods of an object like the Graphics object named g? You do that with a dot operator (.) like this: g.drawString(), where here you are invoking g's drawString() method to "draw" a string of text on the screen (text is handled like any other type of graphics in a windows environment—that is, it is drawn on the screen rather than "printed," just as you would draw a rectangle or circle). Supply three parameters to the drawString() method—the string of text you want to display, and the (x, y) location of that string's lower-left corner (called the starting point of the string's *baseline*) in pixels on the screen, passed in two integer values. As shown in Figure 1.3, you can draw your string at the pixel location (60, 30), where (0, 0) is the upper-left corner of the applet's display.

N **NOTE**   The coordinate system in a Java program is set up with the origin (0, 0) at the upper-left, with x increasing horizontally to the right, and y increasing vertically downwards; this fact will be important throughout the book. If it seems backwards to you, you might try thinking of it in terms of reading a page of text, like this one, where you start at the upper-left and work your way to the right and down. The units of measurement in Java coordinate systems are almost always screen pixels.

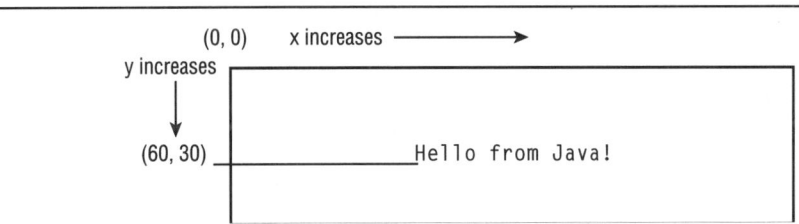

FIGURE 1.3:   Drawing a string at (60,30)

This means that you add a call to the drawString() method this way:

```
import java.awt.Graphics;
public class hello extends java.applet.Applet
{
    public void paint( Graphics g )
    {
        g.drawString( "Hello from Java!", 60, 30 );
    }
}
```

Note that Java uses the same convention as C or C++ to indicate that a code statement is finished: it ends the statement with a semicolon (;).

 **TIP**   In general, Java adheres very strongly to C++ coding conventions. If you know C++, you already know a great deal of Java.

You have completed the code necessary for this applet, which is also to say you have completed the code for the new class, hello. When the Java compiler creates `hello.class`, the entire specification of the new class will be in that file. This is the actual binary file that you upload to your Internet Service Provider so it may be included in your Web page. A Java-enabled Web browser takes this class specification and creates an object of that class and then gives it control to display itself and, if applicable, handle user input.

But how? You have not yet completed the dissection of the first example; all you have done so far is to trace the development of `hello.java` into `hello.class`. How did you get the applet to be displayed in the Applet Viewer?

Understanding the Applet's Web Page

The Applet Viewer took the `hello.class` applet and displayed it in a Web page, as shown in Figure 1.4.

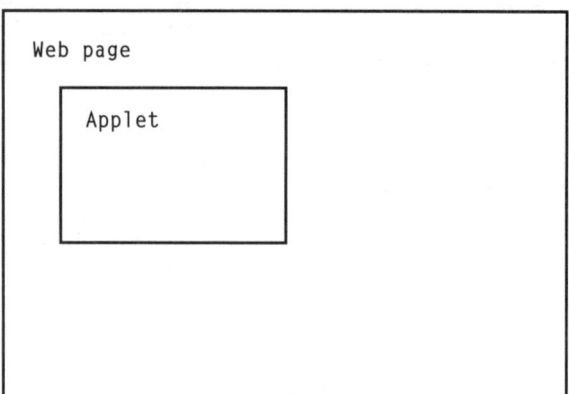

FIGURE 1.4:   Displaying an applet in a Web page

How did it get there? You created a Web page for your applet and then opened that Web page in the Applet Viewer, which then displayed your applet. That Web page looks like this:

```
<html>

<!- Web page written for the Sun Applet Viewer>

<head>
<title>hello</title>
</head>

<body>
<hr>

<applet
code=hello.class
width=200
height=200>

</applet>

<hr>
</body>
</html>
```

Web pages are written in HTML (HyperText Markup Language). Because applets appear in Web pages, we will take the time to briefly work through the above page to make sure you know what's going on. If you're familiar with HTML, you can skip much of this review, but you should take a look at how to use the `<applet>` tag to embed applets in Web pages.

Connecting Java and HTML

Let's take apart the Web page you created for the applet now, starting with the `<html>` tag:

```
<html>
    .
    .
    .
```

Instructions in .html pages are placed into tags surrounded by angle brackets: < and >. The tags hold directions to the Web browser and are not displayed on the screen. Here, the <html> tag indicates to the Web browser that this .html file is written in HTML.

Next comes a comment. Comments in .html pages are written using the ! symbol like this: <! This is a comment.>. Indicate that this is a Web page written so we can use the Sun Applet Viewer, like this:

```
<html>

<!- Web page written for the Sun Applet Viewer>
        .
        .
        .
```

Next comes the header portion of the Web page, which you declare with the <head> tag, ending the header section with the corresponding end header tag, </head> (many HTML tags are used in pairs like this, such as <head> and </head> or <center> and </center> to center text and images). In this case, the .html file gets the title (set up with the <title> tag) *hello*, to match your applet:

```
<html>

<!- Web page written for the Sun Applet Viewer>

➡<head>
➡<title>h*ello</title>
➡</head>
        .
        .
        .
```

The title is the name given to a Web page, and it's usually displayed in the Web browser's title bar. Next comes the body of the Web page. Here is where all the actual items for display will go. You start the page off with a ruler line (visible in Figure 1.4), using the <hr> tag:

```
<html>

<!- Web page written for the Sun Applet Viewer>

<head>
<title>hello</title>
</head>
```

```
→<body>
→<hr>
    .
    .
    .
```

Now we come to the applet. Applets are embedded with the `<applet>` tag, and here you use the *code* keyword to indicate that this applet is supported by the `hello.class` file. You indicate the size of the applet as 200×200 pixels (you can choose any size you like here) this way:

```
<html>

<!- Web page written for the Sun Applet Viewer>
<head>
<title>hello</title>
</head>

<body>
<hr>
→<applet
→code=hello.class
→width=200
→height=200>
→</applet>
    .
    .
    .
```

 TIP   You can also use the `java.applet.Applet.resize()` method to request that the Web browser resize applets.

The `<applet>` tag is important, so let's take a closer look at it now. Here's how the `<applet>` tag works in general (the items in square brackets are optional, and the others are required):

```
<APPLET
    [ALIGN = LEFT or RIGHT or TOP or TEXTTOP or MIDDLE or
        ABSMIDDLE  or BASELINE or BOTTOM or ABSBOTTOM]
        [ALT = AlternateText]
        CODE = AppletName.class
        [CODEBASE = URL of .class file]
        HEIGHT = AppletPixelsHeight
        [HSPACE = PixelSpaceToLeftOfApplet]
        [NAME = AppletInstanceName]
        [VSPACE = PixelSpaceAboveApplet]
```

```
        WIDTH = AppletPixelsWidth
    >
    [<PARAM NAME = Parameter1 VALUE = VALUE1]
    [<PARAM NAME = Parameter2 VALUE = VALUE2]
            .
            .
            .

</APPLET>
```

TIP   You can specify the URL of the applet's `.class` file with the `CODEBASE` keyword. This is often useful if you want to store your applets together in a directory in your ISP, away from the `.html` files.

Indicate to the Web browser here how much space you'll need for your applet, using the `HEIGHT` and `WIDTH` keywords. You can also pass parameters to applets with the PARAM keyword like this: `<applet> PARAM today = "friday" </applet>`. Passing parameters in this way allows you to customize your applets to fit different Web pages because you can read the parameters from inside an applet and make use of them. I'll show you how this works in an example later in the book.

TIP   There are enhancements to the `<applet>` tag in Java 1.2, such as the ability to pass the name of `.jar` files as parameters. You'll learn more about this later on.

Not all Web browsers support Java. In practice, this means that those browsers just ignore the `<applet>` tag. This, in turn, means that you can place text between the `<applet>` and `</applet>` tags that will be displayed in non-Java browsers (and not in Java-enabled browsers), like this:

```
<applet code=hello>
Your Web browser does not support Java, so you can't see my applets,
sorry!
</applet>
```

Using the `<applet>` tag, you can embed applets in Web pages, as Java has done in this temporary page. Finish off the Web page with the `</body>` and `</html>` tags as follows:

```
<html>

<!- Web page written for the Sun Applet Viewer>
```

```
<head>
<title>hello</title>
</head>

<body>
<hr>

<applet
code=hello.class
width=200
height=200>

</applet>

<hr>
→</body>
→</html>
```

This completes our first example—you've had a glimpse into the process of creating and running an applet. It was as quick and easy as that—you created and ran your first applet.

In this Skill, the example applet demonstrated only the easiest way to get an applet to work. Let's continue on to get a better idea of how you'll be working with Java throughout the book as you give your applet more power in Skill 2.

Are You up to Speed?

Now you can. . .

- ☑ **create your own Java source code files**

- ☑ **understand the inner workings of a simple applet**

- ☑ **create a small working Java applet**

- ☑ **use the Applet Viewer to embed an applet in a Web page**

- ☑ **understand the basic object-oriented programming topics that will be useful throughout the book**

Handling Java Text Fields

- Adding buttons and other Java controls
- Adding and using text fields
- Using Java class constructors
- Using the *new* operator
- Using the *init()* function
- Initializing Java controls

n Skill 1, you saw the basics of a simple Java applet. In Skill 2, you're going to add *controls* to programs. Controls are the interactive items you use in applets, like text boxes, buttons, and scrolling list boxes, and they're very powerful parts of Java programs. After exploring text boxes (called *text fields* in Java) in this skill, we'll see how to integrate them with buttons in Skill 3. For example, we'll see how to create an applet with a text field and a button marked Click Here, as shown in Figure 2.1. Text fields and buttons are two of the most important and fundamental controls.

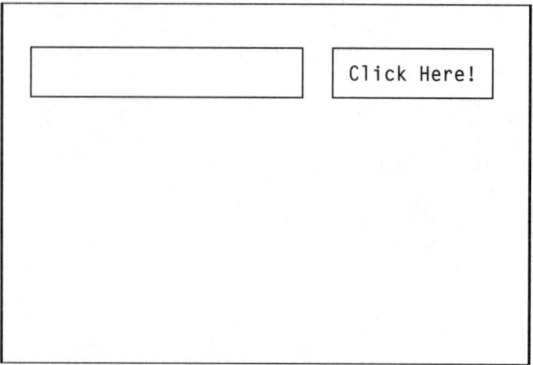

FIGURE 2.1:   An applet with a text field and a button

When the user clicks the Click Here button, you can place a new message that reads, "Welcome to Java" in the text field, as shown in Figure 2.2.

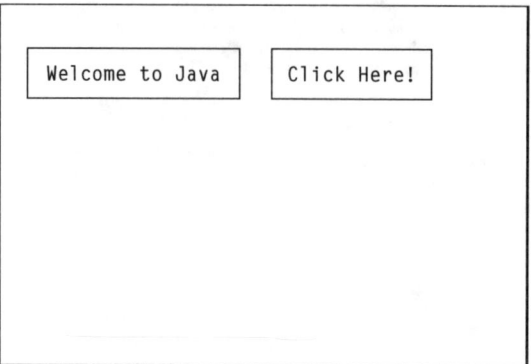

FIGURE 2.2:   When the user clicks the Click Here button, a message appears in the text field.

Using controls is a very strong technique in Java—in fact, using controls is often the whole point of an applet.

Declaring a Text Field

In this example, the first control you add to an applet will be the text field. Familiar to all Windows users, a *text field* is just a box that can hold text. (Text fields are also called text boxes and edit controls.) Your goal might be to place a text field in your applet, as shown in Figure 2.3. You can even start the text field out with the message, "Welcome to Java," as shown in Figure 2.4. After this text field appears, the users can edit the text as they like, using the mouse and keyboard.

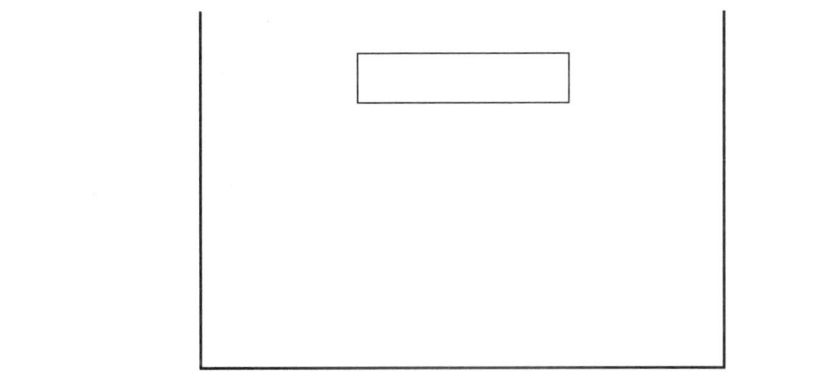

FIGURE 2.3: An applet with an empty text field

TIP   Sometimes you may not want the user to edit the text you display in a Java program. In that case, you can use the TextField setEditable() method, which allows you to make text fields read-only. In addition, you can use *Label* controls, instead of text fields. Label controls display text that cannot be altered by the user. We'll learn about these controls in Skill 4.

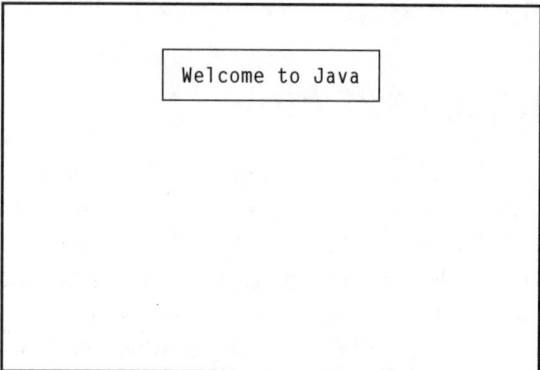

Welcome to Java

FIGURE 2.4: The message "Welcome to Java" can be displayed in a text field.

Create a new subdirectory now to contain the code for your text field example, naming it `text`. Now create a new file, named `text.java`, with your editor. You can start your new text field program the same way you started the `hello.java` file:

```
import java.awt.*;

public class text extends java.applet.Applet
{
    .
    .
    .
}
```

Here, you import all the classes in the Java AWT package with the statement `import java.awt.*`. These are the classes that will let you add text fields and buttons to your applet—for example, two of the classes in this package that you will use are `Button` and `TextField`. In addition, you will declare a new public class named `text` as your applet's main class, based on the `java.applet.Applet` class.

Next, you create your text field. First you have to declare it, setting up an object named, for example, `text1` of the `TextField` class:

```
import java.awt.*;

public class text extends java.applet.Applet
{
➜       TextField text1;
            .
            .
            .
}
```

The above declares your new text field, named `text1`. The methods of the Java class `TextField`, which is the class you will use for text fields, appear in Table 2.1.

 **NOTE**

Note the distinction between the terms `TextField` and `text1`. `TextField` is a Java class, and `text1` is the object of that class that we will actually work with.

Skill 2

T A B L E 2 . 1 : Java TextField class methods

Method	Does This
addActionListener(ActionListener)	Adds action listener to text field
addNotify()	Creates TextField's peer
echoCharIsSet()	Returns true if TextField has echoing
getColumns()	Returns the number of columns
getEchoChar()	Returns the echoing character
getMinimumSize()	Returns minimum size for TextField
getMinimumSize(int)	Returns minimum size needed for TextField with specified columns
getPreferredSize()	Returns preferred size for TextField
getPreferredSize(int)	Returns preferred size for TextField with the specified columns
minimumSize()	Deprecated. Replaced by getMinimumSize()
minimumSize(int)	Deprecated. Replaced by getMinimumSize(int)
paramString()	Returns the String of parameters for TextField
preferredSize()	Deprecated. Replaced by getPreferredSize()
preferredSize(int)	Deprecated. Replaced by getPreferredSize(int)
processActionEvent(ActionEvent)	Processes action events by dispatching them to ActionListener objects
processEvent(AWTEvent)	Processes events on text field
removeActionListener(ActionListener)	Removes the specified action listener
setColumns(int)	Sets number of columns in TextField
setEchoChar(char)	Sets echo character for TextField
setEchoCharacter(char)	Deprecated. Replaced by setEchoChar(char)

Placing text1 in your applet makes it a *global class variable*. What I mean by global is that it will be available to all the methods (built-in functions) of the text class and to all the code in those methods, because it is declared outside any such method.

As far as variables go, a variable is just a place set aside in memory for data; you will find that variable's numeric data types in Java are just the same as most standard Basic, C, or C++ implementations. For example, to set aside space for integer data, we set up an integer variable of type int:

```
int the_integer;
```

To place values in a variable, just assign them to that variable as follows:

```
the_integer = 5;
```

The built-in Java numeric data types like int and float appear in Table 2.2.

TABLE 2.2: The Java numeric data types

Type	Bits	Means
byte	8	Holds a byte of data
Short	16	Short integer
Int	32	Integer value
Long	64	Long integer
Float	32	Floating point value
Double	64	Double precision floating point value

TABLE 2.2 *CONTINUED*: The Java numeric data types

Type	Bits	Means
Char	16	Unicode character
Boolean	—	Takes true or false values

 **NOTE**   You can declare a class's data as private, protected, or public, just as you can for a class's methods.

Initializing with the *init()* Method

Declaring a text field just sets aside memory for it and does nothing to display it in your applet. You have to handle that yourself in the init() method.

When you want to initialize an applet, by, for example, adding text fields to it, you do that in the init() method. As you'll see throughout this book, all kinds of initialization can take place in the init() function. It runs automatically when the applet starts, so you should place code that you want run first in the init() function. To use init(), just add it to your class as follows:

```
import java.awt.*;

public class text extends java.applet.Applet
{
    TextField text1;

    public void init()
    {
        .
        .
        .
    }

}
```

Note that the init() function is like any other function, except that it doesn't return a value (which is why the return type is listed as void above) and it runs automatically when the applet starts. Your task in init() is to create the new text field and install it in your applet. Creating Java controls is a two-step process: first declare the new object as you have done above, and then create the new object in the init() function, using the Java new operator.

Handling Memory with the *new* Operator

The Java new operator is just like the C++ new operator; it is used to allocate memory for objects, variables, arrays—for anything you'd like. If you know C, the new operator largely replaces malloc(), calloc(), and all the memory allocation functions—and it is much easier to work with.

 NOTE   While the standard memory-allocating functions like malloc() and calloc() in C are functions, the new operator is indeed an operator (like +, —, and so on), not a function. This operator is a built-in part of Java and does not come from any class library.

Let's put the new operator to work. Create your new object named text1 in your applet's init() method, using the following syntax:

```
import java.awt.*;

public class text extends java.applet.Applet
{
    TextField text1;

    public void init()
    {
        text1 = new TextField();
            .
            .
            .
    }

}
```

This syntax creates a new TextField object and places it in the text1 variable. This is a two-step process that you'll see many times in this book: you first *declare* a control's object and then use the new operator to *create* that object in the init() method.

The above new line of code creates a new text field, but it's only one character wide. To make the text field, say, 20 characters wide, pass a value of 20 to the `TextField` class's *constructor*.

What Are Java Constructors?

Using constructors is a very popular technique in object-oriented programming; a constructor for a particular class is simply a method that is automatically run when you create an object of that class, and its purpose is to initialize that object as you want it. That is, constructors are used to initialize objects. A class's constructor is called when a new object is being created of that class, and you can set the object up as you like it. Because a constructor is a method, you can pass data to constructors (if they are written to accept such data), allowing us to set up an object as you want when that object is created. In this case, you'll pass a value of 20 to your new text field's constructor. You can do that using the following syntax:

```
import java.awt.*;

public class text extends java.applet.Applet
{
    TextField text1;

    public void init()
    {
→       text1 = new TextField(20);
            .
            .
            .
    }
```

This makes your new text field 20 characters wide. If you wanted to set up an initial string in the text field instead of using a set number of characters, you could just pass that string to `TextField`'s constructor as follows:

```
text1 = new TextField("Welcome to Java");
```

Overloading Java Methods

If you are not familiar with C++, this might seem odd—how can you call a function with a numeric value like 20 *or* a string like "Welcome to Java"? The reason is that in Java, as in C++, you can *overload* functions. This means that you can set up a function to be called with different types and numbers of parameters. The Java compiler determines which version of the function to call depending on what parameters—and how many of them—you pass. For that reason, both these lines are valid Java code:

```
text1 = new TextField(20);
text2 = new TextField("Welcome to Java");
```

NOTE   Don't confuse overloading functions with overriding them. Overloading a function means that the function can be called with different parameter lists, while overriding a function redefines the version of the function that appears in the class's base class.

Now that you've created your new text field, the next step is to *add* it to your applet's display. In Skill 3, I'll show you that Java handles the display (or *layout*) of your controls automatically, although you will take more control of this process as time goes on. To add your text field to your applet's display, use the add( ) method as follows, where you add the new control text1 to your applet's default layout:

```
import java.awt.*;

public class text extends java.applet.Applet
{
    TextField text1;

    public void init()
    {
            text1 = new TextField(20);
  ➜         add(text1);
            .
            .
            .

    }

}
```

Now your new text field appears in the applet, as shown in Figure 2.5. Figure 2.6 shows the text you'll be adding to the text field.

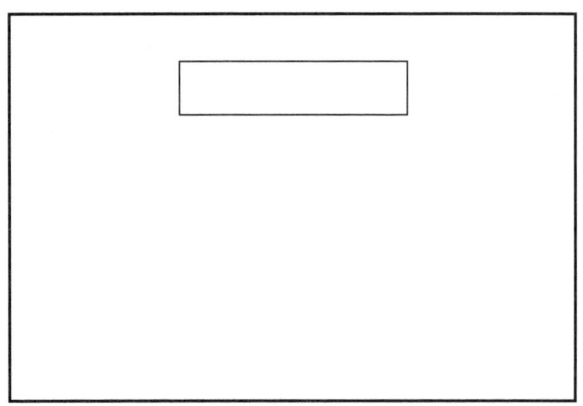

FIGURE 2.5:   Your new text field

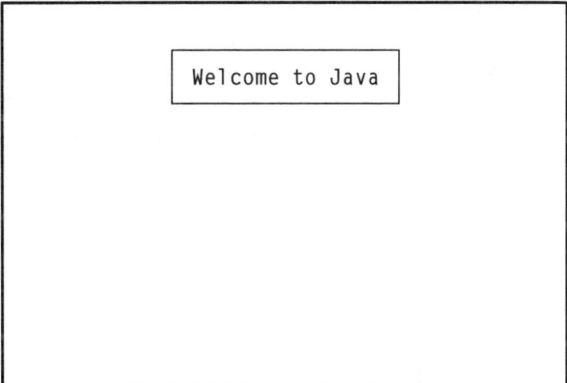

FIGURE 2.6:   You want to add the text "Welcome to Java".

Add the text shown in Figure 2.6 to the text field as follows, using the
TextField class's setText() method (see Table 2.1).

```java
import java.awt.*;

public class text extends java.applet.Applet
{
    TextField text1;

    public void init()
    {
        text1 = new TextField(20);
        add(text1);
➜       text1.setText("Welcome to Java");
    }


}
```

NOTE You could place this text into the text box by passing it to the text field's constructor, like this: text1 = new TextField("Welcome to Java");

NOTE Note again the syntax here: text1.setText("Welcome to Java");. This is the
standard way of executing an object's internal method (here, that's the setText()
method of the text1 object) with the dot operator. Again, this is standard C++
terminology, but if you're not used to it, it might take a while before it becomes
second nature. In general, if you want to execute, say, a method named
the_method(), which is a built-in function of an object named the_object, the
correct syntax is: the_object.the_method();.

That's all there is to it! You've created a new text field and added it to your
applet's display. You can also add comments to your program to make it clearer—
Java will ignore anything on a line of code following a // symbol:

```java
import java.awt.*;

public class text extends java.applet.Applet
{
➜   TextField text1;                        //Declare a text field

    public void init()
    {
➜       text1 = new TextField(20);          //Create a text field
➜       add(text1);                         //Add text field to
                                            //  applet
```

➜   `text1.setText("Welcome to Java");`   `//Place text in text`
                                                                      `field`

    `}`

  `}`

Create the `text.class` file now with javac. You'll need a Web page to display your new class file in the Applet Viewer, so create a new .htm file called `text.htm` now, adding the following HTML code to it:

```
<html>

<!- Web page written for the Sun Applet Viewer>

<head>
<title>text</title>
</head>

<body>
<hr>

<applet
    code=text.class
    width=200
    height=200
>
</applet>

<hr>
</body>
</html>
```

You're ready to run the Applet Viewer with this new Web page. The result appears below—you can see your text field, with your message in it. Your first text field applet is a success—the listing for this applet appears in `text.java`.

 **text.java**

```
import java.awt.*;

public class text extends java.applet.Applet
{
    TextField text1;

    public void init()
    {
            text1 = new TextField(20);
            add(text1);
            text1.setText("Welcome to Java");
    }

}
```

 TIP   Java text fields support the standard Windows editing shortcuts like Ctrl+V to paste from the clipboard, Ctrl+X to cut selected text, Ctrl+C to copy selected text, and so on.

Creating and using text fields is a good start. However, it's only a start. Let's turn now to Skill 3, where we'll work with a new Java control: buttons.

Are You up to Speed?

Now you can . . .

☑ **add Java controls to a program and initialize them**

☑ **add and use text fields**

☑ **display multiple lines of text**

☑ **use text areas**

☑ **allocate memory**

☑ **use the Java *new* operator**

SKILL 3

Using Java Buttons

- Using the Java 1.2 delegation-based event model
- Adding and using Java buttons
- Using multiple buttons
- Using Java events
- The Java *String* class
- Adding and using text areas

In Skill 2, you got started with Java controls by taking a look at text fields. Here, you're going to flesh out your programs by adding buttons. Every GUI user is familiar with buttons—you click them to make some action occur. Buttons connect naturally with text fields in Java—when you click a button, you can display something in a text field. These are fundamental GUI controls, so let's start working with buttons now.

Working with Buttons in Java

You have already learned a little about handling text fields. Next, you'll see how to control what happens even more, by using buttons. For example, you might set up a new applet with a text field and a button that has the caption "Click Here!". (See Figure 3.1.) When the user clicks the button, you might display a message such as "Welcome to Java" in your text field, as shown in Figure 3.2.

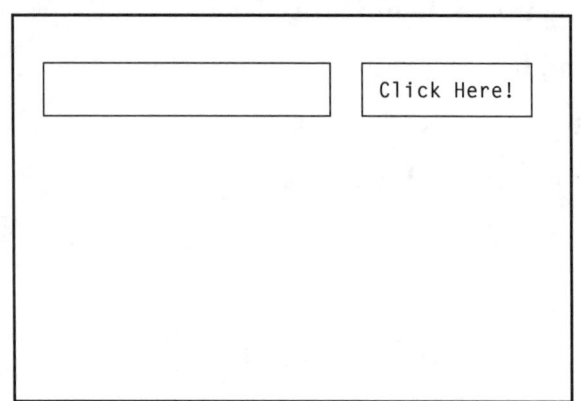

FIGURE 3.1: Using a text field and a button together in an applet

FIGURE 3.2:   "Welcome to Java" appears in the text field.

Let's create this example now. Call your new applet *clicker*, create a new file named `clicker.java`, and start with the usual beginning-of-applet code (note that here you import the `java.applet.Applet` class, which means we can then just extend the `Applet` class, without needing to call it by its full name, `java.applet.Applet`):

```
import java.applet.Applet;
import java.awt.*;

public class clicker extends Applet {
    .
    .
    .
}
```

Start by adding the text field for your new applet, which, as before, you can name `text1`. Declare that new control at the beginning of our class's declaration. This is where you will place all your control's declarations, to make them global class variables because you need to reach them from more than one method:

```
import java.applet.Applet;
import java.awt.*;

public class clicker extends Applet {

➜    TextField text1;
```

.
.
.

Next, create the new text field with the new operator and add it to your applet's display with the add( ) method:

```
import java.applet.Applet;
import java.awt.*;

public class clicker extends Applet {

TextField text1;

    public void init(){
        text1 = new TextField(20);
        add(text1);
            .
            .
            .

    }

}
```

Adding a Button to a Program

You've created your text field. Now, add the new button with the caption "Click Here!", as shown in Figure 3.3.

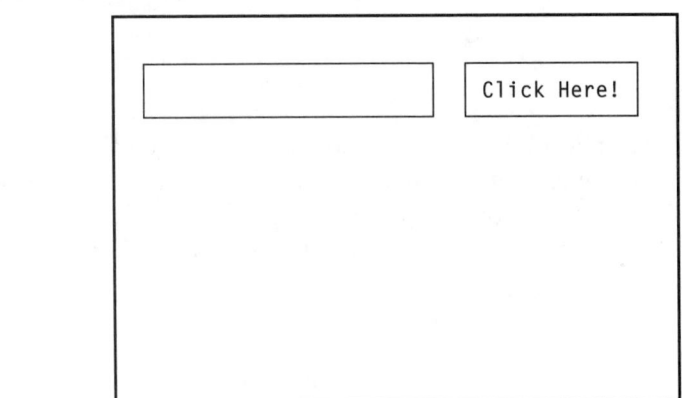

FIGURE 3.3: Add the Click Here! button to clicker.java.

We add a new button with the Java `Button` class, naming our new button object `button1`, and declaring it at the beginning of our class, as we do with all controls:

```
import java.applet.Applet;
import java.awt.*;

public class clicker extends Applet {

    TextField text1;
    Button button1;

    public void init(){
        text1 = new TextField(20);
        add(text1);
            .
            .
            .
    }

}
```

The methods of the Java `Button` class appear in Table 3.1.

TABLE 3.1: Java Button class methods

Method	Does This
Button()	Constructs a Button with no label
Button(String)	Constructs a Button with the given label
addActionListener(ActionListener)	Adds the action listener to the button
addNotify()	Creates peer of a button
getActionCommand()	Returns the name of the action event fired by a button
getLabel()	Gets label of a button
paramString()	Returns parameter String
processActionEvent(ActionEvent)	Processes action events occurring by dispatching them to the ActionListener objects
processEvent(AWTEvent)	Processes events
pemoveActionListener(ActionListener)	Removes the given action listener
setActionCommand(String)	Sets the command name of the action event fired by a button
setLabel(String)	Sets the label

TIP   You can set a button's caption on-the-fly with setLabel(), allowing you to change the options you offer to the user as required.

Next, create the button and add it to your applet. Give the button a caption of "Click Here!" by passing that text to the Button class's constructor as follows:

```
import java.applet.Applet;
import java.awt.*;

public class clicker extends Applet {

    TextField text1;
    Button button1;

    public void init(){
        text1 = new TextField(20);
        add(text1);
        button1 = new Button("Click Here!");
        add(button1);
            .
            .
            .

    }

}
```

Now you have two controls: the text field and the button. The next step is to actually connect the button to the text field in code.

What Are Java Events?

When the user clicks a button, types text, uses the mouse, or performs any other interface-related action in your applet, an interface *event* occurs; if you have programmed in Windows, you probably know about such interface events already. When an event occurs in your applet, such as when the user clicks the mouse, the applet is notified, and you can take the appropriate action. That's the way programming goes in *Graphics User Interface* (GUI) programs like those written for Windows—we respond to user events when they happen because the user directs the program flow by manipulating the controls in the applet. In this case, you can find out what events—like mouse movements or button clicks—occur as your applet runs by using the *ActionListener* interface.

If you've programmed in Java 1.0, you were probably expecting us to use an action() method here, to handle button clicks, but the action() method is now considered *deprecated*—obsolete! This is a fundamental change. The new technique in Java 1.1 and Java 1.2 is the use of the *delegation-based event model*. To use this technique, we indicate that our applet class will *implement* the ActionListener interface (this is somewhat like saying that we are deriving our applet's class based on ActionListener—I'll show you more about implementing interfaces when I cover multi-threading).

NOTE   Java does not support multiple inheritance—that is, deriving one class from two others, like the Applet class and some hypothetical ActionListener class, at the same time. Java declares ActionListener as an interface to let you use the ActionListener methods; this means you can *extend* the Applet *class* to create your applet, and *implement* the ActionListener *interface* to use the Action-Listener methods as well. I'll show you more about this later.

Implementing that interface looks like this, where you also import the java.awt.event package that holds the ActionListener interface:

```
 import java.applet.Applet;
 import java.awt.*;
→import java.awt.event.*;

→public class clicker extends Applet implements ActionListener{

    TextField text1;
    Button button1;

    public void init(){
        text1 = new TextField(20);
        add(text1);
        button1 = new Button("Click Here!");
        add(button1);
            .
            .
            .
    }
}
```

TIP   The class that implements the ActionListener interface does not have to be the applet's main class—you can create an entirely new class to do that. In larger programs it's often a good idea to do so because it helps break up the code. One of the primary differences between Java 1.0 and Java 1.2 is that in Java 1.0 all the code that handled events had to go into the action() method, whereas in Java 1.2 you can create Listener objects to handle events. You can use many Listener objects in a Java program to handle a great variety of events.

The delegation-based event model works like this: Events are passed from source controls to listener objects. That means you will connect a *Listener* to your button, button1. When an event occurs, the listener object will "hear" it. In this case, you will make the listener object the applet object itself by connecting your applet to button1 as a listener; do that with the button's addActionListener() method. But to indicate that you want the applet itself to be the button's listener, you would need to be able to pass the applet itself as an argument to addActionListener(). How do you do that?

The *this* Keyword

You do that with the this keyword, which is a keyword that refers to the current object you're in. This means that you set up your ActionListener as follows:

```java
import java.applet.Applet;
import java.awt.*;
import java.awt.event.*;

public class clicker extends Applet implements ActionListener{

    TextField text1;
    Button button1;

    public void init(){
        text1 = new TextField(20);
        add(text1);
        button1 = new Button("Click Here!");
        add(button1);
        button1.addActionListener(this);
    }
}
```

We've set up our ActionListener; now, when there are button events, they will be sent to our applet. But how do we make use of the button events?

Using Button Events

Catch the events sent to you by overriding the ActionListener interface's actionPerformed() method and adding your own version, which looks like this:

```java
import java.applet.Applet;
import java.awt.*;
import java.awt.event.*;

public class clicker extends Applet implements ActionListener {

    TextField text1;
    Button button1;

    public void init(){
        text1 = new TextField(20);
        add(text1);
        button1 = new Button("Click Here!");
        add(button1);
        button1.addActionListener(this);
    }

    public void actionPerformed(ActionEvent event){
        .
        .
        .

    }
}
```

This is the method that will be called when the user clicks your button. The ActionEvent object that is passed to you here holds information about the event that occurred. For example, if you have a number of buttons, clicking any one will call this method—how do you make sure that your button, button1, was clicked?

You can check which button was clicked with the ActionEvent class's getSource() method. This method returns the control that caused the event, and you can check to see if that control is button1:

```java
import java.applet.Applet;
import java.awt.*;
import java.awt.event.*;

public class clicker extends Applet implements ActionListener {

    TextField text1;
    Button button1;
```

```
public void init(){
    text1 = new TextField(20);
    add(text1);
    button1 = new Button("Click Here!");
    add(button1);
    button1.addActionListener(this);
}

public void actionPerformed(ActionEvent event){
    if(event.getSource() == button1){
            .
            .
            .

    }
  }
}
```

If the control that created the Java event is button1, the code you place in the code block—the code surrounded by the { and } braces following the if statement—will be executed. That's because you use the Java *equality* operator (= =) to compare the control returned by event.getSource() and button1.

 **NOTE**   In Java, if statements work the same way they do in just about any other programming language: if the expression in the parentheses of the if statement is true, the code in the code block is executed:

```
if(conditional){
[code block]
}
```

If button1 was indeed clicked, you want to display your message: "Welcome to Java," and you do that by first setting up a Java *String* object named msg (which, since we define it in actionPerformed(), will only be available in that procedure, making it a *local* variable), holding that text and then displaying that string in the text field using the TextField's setText() method:

```
import java.applet.Applet;
import java.awt.*;
import java.awt.event.*;

public class clicker extends Applet implements ActionListener {

    TextField text1;
    Button button1;
```

```
        public void init(){
            text1 = new TextField(20);
            add(text1);
            button1 = new Button("Click Here!");
            add(button1);
            button1.addActionListener(this);
        }

        public void actionPerformed(ActionEvent event){
➜           String msg = new String ("Welcome to Java");
            if(event.getSource() == button1){
➜               text1.setText(msg);
            }
        }
    }
```

You might also note here that we combined the two usual steps—declaring and creating an object—into one line with the msg variable.

The String class is a super-handy Java class that handles text strings for you. The methods of this class appear in Table 3.2, and it's worth taking a look at that table to see what's available.

TABLE 3.2: The Java String class methods

Method	Does This
String()	Constructs new String
String(byte[])	Constructs new String by converting the array of bytes into the string
String(byte[], ByteToCharConverter)	Construct new String converting the array of bytes using given character encoding converter
String(byte[], int)	Constructs new String from given array of bytes. Deprecated
String(byte[], int, int)	Constructs new String by converting the subarray using default character-encoding converter
String(byte[], int, int, ByteToCharConverter)	Constructs new String by converting the speci fied subarray of bytes using the given character-encoding converter
String(byte[], int, int, int)	Constructs new String from given subarray of bytes. Deprecated
String(char[])	Constructs new String from given array of characters

TABLE 3.2 CONTINUED: The Java `String` class methods

Method	Does This
`String(char[], int, int)`	Constructs new `String` from given subarray of characters
`String(String)`	Constructs new `String` copying given `String`
`String(StringBuffer)`	Constructs new `string` from contents of given string buffer
`charAt(int)`	Returns character at the given index
`compareTo(String)`	Compares String to another String
`concat(String)`	Concatenates given `string` to the end of this `String`
`copyValueOf(char[])`	Returns a `String` mode from given character array
`copyValueOf(char[], int, int)`	Returns a `String` that is equivalent to the specified character array
`endsWith(String)`	Determines if `String` ends with a suffix
`equals(Object)`	Compares `String` to the given object
`equalsIgnoreCase(String)`	Compares this `String` to another object
`getBytes()`	Apply the character-encoding converter to `String` storing result in a byte array
`getBytes(CharToByteConverter)`	Apply the given character-encoding converter to this `String`, storing result bytes in a new byte array
`getBytes(int, int, byte[], int)`	Copies characters from this `String` into the specified byte array. Deprecated
`getBytes(String)`	Convert this `String` into bytes according to the specified character encoding, storing the result into a new byte array
`getChars(int, int, char[], int)`	Copies characters from this `String` into the specified character array
`hashCode()`	Returns a hashcode for `String`
`indexOf(int)`	Returns index in `String` of first occurrence of the given character
`indexOf(int, int)`	Returns index in `String` of first occurrence of the given character, starting at `fromIndex`

TABLE 3.2 CONTINUED: The Java String class methods

Method	Does This
indexOf(String)	Returns index in String of first occurrence of given substring
indexOf(String, int)	Returns index in String of first occurrence of given substring
intern()	Returns a String that is equal to this String but that is guaranteed to be from the unique String pool
lastIndexOf(int)	Returns index in String of last occurrence of given character
lastIndexOf(int, int)	Returns index in String of last occurrence of given character
lastIndexOf(String)	Returns index within String of rightmost occurrence of given substring
lastIndexOf(String, int)	Returns index in String of last occurrence of given substring
length()	Returns length of this String
regionMatches(boolean, int, String, int, int)	Determines if a region of String matches given region of given String
regionMatches(int, String, int, int)	Determines if a region of String matches given region of given String
replace(char, char)	Converts this String by replacing all occurrences of oldChar with newChar
startsWith(String)	Determines if this String starts with some prefix
startsWith(String, int)	Determines if this String starts with some prefix
substring(int)	Returns substring of a String
substring(int, int)	Returns substring of a String
toCharArray()	Converts String to a character array
toLowerCase()	Converts characters in this String to lowercase (using the rules of the default locale)
toLowerCase(Locale)	Converts all of the characters in this String to lowercase using the rules of the given locale
toString()	Converts the object (in this case already a String) to a String
toUpperCase()	Converts all of the characters in this String to uppercase using the rules of the default locale

Skill 3

TABLE 3.2 CONTINUED: The Java String class methods

Method	Does This
toUpperCase(Locale)	Converts all of the characters in this String to uppercase using the rules of the given locale
trim()	Trims leading and trailing white space from this String
valueOf(boolean)	Returns a String object that represents the state of the given boolean
valueOf(char)	Returns a String object that contains a single character
valueOf(char[])	Returns a String that is equivalent to the given character array
valueOf(char[], int, int)	Returns a String that is equivalent to the given character array
valueOf(double)	Returns a String that represents the value of the double
valueOf(float)	Returns a String that represents the value of the float
valueOf(int)	Returns a String that represents the value of the integer
valueOf(long)	Returns a String that represents the value of the long

 TIP   The String class's methods now make use of the Java 1.1 Internationalization techniques, like using character-encoding converters and being locale-aware. Using the Java Locale class, you can set the formation of Strings with constants like Locale.FRENCH, Locale.GERMAN, and so on.

Now your new applet is complete. Build it now and run it. Click the button and watch the "Welcome to Java" message appear in the text field as shown below. The code for this applet appears in clicker.java.

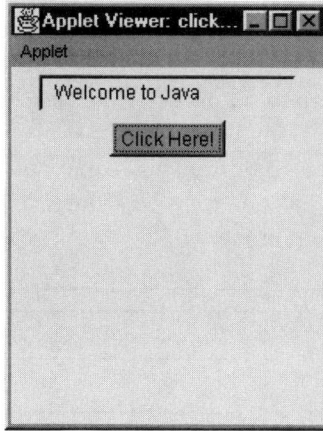

clicker.java

```
import java.applet.Applet;
import java.awt.*;
import java.awt.event.*;

public class clicker extends Applet implements ActionListener {

    TextField text1;
    Button button1;

    public void init(){
        text1 = new TextField(20);
        add(text1);
        button1 = new Button("Click Here!");
        add(button1);
        button1.addActionListener(this);
    }

    public void actionPerformed(ActionEvent event){
        String msg = new String ("Welcome to Java");
        if(event.getSource() == button1){
            text1.setText(msg);
        }
    }
}
```

So far, you've seen how to add both a text field and a button to your applet. Now let's turn to the next case—multiple buttons.

How to Handle Multiple Buttons

Say you want to set up a new applet that has two buttons, labeled "Welcome to" and "Java", along with a text box, as shown in Figure 3.4. When the user clicks the Welcome To button, you can display "Welcome to" in the text box, as shown in Figure 3.5. When they click the Java button, you can display "Java" in the text box, as shown in Figure 3.6.

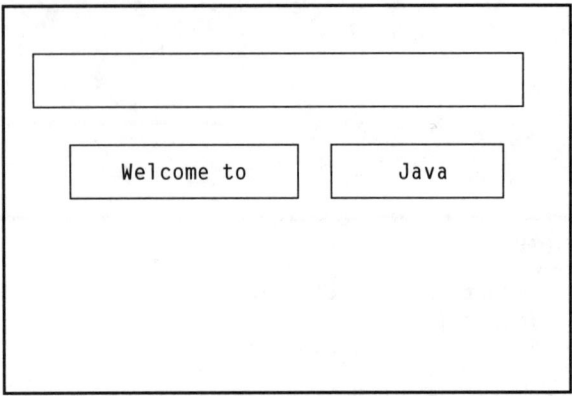

FIGURE 3.4: An applet with a text box and two buttons

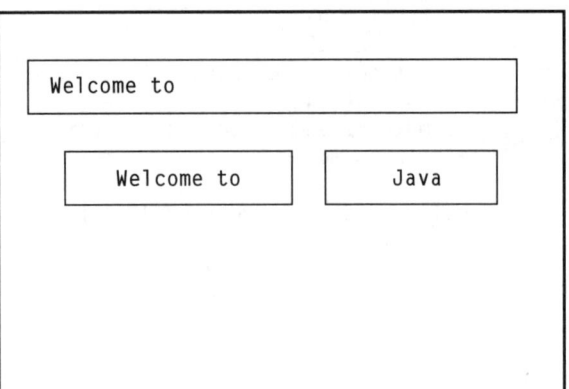

FIGURE 3.5: Click the Welcome To button and "Welcome to" appears in the text box.

FIGURE 3.6:   Click the Java button and "Java" appears in the text box.

Creating *clickers.java*

This exercise will give you the chance to see how to keep buttons separate and to learn a new and faster method of determining which button was clicked. Let's put this together now. Create a new file called `clickers.java`. You'll need two buttons, `button1` and `button2`, and a text field, `text1`. Add those to the beginning of your class definition as follows:

```
import java.applet.Applet;
import java.awt.*;
import java.awt.event.*;

public class clickers extends Applet {

→    TextField text1;
→    Button button1, button2;
         .
         .
         .

}
```

Next, create and add those controls to your applet in an `init()` method as you did in the last two examples:

```java
import java.applet.Applet;
import java.awt.*;
import java.awt.event.*;

public class clickers extends Applet {

    TextField text1;
    Button button1, button2;

➜   public void init(){

        .

        .

        .

➜   }
}
```

In this case, you want a text field and two buttons, one button with the caption "Welcome to" and the other with the caption "Java":

```java
import java.applet.Applet;
import java.awt.*;
import java.awt.event.*;

public class clickers extends Applet {

    TextField text1;
    Button button1, button2;

    public void init(){
➜       text1 = new TextField(20);
➜       add(text1);
➜       button1 = new Button("Welcome to");
➜       add(button1);
➜       button2 = new Button("Java");
➜       add(button2);
    }
}
```

At this point, you've added all the controls you'll need to your applet, as shown in Figure 3.7.

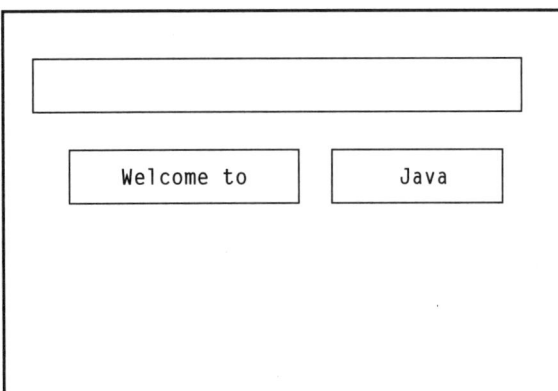

FIGURE 3.7:   Your applet contains three controls: two buttons and a text field.

Making *clickers.java* Work

Now it's time to get the new controls working. As before, do that by adding the actionPerformed() method to our class now, as well as the keywords implements ActionListener:

```
import java.applet.Applet;
import java.awt.*;
import java.awt.event.*;

public class clickers extends Applet implements ActionListener{

    TextField text1;
    Button button1, button2;

    public void init(){
        text1 = new TextField(20);
        add(text1);
        button1 = new Button("Welcome to");
        add(button1);
        button2 = new Button("Java");
        add(button2);
    }
```

```
→    public void actionPerformed(ActionEvent e){
                  .
                  .
                  .
→    }
    }
```

In addition to adding the `actionPerformed()` method and your keywords, you will connect your buttons to the ActionListener now—note that both buttons will be connected to the same ActionListener this way, as we use `addActionListener()`:

```
import java.applet.Applet;
import java.awt.*;
import java.awt.event.*;

→public class clickers extends Applet implements ActionListener{

    TextField text1;
    Button button1, button2;

    public void init(){
        text1 = new TextField(20);
        add(text1);
        button1 = new Button("Welcome to");
        add(button1);
→       button1.addActionListener(this);
        button2 = new Button("Java");
        add(button2);
→       button2.addActionListener(this);
    }

    public void actionPerformed(ActionEvent e){
                  .
                  .
                  .
    }
    }
```

Now your buttons are connected to the `actionPerformed()` method. The next step is to determine which button caused the click event that caused `actionPerformed()` to be called, and you can do that with the ActionEvent class's `getSource()` method. Here, the two buttons are `button1` and `button2`. Check to see which one was clicked as follows:

```
import java.applet.Applet;
import java.awt.*;
import java.awt.event.*;
```

```
public class clickers extends Applet implements ActionListener {

    TextField text1;
    Button button1, button2;

    public void init(){
        text1 = new TextField(20);
        add(text1);
        button1 = new Button("Welcome to");
        add(button1);
        button1.addActionListener(this);
        button2 = new Button("Java");
        add(button2);
        button2.addActionListener(this);
    }

    public void actionPerformed(ActionEvent e){
➜        if(e.getSource() == button1){

             .
             .
             .

➜        }
➜        if(e.getSource() == button2){

             .
             .
             .

➜        }
    }
}
```

In case button1 *was* clicked, place the text "Welcome to" in the text field text1
like this:

```
import java.applet.Applet;
import java.awt.*;
import java.awt.event.*;

public class clickers extends Applet implements ActionListener {

    TextField text1;
    Button button1, button2;

    public void init(){
        text1 = new TextField(20);
        add(text1);
        button1 = new Button("Welcome to");
        add(button1);
        button1.addActionListener(this);
        button2 = new Button("Java");
        add(button2);
```

```
        button2.addActionListener(this);
    }

    public void actionPerformed(ActionEvent e){
        if(e.getSource() == button1){
➜           text1.setText("Welcome to");
        }
        if(e.getSource() == button2){
            .
            .
            .
        }
    }
}
```

We can do the same for button2, which places the text "Java" in text1, as follows:

```
import java.applet.Applet;
import java.awt.*;
import java.awt.event.*;

public class clickers extends Applet implements ActionListener {

    TextField text1;
    Button button1, button2;

    public void init(){
        text1 = new TextField(20);
        add(text1);
        button1 = new Button("Welcome to");
        add(button1);
        button1.addActionListener(this);
        button2 = new Button("Java");
        add(button2);
        button2.addActionListener(this);
    }

    public void actionPerformed(ActionEvent e){
        if(e.getSource() == button1){
            text1.setText("Welcome to");
        }
        if(e.getSource() == button2){
➜           text1.setText("Java");
        }
    }
}
```

Your applet is complete. Build that applet now and execute it, as shown below. As you designed it, when the user clicks the Welcome To button, "Welcome to" appears in the text field; when they click the Java button, "Java" appears in the text field. Your applet is working. The listing for this applet appears in `clickers.java`.

clickers.java

```java
import java.applet.Applet;
import java.awt.*;
import java.awt.event.*;

public class clickers extends Applet implements ActionListener {

    TextField text1;
    Button button1, button2;

    public void init(){
        text1 = new TextField(20);
        add(text1);
        button1 = new Button("Welcome to");
        add(button1);
        button1.addActionListener(this);
        button2 = new Button("Java");
        add(button2);
        button2.addActionListener(this);
    }

    public void actionPerformed(ActionEvent e){
        if(e.getSource() == button1){
            text1.setText("Welcome to");
```

```
        }
        if(e.getSource() == button2){
            text1.setText("Java");
        }
    }
}
```

While we're working on text fields and buttons, let's take a look at the multi-line text field called a *text area*. Java uses a text area to support text that takes up more than one line.

Handling Java Text Areas

A text area really works in almost the same way that a text field does, but it can have several lines, as shown in Figure 3.8.

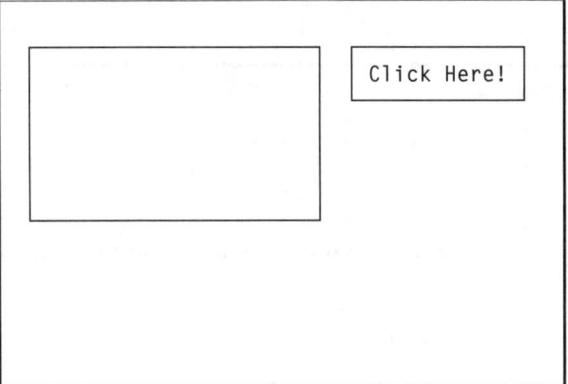

FIGURE 3.8:   An empty text area

This is the control to use when you have multiple lines of text to display, such as a set of instructions, or when you let the user edit a large amount of text. Text fields can do the same job, but for large amounts of text—especially text that has carriage returns or paragraphs—text areas are the way to go.

Creating *txtarea.java*

Let's put together an example applet using a text area. When the user clicks a button labeled "Click Here", you can place a message saying: "Welcome to Java" in the text area, as shown in Figure 3.9.

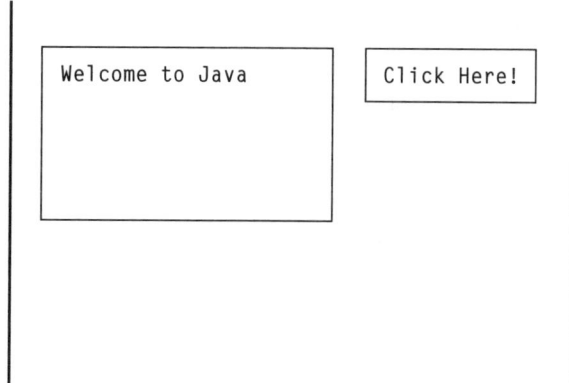

FIGURE 3.9: When the user clicks the button, "Welcome to Java" appears in the text area.

Handle a text area much as you would handle a text field; let's see one in action. Create a new file named `txtarea.java`. Open that file now and add the usual starting code:

```
import java.applet.Applet;
import java.awt.*;
import java.awt.event.*;

public class txtarea extends Applet {
    .
    .
    .
}
```

As with previous examples, add a button, `button1`, to your applet. Next, add a text area object of the Java class `TextArea`, calling that object, say, `textarea1`, giving it five rows and twenty columns, and starting it off with an empty string,

" " to display. (That is, the text area will appear blank.) We pass those values, " ", 5, and 20, as *parameters* to the TextArea constructor:

```
import java.applet.Applet;
import java.applet.Applet;
import java.awt.*;
import java.awt.event.*;

public class txtarea extends Applet {

→    TextArea textarea1;
→    Button button1;

     public void init(){
→        textarea1 = new TextArea("", 5, 20);
→        add(textarea1);
→        button1 = new Button("Click Here!");
         add(button1);
            .
            .
            .
     }
```

The Java TextArea class methods appear in Table 3.3.

T A B L E 3.3: TextArea class methods

Method	Does This
TextArea()	Constructs new TextArea
TextArea(int, int)	Deprecated. Replaced by TextArea(String, int, int)
TextArea(String)	Constructs new TextArea with the specified text
TextArea(String, int, int)	Constructs new TextArea with given text and number of rows and columns
TextArea(String, int, int, int)	Constructs new TextArea with given text and number of rows, columns, and scrollbar "visibility"
addNotify()	Creates TextArea's peer
append(String)	Appends given text to end of TextArea
appendText(String)	Deprecated. Replaced by append(String)

TABLE 3.3 CONTINUED: TextArea class methods

Method	Does This
getColumns()	Returns number of columns in TextArea
getMinimumSize()	Returns minimum size Dimensions of TextArea
getMinimumSize(int, int)	Returns given minimum size Dimensions of TextArea
getPreferredSize()	Returns the preferred Dimensions of TextArea
getPreferredSize(int, int)	Returns given row and column Dimensions of TextArea
getRows()	Returns the number of rows in the TextArea
getScrollbarVisibility()	Returns enumerated value describing which scrollbars TextArea has
insert(String, int)	Inserts the given text at the given position
insertText(String, int)	Deprecated. Replaced by insert(String, int)
minimumSize()	Deprecated. Replaced by getMinimumSize()
minimumSize(int, int)	Deprecated. Replaced by getMinimumSize (int, int)
paramString()	Returns the String of parameters for this TextArea
preferredSize()	Deprecated. Replaced by getPreferredSize()
preferredSize(int, int)	Deprecated. Replaced by getPreferredSize (int, int)
replaceRange(String, int, int)	Replaces text from the indicated start to end position with the new text given
replaceText(String, int, int)	Deprecated. Replaced by replaceRange (String, int, int)
setColumns(int)	Sets the number of columns for TextArea

Making *txtarea.java* Work

Now add the keywords implements ActionListener and make the applet's main class a listener for the Click Here! button:

```
import java.applet.Applet;
import java.awt.*;
```

Skill 3

```
 import java.awt.event.*;

→public class txtarea extends Applet implements ActionListener{

    TextArea textarea1;
    Button button1;

    public void init(){
        textarea1 = new TextArea("", 5, 20);
        add(textarea1);
        button1 = new Button("Click Here!");
        add(button1);
→       button1.addActionListener(this);
    }
 }
```

In addition, you'll need an `actionPerformed()` method to catch button clicks:

```
import java.awt.*;
import java.awt.event.*;

public class txtarea extends Applet implements ActionListener {

    TextArea textarea1;
    Button button1;

    public void init(){
        textarea1 = new TextArea("", 5, 20);
        add(textarea1);
        button1 = new Button("Click Here!");
        add(button1);
        button1.addActionListener(this);
    }

→   public void actionPerformed (ActionEvent e){
                .
                .
                .

→   }
 }
```

If the button is indeed clicked, you can place your "Welcome to Java" text into the text area. Instead of using `setText()` to set the text of your text area as you did for text fields, you will use the `TextArea` class's `insert()` method.

> **TIP**   The insert() method, which lets you insert text at a specific location, is unique to text areas—text fields do not have this method. With insert(), you treat all the text in the text area as one long string, each character counting as one place, and you indicate the position at which you want to insert your new text by passing that location as an integer to insert().

You can insert your text at a specified position in the text area. In this case, place the "Welcome to Java" message at the beginning of the text area so you pass a location of 0. We create a new String object named msg and then display that string using insert() to place it into the text area:

```java
import java.applet.Applet;
import java.awt.*;
import java.awt.event.*;

public class txtarea extends Applet implements ActionListener {

    TextArea textarea1;
    Button button1;

    public void init(){
        textarea1 = new TextArea("", 5, 20);
        add(textarea1);
        button1 = new Button("Click Here!");
        add(button1);
        button1.addActionListener(this);
    }

    public void actionPerformed (ActionEvent e){
        String msg = "Welcome to Java";
        if(e.getSource() == button1){
            textarea1.insert(msg, 0);
        }
    }
}
```

Run the new applet, as shown below. As you can see, your new text area is working. Now you're able to support not only buttons and text fields, but text areas as well. If the user were to edit the text in the text area, they'd find out that it supports multiple lines and that they can use the Enter key as they type. The listing for this applet appears in txtarea.java.

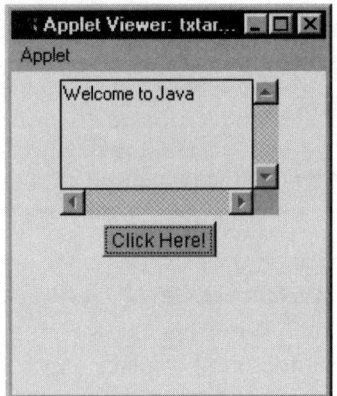

ⓒ txtarea.java

```java
import java.applet.Applet;
import java.awt.*;
import java.awt.event.*;

public class txtarea extends Applet implements ActionListener {

    TextArea textarea1;
    Button button1;

    public void init(){
        textarea1 = new TextArea("", 5, 20);
        add(textarea1);
        button1 = new Button("Click Here!");
        add(button1);
        button1.addActionListener(this);
    }

    public void actionPerformed (ActionEvent e){
        String msg = "Welcome to Java";
        if(e.getSource() == button1){
            textarea1.insert(msg, 0);
        }
    }
}
```

This completes our guided tour of buttons and text fields. You've learned how to add controls to our programs, use text boxes, use buttons, and use text areas.

Let's turn now to Skill 4, in which you will start working with a new Java control: check boxes.

Are You up to Speed?

Now you can. . .

- ☑ add and use a button in a program
- ☑ store strings of text in a program, using the Java *String* class
- ☑ use Java events to interact with the user
- ☑ handle multiple buttons in the *actionPerformed()* method
- ☑ display multiple lines of text
- ☑ add and use text areas

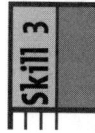

Skill 3

SKILL 4

Using Java Layouts and Check Boxes

- Building programs with check boxes
- Using Java layouts to arrange controls
- Converting text from text fields to numbers
- Reading input from text fields
- Using the Java *Label* control
- Working with the GridLayout manager

You've already come far: you've worked with text fields, text areas, and buttons. However, there are many more powerful Java controls, and one of those is the check box. In this skill, we're going to take a look at check boxes. This new control is important by itself, but you'll also learn more about coordinating controls (handling and arranging a number of controls together) in a Java program. The reason you'll learn more about coordinating controls like this is that controls like check boxes and radio buttons are meant to be handled in *groups*. You often use check boxes to choose one or more selections among a group of selections, and radio buttons are even more group-oriented—they are used to allow the user to select one option among many.

What Is a Java Layout?

In Skills 1 through 3 you did not perform any special placement of text fields and buttons in your applets—Java handled the placement of controls for you. That is both good and bad—it's good if things work out the way you want them, but bad otherwise.

You have been using Java's default *layout manager*, the FlowLayout manager. Layout managers control the placement of controls in an applet. You can select which layout manager to use, and that's a good thing because often the default layout manager will not arrange your controls the way you want them.

Let's take a look at an example. In this case, you want to build a small adding calculator applet. All you'll do is take two integers from the user, add them together, and display the result. This applet will require you to handle both text and numeric input, as well as layout managers. Let's get started now.

Building the Adder Applet

Your goal is simply to create a Java applet that acts as an adding calculator. You can make this calculator up of text fields and buttons: one text field for the first number, one for the second, a button for the equals sign, and another text field for the answer. To add 2 + 2, the user will enter that data into the first two text fields, as shown in Figure 4.1. Then, when they click the button whose caption is "=", they will see the result in the bottom text field, as shown in Figure 4.2.

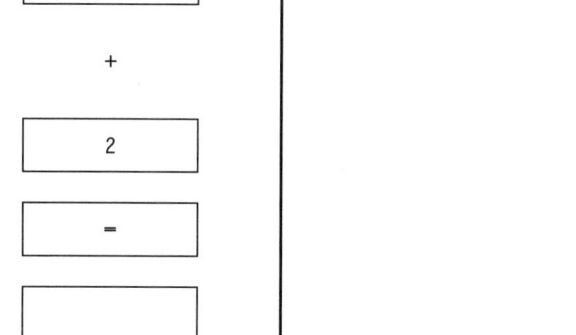

FIGURE 4.1: The user enters data into the first two text fields of our applet.

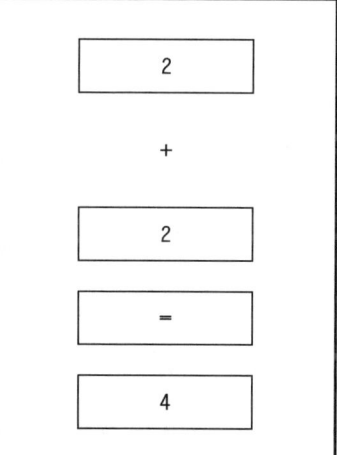

FIGURE 4.2: When the user clicks the = button, the sum of the first two text fields appears in the third text field.

The *Label* Control

You may wonder at first how to place a plus sign between the top two text boxes and may assume that you should use the `drawString()` method as you did in Skill 1, but in fact you'll place the plus sign in a new type of control: a `Label` control. This control is a control like any other—it displays text and nothing more. The methods of the `Label` control appear in Table 4.1.

T A B L E 4.1: The Label class methods

Method	Does This
`Label()`	Constructs an empty label
`Label(String)`	Constructs a label with given text
`Label(String, int)`	Constructs a label with given text and alignment (`Label.RIGHT`, `Label.CENTER`, or `Label.LEFT`)
`addNotify()`	Creates a peer for Label
`getAlignment()`	Gets alignment of Label
`getText()`	Gets caption of Label
`paramString()`	Returns parameter string of Label
`setAlignment(int)`	Sets alignment for Label (`Label.RIGHT`, `Label.CENTER`, or `Label.LEFT`)
`setText(String)`	Sets text in Label

TIP Note that you can set the text of a label control with the `setText()` method just as you can in a text field. You can also align the text in the label to the right, left, or center by passing one of the Label class's pre-defined constants to the constructor or the `setAlignment()` method: `Label.RIGHT`, `Label.LEFT`, or `Label.CENTER`.

Let's start this project. Create a new file named `adder.java` now, and add the usual starting code, including a new class named `adder`:

```
import java.applet.Applet;
import java.awt.*;
import java.awt.event.*;

public class adder extends Applet {

}
```

First, add all the controls you'll need, including the new label, `pluslabel`, like this:

```
import java.applet.Applet;
import java.awt.*;
import java.awt.event.*;

public class adder extends Applet {

    TextField text1, text2, answertext;
    Label pluslabel;
    Button button1;
        .
        .
        .

}
```

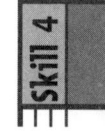

Next, you have to initialize these controls in the `init()` method, so add that method now:

```
import java.applet.Applet;
import java.awt.*;
import java.awt.event.*;

public class adder extends Applet {

    TextField text1, text2, answertext;
    Label pluslabel;
    Button button1;

    public void init(){
        .
        .
        .

    }

}
```

Your first job is to add the top text field, `text1`. You do so in the `init()` method as follows:

```
import java.applet.Applet;
import java.awt.*;
import java.awt.event.*;

public class adder extends Applet {

    TextField text1, text2, answertext;
    Label pluslabel;
    Button button1;
```

```
        public void init(){

→           text1 = new TextField(10);
→           add(text1);
                    .
                    .
                    .
        }

    }
```

 **NOTE**   When you use the add() method, you are adding controls to our applet using the default layout manager, which is called the *FlowLayout* manager.

You've added the first text field. Next, you can add the plus sign that is supposed to appear between the top two text fields.

Adding a Java *Label* Control

You've already declared the label control that will display your plus sign as an object of the Java class Label, and called it pluslabel:

```
import java.applet.Applet;
import java.awt.*;
import java.awt.event.*;

public class adder extends Applet implements ActionListener {

    TextField text1, text2, answertext;
→   Label pluslabel;
    Button button1;
        .
        .
        .
```

Now, in the init() method, you can create this label object and add it to your applet's layout. Do so as follows:

```
import java.applet.Applet;
import java.awt.*;
import java.awt.event.*;

public class adder extends Applet {

    TextField text1, text2, answertext;
    Label pluslabel;
    Button button1;
```

```
public void init(){

    text1 = new TextField(10);
    add(text1);

→   pluslabel = new Label("+");
→   add(pluslabel);
            .
            .
            .

}
```

Label controls are very useful, as their name indicates, when you want to label anything, including other controls. They present you with an easy way to display text without having to worry about redrawing that text when the applet is uncovered or redisplayed.

Now add the other controls: the second text field, the equals button, and the answer text field. In init(), add the controls as follows:

```
import java.applet.Applet;
import java.awt.*;
import java.awt.event.*;

public class adder extends Applet {

    TextField text1, text2, answertext;
    Label pluslabel;
    Button button1;

    public void init(){

        text1 = new TextField(10);
        add(text1);

        pluslabel = new Label("+");
        add(pluslabel);

→       text2 = new TextField(10);
→       add(text2);

→       button1 = new Button("=");
→       add(button1);

→       answertext = new TextField(10);
→       add(answertext);
    }
}
```

At this point, then, you've added all the controls we'll need. The next step is to connect the controls to our code and make your adding calculator work.

Writing the Adder Applet

You make your calculator work by responding to the user when they click the = button. To do that, implement the ActionListener interface, connect your button to it, and add the `actionPerformed()` method to your applet now:

```java
import java.applet.Applet;
import java.awt.*;
import java.awt.event.*;

public class adder extends Applet implements ActionListener {

    TextField text1, text2, answertext;
    Label pluslabel;
    Button button1;

    public void init(){

        text1 = new TextField(10);
        add(text1);

        pluslabel = new Label("+");
        add(pluslabel);

        text2 = new TextField(10);
        add(text2);

        button1 = new Button("=");
        add(button1);
        button1.addActionListener(this);

        answertext = new TextField(10);
        add(answertext);

    }

    public void actionPerformed(ActionEvent e) {
        .
        .
        .
    }

}
```

When the user clicks the = button, you want to read the two integers in the top two text fields, add them, and display the result in the bottom text field (the `answertext` text field). Start in the `actionPerformed()` method by making sure that the = button (`button1`) was the button that was clicked:

```java
import java.applet.Applet;
import java.awt.*;
import java.awt.event.*;

public class adder extends Applet implements ActionListener {

    TextField text1, text2, answertext;
    Label pluslabel;
    Button button1;

    public void init(){

        text1 = new TextField(10);
        add(text1);

        pluslabel = new Label("+");
        add(pluslabel);

        text2 = new TextField(10);
        add(text2);

        button1 = new Button("=");
        add(button1);
        button1.addActionListener(this);

        answertext = new TextField(10);
        add(answertext);

    }

    public void actionPerformed(ActionEvent e) {
        if(e.getSource() == button1){
            .
            .
            .

        }
    }

}
```

When the = button is clicked, go on to read the integers the user placed in the top two text fields, `text1` and `text2`. How do you do that?

Reading Numeric Data from Text Fields

You saw in Skill 3 that you can place text in a text field with the setText() method. To read text, it turns out you can use the text field's getText() method like this: text1.getText(). This syntax returns the string of text in the text field text1. For example, if the user has placed "2" in text1, you get "2" back—but that is a text string, and *not* a numeric value. How do you convert the string "2" to the actual number 2? You do that with the Java Integer class.

The Java Integer class has a method called parseInt() that takes text and returns an integer value. For example, you can get the text in the text field text1 this way:

```
text1.getText()
```

And you can convert that text to an integer value this way:

```
Integer.parseInt(text1.getText())
```

 **TIP**   Besides the parseInt() method, Java also has a parseLong() method, and a parseNumbers() method for floating point values. You can do other things with classes like Integer too—if you want to check the maximum or minimum possible values an integer can hold, just look at that class's constants named MAX_VALUE or MIN_VALUE like this: int big_number = Integer.MAX_VALUE;.

In your applet, this means that you can now take the integer in text1, add it to the integer in text2, and store the result in a new integer called sum as follows:

```
import java.applet.Applet;
import java.awt.*;
import java.awt.event.*;

public class adder extends Applet implements ActionListener {

    TextField text1, text2, answertext;
    Label pluslabel;
    Button button1;

    public void init(){

        text1 = new TextField(10);
        add(text1);
```

```
        pluslabel = new Label("+");
        add(pluslabel);

        text2 = new TextField(10);
        add(text2);

        button1 = new Button("=");
        add(button1);
        button1.addActionListener(this);

        answertext = new TextField(10);
        add(answertext);

    }

    public void actionPerformed(ActionEvent e) {
        if(e.getSource() == button1){
            int sum = Integer.parseInt(text1.getText()) +
    Integer.parseInt(text2.getText());
                .
                .
                .
        }
    }

}
```

TIP

You may be surprised to see (unless you program in C++) that you can declare new variables like sum right in the middle of your code, rather than having to do it at the beginning of the function. This is a very useful aspect of Java—if you declare variables in a specific block of code (blocks of code are set apart with { and }), then the variables you declare inside that block of code are created when you enter that block and destroyed when you leave. In practical terms, that means you can declare variables as you like throughout a Java program.

Now that you have the answer you want to display in the integer named sum, convert that value to a string so you can display it in the answer text field.

Putting Numeric Data into Text Fields

At this point, you need to take an integer value (in the variable named sum) and convert it to a string that you can display in the text field answertext. The Java String class will help you here because it has a method called valueOf() designed for just this case. You can pass a number to the valueOf() method, and receive a string of text representing that number. In code, that looks like this:

```java
import java.applet.Applet;
import java.awt.*;
import java.awt.event.*;

public class adder extends Applet implements ActionListener {

    TextField text1, text2, answertext;
    Label pluslabel;
    Button button1;

    public void init(){

        text1 = new TextField(10);
        add(text1);

        pluslabel = new Label("+");
        add(pluslabel);

        text2 = new TextField(10);
        add(text2);

        button1 = new Button("=");
        add(button1);
        button1.addActionListener(this);

        answertext = new TextField(10);
        add(answertext);

    }

    public void actionPerformed(ActionEvent e) {
        if(e.getSource() == button1){
→           int sum = Integer.parseInt(text1.getText()) +
    Integer.parseInt(text2.getText());
→           answertext.setText(String.valueOf(sum));
        }
    }

}
```

TIP   The String class method valueOf() is overloaded to handle not only integers, but longs, doubles, and floats as well.

Your applet is ready to go. The listing for this applet appears in adder.java.

adder.java, version 1

```
import java.applet.Applet;
import java.awt.*;
import java.awt.event.*;

public class adder extends Applet implements ActionListener {

    TextField text1, text2, answertext;
    Label pluslabel;
    Button button1;

    public void init(){

        text1 = new TextField(10);
        add(text1);

        pluslabel = new Label("+");
        add(pluslabel);

        text2 = new TextField(10);
        add(text2);

        button1 = new Button("=");
        add(button1);
        button1.addActionListener(this);

        answertext = new TextField(10);
        add(answertext);

    }

    public void actionPerformed(ActionEvent e) {
        if(e.getSource() == button1){
            int sum = Integer.parseInt(text1.getText()) +
Integer.parseInt(text2.getText());
            answertext.setText(String.valueOf(sum));
        }
    }

}
```

Skill 4

Build the applet and run it, creating the display shown below (your results will depend on the width you set for the applet's page in the applet viewer).

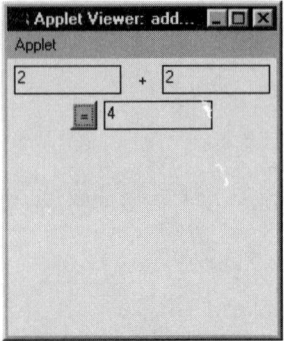

As you can see, the calculator functions, but it looks all wrong—the controls are all on two lines and look scrambled. That's because you are using the default layout manager. As shown in Figure 4.3, this layout manager just adds controls to an applet like you might add text to a document in a word processor—row by row, like words on a page. When it comes to the end of a row, it simply wraps the next controls around to the next line, as shown in Figure 4.4.

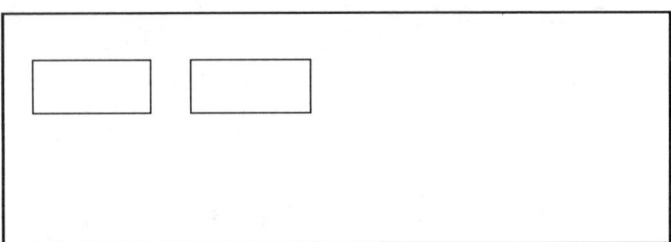

FIGURE 4.3:   The default layout manager adds controls to an applet row by row, like words on a page.

Up until now, that has been sufficient layout control, but the adding calculator demands more control of the layout. Let's take a look at a new layout manager—the GridLayout manager—now.

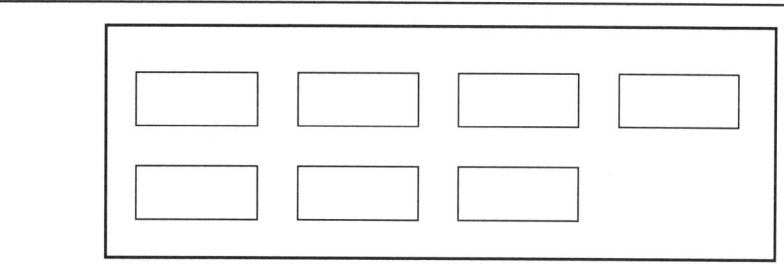

FIGURE 4.4:   When the default layout manager comes to the end of a row, it wraps the next controls.

Working with the Java Grid Layout

The controls on your calculator must be placed as shown in Figure 4.5: vertically, not horizontally. You can place them vertically by replacing the default FlowLayout manager in your applet with another layout manager—the GridLayout manager.

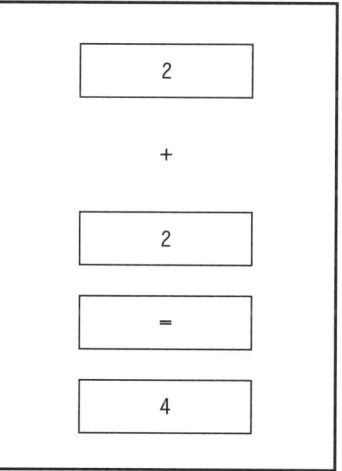

FIGURE 4.5:   Your controls must be arranged vertically.

Using the GridLayout Manager

The FlowLayout manager simply places controls in an applet one by one, wrapping them at the end of a row. The GridLayout manager, on the other hand, is often more useful, because it places controls in a grid, as shown in Figure 4.6. To arrange your adding calculator's controls vertically, add them to your applet in a grid of dimensions 9x3, as shown in Figure 4.7.

FIGURE 4.6:   The GridLayout manager places controls on a grid.

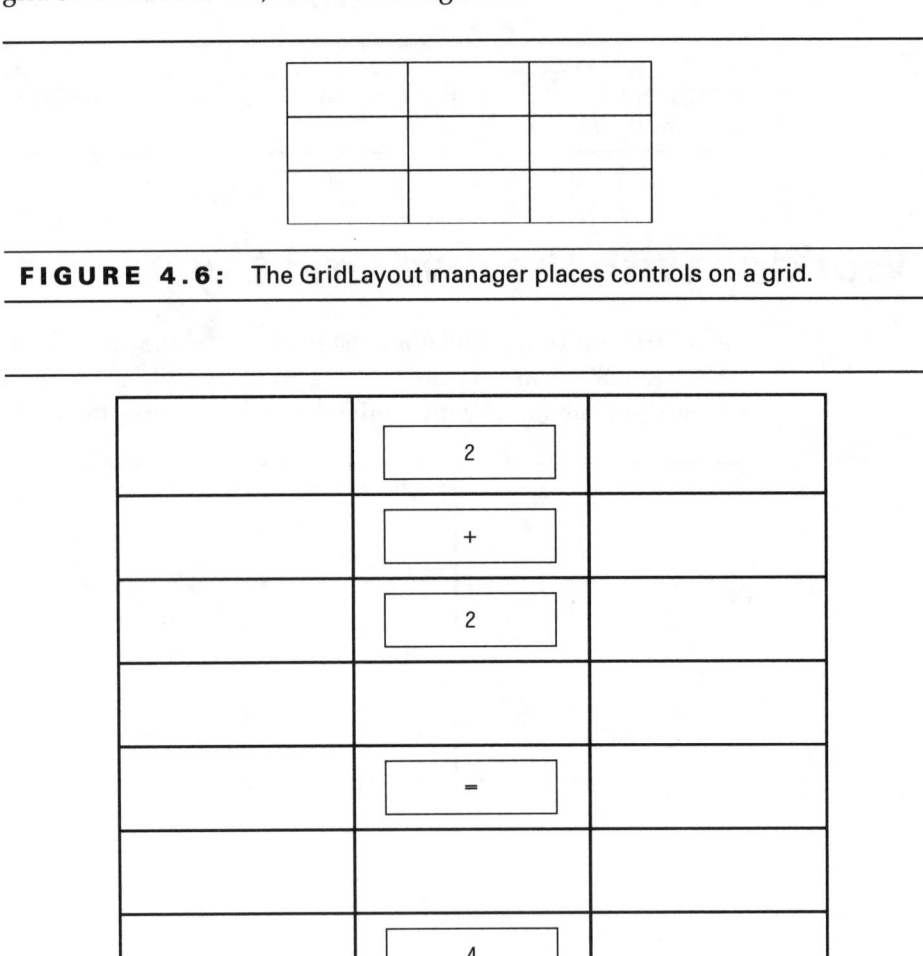

FIGURE 4.7:   Your calculator with padded cells arranged in a grid

To add your calculator's controls to your applet in a 9x3 grid, install the GridLayout manager in your applet and then add the controls to it. As you add controls to the layout manager, it will place them in the grid, one after the other, row by row. That means that you have to fill all of the entries in the grid, not just the entries that hold the controls you want to display. One way of solving this problem is to use a set of labels without any text that act as spacers. Add these labels now, giving them the names shown in Figure 4.8.

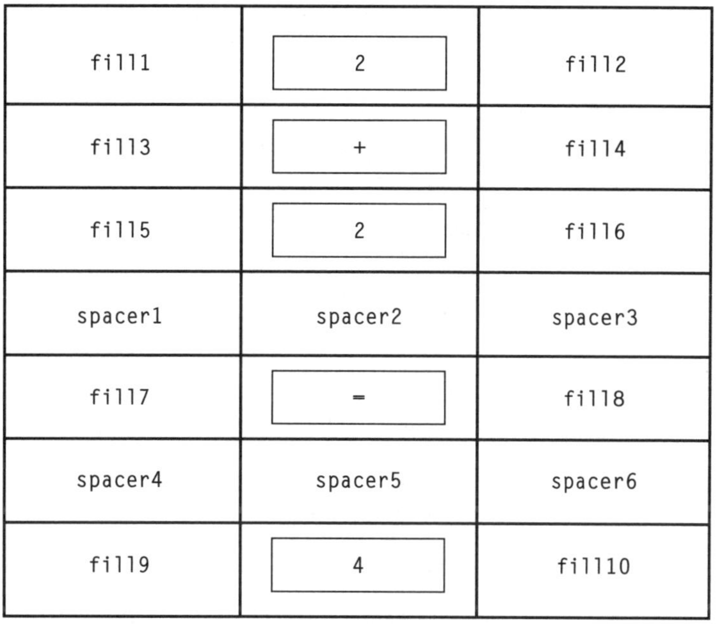

fill1	2	fill2
fill3	+	fill4
fill5	2	fill6
spacer1	spacer2	spacer3
fill7	=	fill8
spacer4	spacer5	spacer6
fill9	4	fill10

FIGURE 4.8: Adding labels to every entry in the grid

Add these spacer labels to the **adder** class as shown below.

```
import java.applet.Applet;
import java.applet.Applet;
import java.awt.*;
import java.awt.event.*;

public class adder2 extends Applet implements ActionListener {

    TextField text1, text2, answertext;
    Label pluslabel, fill1, fill2, fill3, fill4, fill5,
```

```
→    fill6, fill7, fill8, fill9, fill10;
→    Label spacer1, spacer2, spacer3, spacer4, spacer5, spacer6;
     Button button1;
         .
         .
         .
}
```

Now you can install the GridLayout manager as your new layout manager.

Adding a GridLayout Manager

Install the GridLayout manager (replacing the default FlowLayout manager) in
the init() method before you have added any controls to the layout. In this case,
you want a grid of 9 rows and 3 columns, and you set that up with the setLayout()
method as follows:

```
import java.applet.Applet;
import java.awt.*;
import java.awt.event.*;

public class adder2 extends Applet implements ActionListener {

    TextField text1, text2, answertext;
    Label pluslabel, fill1, fill2, fill3, fill4, fill5,
    fill6, fill7, fill8, fill9, fill10;
    Label spacer1, spacer2, spacer3, spacer4, spacer5, spacer6;
    Button button1;

    public void init(){

→        setLayout(new GridLayout(9, 3));
             .
             .
             .
    }
}
```

Now your applet uses a grid layout. Add the other controls, including the
spacer labels, the same way (note in particular that to place the plus sign in the
middle of its label you include the class constant Label.CENTER in the call to the
Label class's constructor):

```
import java.applet.Applet;
import java.awt.*;
import java.awt.event.*;
```

```
public class adder2 extends Applet implements ActionListener {

    TextField text1, text2, answertext;
    Label pluslabel, fill1, fill2, fill3, fill4, fill5,
    fill6, fill7, fill8, fill9, fill10;
    Label spacer1, spacer2, spacer3, spacer4, spacer5, spacer6;
    Button button1;

    public void init(){

        setLayout(new GridLayout(9, 3));

        fill1 = new Label();
        add(fill1);
        text1 = new TextField(10);
        add(text1);
        fill2 = new Label();
        add(fill2);

        fill3 = new Label();
        add(fill3);
        pluslabel = new Label("+", Label.CENTER);
        add(pluslabel);
        fill4 = new Label();
        add(fill4);

        fill5 = new Label();
        add(fill5);
        text2 = new TextField(10);
        add(text2);
        fill6 = new Label();
        add(fill6);

        spacer1 = new Label();
        add(spacer1);
        spacer2 = new Label();
        add(spacer2);
        spacer3 = new Label();
        add(spacer3);

        fill7 = new Label();
        add(fill7);
        button1 = new Button("=");
        add(button1);
        button1.addActionListener(this);
        fill8 = new Label();
        add(fill8);
```

Skill 4

```
→        spacer4 = new Label();
→        add(spacer4);
→        spacer5 = new Label();
→        add(spacer5);
→        spacer6 = new Label();
→        add(spacer6);

→        fill9 = new Label();
→        add(fill9);
→        answertext = new TextField(10);
→        add(answertext);
→        fill10 = new Label();
→        add(fill10);
→    }
}
```

Now your controls will be aligned vertically. Build and run the new version of the numbers applet now. As you can see in the graphic below, your controls are placed as you want them—your grid layout example is a success. The code for this applet appears in adder.java.

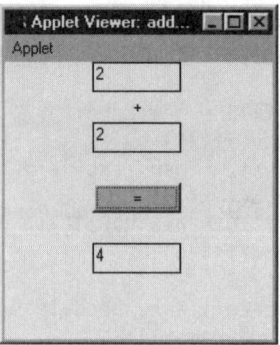

 adder.java, version 2 (with layout)

```
import java.applet.Applet;
import java.awt.*;
import java.awt.event.*;

public class adder2 extends Applet implements ActionListener {

    TextField text1, text2, answertext;
```

```
Label pluslabel, fill1, fill2, fill3, fill4, fill5,
fill6, fill7, fill8, fill9, fill10;
Label spacer1, spacer2, spacer3, spacer4, spacer5, spacer6;
Button button1;

public void init(){

    setLayout(new GridLayout(9, 3));

    fill1 = new Label();
    add(fill1);
    text1 = new TextField(10);
    add(text1);
    fill2 = new Label();
    add(fill2);

    fill3 = new Label();
    add(fill3);
    pluslabel = new Label("+", Label.CENTER);
    add(pluslabel);
    fill4 = new Label();
    add(fill4);

    fill5 = new Label();
    add(fill5);
    text2 = new TextField(10);
    add(text2);
    fill6 = new Label();
    add(fill6);

    spacer1 = new Label();
    add(spacer1);
    spacer2 = new Label();
    add(spacer2);
    spacer3 = new Label();
    add(spacer3);

    fill7 = new Label();
    add(fill7);
    button1 = ncw Button("=");
    add(button1);
    button1.addActionListener(this);
    fill8 = new Label();
    add(fill8);

    spacer4 = new Label();
    add(spacer4);
    spacer5 = new Label();
```

Skill 4

```
            add(spacer5);
            spacer6 = new Label();
            add(spacer6);

            fill9 = new Label();
            add(fill9);
            answertext = new TextField(10);
            add(answertext);
            fill10 = new Label();
            add(fill10);
        }

    public void actionPerformed(ActionEvent e){
        if(e.getSource() == button1){
→           int sum = Integer.parseInt(text1.getText()) +
  Integer.parseInt(text2.getText());
            answertext.setText(String.valueOf(sum));
        }
    }
}
```

Now that you are somewhat familiar with layouts, let's press on to work with check boxes, which are often used in special layouts, as you'll soon see.

Building Programs with Check Boxes

We will begin check boxes with a simple check box example. In this case, you'll just put five check boxes into your applet, as shown in Figure 4.9. When the user clicks one of these check boxes, you can indicate that action in a text field, as shown in Figure 4.10.

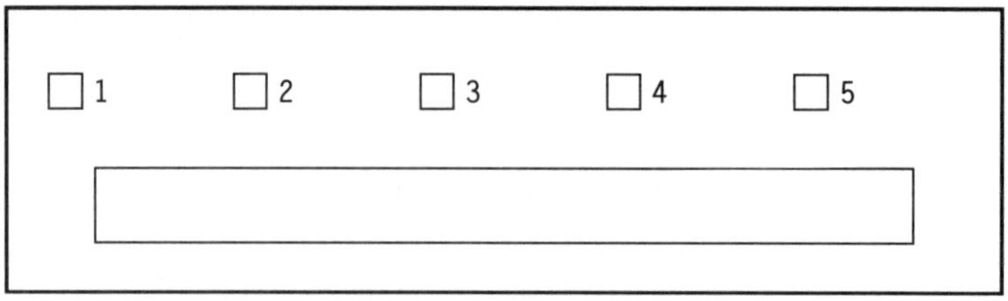

FIGURE 4.9:   An applet with five check boxes and a text field

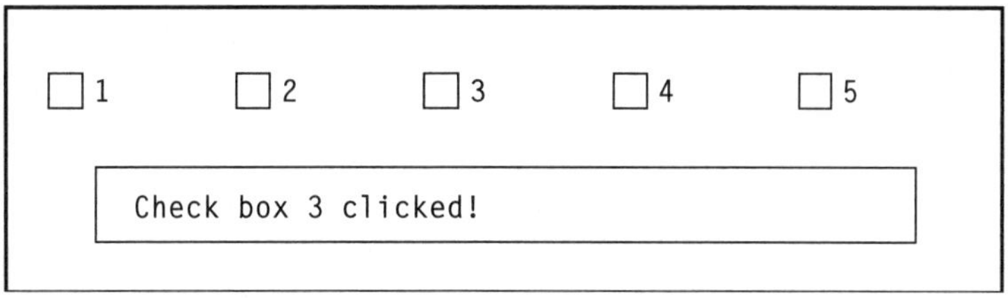

FIGURE 4.10: When the user clicks check box 3, the message "Check box 3 clicked!" appears in the text field.

Now you'll create a new applet called *checker*. Create a new file named checker.java and create a new class named checker as shown below:

```
import java.applet.Applet;
import java.awt.*;
import java.awt.event.*;

public class checker extends Applet {

}
```

Now you can declare the five check boxes you'll need—naming them, checkbox1 to checkbox5—and the text field, called text1, that you'll use to report when the user clicks a check box. Check boxes are created with the Java Checkbox class, so declare your five check boxes as follows:

```
import java.applet.Applet;
import java.awt.*;
import java.awt.event.*;

public class checker extends Applet{
→Checkbox checkbox1, checkbox2, checkbox3, checkbox4, checkbox5;
→    TextField text1;
         .
         .
         .
    }
```

The Java Checkbox class methods appear in Table 4.2.

As with other controls, you actually create and add the new check boxes to your applet in the `init()` method, so create that method now:

```
import java.applet.Applet;
import java.awt.*;
import java.awt.event.*;

public class checker extends Applet {
```
→   `Checkbox checkbox1, checkbox2, checkbox3, checkbox4, checkbox5;`
              `TextField text1;`

→   `public void init(){`

→   `}`

     `}`

T A B L E 4.2: The Checkbox class methods

Method	Does This
`Checkbox()`	Constructs a Checkbox with an empty label
`Checkbox(String)`	Constructs a Checkbox with the given label
`Checkbox(String, boolean)`	Constructs a Checkbox with the given label
`Checkbox(String, boolean, CheckboxGroup)`	Constructs a Checkbox with the given label, set to the given state, and in the given check box group
`Checkbox(String, CheckboxGroup, boolean)`	Deprecated. Replaced by `Checkbox(String, boolean, CheckboxGroup)`
`addItemListener(ItemListener)`	Adds the given item listener to receive item events from this Checkbox
`addNotify()`	Creates the peer of the Checkbox
`getCheckboxGroup()`	Returns the Checkbox group
`getLabel()`	Gets the label of the Checkbox
`getSelectedObjects()`	Returns an array (length 1) containing the selected Checkbox's label or null if the Checkbox is not selected
`getState()`	Returns the boolean state of the Checkbox
`paramString()`	Returns the parameter String of this Checkbox
`processEvent(AWTEvent)`	Processes events on this Checkbox

TABLE 4.2 CONTINUED: The Checkbox class methods

Method	Does This
processItemEvent(ItemEvent)	Processes item events occurring on this Checkbox by dispatching them to any registered ItemListener objects
removeItemListener(ItemListener)	Removes the given item listener so that it no longer receives item events from this Checkbox
setCheckboxGroup(CheckboxGroup)	Sets the CheckboxGroup to the given group
setLabel(String)	Sets this Checkbox's label to be the given string
setState(Boolean)	Sets the check box's state.

All you have to do here is add the check boxes and the text field. Add the check box checkbox1 like this:

```
import java.applet.Applet;
import java.awt.*;
import java.awt.event.*;

public class checker extends Applet {

    Checkbox checkbox1, checkbox2, checkbox3, checkbox4, checkbox5;
    TextField text1;

    public void init(){

➜       checkbox1 = new Checkbox("1");
➜       add(checkbox1);
            .
            .
            .

    }
}
```

Note that you can give the check box a label (here that label is simply 1) by passing a string to the Checkbox class's constructor, as you did above. All that remains now is to add the other check boxes and the text field:

```
import java.applet.Applet;
import java.awt.*;
import java.awt.event.*;

public class checker extends Applet {
```

```
        Checkbox checkbox1, checkbox2, checkbox3, checkbox4, checkbox5;
        TextField text1;

        public void init(){

            checkbox1 = new Checkbox("1");
            add(checkbox1);
➜           checkbox2 = new Checkbox("2");
➜           add(checkbox2);
➜           checkbox3 = new Checkbox("3");
➜           add(checkbox3);
➜           checkbox4 = new Checkbox("4");
➜           add(checkbox4);
➜           checkbox5 = new Checkbox("5");
➜           add(checkbox5);
➜           text1 = new TextField(20);
➜           add(text1);
        }
    }
```

Now your new check boxes are installed. The next step is to connect them to
the code. You might expect to use an ActionListener interface, but in fact, you use
a different interface with check boxes because unlike buttons, check boxes can be
either checked or unchecked (and the way to test their state is with the **getState()**
method). The interface you use here is called **ItemListener**, and you implement
that as follows:

```
    import java.applet.Applet;
    import java.awt.*;
    import java.awt.event.*;

➜public class checker extends Applet implements ItemListener{

        Checkbox checkbox1, checkbox2, checkbox3, checkbox4, checkbox5;
        TextField text1;

        public void init(){

            checkbox1 = new Checkbox("1");
            add(checkbox1);
            checkbox2 = new Checkbox("2");
            add(checkbox2);
            checkbox3 = new Checkbox("3");
            add(checkbox3);
            checkbox4 = new Checkbox("4");
            add(checkbox4);
```

```
        checkbox5 = new Checkbox("5");
        add(checkbox5);
        text1 = new TextField(20);
        add(text1);
    }
}
```

Make your applet into the listener for your check boxes (that is, our applet will handle the events that occur when the check boxes are clicked or unclicked) with the check box addItemListener() method this way:

```
import java.applet.Applet;
import java.awt.*;
import java.awt.event.*;

public class checker extends Applet implements ItemListener {

    Checkbox checkbox1, checkbox2, checkbox3, checkbox4, checkbox5;
    TextField text1;

    public void init(){

        checkbox1 = new Checkbox("1");
        add(checkbox1);
→       checkbox1.addItemListener(this);
        checkbox2 = new Checkbox("2");
        add(checkbox2);
→       checkbox2.addItemListener(this);
        checkbox3 = new Checkbox("3");
        add(checkbox3);
→       checkbox3.addItemListener(this);
        checkbox4 = new Checkbox("4");
        add(checkbox4);
→       checkbox4.addItemListener(this);
        checkbox5 = new Checkbox("5");
        add(checkbox5);
→       checkbox5.addItemListener(this);
        text1 = new TextField(20);
        add(text1);
    }
}
```

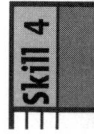

Now you've added your new check boxes to the applet and connected them up to your applet so that check box events will be sent to your applet. You're almost done; all you have to do now is to handle the check box events. The method to override when using the ItemListener interface (so you will be notified when check boxes are checked) is itemStateChanged(), and you add that now:

```
import java.applet.Applet;
import java.awt.*;
import java.awt.event.*;

public class checker extends Applet implements ItemListener {

    Checkbox checkbox1, checkbox2, checkbox3, checkbox4, checkbox5;
    TextField text1;

    public void init(){

        checkbox1 = new Checkbox("1");
        add(checkbox1);
        checkbox1.addItemListener(this);
        checkbox2 = new Checkbox("2");
        add(checkbox2);
        checkbox2.addItemListener(this);
        checkbox3 = new Checkbox("3");
        add(checkbox3);
        checkbox3.addItemListener(this);
        checkbox4 = new Checkbox("4");
        add(checkbox4);
        checkbox4.addItemListener(this);
        checkbox5 = new Checkbox("5");
        add(checkbox5);
        checkbox5.addItemListener(this);
        text1 = new TextField(20);
        add(text1);
    }

    public void itemStateChanged(ItemEvent e) {
            .
            .
            .
    }
}
```

itemStateChanged() is the method that will be called if the user clicks one of your check boxes and you are passed an object of class ItemEvent in that method. You can examine which check box was clicked with the ItemEvent class's getItemSelectable() method for checkbox1, as follows:

```
import java.applet.Applet;
import java.awt.*;
import java.awt.event.*;
```

```
public class checker extends Applet implements ItemListener {

    Checkbox checkbox1, checkbox2, checkbox3, checkbox4, checkbox5;
    TextField text1;

    public void init(){

        checkbox1 = new Checkbox("1");
        add(checkbox1);
        checkbox1.addItemListener(this);
        checkbox2 = new Checkbox("2");
        add(checkbox2);
        checkbox2.addItemListener(this);
        checkbox3 = new Checkbox("3");
        add(checkbox3);
        checkbox3.addItemListener(this);
        checkbox4 = new Checkbox("4");
        add(checkbox4);
        checkbox4.addItemListener(this);
        checkbox5 = new Checkbox("5");
        add(checkbox5);
        checkbox5.addItemListener(this);
        text1 = new TextField(20);
        add(text1);
    }

    public void itemStateChanged(ItemEvent e) {
➔       if(e.getItemSelectable() == checkbox1){
                    .
                    .
                    .
        }
    }
}
```

If checkbox1 is clicked, you can place a message in the text field saying: "Check box 1 clicked!" using the TextField setText() method, as follows:

```
import java.applet.Applet;
import java.awt.*;
import java.awt.event.*;

public class checker extends Applet implements ItemListener {

    Checkbox checkbox1, checkbox2, checkbox3, checkbox4, checkbox5;
    TextField text1;

    public void init(){
```

```
            checkbox1 = new Checkbox("1");
            add(checkbox1);
            checkbox1.addItemListener(this);
            checkbox2 = new Checkbox("2");
            add(checkbox2);
            checkbox2.addItemListener(this);
            checkbox3 = new Checkbox("3");
            add(checkbox3);
            checkbox3.addItemListener(this);
            checkbox4 = new Checkbox("4");
            add(checkbox4);
            checkbox4.addItemListener(this);
            checkbox5 = new Checkbox("5");
            add(checkbox5);
            checkbox5.addItemListener(this);
            text1 = new TextField(20);
            add(text1);
        }

    public void itemStateChanged(ItemEvent e) {
        if(e.getItemSelectable() == checkbox1){
➔           text1.setText("Check box 1 clicked!");
        }         .
                  .
                  .

    }
}
```

You can respond to clicks on the other check boxes in the same way:

```
import java.applet.Applet;
import java.awt.*;
import java.awt.event.*;

public class checker extends Applet implements ItemListener {

    Checkbox checkbox1, checkbox2, checkbox3, checkbox4, checkbox5;
    TextField text1;

    public void init(){

        checkbox1 = new Checkbox("1");
        add(checkbox1);
        checkbox1.addItemListener(this);
        checkbox2 = new Checkbox("2");
        add(checkbox2);
        checkbox2.addItemListener(this);
        checkbox3 = new Checkbox("3");
```

```
        add(checkbox3);
        checkbox3.addItemListener(this);
        checkbox4 = new Checkbox("4");
        add(checkbox4);
        checkbox4.addItemListener(this);
        checkbox5 = new Checkbox("5");
        add(checkbox5);
        checkbox5.addItemListener(this);
        text1 = new TextField(20);
        add(text1);
    }

    public void itemStateChanged(ItemEvent e) {
        if(e.getItemSelectable() == checkbox1){
            text1.setText("Check box 1 clicked!");
        }
➜        if(e.getItemSelectable() == checkbox2){
➜            text1.setText("Check box 2 clicked!");
➜        }
➜        if(e.getItemSelectable() == checkbox3){
➜            text1.setText("Check box 3 clicked!");
➜        }
➜        if(e.getItemSelectable() == checkbox4){
➜            text1.setText("Check box 4 clicked!");
➜        }
➜        if(e.getItemSelectable() == checkbox5){
➜            text1.setText("Check box 5 clicked!");
➜        }
    }
}
```

Your check box example is ready to go. Build the new applet now and run it, as shown below. As you can see, when the user clicks a check box, your applet responds and indicates what happened. Your check box example works exactly as you want it to. The code for this applet appears in checker.java.

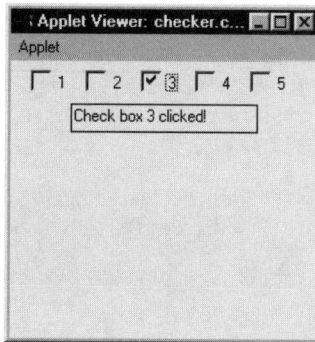

TIP   To see at any time whether a check box is clicked or not, you can use the getState() method like this: checkbox1.getState(), which returns true if the check box is checked and false otherwise.

checker.java

```java
import java.applet.Applet;
import java.awt.*;
import java.awt.event.*;

public class checker extends Applet implements ItemListener {

    Checkbox checkbox1, checkbox2, checkbox3, checkbox4, checkbox5;
    TextField text1;

    public void init(){

        checkbox1 = new Checkbox("1");
        add(checkbox1);
        checkbox1.addItemListener(this);
        checkbox2 = new Checkbox("2");
        add(checkbox2);
        checkbox2.addItemListener(this);
        checkbox3 = new Checkbox("3");
        add(checkbox3);
        checkbox3.addItemListener(this);
        checkbox4 = new Checkbox("4");
        add(checkbox4);
        checkbox4.addItemListener(this);
        checkbox5 = new Checkbox("5");
        add(checkbox5);
        checkbox5.addItemListener(this);
        text1 = new TextField(20);
        add(text1);
    }

    public void itemStateChanged(ItemEvent e) {
        if(e.getItemSelectable() == checkbox1){
            text1.setText("Check box 1 clicked!");
        }
        if(e.getItemSelectable() == checkbox2){
            text1.setText("Check box 2 clicked!");
        }
        if(e.getItemSelectable() == checkbox3){
```

```
            text1.setText("Check box 3 clicked!");
        }
        if(e.getItemSelectable() == checkbox4){
            text1.setText("Check box 4 clicked!");
        }
        if(e.getItemSelectable() == checkbox5){
            text1.setText("Check box 5 clicked!");
        }
    }
}
```

You've had a good introduction to check boxes in the checkers applet. Now you're able to use check boxes in your Java programs. In the next Skill you will turn to the other control that acts very much like check boxes: radio buttons. Check boxes and radio buttons are often used together.

Are You up to Speed?

Now you can. . .

- ☑ allow the user to use check boxes in Java programs
- ☑ display text in a Java program
- ☑ add and use labels
- ☑ use Java layouts
- ☑ read input from text fields
- ☑ use Java methods to convert the text you read from text fields to a number
- ☑ install and use the GridLayout manager in Java programs

SKILL 5

Working with Radio Buttons

- Adding Java panels in a program
- Placing controls in a panel
- Reaching controls in other panels
- Grouping radio buttons together
- Using the *CheckboxGroup* class

In Skill 4, we took a look at Java check boxes. Here, you're going to learn about radio buttons. In addition, you'll start to learn how to group controls together, both with the `CheckboxGroup` class and the `Panel` class. You'll bring radio buttons and check boxes together in a relatively large-scale example. Let's start at once with a guided tour of radio buttons.

Building Programs with Radio Buttons

Radio buttons (also called option buttons) are much like check boxes, but there is an important difference. You can check a number of check boxes at the same time, as shown in Figure 5.1. Radio buttons (or *option buttons*), however, operate in a group, and only one can be clicked at one time, as shown in Figure 5.2.

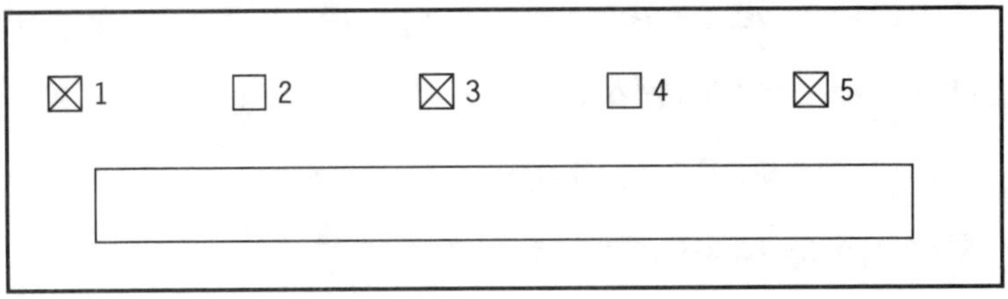

FIGURE 5.1:   You can check more than one check box at a time.

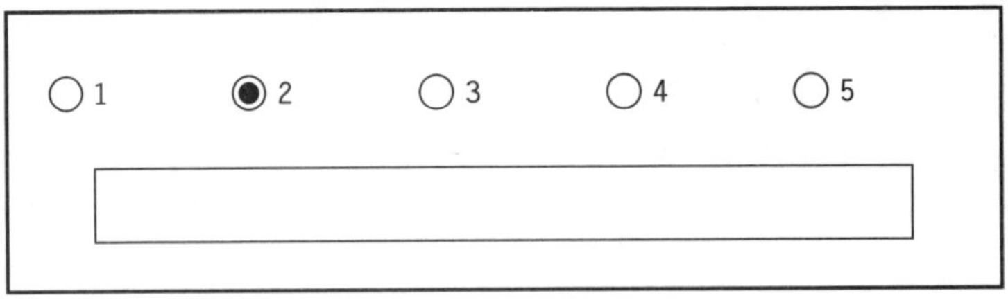

FIGURE 5.2:   Only one radio button can be active at a time.

To associate radio buttons with each other, use a `CheckboxGroup` object. When you add radio buttons to a group, the `CheckboxGroup` class's internal methods will make sure that only one of the radio buttons is checked at any time automatically—you won't have to worry about "unchecking" radio buttons when one of a group is checked.

The Radios Applet

To see radio buttons at work, let's write a new applet much like the check box applet that will present radio buttons, instead of check boxes, to the user. When the user clicks one of the radio buttons, you can report that fact, as shown in Figure 5.3.

FIGURE 5.3: When the user clicks a button, a message appears in the text field.

Create a new project now named `radios.java` and create the new class named `radios`, like this:

```
import java.applet.Applet;
import java.awt.*;
import java.awt.event.*;

public class radios extends Applet {
        .
        .
        .
}
```

You might be expecting a new Java class called `RadioButton` or something like that. However, in Java, radio buttons are actually just check boxes that have been added to a check box group. When you add check boxes to a check box group, they change their appearance automatically and become radio buttons. That means that you can create five new `Checkbox` objects for your radio controls:

```
import java.applet.Applet;
import java.awt.*;
import java.awt.event.*;


public class radios extends Applet {

Checkbox checkbox1, checkbox2, checkbox3, checkbox4, checkbox5;
}
```

Next, you will need an object of class CheckboxGroup to add your check boxes to (so they can act in a coordinated fashion). The CheckboxGroup class methods appear in Table 5.1. In your applet, you declare a new object of class CheckboxGroup, which you can name checkboxgroup1, and you declare the text field:

```java
import java.applet.Applet;
import java.awt.*;
import java.awt.event.*;

public class radios extends Applet {

→     CheckboxGroup checkboxgroup1;
       Checkbox checkbox1, checkbox2, checkbox3, checkbox4, checkbox5;
→     TextField text1;

}
```

TABLE 5.1: The CheckboxGroup Class Methods

Method	Does This
CheckboxGroup()	Creates a CheckboxGroup
getCurrent()	Gets current selection. Deprecated
getSelectedCheckbox()	Gets current selected check box
setCurrent(Checkbox)	Sets current selection to indicated Checkbox. Deprecated
setSelectedCheckbox()	Sets the current choice to the specified Checkbox
toString()	Returns string of CheckboxGroup's options

Next, set up your controls in the init() method by adding that method to your applet now:

```java
import java.applet.Applet;
import java.awt.*;
import java.awt.event.*;

public class radios extends Applet {

       CheckboxGroup checkboxgroup1;
       Checkbox checkbox1, checkbox2, checkbox3, checkbox4, checkbox5;
       TextField text1;

→     public void init(){
           .
           .
           .
```

→   }
}

Create your new CheckboxGroup object, checkbox1:

```java
import java.applet.Applet;
import java.awt.*;
import java.awt.event.*;

public class radios extends Applet {

    CheckboxGroup checkboxgroup1;
    Checkbox checkbox1, checkbox2, checkbox3, checkbox4, checkbox5;
    TextField text1;

    public void init(){

    checkboxgroup1 = new CheckboxGroup();
                    .
                    .
                    .
    }

}
```

→ (arrow marking the `checkboxgroup1 = new CheckboxGroup();` line)

Connecting Check Boxes to a *CheckBoxGroup*

Now you are ready to add your radio buttons to this new check box group. You do that when you create each check box, passing your CheckboxGroup object to the constructor of the Checkbox class. This attaches the new check box to the check box group and turns that check box into a radio button. For example, you add the first radio button and give it the simple caption "1", as follows:

 **NOTE**   The last parameter indicates if the radio button should appear initially checked, and you pass a value of false to indicate that it should appear unchecked initially.

```java
import java.applet.Applet;
import java.awt.*;
import java.awt.event.*;

public class radios extends Applet {

    CheckboxGroup checkboxgroup1;
    Checkbox checkbox1, checkbox2, checkbox3, checkbox4, checkbox5;
    TextField text1;

    public void init(){
```

```
                  checkboxgroup1 = new CheckboxGroup();

➔                 checkbox1 = new Checkbox("1", false, checkboxgroup1);
➔                 add(checkbox1);
                          .
                          .
                          .
          }

      }
```

Now you can add the rest of the radio buttons and the text field you'll use to report on user activities:

```
    import java.applet.Applet;
    import java.awt.*;
    import java.awt.event.*;

    public class radios extends Applet {

        CheckboxGroup checkboxgroup1;
        Checkbox checkbox1, checkbox2, checkbox3, checkbox4, checkbox5;
        TextField text1;

        public void init(){

            checkboxgroup1 = new CheckboxGroup();

            checkbox1 = new Checkbox("1", false, checkboxgroup1);
            add(checkbox1);

➔           checkbox2 = new Checkbox("2", false, checkboxgroup1);
➔           add(checkbox2);

➔           checkbox3 = new Checkbox("3", false, checkboxgroup1);
➔           add(checkbox3);

➔           checkbox4 = new Checkbox("4", false, checkboxgroup1);
➔           add(checkbox4);

➔           checkbox5 = new Checkbox("5", false, checkboxgroup1);
➔           add(checkbox5);

➔           text1 = new TextField(20);
➔           add(text1);

        }
    }
```

At this point, then, you've installed your radio buttons. The next step is to respond when they are clicked, and you do that just as you did in your previous example on check boxes, in itemStateChanged(). First, make your applet into the ItemListener for the radio buttons:

```
import java.applet.Applet;
import java.awt.*;
import java.awt.event.*;

public class radios extends Applet implements ItemListener{

    CheckboxGroup checkboxgroup1;
    Checkbox checkbox1, checkbox2, checkbox3, checkbox4, checkbox5;
    TextField text1;

    public void init(){

        checkboxgroup1 = new CheckboxGroup();

        checkbox1 = new Checkbox("1", false, checkboxgroup1);
        add(checkbox1);
        checkbox1.addItemListener(this);

        checkbox2 = new Checkbox("2", false, checkboxgroup1);
        add(checkbox2);
        checkbox2.addItemListener(this);

        checkbox3 = new Checkbox("3", false, checkboxgroup1);
        add(checkbox3);
        checkbox3.addItemListener(this);

        checkbox4 = new Checkbox("4", false, checkboxgroup1);
        add(checkbox4);
        checkbox4.addItemListener(this);

        checkbox5 = new Checkbox("5", false, checkboxgroup1);
        add(checkbox5);
        checkbox5.addItemListener(this);

        text1 = new TextField(20);
        add(text1);

    }
```

Skill 5

Now add the itemStateChanged() method. Here, you just report back to the user in your text field, indicating which radio button was clicked:

```java
import java.applet.Applet;
import java.awt.*;
import java.awt.event.*;

public class radios extends Applet implements ItemListener {

    CheckboxGroup checkboxgroup1;
    Checkbox checkbox1, checkbox2, checkbox3, checkbox4, checkbox5;
    TextField text1;

    public void init(){

        checkboxgroup1 = new CheckboxGroup();

        checkbox1 = new Checkbox("1", false, checkboxgroup1);
        add(checkbox1);
        checkbox1.addItemListener(this);

        checkbox2 = new Checkbox("2", false, checkboxgroup1);
        add(checkbox2);
        checkbox2.addItemListener(this);

        checkbox3 = new Checkbox("3", false, checkboxgroup1);
        add(checkbox3);
        checkbox3.addItemListener(this);

        checkbox4 = new Checkbox("4", false, checkboxgroup1);
        add(checkbox4);
        checkbox4.addItemListener(this);

        checkbox5 = new Checkbox("5", false, checkboxgroup1);
        add(checkbox5);
        checkbox5.addItemListener(this);

        text1 = new TextField(20);
        add(text1);

    }

    public void itemStateChanged(ItemEvent e){
➡        if(e.getItemSelectable() == checkbox1){
➡            text1.setText("Radio button 1 clicked!");
➡        }
➡        if(e.getItemSelectable() == checkbox2){
```

```
→              text1.setText("Radio button 2 clicked!");
→          }
→          if(e.getItemSelectable() == checkbox3){
→              text1.setText("Radio button 3 clicked!");
→          }
→          if(e.getItemSelectable() == checkbox4){
→              text1.setText("Radio button 4 clicked!");
→          }
→          if(e.getItemSelectable() == checkbox5){
→              text1.setText("Radio button 5 clicked!");
→          }
         }
    }
```

There you have it—build this new radio button applet and run it, as shown below. You can see the radio buttons in this applet—and only one may be selected at a time. When the user clicks a new radio button, the one that had been selected before is cleared, and the just-clicked radio button is selected instead. Your radio button example is a success. The code for this applet appears in radios.java.

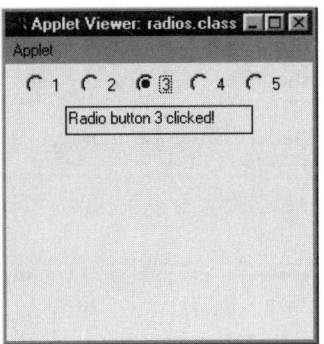

radios.java

```
import java.applet.Applet;
import java.awt.*;
import java.awt.event.*;

public class radios extends Applet implements ItemListener {

    CheckboxGroup checkboxgroup1;
```

```
Checkbox checkbox1, checkbox2, checkbox3, checkbox4, checkbox5;
TextField text1;

public void init(){

    checkboxgroup1 = new CheckboxGroup();

    checkbox1 = new Checkbox("1", false, checkboxgroup1);
    add(checkbox1);
    checkbox1.addItemListener(this);

    checkbox2 = new Checkbox("2", false, checkboxgroup1);
    add(checkbox2);
    checkbox2.addItemListener(this);

    checkbox3 = new Checkbox("3", false, checkboxgroup1);
    add(checkbox3);
    checkbox3.addItemListener(this);

    checkbox4 = new Checkbox("4", false, checkboxgroup1);
    add(checkbox4);
    checkbox4.addItemListener(this);

    checkbox5 = new Checkbox("5", false, checkboxgroup1);
    add(checkbox5);
    checkbox5.addItemListener(this);

    text1 = new TextField(20);
    add(text1);

}

public void itemStateChanged(ItemEvent e){
    if(e.getItemSelectable() == checkbox1){
        text1.setText("Radio button 1 clicked!");
    }
    if(e.getItemSelectable() == checkbox2){
        text1.setText("Radio button 2 clicked!");
    }
    if(e.getItemSelectable() == checkbox3){
        text1.setText("Radio button 3 clicked!");
    }
    if(e.getItemSelectable() == checkbox4){
        text1.setText("Radio button 4 clicked!");
    }
    if(e.getItemSelectable() == checkbox5){
        text1.setText("Radio button 5 clicked!");
    }
}
}
```

Now that you have some experience in handling both check boxes and radio buttons in isolation, the next step is to see them at work in an applet, arranged into groups as they normally are. To do so, you'll first learn to arrange controls in *panels* and then arrange the panels themselves.

Building Programs with Panels

Layout managers are only part of the story of organizing controls in an applet. Another part of the story concerns the Panel class. A panel is just a rectangular region that contains controls. For example, you could design a panel with four check boxes and then display that panel in an applet, as shown in Figure 5.4. In many ways, you can think of a panel as a new control that contains other controls. This means that you could add more panels to your applet just as easily as you added the first one, as shown in Figure 5.5.

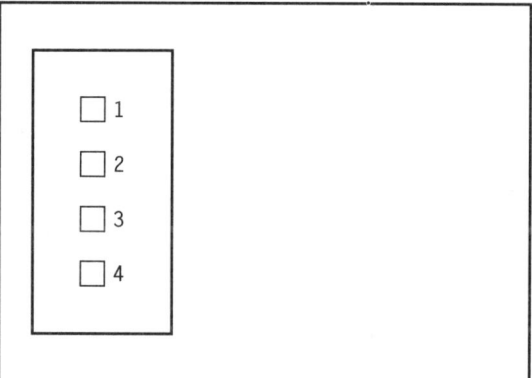

FIGURE 5.4:   A panel with four check boxes

This technique is perfect for groups of controls like radio buttons or check boxes, because it keeps the group of controls together. Watch this technique at work now as you create a new example that uses panels.

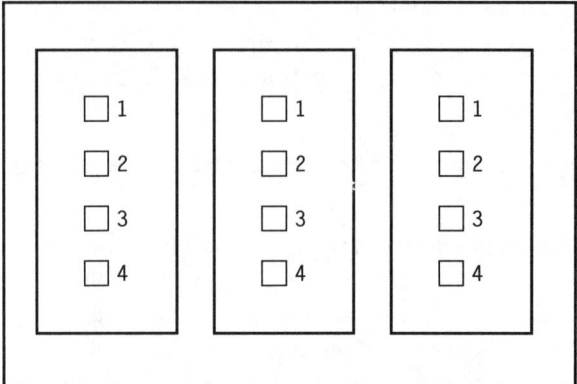

FIGURE 5.5:   Adding several panels to our applet

Creating a Panel

Create a new file named checkpanels.java. You can construct the example you just outlined above, so your first job is to create a new type of panel with the four check boxes you want in it—call this new class checkboxpanel, and use this panel in our applet. Create this class by deriving it from the Java Panel class—add this code to the checkpanels.java file now:

```
class checkboxpanel extends Panel {
    .
    .
    .
}
```

This is the first time that you have created a new class in your programs. This new class will be used by the main applet class, and because you are defining this new class in the same file as the applet's code, you won't have to use the Java import statement to import this new class. When you compile checkpanels .java, two .class files will be created: checkboxpanel.class (your new class) and the applet class itself, checkpanels.class. When the applet is run, the code in the applet, checkpanels.class, will load the code in checkboxpanel.class as needed.

Add the four check boxes you want in this class as you have added controls in the past—by first declaring them at the beginning of your new class's definition:

```
class checkboxpanel extends Panel {
➡    Checkbox check1, check2, check3, check4;
              .
              .
              .

    }
```

Now create and add the new checkboxes to this panel. It turns out that you do that not in the panel's init() method but in its constructor (the Panel class does not support an init() method). A Java constructor is run when an object of the class is created, and you define it as just a method with the exact same name of the class itself. Constructors never have a return value, but may have parameters used for initializing the new object being created, and can be overloaded based on the number and type of parameters. This is similar to what you see in the Java classes you've already discussed. In this case, that's checkboxpanel, so set up the constructor for this class and name that constructor checkboxpanel():

```
class checkboxpanel extends Panel {

➡    checkboxpanel(){
              .
              .
              .
➡    }
    }
```

That's your new class's constructor. In that constructor, create and add your new check boxes, as follows:

```
class checkboxpanel extends Panel {
➡    Checkbox check1, check2, check3, check4;

    checkboxpanel(){
➡        check1 = new Checkbox("1");
➡        add(check1);
➡        check2 = new Checkbox("2");
➡        add(check2);
➡        check3 = new Checkbox("3");
➡        add(check3);
➡        check4 = new Checkbox("4");
➡        add(check4);
    }
    }
```

Skill 5

Now you've created the new panel class buttons. A panel of this class will look like this:

You can treat these new panels much like controls in our applet. For example, to add three of these panels to our applet as, say, panel1, panel2, and panel3, you start by declaring them like this in our applet's main class, checkpanels:

```
import java.applet.Applet;
import java.awt.*;

public class checkpanels extends Applet {

      checkboxpanel panel1, panel2, panel3;
            .
            .
            .
}

class checkboxpanel extends Panel {
    Checkbox check1, check2, check3, check4;

    checkboxpanel(){
        check1 = new Checkbox("1");
        add(check1);
        check2 = new Checkbox("2");
        add(check2);
        check3 = new Checkbox("3");
        add(check3);
        check4 = new Checkbox("4");
        add(check4);
    }
}
```

Next, you have to initialize these panels in the `init()` method. You will use the GridLayout manager with 1 row and 3 columns to make these panels appear side by side, so start off by installing that manager first:

```java
import java.applet.Applet;
import java.awt.*;

public class checkpanels extends Applet {

    checkboxpanel panel1, panel2, panel3;

    public void init(){
        setLayout(new GridLayout(1, 3));
            .
            .
            .

    }
}

class checkboxpanel extends Panel {
    Checkbox check1, check2, check3, check4;

    checkboxpanel(){
        check1 = new Checkbox("1");
        add(check1);
        check2 = new Checkbox("2");
        add(check2);
        check3 = new Checkbox("3");
        add(check3);
        check4 = new Checkbox("4");
        add(check4);
    }
}
```

Now create and add your three checkbox panels, `panel1`, `panel2`, and `panel3` of your new class `checkpanels` to the applet:

```java
import java.applet.Applet;
import java.awt.*;

public class checkpanels extends Applet {

    checkboxpanel panel1, panel2, panel3;

    public void init(){
        setLayout(new GridLayout(1, 3));
```

Skill 5

```
→        panel1 = new checkboxpanel();
→        panel2 = new checkboxpanel();
→        panel3 = new checkboxpanel();
→        add(panel1);
→        add(panel2);
→        add(panel3);
    }

}

class checkboxpanel extends Panel {
    Checkbox check1, check2, check3, check4;

    checkboxpanel(){
        check1 = new Checkbox("1");
        add(check1);
        check2 = new Checkbox("2");
        add(check2);
        check3 = new Checkbox("3");
        add(check3);
        check4 = new Checkbox("4");
        add(check4);
    }
}
```

That's all there is to it—now you've created a new panel type, added controls to the panel, and added panels of that type to your applet. As you can see in the graphic below, you have successfully installed three panels in your applet. Your checkpanels applet is a success. The code for this applet appears in checkpanels.java.

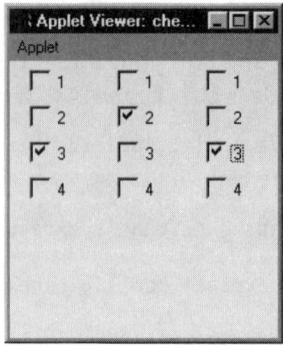

C **checkpanels.java**

```java
import java.applet.Applet;
import java.awt.*;

public class checkpanels extends Applet {

    checkboxpanel panel1, panel2, panel3;

    public void init(){
        setLayout(new GridLayout(1, 3));
        panel1 = new checkboxpanel();
        panel2 = new checkboxpanel();
        panel3 = new checkboxpanel();
        add(panel1);
        add(panel2);
        add(panel3);
    }

}

class checkboxpanel extends Panel {
    Checkbox check1, check2, check3, check4;

    checkboxpanel(){
        check1 = new Checkbox("1");
        add(check1);
        check2 = new Checkbox("2");
        add(check2);
        check3 = new Checkbox("3");
        add(check3);
        check4 = new Checkbox("4");
        add(check4);
    }
}
```

As you can see, panels make up a powerful technique for grouping controls together. You'll use panels in your next example, in which you will bring Skill 5 together with Skill 4 by using radio buttons, check boxes, panels, and layouts all in the same applet.

Putting Check Boxes and Radio Buttons Together

Let's say that you decide to set up a sandwich shop on the Web. In particular, you want to embed an applet in a Web page giving customers the price of various sandwiches. That applet might look something like Figure 5.6, in which you let the customer select from one of three sandwich options, and let the applet indicate the ingredients in each sandwich and give the customer a price for what they have selected.

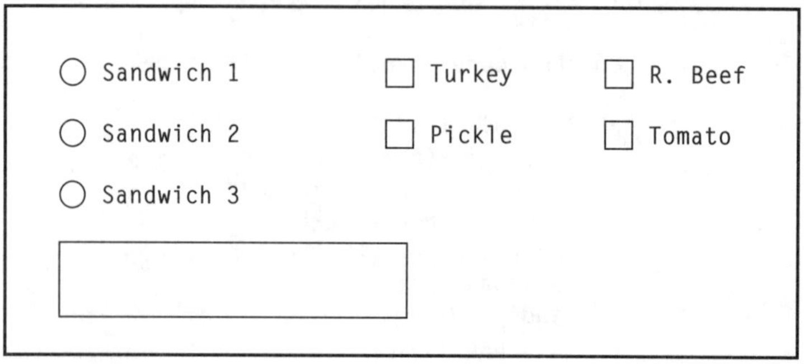

FIGURE 5.6:   An online sandwich shop

For example, if the user clicks the Sandwich 1 radio button, you set the corresponding check boxes to indicate what's in this sandwich, and indicate the total price in a text field, as shown in Figure 5.7. If the user then clicks another radio button, all the other check boxes are cleared, a new set of sandwich ingredients is indicated, and a new price appears, as shown in Figure 5.8. You can put the controls in your applet into two panels, as shown in Figure 5.9. Panel1 will be the user menu list and price and Panel2 will be the ingredient list.

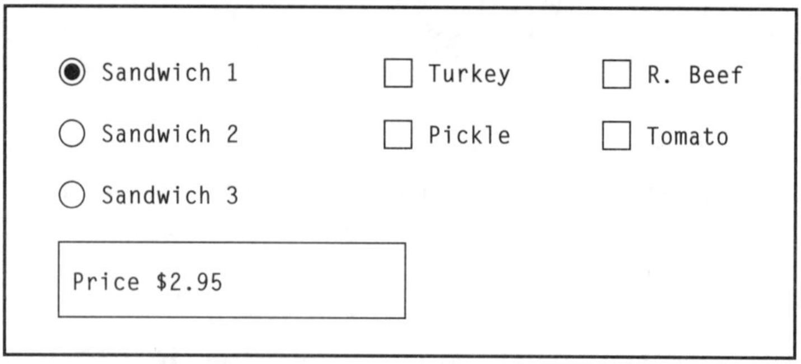

FIGURE 5.7:   When the user selects a sandwich, the applet indicates the ingredients and price of the sandwich.

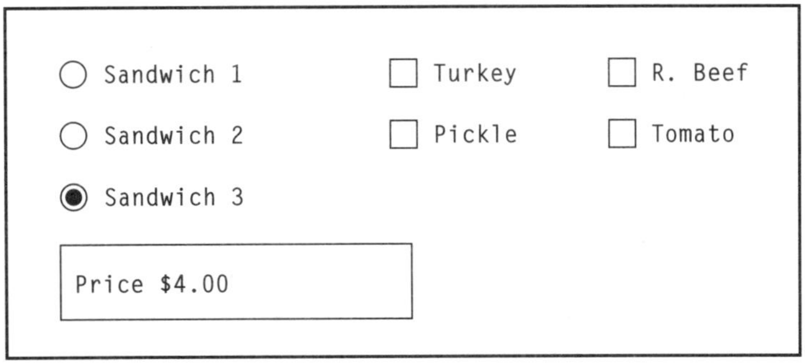

```
  ○  Sandwich 1        □  Turkey       □  R. Beef

  ○  Sandwich 2        □  Pickle       □  Tomato

  ◉  Sandwich 3

  ┌─────────────────────┐
  │ Price $4.00         │
  └─────────────────────┘
```

FIGURE 5.8:   When the user selects a new sandwich, the applet displays information about the new sandwich.

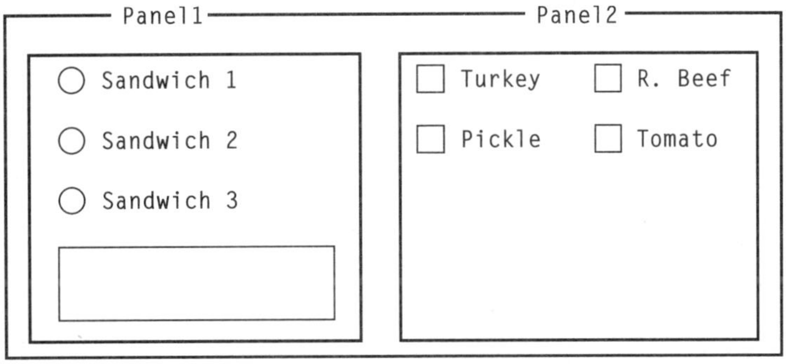

Skill 5

```
┌─ Panel1 ─────────────────┬─ Panel2 ─────────────────┐
│  ○  Sandwich 1           │  □  Turkey    □  R. Beef  │
│                          │                           │
│  ○  Sandwich 2           │  □  Pickle    □  Tomato   │
│                          │                           │
│  ○  Sandwich 3           │                           │
│  ┌───────────────────┐   │                           │
│  │                   │   │                           │
│  └───────────────────┘   │                           │
└──────────────────────────┴───────────────────────────┘
```

FIGURE 5.9:   You'll divide your controls into two panels.

To see this idea in action, create a new applet named sandwich.java. You will begin by designing the new panels, starting with the panel with the radio buttons and the text field.

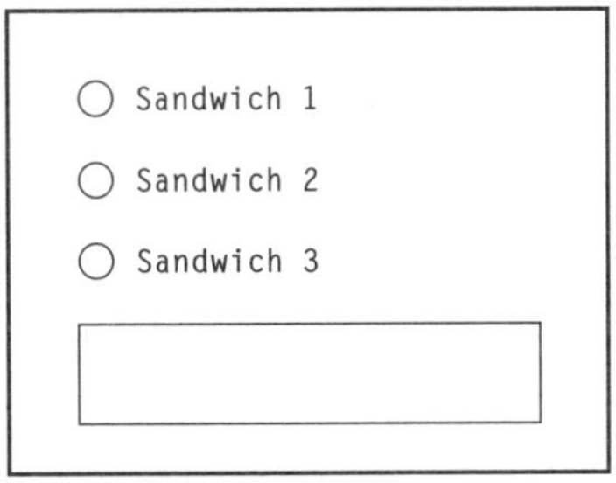

```
┌──────────────────────────┐
│   ○  Sandwich 1          │
│   ○  Sandwich 2          │
│   ○  Sandwich 3          │
│   ┌──────────────────┐   │
│   │                  │   │
│   └──────────────────┘   │
└──────────────────────────┘
```

Creating the Menu Panel

You design the new panels as you did in your previous panels applet, by deriving a new class named, for instance, Menu, from the Java Panel class (add this new class to the sandwich.java file):

```
class Menu extends Panel {
    .
    .
    .
}
```

Now add the controls you'll need—note that since this panel holds radio buttons, you'll need a check box group object:

```
class Menu extends Panel {
    CheckboxGroup CGroup;
    Checkbox sandwich1, sandwich2, sandwich3;
    TextField Pricebox;
        .
        .
        .
}
```

Now add your controls to the new Panel class in that class's constructor:

```
class Menu extends Panel {
    CheckboxGroup CGroup;
    Checkbox Sandwich1, Sandwich2, Sandwich3;
    TextField Pricebox;

    Menu(){
➜       CGroup = new CheckboxGroup();
➜       add(Sandwich1 = new Checkbox("Sandwich 1", CGroup, false));
➜       add(Sandwich2 = new Checkbox("Sandwich 2", CGroup, false));
➜       add(Sandwich3 = new Checkbox("Sandwich 3", CGroup, false));
➜       Pricebox = new TextField(15);
➜       add(Pricebox);
    }
}
```

That's it—you've set up your first panel:

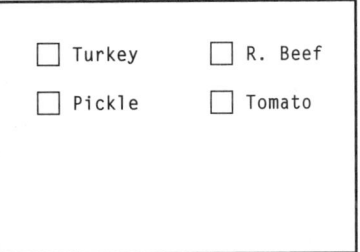

Creating the Ingredients Panel

The other panel you need looks like this, with four labeled check boxes:

You can call this new panel class `Ingredients` and add the definition of this new class to the `sandwich.java` file. All you'll need in this new class are four check boxes, labeled with the ingredients in your sandwiches, so that class looks like this:

```
class Ingredients extends Panel {

Checkbox Ingredient1, Ingredient2, Ingredient3, Ingredient4;

    Ingredients(){
        add(Ingredient1 = new Checkbox("Turkey"));
        add(Ingredient2 = new Checkbox("R.Beef"));
        add(Ingredient3 = new Checkbox("Pickle"));
        add(Ingredient4 = new Checkbox("Tomato"));
    }
}
```

And that takes care of the Ingredients panel.

Adding Panels to the *sandwich* Class

At this point, then, our new panels are ready to add to the sandwich class. Add
that class now and declare a panel of each of our new panel classes as follows:

```
import java.applet.Applet;
import java.awt.*;
import java.awt.event.*;

public class sandwich extends Applet {

→    Menu Panel1;
→    Ingredients Panel2;
         .
         .
         .

}

class Menu extends Panel {
    CheckboxGroup CGroup;
    Checkbox Sandwich1, Sandwich2, Sandwich3;
    TextField Pricebox;

    Menu(){
        CGroup = new CheckboxGroup();
        add(Sandwich1 = new Checkbox("Sandwich 1", CGroup, false));
        add(Sandwich2 = new Checkbox("Sandwich 2", CGroup, false));
        add(Sandwich3 = new Checkbox("Sandwich 3", CGroup, false));
        Pricebox = new TextField(15);
        add(Pricebox);
    }
}

class Ingredients extends Panel {
    Checkbox Ingredient1, Ingredient2, Ingredient3, Ingredient4;

    Ingredients(){
        add(Ingredient1 = new Checkbox("Turkey"));
        add(Ingredient2 = new Checkbox("R.Beef"));
        add(Ingredient3 = new Checkbox("Pickle"));
        add(Ingredient4 = new Checkbox("Tomato"));
    }
}
```

Now you can create and add those panels. To make sure they appear side by side, you'll use the GridLayout manager. Install that manager now in the applet's `init()` method:

```java
import java.applet.Applet;
import java.awt.*;
import java.awt.event.*;

public class sandwich extends Applet {

    Menu Panel1;
    Ingredients Panel2;

    public void init(){
        setLayout(new GridLayout(1, 2));
                .
                .
                .
    }
}
```

Then simply add your two new panels, like this:

```java
import java.applet.Applet;
import java.awt.*;
import java.awt.event.*;

public class sandwich extends Applet {

    Menu Panel1;
    Ingredients Panel2;

    public void init(){
        setLayout(new GridLayout(1, 2));
        Panel1 = new Menu();
        Panel2 = new Ingredients();
        add(Panel1);
        add(Panel2);
                .
                .
                .
    }

}
```

At this point, your applet will look like Figure 5.10.

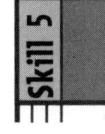

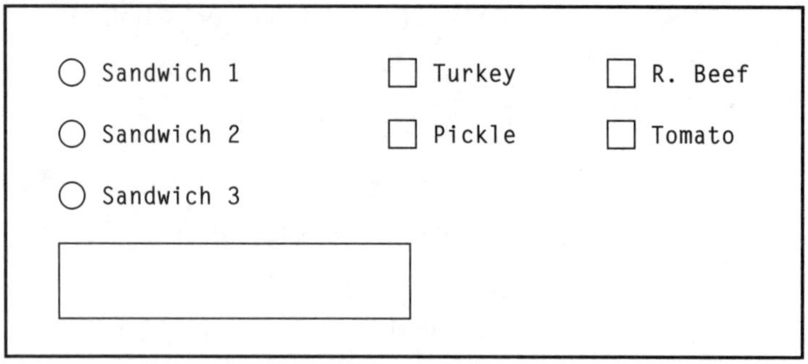

```
  ○ Sandwich 1        □ Turkey        □ R. Beef

  ○ Sandwich 2        □ Pickle        □ Tomato

  ○ Sandwich 3

  ┌─────────────────────────────┐
  │                             │
  │                             │
  └─────────────────────────────┘
```

FIGURE 5.10: Your applet so far

 **NOTE**   Panels do not have any predefined outlines that appear around them in an applet. They are really just constructs to arrange controls, not GUI objects.

Connecting the Buttons in Code

You haven't done anything yet to make this applet functional—you still need to connect up the buttons. You start that process as you did in our earlier example, by adding the ItemListener interface to our applet:

```
import java.applet.Applet;
import java.awt.*;
import java.awt.event.*;

→public class sandwich extends Applet implements ItemListener{

    Menu Panel1;
    Ingredients Panel2;

    public void init(){
        setLayout(new GridLayout(1, 2));
        Panel1 = new Menu();
        Panel2 = new Ingredients();
        add(Panel1);
        add(Panel2);
    }

}
```

Now you have to connect the option button's `ItemListener` interfaces to your applet. In code, the option buttons are named `Sandwich1`, `Sandwich2`, and `Sandwich3`, but you can't just execute a statement such as:

```
Sandwich1.addItemListener(this)
```

because `Sandwich1` is not an object in your applet, but in the `Panel1` object. That means you will reach those option buttons another way, using the Java dot operator (.):

```
import java.applet.Applet;
import java.awt.*;
import java.awt.event.*;

→public class sandwich extends Applet implements ItemListener{

    Menu Panel1;
    Ingredients Panel2;

    public void init(){
        setLayout(new GridLayout(1, 2));
        Panel1 = new Menu();
        Panel2 = new Ingredients();
        add(Panel1);
→       Panel1.Sandwich1.addItemListener(this);
→       Panel1.Sandwich2.addItemListener(this);
→       Panel1.Sandwich3.addItemListener(this);
        add(Panel2);
    }
}
```

Next, add the `itemStateChanged()` method to handle radio-button clicks:

```
import java.applet.Applet;
import java.awt.*;
import java.awt.event.*;

public class sandwich extends Applet implements ItemListener {

    Menu Panel1;
    Ingredients Panel2;

    public void init(){
        setLayout(new GridLayout(1, 2));
        Panel1 = new Menu();
        Panel2 = new Ingredients();
        add(Panel1);
        Panel1.Sandwich1.addItemListener(this);
```

Skill 5

```
        Panel1.Sandwich2.addItemListener(this);
        Panel1.Sandwich3.addItemListener(this);
        add(Panel2);
    }


→   public void itemStateChanged(ItemEvent e) {
                    .
                    .
                    .
→   }
    }
```

Now you need to handle the case in which the user clicks the radio button
marked "Sandwich 1". Use the following syntax to check whether that button
was clicked:

```
import java.applet.Applet;
import java.awt.*;
import java.awt.event.*;

public class sandwich extends Applet implements ItemListener {

    Menu Panel1;
    Ingredients Panel2;

    public void init(){
        setLayout(new GridLayout(1, 2));
        Panel1 = new Menu();
        Panel2 = new Ingredients();
        add(Panel1);
        Panel1.Sandwich1.addItemListener(this);
        Panel1.Sandwich2.addItemListener(this);
        Panel1.Sandwich3.addItemListener(this);
        add(Panel2);
    }


        public void itemStateChanged(ItemEvent e) {
→       if(e.getItemSelectable() == Panel1.Sandwich1){

→           }
        }
    }
```

If, in fact, the "Sandwich 1" radio button is clicked, you want the check boxes to
indicate what is in the sandwich, as shown in Figure 5.11.

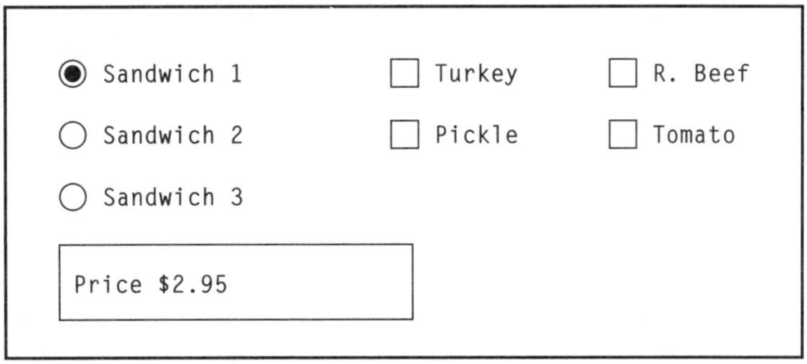

FIGURE 5.11: When the user clicks the "Sandwich 1" button, the check boxes should indicate what's in the sandwich.

If the "Sandwich 1" radio button was clicked, you will set the check boxes appropriately in Panel2. The check boxes are actually objects internal to the Panel2 object that you have named Ingredient1 to Ingredient4, so address them as Panel2.Ingredient1 to Panel2.Ingredient4. You can use the check box method setState() to set the check boxes as you want them—passing a value of true makes them appear checked, and a value of false makes them appear unchecked—as well as place the price in the text field:

```
import java.applet.Applet;
import java.awt.*;
import java.awt.event.*;

public class sandwich extends Applet implements ItemListener {

    Menu Panel1;
    Ingredients Panel2;

    public void init(){
        setLayout(new GridLayout(1, 2));
        Panel1 = new Menu();
        Panel2 = new Ingredients();
        add(Panel1);
        Panel1.Sandwich1.addItemListener(this);
        Panel1.Sandwich2.addItemListener(this);
        Panel1.Sandwich3.addItemListener(this);
        add(Panel2);
    }
```

```
       public void itemStateChanged(ItemEvent e) {
           if(e.getItemSelectable() == Panel1.Sandwich1){
➜              Panel2.Ingredient1.setState(true);
➜              Panel2.Ingredient2.setState(false);
➜              Panel2.Ingredient3.setState(true);
➜              Panel2.Ingredient4.setState(false);
➜              Panel1.Pricebox.setText("Price: $2.95");
   }
       }
   }
```

That is how you handle the "Sandwich 1" button. The other sandwich buttons are the same with different options, so the code to activate them looks like this:

```
import java.applet.Applet;
import java.awt.*;
import java.awt.event.*;

public class sandwich extends Applet implements ItemListener {

    Menu Panel1;
    Ingredients Panel2;

    public void init(){
        setLayout(new GridLayout(1, 2));
        Panel1 = new Menu();
        Panel2 = new Ingredients();
        add(Panel1);
        Panel1.Sandwich1.addItemListener(this);
        Panel1.Sandwich2.addItemListener(this);
        Panel1.Sandwich3.addItemListener(this);
        add(Panel2);
    }


    public void itemStateChanged(ItemEvent e) {
        if(e.getItemSelectable() == Panel1.Sandwich1){
            Panel2.Ingredient1.setState(true);
            Panel2.Ingredient2.setState(false);
            Panel2.Ingredient3.setState(true);
            Panel2.Ingredient4.setState(false);
            Panel1.Pricebox.setText("Price: $2.95");
        }
➜       if(e.getItemSelectable() == Panel1.Sandwich2){
➜           Panel2.Ingredient1.setState(false);
➜           Panel2.Ingredient2.setState(true);
➜           Panel2.Ingredient3.setState(true);
➜           Panel2.Ingredient4.setState(true);
```

```
→          Panel1.Pricebox.setText("Price: $2.95");
→      }
→      if(e.getItemSelectable() == Panel1.Sandwich3){
→          Panel2.Ingredient1.setState(true);
→          Panel2.Ingredient2.setState(true);
→          Panel2.Ingredient3.setState(true);
           Panel2.Ingredient4.setState(true);
→          Panel1.Pricebox.setText("Price: $4.00");
→      }
    }
  }
```

You've completed your `sandwich.java` example applet, which uses panels, check boxes, radio buttons, and a grid layout. The completed applet is shown below. When the user clicks various system options, the applet shows the corresponding price and ingredients. Your applet is a success. The code for this applet appears in `sandwich.java`.

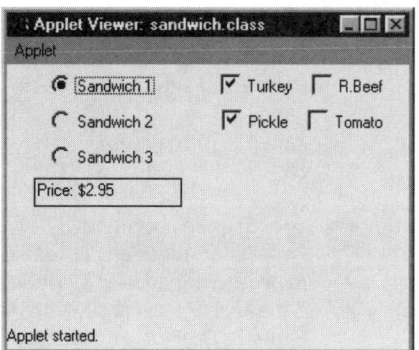

sandwich.java

```java
import java.applet.Applet;
import java.awt.*;
import java.awt.event.*;

public class sandwich extends Applet implements ItemListener {

    Menu Panel1;
    Ingredients Panel2;
```

```java
public void init(){
    setLayout(new GridLayout(1, 2));
    Panel1 = new Menu();
    Panel2 = new Ingredients();
    add(Panel1);
    Panel1.Sandwich1.addItemListener(this);
    Panel1.Sandwich2.addItemListener(this);
    Panel1.Sandwich3.addItemListener(this);
    add(Panel2);
}


public void itemStateChanged(ItemEvent e) {
    if(e.getItemSelectable() == Panel1.Sandwich1){
        Panel2.Ingredient1.setState(true);
        Panel2.Ingredient2.setState(false);
        Panel2.Ingredient3.setState(true);
        Panel2.Ingredient4.setState(false);
        Panel1.Pricebox.setText("Price: $2.95");
    }
    if(e.getItemSelectable() == Panel1.Sandwich2){
        Panel2.Ingredient1.setState(false);
        Panel2.Ingredient2.setState(true);
        Panel2.Ingredient3.setState(true);
        Panel2.Ingredient4.setState(true);
        Panel1.Pricebox.setText("Price: $2.95");
    }
    if(e.getItemSelectable() == Panel1.Sandwich3){
        Panel2.Ingredient1.setState(true);
        Panel2.Ingredient2.setState(true);
        Panel2.Ingredient3.setState(true);
        Panel2.Ingredient4.setState(true);
        Panel1.Pricebox.setText("Price: $4.00");
    }
}
}

class Menu extends Panel {
    CheckboxGroup CGroup;
    Checkbox Sandwich1, Sandwich2, Sandwich3;
    TextField Pricebox;

    Menu(){
        CGroup = new CheckboxGroup();
        add(Sandwich1 = new Checkbox("Sandwich 1", CGroup, false));
        add(Sandwich2 = new Checkbox("Sandwich 2", CGroup, false));
        add(Sandwich3 = new Checkbox("Sandwich 3", CGroup, false));
        Pricebox = new TextField(15);
```

```
            add(Pricebox);
        }
    }

    class Ingredients extends Panel {
        Checkbox Ingredient1, Ingredient2, Ingredient3, Ingredient4;

        Ingredients(){
            add(Ingredient1 = new Checkbox("Turkey"));
            add(Ingredient2 = new Checkbox("R.Beef"));
            add(Ingredient3 = new Checkbox("Pickle"));
            add(Ingredient4 = new Checkbox("Tomato"));
        }
    }
```

Now you're working with check boxes, radio buttons, and panels. You've also gained some practical experience accessing members of another class by reaching the buttons in your panels from your applet class. Now let's turn to another powerful Java control—scroll bars—in Skill 6.

Are You up to Speed?

Now you can. . .

☑ **add and use radio buttons for more power in your Java programs**

☑ **use the *Panel* class as a base class to derive your own panel class to group Java controls together**

☑ **use the *CheckboxGroup* class to group radio buttons together so that only one of them will appear checked at any time**

☑ **reach objects embedded in other object**

SKILL 6

Adding Scroll Bars

- Adding and using scroll bars in Java programs
- Updating scroll settings to match scrolling actions
- Coordinating multiple scroll bars
- Using the BorderLayout manager
- Using AdjustmentListeners

Skill 5 provided you with a good introduction to the use of radio buttons, and showed you how to put radio buttons and check boxes together in the sandwich applet. In this Skill, you're going to continue the guided tour of Java by examining a new control: scroll bars. As any user of a windowed environment can tell you, scroll bars are very important controls. You'll also examine some additional Java layout techniques—layouts are an important part of Java programming, and you'll become more familiar with what Java has to offer us here. You'll also be introduced to the new ScrollPane class.

Adding Scroll Bars to Programs

Let's start off with a scroll bar example. There are two types of scroll bar controls—horizontal and vertical scroll bars, and you'll see both here. For example, let's create a new applet named scroller that contains both types of scroll bars, as shown in Figure 6.1. When the user moves a scroll bar, we'll report on the new horizontal or vertical position of the bars in a text field, as shown in Figure 6.2.

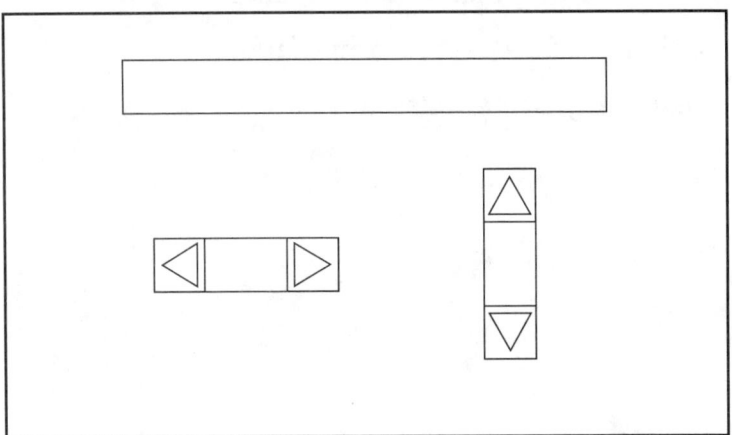

FIGURE 6.1:   Our applet will contain a vertical scroll bar and a horizontal scroll bar.

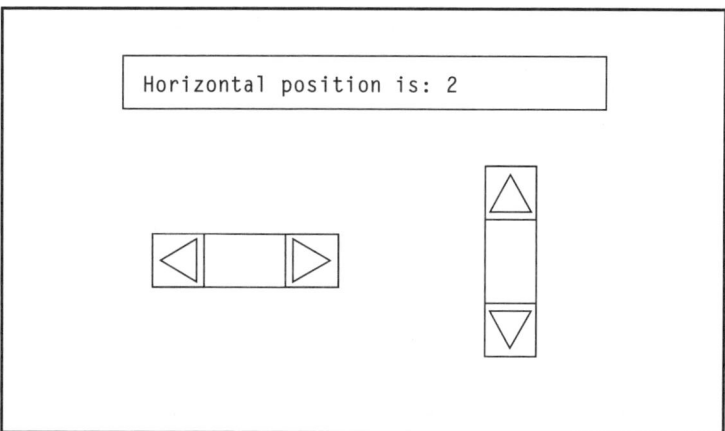

FIGURE 6.2: The text field will report the new position of the scroll bar.

This will be an easy example. Create a new file named scroller.java. Begin by adding the text field we'll need, text1, and the two scroll bars, scroll1 and scroll2, which are objects of the Java Scrollbar class:

```
import java.applet.Applet;
import java.awt.event.*;
import java.awt.*;

public class scroller extends Applet {

    TextField text1;
    Scrollbar scroll1, scroll2;
         .
         .
         .
}
```

The Java Scrollbar class's methods appear in Table 6.1.

TABLE 6.1: The Scrollbar class methods

Method	Does This
Scrollbar()	Constructs a Scrollbar (vertical)
Scrollbar(int)	Constructs a Scrollbar with specified orientation: Scrollbar.HORIZONTAL or Scrollbar.VERTICAL
Scrollbar(int, int, int, int, int)	Constructs a Scrollbar with given orientation, initial value, scroll thumb size, minimum and maximum values
AddAdjustmentListener (AdjustmentListener)	Adds new adjustment listener to get adjustment events from this Scrollbar
addNotify()	Adds the Scrollbar's peer
GetBlockIncrement()	Gets block increment for Scrollbar
GetLineIncrement()	Deprecated. Gets line-by-line increment for Scrollbar
getMaximum()	Gets maximum setting of Scrollbar
getMinimum()	Gets minimum setting of Scrollbar
getOrientation()	Gets orientation of Scrollbar
getPageIncrement()	Deprecated. Gets page-by-page increment for Scrollbar
getUnitIncrement()	Gets unit increment for Scrollbar
getValue()	Gets current value of Scrollbar
getVisible()	Deprecated. Gets the visible portion of Scrollbar
getVisibleAmount()	Gets visible amount of Scrollbar
paramString()	Gets string parameters for Scrollbar
ProcessAdjustmentEvent (AdjustmentEvent)	Processes adjustment events of scroll bar, dispatching them to AdjustmentListener objects
processEvent(AWTEvent)	Processes events of Scrollbar
removeAdjustmentListener (AdjustmentListener)	Removes the specified adjustment listener so that it no longer gets adjustment events
setBlockIncrement(int)	Sets block increment for Scrollbar
setLineIncrement(int)	Deprecated. Sets line-by-line increment for Scrollbar
setMaximum(int)	Sets maximum value for Scrollbar
setMinimum(int)	Sets minimum value for Scrollbar

TABLE 6.1 CONTINUED: The Scrollbar class methods

Method	Does This
setOrientation(int)	Sets orientation for Scrollbar
setPageIncrement(int)	Deprecated. Sets page-by-page increment for Scrollbar
setUnitIncrement(int)	Sets unit increment for Scrollbar
setValue(int)	Sets value of Scrollbar to given value
setValues(int, int, int, int)	Sets values for Scrollbar
setVisibleAmount(int)	Sets visible amount of Scrollbar

Installing Scroll Bars

In the init() method, you will add scroll bars and text fields to the applet. You'll start with the text field you'll need to report the scroll bars' positions, text1:

```
import java.applet.Applet;
import java.awt.event.*;
import java.awt.*;

public class scroller extends Applet {

    TextField text1;
    Scrollbar scroll1, scroll2;

    public void init(){
        text1 = new TextField(20);
        add(text1);
            .
            .
            .

    }
}
```

Now you will continue constructing your horizontal scroll bar, scroll1, by passing these parameters to its constructor (see Table 6.1): its orientation (you use the pre-defined Scrollbar class constants Scrollbar.HORIZONTAL or Scrollbar VERTICAL—these constants are built into the Scrollbar class), the scroll bar's initial value (i.e., the location of the scroll box in the scroll bar—called the *thumb*),

Skill 6

the size of the scroll thumb in pixels, and the scroll bar's minimum possible value (use 1) and its maximum possible value (use 100):

```java
import java.applet.Applet;
import java.awt.event.*;
import java.awt.*;


public class scroller extends Applet {

        TextField text1;
        Scrollbar scroll1, scroll2;

        public void init(){
                text1 = new TextField(20);
                add(text1);

                scroll1 = new Scrollbar(Scrollbar.HORIZONTAL, 1, 10, 1, 100);
                add(scroll1);
                        .
                        .
                        .

        }
}
```

TIP Using the setValues() method, you can change a scroll bar's maximum and minimum possible values while your applet is running. You can also scroll the scroll bar from code with the setValue() method. (It's a common error to confuse setValue() with setValues(), but note that these are two different methods.)

Using this code, you will create a new horizontal scroll bar whose values can range from 1 to 100, and whose initial value is 1.

In the same way, you can create a similar scroll bar, scroll2, which has the same value range but is vertical:

```java
import java.applet.Applet;
import java.awt.event.*;
import java.awt.*;


public class scroller extends Applet {

        TextField text1;
        Scrollbar scroll1, scroll2;
```

```
        public void init(){
            text1 = new TextField(20);
            add(text1);
            scroll1 = new Scrollbar(Scrollbar.HORIZONTAL, 1, 10, 1, 100);
            add(scroll1);

➜           scroll2 = new Scrollbar(Scrollbar.VERTICAL, 1, 10, 1, 100);
➜           add(scroll2);
        }
    }
```

That's it—your scroll bars will now appear in your applet now.

Connecting Scroll Bars to Code

The next step is to connect them to code, and you might think that's done with an ActionListener or ItemListener interface—but in fact, the *AdjustmentListener* interface is used this time, because scroll bars are considered *adjustable* controls. Use the addAdjustmentListener() method of the Scrollbar class like you used the addItemListener() and addActionListener().

```
import java.applet.Applet;
import java.awt.event.*;
import java.awt.*;


➜public class scroller extends Applet implements AdjustmentListener {

    TextField text1;
    Scrollbar scroll1, scroll2;

    public void init(){
        text1 = new TextField(20);
        add(text1);
        scroll1 = new Scrollbar(Scrollbar.HORIZONTAL, 1, 10, 1, 100);
        add(scroll1);
➜           scroll1.addAdjustmentListener(this);
        scroll2 = new Scrollbar(Scrollbar.VERTICAL, 1, 10, 1, 100);
        add(scroll2);
➜           scroll2.addAdjustmentListener(this);
    }


    }
```

You can determine which scroll bar caused the event by overriding the adjustmentValueChanged() method. That method takes a parameter of class AdjustmentEvent:

```java
import java.applet.Applet;
import java.awt.event.*;
import java.awt.*;


public class scroller extends Applet implements AdjustmentListener {

    TextField text1;
    Scrollbar scroll1, scroll2;

    public void init(){
        text1 = new TextField(20);
        add(text1);
        scroll1 = new Scrollbar(Scrollbar.HORIZONTAL, 1, 10, 1, 100);
        add(scroll1);
        scroll1.addAdjustmentListener(this);
        scroll2 = new Scrollbar(Scrollbar.VERTICAL, 1, 10, 1, 100);
        add(scroll2);
        scroll2.addAdjustmentListener(this);
    }

    public void adjustmentValueChanged(AdjustmentEvent e){
            .
            .
            .

    }
}
```

You can determine which scroll bar caused the event with the AdjustableEvent class's getAdjustable() method the following way, where you check to see if scroll1 caused the scroll event:

```java
import java.applet.Applet;
import java.awt.event.*;
import java.awt.*;


public class scroller extends Applet implements AdjustmentListener {

    TextField text1;
    Scrollbar scroll1, scroll2;

    public void init(){
```

```
        text1 = new TextField(20);
        add(text1);
        scroll1 = new Scrollbar(Scrollbar.HORIZONTAL, 1, 10, 1, 100);
        add(scroll1);
        scroll1.addAdjustmentListener(this);
        scroll2 = new Scrollbar(Scrollbar.VERTICAL, 1, 10, 1, 100);
        add(scroll2);
        scroll2.addAdjustmentListener(this);
    }

    public void adjustmentValueChanged(AdjustmentEvent e){
➜       if(e.getAdjustable() == scroll1) {
                                .
                                .
                                .
➜         }
      }
  }
```

The first step is to set the scroll bar's thumb position to the place the user scrolled it to. That might seem funny, but it turns out that unless you update the scroll bar's thumb yourself, it will spring back when the user releases it to the position it occupied before it was scrolled. The reason that you have to move it yourself is that the user may have moved the thumb to some location you consider "forbidden," and Java allows you the option of not accepting the user's scroll actions in that case. To set the thumb's new location, use the Scrollbar class's setValue() method, and to get its current value, use the getValue() method. To place the thumb at the location the user moved it to, execute this code:

```
import java.applet.Applet;
import java.awt.event.*;
import java.awt.*;


public class scroller extends Applet implements AdjustmentListener {

    TextField text1;
    Scrollbar scroll1, scroll2;

    public void init(){
        text1 = new TextField(20);
        add(text1);
        scroll1 = new Scrollbar(Scrollbar.HORIZONTAL, 1, 10, 1, 100);
        add(scroll1);
        scroll1.addAdjustmentListener(this);
        scroll2 = new Scrollbar(Scrollbar.VERTICAL, 1, 10, 1, 100);
```

```
                    add(scroll2);
                    scroll2.addAdjustmentListener(this);
                }

        public void adjustmentValueChanged(AdjustmentEvent e){
            if(e.getAdjustable() == scroll1) {
  →             scroll1.setValue(scroll1.getValue());
                                    .
                                    .
                                    .

            }
        }
    }
```

WARNING   Don't forget to set the scroll bar thumb to its new value when it has been scrolled, or it will appear to "jump" back on its own when the user releases it.

Because scroll1, the horizontal scroll bar, was scrolled, we need to display the new setting of that scroll bar in the text field text1 . To do so, convert the value of scroll1 to an integer and display it in text1 this way:

```
import java.applet.Applet;
import java.awt.event.*;
import java.awt.*;


public class scroller extends Applet implements AdjustmentListener {

    TextField text1;
    Scrollbar scroll1, scroll2;

    public void init(){
        text1 = new TextField(20);
        add(text1);
        scroll1 = new Scrollbar(Scrollbar.HORIZONTAL, 1, 10, 1, 100);
        add(scroll1);
        scroll1.addAdjustmentListener(this);
        scroll2 = new Scrollbar(Scrollbar.VERTICAL, 1, 10, 1, 100);
        add(scroll2);
        scroll2.addAdjustmentListener(this);
    }

    public void adjustmentValueChanged(AdjustmentEvent e){
        if(e.getAdjustable() == scroll1) {
```

```
                    scroll1.setValue(scroll1.getValue());
→                   text1.setText("Horizontal position: " +
        scroll1.getValue());
                }
            }
        }
```

TIP   You can concatenate—that is, join—strings in Java with the + operator as in the line text1.setText("horizontal position:" + scroll1.getValue());.

Do the same for `scroll2` as you did for `scroll1` with the following code to display `scroll2`'s value:

```
import java.applet.Applet;
import java.awt.event.*;
import java.awt.*;


public class scroller extends Applet implements AdjustmentListener {

    TextField text1;
    Scrollbar scroll1, scroll2;

    public void init(){
        text1 = new TextField(20);
        add(text1);
        scroll1 = new Scrollbar(Scrollbar.HORIZONTAL, 1, 10, 1, 100);
        add(scroll1);
        scroll1.addAdjustmentListener(this);
        scroll2 = new Scrollbar(Scrollbar.VERTICAL, 1, 10, 1, 100);
        add(scroll2);
        scroll2.addAdjustmentListener(this);
    }

    public void adjustmentValueChanged(AdjustmentEvent e){
        if(e.getAdjustable() == scroll1) {

            scroll1.setValue(scroll1.getValue());
            text1.setText("Horizontal position: " +
    scroll1.getValue()); }
→       if(e.getAdjustable() == scroll2) {
→           scroll2.setValue(scroll2.getValue());
→           text1.setText("Vertical position: " +
    scroll2.getValue());
→       }
        }
    }
```

Your scroll bar applet is ready to go. As shown below, the user can move the scroll bar thumbs, and their new position will be reported in the text fields. Your scrolling applet is a success! The code for this applet appears in `scroller.java`.

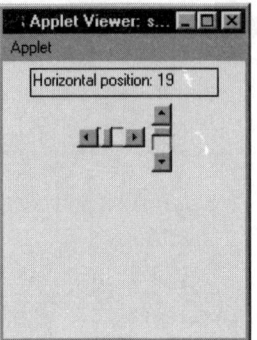

scroller.java

```java
import java.applet.Applet;
import java.awt.event.*;
import java.awt.*;


public class scroller extends Applet implements AdjustmentListener {

    TextField text1;
    Scrollbar scroll1, scroll2;

    public void init(){
        text1 = new TextField(20);
        add(text1);
        scroll1 = new Scrollbar(Scrollbar.HORIZONTAL, 1, 10, 1, 100);
        add(scroll1);
        scroll1.addAdjustmentListener(this);
        scroll2 = new Scrollbar(Scrollbar.VERTICAL, 1, 10, 1, 100);
        add(scroll2);
        scroll2.addAdjustmentListener(this);
    }
```

```
public void adjustmentValueChanged(AdjustmentEvent e){
    if(e.getAdjustable() == scroll1) {
        scroll1.setValue(scroll1.getValue());
        text1.setText("Horizontal position: " +
scroll1.getValue());
    }
    if(e.getAdjustable() == scroll2) {
        scroll2.setValue(scroll2.getValue());
    }
}
}
```

There is a special Java layout manager—the BorderLayout manager—that is perfect for use with scroll bars, although even many Java experts do not know about it. Let's use this layout to add power to the following applet.

Using Scroll Bars and BorderLayouts

The BorderLayout manager will allow you to surround your applet with scroll bars, as shown in Figure 6.3. When the user scrolls the horizontal or vertical scroll bars, you can report the new settings of the changed scroll bar in the text field, as shown in Figure 6.4.

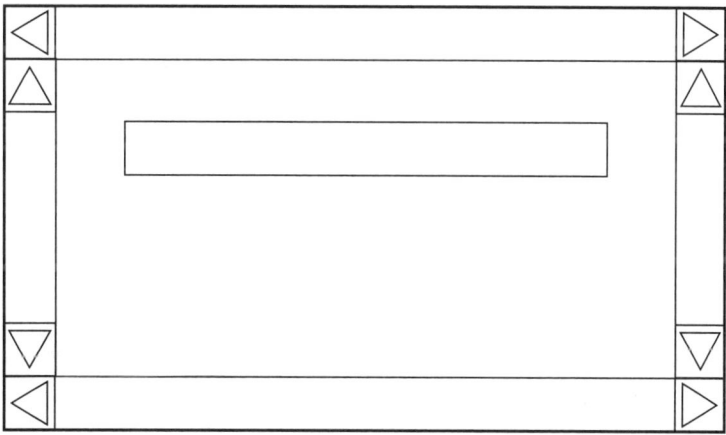

FIGURE 6.3:   Using the BorderLayout manager to place the scroll bars

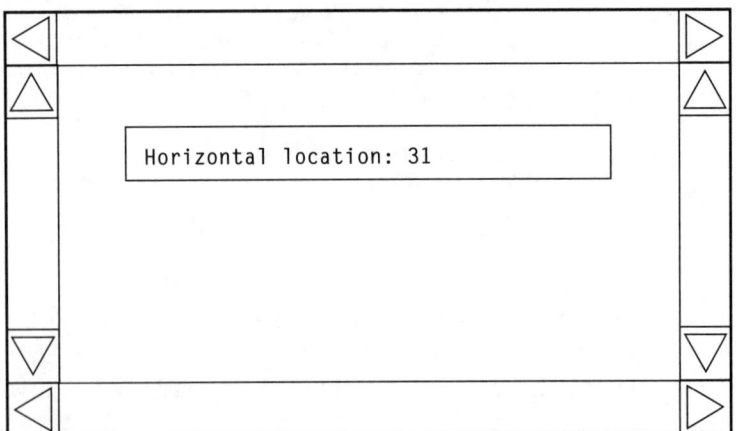

FIGURE 6.4:   Reporting the new position of the scroll bar

Let's see this feature in action. Create a new file named, say, `scrollborder`
`.java`. You declare the controls you need—two horizontal scroll bars `hScroll1`
and `hScroll2`, and two vertical scroll bars, `vScroll1` and `vScroll2`—as follows:

```
import java.applet.Applet;
import java.awt.*;
import java.awt.event.*;

public class scrollborder extends Applet implements AdjustmentListener
{
```

➡   `Scrollbar hScroll1, hScroll2, vScroll1, vScroll2;`

```
           .
           .
           .
}
```

You want to display a text field in the center of the applet. To accommodate
this, you will place a text field in a panel (named `Panel1`) of a new class named
`textpanel`:

```
import java.applet.Applet;
import java.awt.*;
import java.awt.event.*;

public class scrollborder extends Applet implements AdjustmentListener
{

        Scrollbar hScroll1, hScroll2, vScroll1, vScroll2;
```

```
➜        textPanel Panel1;
              .
              .
              .
    }
```

Create your `textpanel` class now. To do so, add this code to the end of the `scrollborder.java` file:

```
class textpanel extends Panel {

}
```

You learned how to work with panels in Skill 5. All you need here is a text field, which you might call `Text1`:

```
class textPanel extends Panel {
➜      TextField Text1;

       textPanel(){
➜          Text1 = new TextField(20);
➜          add(Text1);
       }
    }
```

Now that your new panel class is ready, you can set up your new layout. This layout will consist of four scroll bars surrounding your central panel, and as you'll see, that's easy to set up with the BorderLayout manager. First, install that as your new layout manager in the applet's `init()` method:

```
import java.applet.Applet;
import java.awt.*;
import java.awt.event.*;

public class scrollborder extends Applet implements AdjustmentListener
{

      Scrollbar hScroll1, hScroll2, vScroll1, vScroll2;
      textPanel Panel1;

      public void init(){
➜          setLayout(new BorderLayout());
                .
                .
                .

      }

}
```

Skill 6

You can now add your controls to this new layout. When you add controls to the BorderLayout manager, you specify where the new control goes—around the edges of the applet, which are designated north, south, east, and west, or in the center, as shown in Figure 6.5.

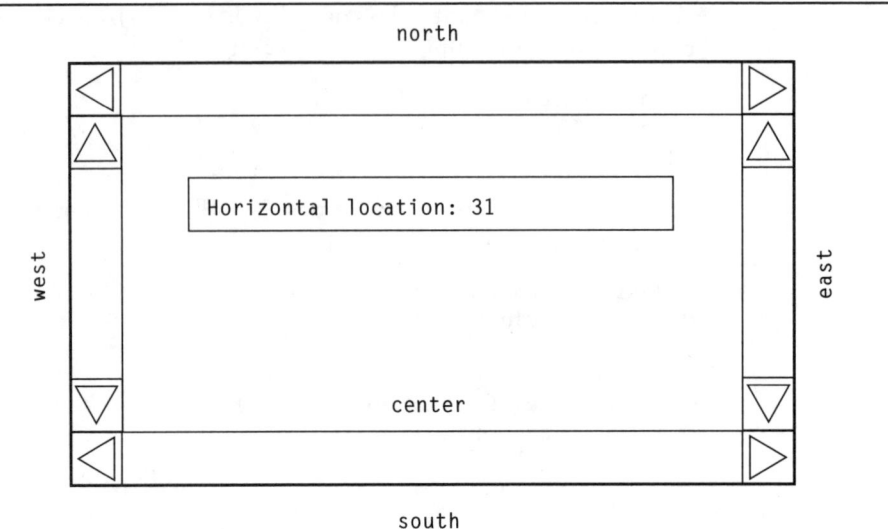

FIGURE 6.5:   Locations in the layout are designated as north, south, east, west, and center.

For example, create and add a scroll bar on the top of the applet—the "North" position—like this, where you also connect your applet as its AdjustmentListener:

```
import java.applet.Applet;
import java.awt.*;
import java.awt.event.*;

public class scrollborder extends Applet implements AdjustmentListener
{

     Scrollbar hScroll1, hScroll2, vScroll1, vScroll2;
     textPanel Panel1;

     public void init(){
          setLayout(new BorderLayout());
```

```
→          hScroll1 = new Scrollbar(Scrollbar.HORIZONTAL, 1, 1, 1, 200);
→          add("North", hScroll1);
→          hScroll1.addAdjustmentListener(this);
                   .
                   .
                   .

       }
}
```

Continue on, adding the other scroll bars, and the Panel1 object in the center of our applet:

```
import java.applet.Applet;
import java.awt.*;
import java.awt.event.*;

public class scrollborder extends Applet implements AdjustmentListener
{

       Scrollbar hScroll1, hScroll2, vScroll1, vScroll2;
       textPanel Panel1;

       public void init(){
           setLayout(new BorderLayout());

           hScroll1 = new Scrollbar(Scrollbar.HORIZONTAL, 1, 1, 1, 200);
           add("North", hScroll1);
           hScroll1.addAdjustmentListener(this);

→          vScroll1 = new Scrollbar(Scrollbar.VERTICAL, 1, 1, 1, 200)
→          add("West", vScroll1);
→          vScroll1.addAdjustmentListener(this);

→          hScroll2 = new Scrollbar(Scrollbar.HORIZONTAL, 1, 1, 1, 200);
→          add("South", hScroll2);
→          hScroll2.addAdjustmentListener(this);

→          vScroll2 = new Scrollbar(Scrollbar.VERTICAL, 1, 1, 1, 200);

→          add("East", vScroll2);
→          vScroll2.addAdjustmentListener(this);

→          Panel1 = new textPanel();
→          add("Center", Panel1);
→          Panel1.Text1.SetLocation(0, 0);
       }
   }
```

Now the scroll bars are laid out correctly in the applet. All that remains is to connect them to the code in the `adjustmentValueChanged()` method. To do this, add the following code to `scrollborder.java`:

```java
import java.applet.Applet;
import java.awt.*;
import java.awt.event.*;

public class scrollborder extends Applet implements AdjustmentListener
{

    Scrollbar hScroll1, hScroll2, vScroll1, vScroll2;
    textPanel Panel1;

    public void init(){
        setLayout(new BorderLayout());

        hScroll1 = new Scrollbar(Scrollbar.HORIZONTAL, 1, 1, 1, 200);
        add("North", hScroll1);
        hScroll1.addAdjustmentListener(this);

        vScroll1 = new Scrollbar(Scrollbar.VERTICAL, 1, 1, 1, 200);
        add("West", vScroll1);
        vScroll1.addAdjustmentListener(this);

        hScroll2 = new Scrollbar(Scrollbar.HORIZONTAL, 1, 1, 1, 200);
        add("South", hScroll2);
        hScroll2.addAdjustmentListener(this);

        vScroll2 = new Scrollbar(Scrollbar.VERTICAL, 1, 1, 1, 200);
        add("East", vScroll2);
        vScroll2.addAdjustmentListener(this);

        Panel1 = new textPanel();
        add("Center", Panel1);
        Panel1.Text1.SetLocation(0, 0);
    }

    public void adjustmentValueChanged(AdjustmentEvent e){
            .
            .
            .

    }
}
```

Note that you should keep the scroll bars coordinated (i.e., if the user scrolls one, you should update the other as well). That looks like this in code:

```
import java.applet.Applet;
import java.awt.*;
import java.awt.event.*;

public class scrollborder extends Applet implements AdjustmentListener
{

    Scrollbar hScroll1, hScroll2, vScroll1, vScroll2;
    textPanel Panel1;

    public void init(){
        setLayout(new BorderLayout());

        hScroll1 = new Scrollbar(Scrollbar.HORIZONTAL, 1, 1, 1, 200);
        add("North", hScroll1);
        hScroll1.addAdjustmentListener(this);

        vScroll1 = new Scrollbar(Scrollbar.VERTICAL, 1, 1, 1, 200);
        add("West", vScroll1);
        vScroll1.addAdjustmentListener(this);

        hScroll2 = new Scrollbar(Scrollbar.HORIZONTAL, 1, 1, 1, 200);
        add("South", hScroll2);
        hScroll2.addAdjustmentListener(this);

        vScroll2 = new Scrollbar(Scrollbar.VERTICAL, 1, 1, 1, 200);
        add("East", vScroll2);
        vScroll2.addAdjustmentListener(this);

        Panel1 = new textPanel();
        add("Center", Panel1);
        Panel1.Text1.SetLocation(0, 0);
    }

    public void adjustmentValueChanged(AdjustmentEvent e){
        if(e.getAdjustable() == hScroll1){

            hScroll1.setValue(hScroll1.getValue());
            hScroll2.setValue(hScroll1.getValue());
        }
        if(e.getAdjustable() == vScroll1){

            vScroll1.setValue(vScroll1.getValue());
            vScroll2.setValue(vScroll1.getValue());
        }
    }
```

Skill 6

```
          if(e.getAdjustable() == hScroll2){

➜                 hScroll2.setValue(hScroll2.getValue());
➜                 hScroll1.setValue(hScroll2.getValue());
          }
          if(e.getAdjustable() == vScroll2){

➜                 vScroll2.setValue(vScroll2.getValue());
➜                 vScroll1.setValue(vScroll2.getValue());
          }
      }

    }
```

Finally, you can report the new scroll bar positions in the appropriate text field as follows:

```
import java.applet.Applet;
import java.awt.*;
import java.awt.event.*;

public class scrollborder extends Applet implements AdjustmentListener
{

    Scrollbar hScroll1, hScroll2, vScroll1, vScroll2;
    textPanel Panel1;

    public void init(){
        setLayout(new BorderLayout());
            .
            .
            .
    }

    public void adjustmentValueChanged(AdjustmentEvent e){
        if(e.getAdjustable() == hScroll1){
            hScroll1.setValue(hScroll1.getValue());
            hScroll2.setValue(hScroll1.getValue());
➜          Panel1.Text1.setText("Horizontal location: " +
    hScroll1.getValue());
        }
        if(e.getAdjustable() == vScroll1){

            vScroll1.setValue(vScroll1.getValue());
            vScroll2.setValue(vScroll1.getValue());
➜          Panel1.Text1.setText("Vertical location: " +
    vScroll1.getValue());
        }
```

```
            if(e.getAdjustable() == hScroll2){
                hScroll2.setValue(hScroll2.getValue());
                hScroll1.setValue(hScroll2.getValue());
➡               Panel1.Text1.setText("Horizontal location: " +
    hScroll2.getValue());
            }
            if(e.getAdjustable() == vScroll2){
                vScroll2.setValue(vScroll2.getValue());
                vScroll1.setValue(vScroll2.getValue());
➡               Panel1.Text1.setText("Vertical location: " +
    vScroll2.getValue());
            }
        }
    }
```

And that's it—your scrollborder applet is finished. Run the scrollborder applet now. As you can see, the scroll bars appear surrounding the central panel. When the user scrolls the scroll bars, the new horizontal and vertical positions appear in the text fields below. The code for this applet appears in scrollborder.java.

 **TIP**   If you want to move controls around in the central panel in response to the action of the surrounding scroll bars, just use the control's SetLocation() method (which most Java controls have). This can give the user the impression they are scrolling the controls around inside the applet.

Skill 6

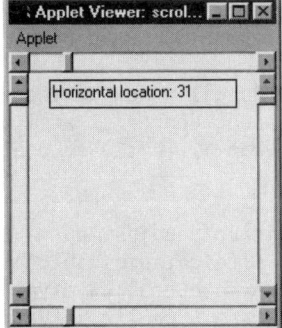

scrollborder.java

```java
import java.applet.Applet;
import java.awt.*;
import java.awt.event.*;

public class scrollborder extends Applet implements AdjustmentListener
{

    Scrollbar hScroll1, hScroll2, vScroll1, vScroll2;
    textPanel Panel1;

    public void init(){
        setLayout(new BorderLayout());

        hScroll1 = new Scrollbar(Scrollbar.HORIZONTAL, 1, 1, 1, 200);
        add("North", hScroll1);
        hScroll1.addAdjustmentListener(this);

        vScroll1 = new Scrollbar(Scrollbar.VERTICAL, 1, 1, 1, 200);
        add("West", vScroll1);
        vScroll1.addAdjustmentListener(this);

        hScroll2 = new Scrollbar(Scrollbar.HORIZONTAL, 1, 1, 1, 200);
        add("South", hScroll2);
        hScroll2.addAdjustmentListener(this);

        vScroll2 = new Scrollbar(Scrollbar.VERTICAL, 1, 1, 1, 200);
        add("East", vScroll2);
        vScroll2.addAdjustmentListener(this);

        Panel1 = new textPanel();
        add("Center", Panel1);
        Panel1.Text1.SetLocation(0, 0);
    }

    public void adjustmentValueChanged(AdjustmentEvent e){
        if(e.getAdjustable() == hScroll1){
            hScroll1.setValue(hScroll1.getValue());
            hScroll2.setValue(hScroll1.getValue());
            Panel1.Text1.setText("Horizontal location: " +
hScroll1.getValue());
        }
        if(e.getAdjustable() == vScroll1){

            vScroll1.setValue(vScroll1.getValue());
            vScroll2.setValue(vScroll1.getValue());
```

```
                    Panel1.Text1.setText("Vertical location: " +
vScroll1.getValue());
            }
          if(e.getAdjustable() == hScroll2){
              hScroll2.setValue(hScroll2.getValue());
              hScroll1.setValue(hScroll2.getValue());
              Panel1.Text1.setText("Horizontal location: " +
hScroll2.getValue());
            }
          if(e.getAdjustable() == vScroll2){
              vScroll2.setValue(vScroll2.getValue());
              vScroll1.setValue(vScroll2.getValue());
              Panel1.Text1.setText("Vertical location: " +
vScroll2.getValue());
            }
        }

    }

class textPanel extends Panel {
    TextField Text1;

    textPanel(){
        Text1 = new TextField(20);
        add(Text1);
    }
}
```

That's it—now you can use scroll bars with the border layout, giving your Java programs a professional air.

Working with the *ScrollPane* Class

Java 1.1 includes a class called ScrollPane, which lets you place a control in the middle of a container object and display it. Scroll bars will appear around the edges of this container as needed. This is something like the example we just developed, except the ScrollPane class scrolls the controls placed in its pane automatically, instead of letting you handle the scrolling events yourself. It's easy to implement, so let's see it at work now—create a new file named scrpane.java, and start it off as usual:

```
import java.applet.Applet;
import java.awt.*;
```

```
public class scrpane extends Applet {

}
```

Now add your ScrollPane object, which you might call scrollpane1:

```
import java.applet.Applet;
import java.awt.*;

public class scrpane extends Applet {

➜        ScrollPane scrollpane1;

         public void init(){
➜            scrollpane1 = new ScrollPane();
                 .
                 .
                 .

         }

}
```

All you have to do is create a new control and add it to your ScrollPane object. You will add a new text field to the ScrollPane object as follows:

```
import java.applet.Applet;
import java.awt.*;

public class scrpane extends Applet {

         ScrollPane scrollpane1;
➜        TextField text1;

         public void init(){
             scrollpane1 = new ScrollPane();
➜           text1 = new TextField("Welcome to Java");
➜           scrollpane1.add(text1);
                 .
                 .
                 .

         }
}
```

The Java ScrollPane class's methods appear in Table 6.2.

TABLE 6.2: The ScrollPane class methods

Method	Does This
ScrollPane()	Creates a new scroll pane container with a display policy of "as needed"
ScrollPane(int)	Create a new scroll pane container
addImpl(Component, Object, int)	Adds the specified component to this scroll pane container
add(Component, int)	Adds given component to this scrollpane container
addNotify()	Creates scroll pane's peer
doLayout()	Lays out container by resizing its child to its preferred size
getHAdjustable()	Returns the Adjustable object that represents the horizontal scroll bar
getHScrollbarHeight()	Returns the height that would be occupied by a horizontal scroll bar
getScrollbarDisplayPolicy()	Returns the display policy for the scroll bars
getScrollPosition()	Returns the current x,y position within the child, which is displayed at the 0,0 location of the scrolled panel's view
getVAdjustable()	Returns the Adjustable object that represents the vertical scroll bar
getViewportSize()	Returns the current size of the scroll pane's view port
getVScrollbarWidth()	Returns the width that would be occupied by a vertical scroll bar
paramString()	Returns the parameter String of this container
printComponents(Graphics)	Prints the component in this scroll pane
setLayout(LayoutManager)	Sets the layout manager for this container
setScrollPosition(int, int)	Scrolls to the given position in the child component
setScrollPosition(Point)	Scrolls to the given position in the child component

Skill 6

All that's left is to add the `ScrollPane` object to your applet, and you do that like this:

```
import java.applet.Applet;
import java.awt.*;

public class scrpane extends Applet {

    ScrollPane scrollpane1;
    TextField text1;

    public void init(){
        scrollpane1 = new ScrollPane();
        text1 = new TextField("Welcome to Java");
        scrollpane1.add(text1);
        add(scrollpane1);
    }

}
```

You can run the applet now, as shown below. As you can see, the `ScrollPane` is active, and by using the scroll bar, the user can scroll your control in the `ScrollPane`. In this way, you can put controls into a `ScrollPane` and let the user scroll as needed. This new applet appears in `scrpane.java`.

scrpane.java

```
import java.applet.Applet;
import java.awt.*;

public class scrpane extends Applet {

    ScrollPane scrollpane1;
    TextField text1;

    public void init(){
        scrollpane1 = new ScrollPane();
        text1 = new TextField("Welcome to Java");
        scrollpane1.add(text1);
        add(scrollpane1);
    }

}
```

That's all there is to it—now you're using the ScrollPane class. We've come far in Skill 6, adding scrolling to our arsenal of Java techniques. That's it for scroll bars for the moment. Let's move on now to another set of powerful Java controls—choice controls and scrolling lists.

Are You up to Speed?

Now you can. . .

- ☑ let the user display more information by using scroll bars in Java programs, allowing the user to manipulate scroll bar thumbs for program input

- ☑ use the BorderLayout manager to handle scroll bars

- ☑ use the *ScrollPane* class to scroll controls easily

- ☑ create multiple scroll bars in one Java program and keep them coordinated as the user manipulates them

- ☑ match the user's scrolling actions by updating scroll bar settings

- ☑ ignore the user's scrolling actions if the user scrolls to a region you consider "forbidden"

Using Choice Controls and Scrolling Lists

- Adding and using *Choice* controls in Java programs
- Adding and using scrolling lists in Java programs
- Passing parameters to an applet
- Determining which selection was made in a scrolling list

In Skill 6, we took a look at handling scroll bars. In this chapter we're going to examine two other popular Java controls, `Choice` controls and Scrolling lists. Both of these controls present a number of options to the user and let them select which one—or ones—they like. We'll also see how to use the built-in Java support for applet *parameters*—values we can pass our applet from the data placed in the `<applet>` tag in the `.html` page. Java adds a great deal of support for parameters for us, and using parameters we can customize our applet to work in many different Web pages without being recompiled. We'll also explore the most powerful—and most complex—of the Java layouts: the GridBagLayout. Let's start now with Java `Choice` controls.

Using *Choice* Controls

The `Choice` control is really just the drop-down list box that Windows users are familiar with. For example, if you had a `Choice` control, the user would see the first choice in the `Choice` control and an arrow button next to it, as shown in Figure 7.1. When the user clicks the arrow button, the list of choices opens, as shown in Figure 7.2. When the user selects a choice (by clicking it), you can display the result in a text field, as shown in Figure 7.3.

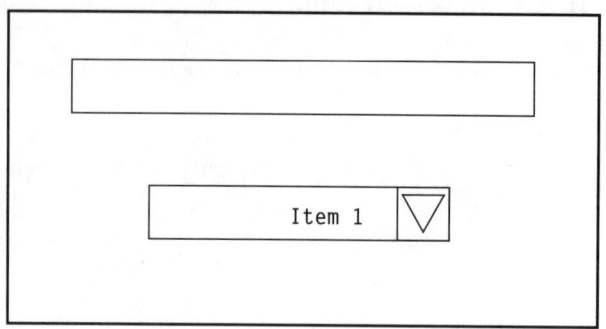

FIGURE 7.1: The `Choice` control

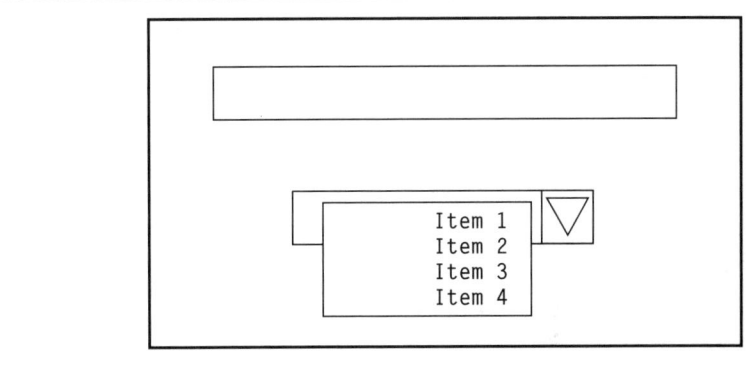

FIGURE 7.2:   Clicking the arrow button displays a list of choices.

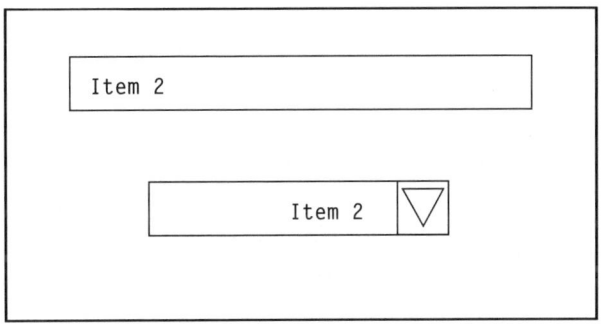

FIGURE 7.3:   You can report which choice was selected.

You will put choice controls to work in a minute. As it turns out, choice controls will give us the chance to first explore another facet of Java—handling parameters. Parameters are values you can pass to an applet and use to customize the applet's behavior. For example, you might pass the items that the Choice control is to display. In this way, you can use the same applet with the same choice control in many different Web pages.

Let's see how this all works. Create a new file named choices.java. Here, you'll pass the choices that the Choice control is to display as parameters embedded in the applet's Web page. Create the Web page choices.htm now. This file will look just like your standard Web page—but with one addition: you'll include param tags giving the values you want to display in the Choice control (i.e., the strings "Item 1" to "Item 4"), giving those strings the names selection1 to selection4:

```
<html>
<head>
<title>choices</title>
</head>
<body>
<hr>
<applet
    code=choices.class
    width=200
    height=200 >
➜    <param name=selection1 value="Item 1">
➜    <param name=selection2 value="Item 2">
➜    <param name=selection3 value="Item 3">
➜    <param name=selection4 value="Item 4">
</applet>
<hr>
</body>
</html>
```

We'll be able to read and make use of those parameters from our applet. If you want to, you can have many different sets of parameters in many different Web pages but still use the same applet. In this way, you can customize the applet's behavior easily.

Now let's write choices.java. Here you'll see how to retrieve the parameters you've set up and place them in your Choice control. Begin by adding the controls you'll need—a Choice control and a text field—this way:

```
import java.applet.Applet;
import java.awt.*;
import java.awt.event.*;

public class choices extends Applet {

➜    Choice choice1;
➜    TextField text1;
            .
            .
            .

}
```

The methods of the Java Choice class appear in Table 7.1.

T A B L E   7 . 1 : The Choice class methods

Method	Does This
Choice()	Constructs a new Choice
add(String)	Adds an item to this Choice
addItem(String)	Deprecated. Replaced by add(String)
addItemListener(ItemListener)	Adds the given item listener to receive item events from this choice
addNotify()	Creates the Choice's peer
countItems()	Deprecated. Replaced by getItemCount()
getItem(int)	Returns the String at given index
getItemCount()	Returns the number of items in this Choice
getSelectedIndex()	Returns index of currently selected item
getSelectedItem()	Returns a String representation of the current choice
getSelectedObjects()	Returns an array (length 1) containing the currently selected object
insert(String, int)	Inserts the item into this choice at the specified position
paramString()	Returns the parameter String of this Choice
processEvent(AWTEvent)	Processes events on this choice
processItemEvent(ItemEvent)	Processes item events occurring on this choice by dispatching them to any registered ItemListener objects
remove(int)	Removes an item from choice's menu
remove(String)	Remove first occurrence of item from the choice menu
removeAll()	Removes all items from the choice menu
removeItemListener(ItemListener)	Removes the item listener
select(int)	Selects the item with the given position
select(String)	Selects the item with the given String

Next, add an init() method and add your new controls there:

```
import java.applet.Applet;
import java.awt.*;
import java.awt.event.*;
```

```
public class choices extends Applet {

    Choice choice1;
    TextField text1;

    public void init(){
→        text1 = new TextField(20);
→        add(text1);
→        choice1 = new Choice();
→        add(choice1);
             .
             .
             .

    }
}
```

Note that before adding the Choice control you can load it with the parameters it reads in directly from the Web page. To do this, just use the getParameter() method. In particular, all you have to do is pass getParameter() the name of the item you want to get (i.e., using the name you gave it in the Web page). Then you can add that new selection to the Choice control this way:

```
import java.applet.Applet;
import java.awt.*;
import java.awt.event.*;

public class choices extends Applet {

    Choice choice1;
    TextField text1;

    public void init(){
        text1 = new TextField(20);
        add(text1);
        choice1 = new Choice();
→        choice1.add(getParameter("selection1"));
→        choice1.add(getParameter("selection2"));
→        choice1.add(getParameter("selection3"));
→        choice1.add(getParameter("selection4"));
        add(choice1);
             .
             .
             .

    }
```

That's it—you've added your selections to the Choice control by retrieving them directly from the Web page.

> **NOTE**   If you've programmed in Java before, you might have expected to add items to the Choice control with the addItem() method, but that method is deprecated in Java 1.2.

At this point, then, your Choice control and text field appear. The next step is to display the choice the user makes, and you do that by adding an Item-Listener to the Choice control:

```
import java.applet.Applet;
import java.awt.*;
import java.awt.event.*;

public class choices extends Applet implements ItemListener {

    Choice choice1;
    TextField text1;

    public void init(){
        text1 = new TextField(20);
        add(text1);
        choice1 = new Choice();
        choice1.add(getParameter("selection1"));
        choice1.add(getParameter("selection2"));
        choice1.add(getParameter("selection3"));
        choice1.add(getParameter("selection4"));
        add(choice1);
        choice1.addItemListener(this);
    }
```

Then add the itemStateChanged() method to your applet so you will be able to read Choice control events:

```
import java.applet.Applet;
import java.awt.*;
import java.awt.event.*;

public class choices extends Applet implements ItemListener {

    Choice choice1;
    TextField text1;

    public void init(){
        text1 = new TextField(20);
        add(text1);
        choice1 = new Choice();
```

```
            choice1.add(getParameter("selection1"));
            choice1.add(getParameter("selection2"));
            choice1.add(getParameter("selection3"));
            choice1.add(getParameter("selection4"));
            add(choice1);
            choice1.addItemListener(this);
        }

➜       public void itemStateChanged(ItemEvent e) {
                    .
                    .
                    .

➜       }
    }
```

Now make sure that `choice1` caused the event:

```
import java.applet.Applet;
import java.awt.*;
import java.awt.event.*;

public class choices extends Applet implements ItemListener {

    Choice choice1;
    TextField text1;

    public void init(){
        text1 = new TextField(20);
        add(text1);
        choice1 = new Choice();
        choice1.add(getParameter("selection1"));
        choice1.add(getParameter("selection2"));
        choice1.add(getParameter("selection3"));
        choice1.add(getParameter("selection4"));
        add(choice1);
        choice1.addItemListener(this);
    }

    public void itemStateChanged(ItemEvent e) {
➜          if(e.getItemSelectable() == choice1){
                    .
                    .
                    .

            }
        }
    }
```

And if so, all that is left is to display the new choice the user has just made in the text field, which you do like this. (Note that you have to indicate that the item you get with `getItemSelectable()` is a `Choice` control with the `(Choice)` cast):

```java
import java.applet.Applet;
import java.awt.*;
import java.awt.event.*;

public class choices extends Applet implements ItemListener {

    Choice choice1;
    TextField text1;

    public void init(){
        text1 = new TextField(20);
        add(text1);
        choice1 = new Choice();
        choice1.add(getParameter("selection1"));
        choice1.add(getParameter("selection2"));
        choice1.add(getParameter("selection3"));
        choice1.add(getParameter("selection4"));
        add(choice1);
        choice1.addItemListener(this);
    }

    public void itemStateChanged(ItemEvent e) {
        if(e.getItemSelectable() == choice1){
→           text1.setText(
    ((Choice)e.getItemSelectable()).getSelectedItem());
        }
    }
}
```

Skill 7

> **NOTE**   Note the use of the term `(Choice)` in the above code. Here, you inform Java that the control you get from the `e.getItemSelectable()` call will be a `Choice` control. You need to tell Java that so you can then use the `Choice` control's `getSelectedItem()` method in the same statement.

And now your selections applet is ready to go. As you can see below, the `Choice` control is active—you've read in the parameters from the Web page and presented them to the user. When the user makes a selection from the `Choice` control, you display that selection in the text field. The code for this applet appears in `choices.java`.

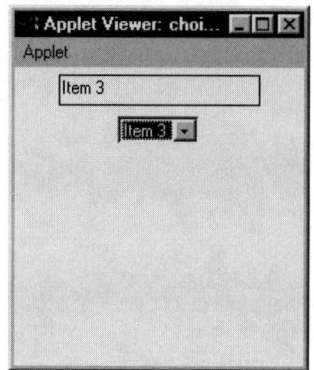

choices.java

```java
import java.applet.Applet;
import java.awt.*;
import java.awt.event.*;

public class choices extends Applet implements ItemListener {

    Choice choice1;
    TextField text1;

    public void init(){
        text1 = new TextField(20);
        add(text1);
        choice1 = new Choice();
        choice1.add(getParameter("selection1"));
        choice1.add(getParameter("selection2"));
        choice1.add(getParameter("selection3"));
        choice1.add(getParameter("selection4"));
        add(choice1);
        choice1.addItemListener(this);
    }

    public void itemStateChanged(ItemEvent e) {
        if(e.getItemSelectable() == choice1){
        text1.setText(
((Choice)e.getItemSelectable()).getSelectedItem());
        }
    }
}
```

We've started well in this chapter with `Choice` controls, and there's more to come. Let's continue now to see how to implement scrolling lists in Java.

Using Scrolling Lists

A scrolling list presents choices that the user may select from using the up and down arrows that appear at right in the `list` control. For example, the user may scroll down to the second choice, as shown in Figure 7.4. If they double-click this choice, you can report their selection in a text field, as shown in Figure 7.5.

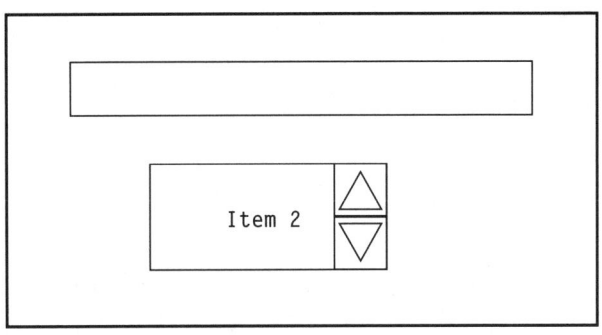

FIGURE 7.4: Selecting from a scrolling list

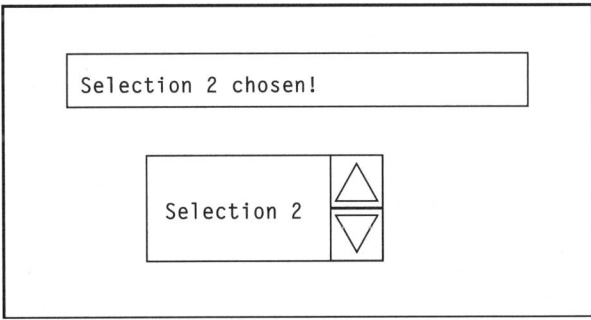

FIGURE 7.5: Reporting a selection in a text field

It will be easy to implement a `Choice` control applet, so let's do that now. Create a new file named `scrolllist.java` for your scrolling list applet and add the applet's main class as usual. Here, you can add the two controls you use, the scrolling list itself (an object of class `List` named `list1`) and a text field (named `text1`) as follows:

```
import java.applet.Applet;
import java.awt.*;
import java.awt.event.*;

public class scrolllist extends Applet {

        List list1;
        TextField text1;
            .
            .
            .
}
```

The Java `List` class methods appear in Table 7.2.

TABLE 7.2: The List class methods

Method	Does This
List()	Creates a new scrolling list initialized with no visible lines
List(int)	Creates a new scrolling list initialized with the given number of visible lines
List(int, boolean)	Creates a new scrolling list initialized with the given number of visible lines and a boolean indicating if multiple selections are allowed or not
add(String)	Adds the given item to the end of scrolling list
add(String, int)	Adds the given item to the scrolling list at the given position
addActionListener(ActionListener)	Adds the given action listener to receive action events from this list
addItem(String)	Deprecated. Replaced by add(String)
addItem(String, int)	Deprecated. Replaced by add(String, int)
addItemListener(ItemListener)	Adds the given item listener to receive item events from this list
addNotify()	Creates the peer for the List

TABLE 7.2 CONTINUED: The List class methods

Method	Does This
allowsMultipleSelections()	Deprecated. Replaced by isMultipleMode()
clear()	Deprecated. Replaced by removeAll()
countItems()	Deprecated. Replaced by getItemCount()
delItem(int)	Deprecated. Replaced by remove(String) and remove(int)
delItems(int, int)	Deprecated. Not for public use in the future
deselect(int)	Deselects the item at the given index
getItem(int)	Gets the item associated with the given index
getItemCount()	Returns the number of items in the list
getItems()	Returns the items in the list
getMinimumSize()	Returns the minimum dimensions needed for the list
getMinimumSize(int)	Returns the minimum dimensions needed for the amount of rows in the list
getPreferredSize()	Returns the preferred dimensions needed for the list
getPreferredSize(int)	Returns the preferred dimensions needed for the list with the given amount of rows
getRows()	Returns the number of visible lines in this list
getSelectedIndex()	Gets the selected item on the list or –1 if no item is selected
getSelectedIndexes()	Returns the selected indexes on the list
getSelectedItem()	Returns the selected item on the list or null if no item is selected
getSelectedItems()	Returns the selected items on the list
getSelectedObjects()	Returns the selected items on the list in an array of Objects
getVisibleIndex()	Gets the index of item that was last made visible
isIndexSelected(int)	Returns true if the item at the given index is selected
isMultipleMode()	Returns true if this list allows multiple selections

TABLE 7.2 CONTINUED: The List class methods

Method	Does This
isSelected(int)	Deprecated. Replaced by isIndexSelected(int)
makeVisible(int)	Forces the item at the given index to be visible
minimumSize()	Deprecated. Replaced by getMinimumSize()
minimumSize(int)	Deprecated. Replaced by getMinimumSize(int)
paramString()	Returns the parameter String of this list
preferredSize()	Deprecated. Replaced by getPreferredSize()
preferredSize(int)	Deprecated. Replaced by getPreferredSize(int)
processActionEvent(ActionEvent)	Processes action events occurring on this component by dispatching them to any registered ActionListener objects
processEvent(AWTEvent)	Processes events on this list
processItemEvent(ItemEvent)	Processes item events occurring on this list by dispatching them to any registered ItemListener objects
remove(int)	Removes an item from the list
remove(String)	Removes the first occurrence of item from the list
removeActionListener(Action Listener)	Removes the given action listener so it no longer receives action events from this list
removeAll()	Removes all items from the list
removeItemListener(ItemListener)	Removes the given item listener so it no longer receives item events from this list
removeNotify()	Removes the peer for this list
replaceItem(String, int)	Replaces the item at the given index
select(int)	Selects the item at the given index
setMultipleMode(boolean)	Sets whether or not this list should allow multiple selections
setMultipleSelections(boolean)	Deprecated. Replaced by setMultipleMode (boolean)

In the `init()` method, just add your new `list` control this way, indicating that you want two lines in your list control, and indicating that you will allow multiple selections by passing a second parameter and setting it to true:

```java
import java.applet.Applet;
import java.awt.*;
import java.awt.event.*;

public class scrolllist extends Applet {

    List list1;
    TextField text1;

    public void init(){
➜        text1 = new TextField(20);
➜        list1 = new List(2, true);
                    .
                    .
                    .


    }
}
```

Next, add the list, the text field, and the selections in the `List` control. You'll add the items to the `List` control with the `List` class's `add()` method this way:

```java
import java.applet.Applet;
import java.awt.*;
import java.awt.event.*;

public class scrolllist extends Applet {

    List list1;
    TextField text1;

    public void init(){
        text1 = new TextField(20);
        add(text1);
        list1 = new List(2, true);
➜        list1.add("Item 1");
➜        list1.add("Item 2");
➜        list1.add("Item 3");
        add(list1);
                    .
                    .
                    .


    }
}
```

In addition, add an ActionListener to your applet's class and the List control:

```
import java.applet.Applet;
import java.awt.*;
import java.awt.event.*;

public class scrolllist extends Applet implements ActionListener{

    List list1;
    TextField text1;

    public void init(){
        text1 = new TextField(20);
        add(text1);
        list1 = new List(2, true);
        list1.add("Item 1");
        list1.add("Item 2");
        list1.add("Item 3");
        add(list1);
        list1.addActionListener(this);
    }
}
```

Now the applet displays the scrolling list control and the text field—your next step is to make the scrolling list active with an actionPerformed() method:

```
import java.applet.Applet;
import java.awt.*;
import java.awt.event.*;

public class scrolllist extends Applet implements ActionListener {

    List list1;
    TextField text1;

    public void init(){
        text1 = new TextField(20);
        add(text1);
        list1 = new List(2, true);
        list1.add("Item 1");
        list1.add("Item 2");
        list1.add("Item 3");
        add(list1);
        list1.addActionListener(this);
    }

    public void actionPerformed(ActionEvent e) {
                    .
                    .
                    .
    }
}
```

If the user has indeed made a selection, you can get the currently selected item in the scrolling list this way:

```
((List) e.getSource()).getSelectedItem()
```

and we display that selection in the text field `text1` as follows:

```
import java.applet.Applet;
import java.awt.*;
import java.awt.event.*;

public class scrolllist extends Applet implements ActionListener {

    List list1;
    TextField text1;

    public void init(){
        text1 = new TextField(20);
        add(text1);
        list1 = new List(2, true);
        list1.add("Item 1");
        list1.add("Item 2");
        list1.add("Item 3");
        add(list1);
        list1.addActionListener(this);
    }

    public void actionPerformed(ActionEvent e) {
        if(e.getSource() == list1){
        text1.setText(((List) e.getSource()).getSelectedItem());
        }
    }
}
```

NOTE   To handle multiple selections (our `list` control is set up to accept multiple selections), you would use `getSelectedItems()` here instead. In this simple example, we're using just a single selection.

You're finished! Your scrolling list applet is ready to run. The user can scroll up and down your list, and when they make a selection, you can report what that selection is, as shown below. The code for this applet appears in `scrolllist.java`.

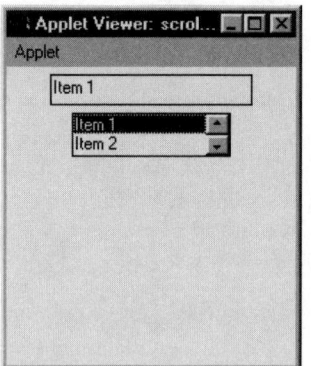

scrolllist.java

```
import java.applet.Applet;
import java.awt.*;
import java.awt.event.*;

public class scrolllist extends Applet implements ActionListener {

    List list1;
    TextField text1;

    public void init(){
        text1 = new TextField(20);
        add(text1);
        list1 = new List(2, true);
        list1.add("Item 1");
        list1.add("Item 2");
        list1.add("Item 3");
        add(list1);
        list1.addActionListener(this);
    }

    public void actionPerformed(ActionEvent e) {
        if(e.getSource() == list1){
        text1.setText(((List) e.getSource()).getSelectedItem());
        }
    }
}
```

We will turn now to the final topic for this chapter—another powerful Java layout manager—the GridBagLayout manager.

Using the GridBagLayout Manager

In this last example of the chapter, we'll explore what is probably the most powerful native Java layout of all—the GridBagLayout. This layout manager lets you specify the position of your controls more exactly than any other layout manager we've seen.

For example, using the GridBagLayout manager, you can create an applet that provides the user with a list of employees. You can display the names of employees in buttons at the top of the applet. When the user clicks a button, you can display the corresponding employee ID number in a text area, as shown in Figure 7.6.

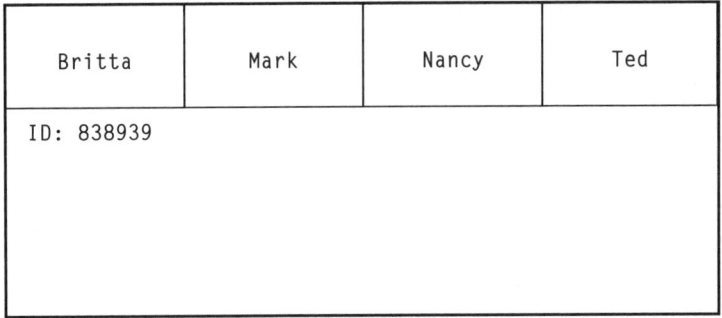

FIGURE 7.6:   Displaying a number in a text field at the click of a button

Let's give this new layout a try. Create a new file now named `employee.java`. You'll also add the controls you'll need—buttons `button1` to `button4`, and a text area named `text1`:

```
import java.applet.Applet;
import java.awt.*;
import java.awt.event.*;

public class employee extends Applet {

        Button button1, button2, button3, button4;
        TextArea text1;
                .
                .
                .

    }
```

Now let's set up our new GridBagLayout manager to see how it works. To do this, create a new object of the GridBagLayout class named gridbag, as follows in the init() method:

```
import java.applet.Applet;
import java.awt.*;
import java.awt.event.*;

public class employee extends Applet {

    Button button1, button2, button3, button4;
    TextArea text1;

    public void init(){

➔        GridBagLayout gridbag = new GridBagLayout();
             .
             .
             .

    }
}
```

You can specify how you want your controls to be arranged under the Grid-BagLayout manager using an object of the Java class GridBagConstraints, as you'll see in the example. Use this object to arrange the controls in a GridBagLayout. In the following code, create an object of that class and name it constraints:

```
import java.applet.Applet;
import java.awt.*;
import java.awt.event.*;

public class employee extends Applet {

    Button button1, button2, button3, button4;
    TextArea text1;

    public void init(){

         GridBagLayout gridbag = new GridBagLayout();
➔        GridBagConstraints constraints = new GridBagConstraints();
             .
             .
             .

    }
}
```

Now you can install your new GridBagLayout in your applet:

```java
import java.applet.Applet;
import java.awt.*;
import java.awt.event.*;

public class employee extends Applet {

    Button button1, button2, button3, button4;
    TextArea text1;

    public void init(){

        GridBagLayout gridbag = new GridBagLayout();
        GridBagConstraints constraints = new GridBagConstraints();
→       setLayout(gridbag);
                .
                .
                .

    }
}
```

The next step is to start specifying how you want your controls to be "constrained" in your new layout, and we'll turn to that now.

Using GridBagConstraints

GridBagLayouts work with the relative "weights" of controls in the x and y directions—for example, since all of these buttons have the same width, they each have the same x weight, as shown in Figure 7.7. If one control is twice as wide as the others, it will have double the x weight, as shown in Figure 7.8.

You can specify x and y weights with the `weightx` and `weighty` members of the `GridBagConstraints` object you named `constraints`. Since all of your buttons have the same height, they have the same value for `weighty`, which we can just set to 1:

```java
import java.applet.Applet;
import java.awt.*;
import java.awt.event.*;

public class employee extends Applet {

    Button button1, button2, button3, button4;
    TextArea text1;
```

```
public void init(){

    GridBagLayout gridbag = new GridBagLayout();
    GridBagConstraints constraints = new GridBagConstraints();
    setLayout(gridbag);
    constraints.weighty = 1;
        .
        .
        .

    }
}
```

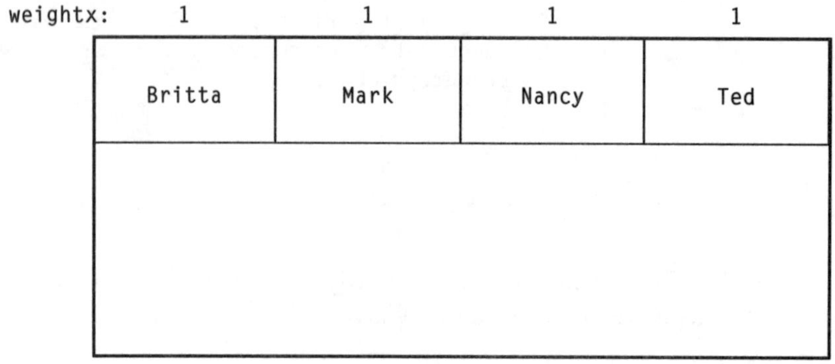

weightx:	1	1	1	1
	Britta	Mark	Nancy	Ted

FIGURE 7.7:   If each button is the same width, then each button has the same x weight.

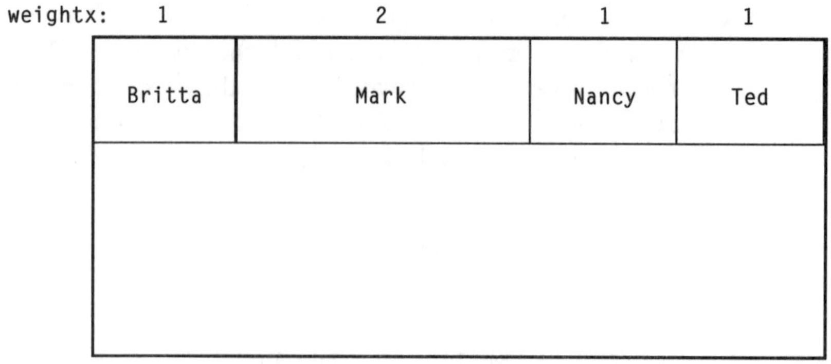

weightx:	1	2	1	1
	Britta	Mark	Nancy	Ted

FIGURE 7.8:   If one button is twice as wide as the others, its x weight is double.

You can specify that the controls in your applet be stretched to fill their allotted space in the layout, and you do that by setting the fill member of your `constraints` object. You could set this data member to the constant `GridBagConstraints` `.HORIZONTAL` to stretch your controls horizontally, to `GridBagConstraints` `.VERTICAL` to stretch them vertically, or to `GridBagConstraints.BOTH` to stretch them in both dimensions to fill the space allotted for them. In this case, let's stretch the controls in both dimensions:

```
import java.applet.Applet;
import java.awt.*;
import java.awt.event.*;

public class employee extends Applet {

    Button button1, button2, button3, button4;
    TextArea text1;

    public void init(){

        GridBagLayout gridbag = new GridBagLayout();
        GridBagConstraints constraints = new GridBagConstraints();
        setLayout(gridbag);
        constraints.weighty = 1;
        constraints.fill = GridBagConstraints.BOTH;
            .
            .
            .

    }
}
```

TIP   In the Java naming convention, the built-in data members of a class are referred to with lowercase letters, while constants use capital letters. Therefore, we know the fill member of a `GridBagConstraints` object is a variable, while `GridBagConstraints.VERTICAL` is a built-in constant of the class.

At this point, you're ready to add your first button to the grid bag. You can do that by giving this first button an x weight of 1, and creating the new button, button1, giving it the caption of the first name in your employee directory, "Britta," and adding an ActionListener to it:

```
import java.applet.Applet;
import java.awt.*;
import java.awt.event.*;
```

```
→public class employee extends Applet implements ActionListener {

       Button button1, button2, button3, button4;
       TextArea text1;

       public void init(){

              GridBagLayout gridbag = new GridBagLayout();
              GridBagConstraints constraints = new GridBagConstraints();
              setLayout(gridbag);
              constraints.weighty = 1;
              constraints.fill = GridBagConstraints.BOTH;

→             constraints.weightx = 1;
→             button1 = new Button("Britta");
→             button1.addActionListener(this);
                          .
                          .
                          .

       }
   }
```

Adding this button to the GridBagLayout is a two-step process. First, set up the grid bag's constraints, using your `constraints` object, and then add the control itself. That looks like this:

```
import java.applet.Applet;
import java.awt.*;
import java.awt.event.*;

public class employee extends Applet implements ActionListener {

       Button button1, button2, button3, button4;
       TextArea text1;

       public void init(){


              GridBagLayout gridbag = new GridBagLayout();
              GridBagConstraints constraints = new GridBagConstraints();
              setLayout(gridbag);
              constraints.weighty = 1;
              constraints.fill = GridBagConstraints.BOTH;

              constraints.weightx = 1;
              button1 = new Button("Britta");
→             gridbag.setConstraints(button1, constraints);
```

```
→           add(button1);
            button1.addActionListener(this);
                       .
                       .
                       .
     }
 }
```

Then add the remaining buttons as follows:

```
import java.applet.Applet;
import java.awt.*;
import java.awt.event.*;

public class employee extends Applet implements ActionListener {

     Button button1, button2, button3, button4;
     TextArea text1;

     public void init(){


          GridBagLayout gridbag = new GridBagLayout();
          GridBagConstraints constraints = new GridBagConstraints();
          setLayout(gridbag);
          constraints.weighty = 1;
          constraints.fill = GridBagConstraints.BOTH;

          constraints.weightx = 1;
          button1 = new Button("Britta");
          gridbag.setConstraints(button1, constraints);
          add(button1);
          button1.addActionListener(this);

→         constraints.weightx = 1;
→         button2 = new Button("Mark");
→         gridbag.setConstraints(button2, constraints);
→         add(button2);
→         button2.addActionListener(this);

→         constraints.weightx = 1;
→         button3 = new Button("Nancy");
→         gridbag.setConstraints(button3, constraints);
→         add(button3);
→         button3.addActionListener(this);

→         constraints.weightx = 1;
→         button4 = new Button("Ted");
```

Skill 7

```
→        constraints.gridwidth = GridBagConstraints.REMAINDER;
→        gridbag.setConstraints(button4, constraints);
→        add(button4);
→        button4.addActionListener(this);
                 .
                 .
                 .

    }
}
```

Note in particular the following line, which you use when adding the final button to the row of buttons:

```
constraints.gridwidth = GridBagConstraints.REMAINDER;
```

This line tells the GridBagLayout that you are done with the current row of controls and that it should take the remainder of the space left for the current (and last) button in this row.

Now that the top row (all buttons) is complete, add the next row, which is made up of the text area control. Again, set `constraints.gridwidth` to `GridBagConstraints.REMAINDER`, this time to indicate that there is only one item in this row—the text area:

```
import java.applet.Applet;
import java.awt.*;
import java.awt.event.*;

public class employee extends Applet implements ActionListener {

    Button button1, button2, button3, button4;
    TextArea text1;

    public void init(){

        GridBagLayout gridbag = new GridBagLayout();
        GridBagConstraints constraints = new GridBagConstraints();
        setLayout(gridbag);
        constraints.weighty = 1;
        constraints.fill = GridBagConstraints.BOTH;

        constraints.weightx = 1;
        button1 = new Button("Britta");
        gridbag.setConstraints(button1, constraints);
        add(button1);
        button1.addActionListener(this);
                 .
                 .
```

```
→        text1 = new TextArea();
→        constraints.gridwidth = GridBagConstraints.REMAINDER;
→        gridbag.setConstraints(text1, constraints);
→        add(text1);
     }
  }
```

Now your GridBag layout is set up. All that remains is to display the correct employee number when the user clicks a button in your applet. As you might expect, you use an `actionPerformed()` method as follows:

```
public class employee extends Applet implements ActionListener {

    Button button1, button2, button3, button4;
    TextArea text1;

    public void init(){


        GridBagLayout gridbag = new GridBagLayout();
        GridBagConstraints constraints = new GridBagConstraints();
        setLayout(gridbag);
        constraints.weighty = 1;
        constraints.fill = GridBagConstraints.BOTH;

        constraints.weightx = 1;
        button1 = new Button("Britta");
        gridbag.setConstraints(button1, constraints);
        add(button1);
        button1.addActionListener(this);
                .
                .
                .
        text1 = new TextArea();
        constraints.gridwidth = GridBagConstraints.REMAINDER;
        gridbag.setConstraints(text1, constraints);
        add(text1);

    }

→    public void actionPerformed(ActionEvent e){
→        if(e.getSource() == button1){
→            text1.setText("ID: 838939");
→        }
→        if(e.getSource() == button2){
→            text1.setText("ID 8533834");
```

```
→        }
→            if(e.getSource() == button3){
→                text1.setText("ID 3583893");
→            }
→            if(e.getSource() == button4){
→                text1.setText("ID 4893439");
→            }
         }
     }
```

Your applet is complete. As you can see below, your controls appear as you want them and in the places you want them. You've set up a GridBagLayout successfully. When you click a button, the corresponding employee number appears. Your employee directory is a success. The code for this applet appears in employee.java.

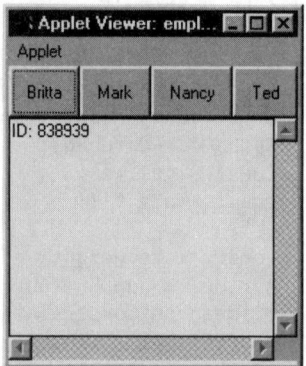

employee.java

```
import java.applet.Applet;
import java.awt.*;
import java.awt.event.*;

public class employee extends Applet implements ActionListener {

    Button button1, button2, button3, button4;
    TextArea text1;

    public void init(){
```

```
    GridBagLayout gridbag = new GridBagLayout();
    GridBagConstraints constraints = new GridBagConstraints();
    setLayout(gridbag);
    constraints.weighty = 1;
    constraints.fill = GridBagConstraints.BOTH;

    constraints.weightx = 1;
    button1 = new Button("Britta");
    gridbag.setConstraints(button1, constraints);
    add(button1);
    button1.addActionListener(this);

    constraints.weightx = 1;
    button2 = new Button("Mark");
    gridbag.setConstraints(button2, constraints);
    add(button2);
    button2.addActionListener(this);

    constraints.weightx = 1;
    button3 = new Button("Nancy");
    gridbag.setConstraints(button3, constraints);
    add(button3);
    button3.addActionListener(this);

    constraints.weightx = 1;
    button4 = new Button("Ted");
    constraints.gridwidth = GridBagConstraints.REMAINDER;
    gridbag.setConstraints(button4, constraints);
    add(button4);
    button4.addActionListener(this);

    text1 = new TextArea();
    constraints.gridwidth = GridBagConstraints.REMAINDER;
    gridbag.setConstraints(text1, constraints);
    add(text1);

}

public void actionPerformed(ActionEvent e){
    if(e.getSource() == button1){
        text1.setText("ID: 838939");
    }
    if(e.getSource() == button2){
        text1.setText("ID 8533834");
    }
    if(e.getSource() == button3){
        text1.setText("ID 3583893");
    }
```

Skill 7

```
                    if(e.getSource() == button4){
                        text1.setText("ID 4893439");
                    }
                }
            }
```

You've come far in this chapter, seeing how to use scrolling lists, Choice controls, the GridBagLayout, applet parameters, and more. Let's turn now to the next chapter, in which we start to explore some new Java techniques—using popup windows and menus.

Are You up to Speed?

Now you can . . .

☑ use *Choice* controls in Java programs to present a drop-down list of options to the user

☑ use scrolling lists to present a scrollable list of options to the user

☑ customize applet performance by passing parameters to applets—this is very useful when you want to use one *.class* file to handle different inputs in different Web pages

☑ use the GridBagLayout

SKILL 8

Creating Windows and Menus

- Working with popup windows
- Using Java menus
- Creating and using popup menus
- Adding menu items to menus
- Showing and hiding windows
- Determining which menu items the user selected

In Skill 7, we took a look at Choice controls and Scrolling Lists. Here, we'll continue our exploration by taking a look at the process of creating windows and menus in Java. These are all very powerful techniques—they enable us to add new windows entirely separate from our applet and to add menus to such windows. In this Skill, we'll also explore popup menus, which appear when the user clicks the right mouse button.

Handling Java Windows

Let's start by learning how to show a new window on the screen. For example, you can create an applet like the one shown in Figure 8.1, with two buttons, Show Window and Hide Window. When the user clicks the Show Window button, you can display a new (free-floating) window with a message in it, as shown in Figure 8.2.

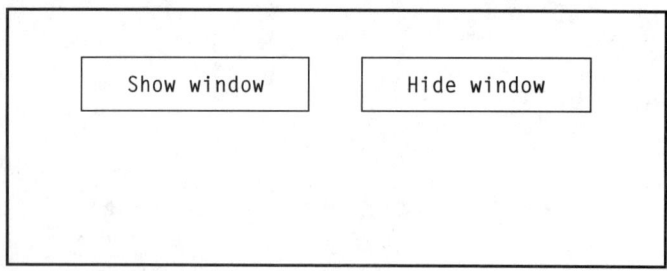

FIGURE 8.1:   An applet with two buttons

When the user clicks the Hide window button, you can hide the window again. Let's put this applet together now. Create a new file named windows.java and add the applet's main class:

```
import java.applet.Applet;
import java.awt.*;
import java.awt.event.*;

public class windows extends Applet {

}
```

The next step is to declare a window object so you can work with it, showing it to the user and hiding it again when required. Let's call this new window object window1. This object will be based on the Java Frame class, which creates a frame window on the screen.

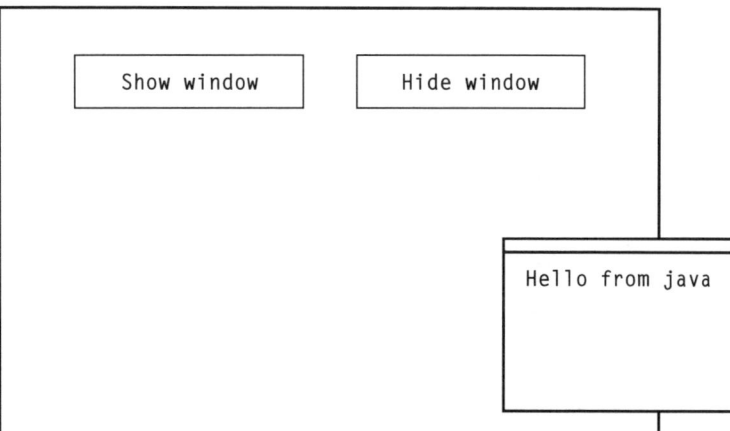

FIGURE 8.2: Clicking the Show window button displays a window with a message in it.

 **NOTE**   Frame windows are surrounded by a frame, which often may be resized.

Now we'll derive our own class, named demoframe, from the Frame class. In this case, the declaration of our window object looks like this:

```
import java.applet.Applet;
import java.awt.*;
import java.awt.event.*;

public class windows extends Applet {

➜       demoframe window1;
              .
              .
              .
}
```

Now that you've declared your window1 object as an object of the new demoframe class, you should write the Java code for this class. Add the following code to the end of the windows.java file now, where you declare the new demoframe class:

```
import java.applet.Applet;
import java.awt.*;
import java.awt.event.*;
```

```
public class windows extends Applet {

    demoframe window1;

}

class demoframe extends Frame {

}
```

The Java Frame class methods appear in Table 8.1.

TABLE 8.1: The Java Frame class methods

Method	Does This
Frame()	Constructs a Frame (starts as invisible)
Frame(String)	Constructs Frame with given title
addNotify()	Creates Frame's peer
dispose()	Disposes of the object
getCursorType()	Gets cursor type. Deprecated
getIconImage()	Gets icon for Frame
getMenuBar()	Gets menu bar for Frame
getTitle()	Gets title of Frame
isResizable()	Gets true if user can resize Frame
paramString()	Gets parameter string of object
remove(MenuComponent)	Removes given menu bar from object
removeWindowListener(WindowListener)	Removes given window listener
setCursor(int)	Sets cursor to a given cursor. Deprecated
setIconImage(Image)	Sets image to show when Frame is iconized
setMenuBar(MenuBar)	Sets menubar for object
setResizable(boolean)	Sets object's resizable flag
setTitle(String)	Sets title for Frame to given title

You'll need a constructor for this new class. The base class, Frame, has a constructor that takes the title you want in the window's title bar as an argument. You can take that argument in your demoframe constructor (recall that a constructor is just a method with the same name as the class) and pass it back to the Frame class's constructor by calling the super() method, which passes parameters to the class's super class (the class it is derived from). This method calls the constructor of a class's base class. The super() method can be used in any derived class's constructor to call the base class constructor (but note that it must be the first line in the derived class's constructor):

```
class demoframe extends Frame {

     demoframe(String title){
➜        super(title);
               .
               .
               .

     }
}
```

Next, you can add the text that you want in this window: "Hello from Java". You can do that by creating and adding a new label like this:

```
class demoframe extends Frame {
➜    Label label1;
     demoframe(String title){
         super(title);
➜        label1 = new Label("Hello from Java");
➜        add(label1);
     }
}
```

However, unlike applets, windows and dialog boxes in Java have no default layout manager. That means you should add your own, and you might use the GridLayout manager this way:

```
class demoframe extends Frame {
     Label label1;
     demoframe(String title){
         super(title);
➜        setLayout(new GridLayout(1, 1));
         label1 = new Label("Hello from Java");
         add(label1);
     }
}
```

And that's it—your new demoframe window class is ready to go.

TIP   Don't forget to set up a layout manager when working with windows or dialog boxes in Java—if the controls you placed in a window or dialog box don't appear, it may be that you forgot to set up a layout manager.

Now you're ready to work with window1, a new window, in your applet. First, add your two new buttons (Show Window and Hide Window) to the applet in its init() method and add the applet as the ActionListener for both:

```
import java.applet.Applet;
import java.awt.*;
import java.awt.event.*;

→public class windows extends Applet implements ActionListener {

        Button button1, button2;
        demoframe window1;

        public void init(){

→           button1 = new Button("Show window");
→           add(button1);
→           button1.addActionListener(this);

→           button2 = new Button("Hide window");
→           add(button2);
→           button2.addActionListener(this);
                        .
                        .
                        .

        }

}

class demoframe extends Frame {
    Label label1;

    demoframe(String title){
        super(title);
        setLayout(new GridLayout(1, 1));
        label1 = new Label("Hello from Java");
        add(label1);
    }
}
```

At this point, then, create `window1`, having already declared it earlier. You can do that by passing a title to the `demoframe` class's constructor:

```
import java.applet.Applet;
import java.awt.*;
import java.awt.event.*;

public class windows extends Applet implements ActionListener {

    Button button1, button2;
    demoframe window1;

    public void init(){

        button1 = new Button("Show window");
        add(button1);
        button1.addActionListener(this);

        button2 = new Button("Hide window");
        add(button2);
        button2.addActionListener(this);

        window1 = new demoframe("Demo window");
                    .
                    .
                    .

    }
}

class demoframe extends Frame {
    Label label1;

    demoframe(String title){
        super(title);
        setLayout(new GridLayout(1, 1));
        label1 = new Label("Hello from Java");
        add(label1);
    }
}
```

You've set up your constructor such that the title "Demo window" is just passed back to the Java `Frame` class's constructor. You can also give the new window an initial size (in pixels) using its `setSize()` method as follows:

```
import java.applet.Applet;
import java.awt.*;
import java.awt.event.*;
```

Skill 8

```
public class windows extends Applet implements ActionListener {

    Button button1, button2;
    demoframe window1;

    public void init(){

        button1 = new Button("Show window");
        add(button1);
        button1.addActionListener(this);

        button2 = new Button("Hide window");
        add(button2);
        button2.addActionListener(this);

        window1 = new demoframe("Demo window");
        window1.setSize(100, 100);

    }

}

class demoframe extends Frame {
    Label label1;

    demoframe(String title){
        super(title);
        setLayout(new GridLayout(1, 1));
        label1 = new Label("Hello from Java");
        add(label1);
    }
}
```

All that remains is to connect your buttons to make the window appear or disappear on command.

To show a window, use its setVisible(true) method, and to hide it again, use its setVisible(false) method. That means you can make your buttons functional by adding an actionPerformed() method this way, where you show or hide the window, window1, like this:

```
import java.applet.Applet;
import java.awt.*;
import java.awt.event.*;

public class windows extends Applet implements ActionListener {

    Button button1, button2;
```

```
demoframe window1;

public void init(){

    button1 = new Button("Show window");
    add(button1);
    button1.addActionListener(this);

    button2 = new Button("Hide window");
    add(button2);
    button2.addActionListener(this);

    window1 = new demoframe("Demo window");
    window1.setSize(100, 100);

}

public void actionPerformed(ActionEvent event){
    if(event.getSource() == button1){
        window1.setVisible(true);
    }
    if(event.getSource() == button2){
        window1.setVisible(false);
    }
}
}
```

Your windows applet is ready to run. When the user clicks the button labeled Show window, the window appears, as also shown below. Now you've seen how to support free-floating windows. The code for this applet appears in `windows.java`.

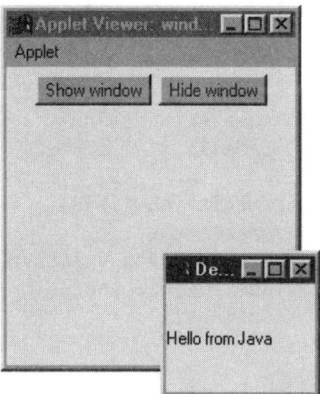

C windows.java

```java
import java.applet.Applet;
import java.awt.*;
import java.awt.event.*;

public class windows extends Applet implements ActionListener {

    Button button1, button2;
    demoframe window1;

    public void init(){

        button1 = new Button("Show window");
        add(button1);
        button1.addActionListener(this);

        button2 = new Button("Hide window");
        add(button2);
        button2.addActionListener(this);

        window1 = new demoframe("Demo window");
        window1.setSize(100, 100);

    }

    public void actionPerformed(ActionEvent event){
        if(event.getSource() == button1){
            window1.setVisible(true);
        }
        if(event.getSource() == button2){
            window1.setVisible(false);
        }
    }
}

class demoframe extends Frame {
    Label label1;

    demoframe(String title){
        super(title);
        setLayout(new GridLayout(1, 1));
        label1 = new Label("Hello from Java");
        add(label1);
    }
}
```

Seeing how to support windows is a good start. We will continue on to learn the workings of another powerful aspect of Java: menus.

Using Menus

In Java, menus need to be attached to a frame window like the one we've just developed. Accordingly, we will start our menu example with a frame window, which can be displayed or hidden. You can use the same two buttons in your new menu applet to show or hide the needed frame window.

When the user clicks the Show Window button, you can display the new frame window that will support your menu. Give your menu system a menu named File. When the user clicks on the File menu, you'll display three items that you can add: "Hello," "from," and "Java," as shown in Figure 8.3.

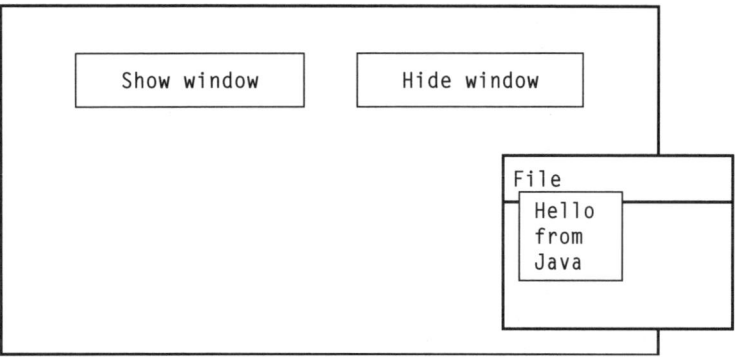

FIGURE 8.3:   The File menu displays three items the user can add.

When the user selects an item in the File menu, you can report in the window what item was selected. For example, if the user selected the Java item, they will see the word "Java," in the window as shown in Figure 8.4.

Let's start this new applet now. Create a file named menudemo.java and place the usual starting code in it:

```
import java.applet.Applet;
import java.awt.*;
import java.awt.event.*;

public class menudemo extends Applet implements ActionListener {

}
```

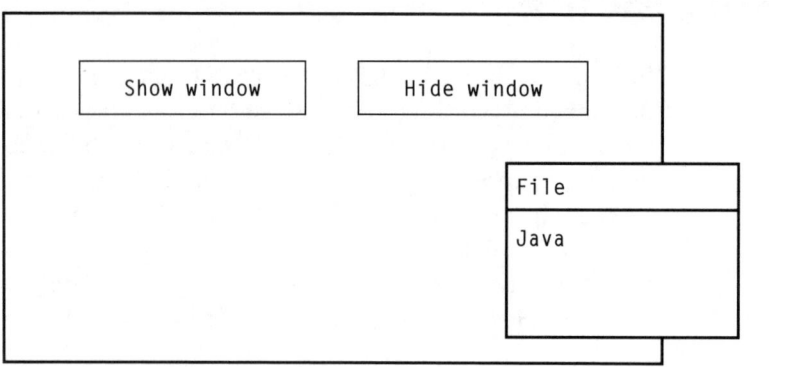

FIGURE 8.4: When the user selects Java, "Java" appears in the window.

You will need a frame window to display your menu with, and you will call that frame window's class `MenuFrame`. You can declare an object of that class named `menuWindow`, as follows:

```
import java.applet.Applet;
import java.awt.*;
import java.awt.event.*;

public class menudemo extends Applet implements ActionListener {

        MenuFrame menuWindow;
               .
               .
               .

}
```

Your next task will be to create the `MenuFrame` class, which will be the frame window that supports your menu. Add that class to the end of `menudemo.java`; because this will be a frame window, you need to extend the Java `Frame` class:

```
import java.applet.Applet;
import java.awt.*;
import java.awt.event.*;

public class menudemo extends Applet implements ActionListener {

        MenuFrame menuWindow;
               .
               .
               .

}
```

```
→class MenuFrame extends Frame {

→}
```

You should begin with a constructor for your new class, so add that now—as before, pass the title of the window back to the base class's constructor (i.e., the Java class Frame's constructor) using, as before, the super() method:

```
class MenuFrame extends Frame {

→       MenuFrame(String title){
→           super(title);
                .
                .
                .

→      }
    }
```

Next, you can add a text field to the window in which to display the user's menu selection. Call that text field **text1** as follows:

```
class MenuFrame extends Frame implements ActionListener {

→       TextField text1;

        MenuFrame(String title){
            super(title);
→           setLayout(new GridLayout(1, 1));
→           add(text1);
                .
                .
                .

        }
    }
```

The next step is to add your menu. You want to add a single menu to your window, the File menu, as shown below:

```
┌──────────────────────────────┐
│ File                         │
├──────────────────────────────┤
│                              │
│                              │
│                              │
│                              │
└──────────────────────────────┘
```

Start by creating an object of the Java class MenuBar. This is the actual object you will add to your window object to show your menu. Call your MenuBar object Menubar1:

```
class MenuFrame extends Frame implements ActionListener {

        MenuBar Menubar1;

        TextField text1;

        MenuFrame(String title){
                super(title);
                text1 = new TextField("");
                setLayout(new GridLayout(1, 1));
                add(text1);
                Menubar1 = new MenuBar();

        }
}
```

The next step is to add a menu—the File menu—to your menubar. To do that, create a new menu of the Java Menu class, called, say, Menu1. Give that new menu the title "File" by passing that string to its constructor:

```
class MenuFrame extends Frame implements ActionListener {

        Menu Menu1;
        MenuBar Menubar1;

        TextField text1;

        MenuFrame(String title){
                super(title);
                text1 = new TextField("");
                setLayout(new GridLayout(1, 1));
                add(text1);
                Menubar1 = new MenuBar();

                Menu1 = new Menu("File");
                        .
                        .
                        .

        }

}
```

The Java Menu class methods appear in Table 8.2.

TABLE 8.2: The Java Menu class methods

Method	Does This
Menu()	Constructs a new Menu with an empty label
Menu(String)	Constructs a new Menu with the given label
Menu(String, boolean)	Constructs a new Menu with the given label
add(MenuItem)	Adds the given item to this menu
add(String)	Adds an item with the given label to this menu
addNotify()	Creates the menu's peer
addSeparator()	Adds a separator line, or a hyphen, to the menu at the current position
countItems()	Deprecated. Replaced by getItemCount()
getItem(int)	Returns the item located at the given index of this menu
getItemCount()	Returns the number of elements in this menu
insert(MenuItem, int)	Inserts the MenuItem to this menu at the given position
insert(String, int)	Inserts an item with the given label to this menu at the given position
insertSeparator(int)	Inserts a separator at the given position
isTearOff()	Returns true if this is a tear-off menu
paramString()	Returns the String parameter of the menu
remove(int)	Deletes the item from this menu at the given index
remove(MenuComponent)	Deletes the given item from this menu
removeAll()	Deletes all items from this menu
removeNotify()	Removes the menu's peer

Now you have a menubar with a File menu in it—it's time to add menu items to this menu:

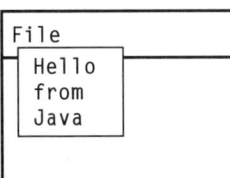

Each of these items is a separate object of the Java `MenuItem` class. In this case, you want to add three items to the File menu, so declare three new `MenuItem` objects, `menuitem1`, `menuitem2`, and `menuitem3`:

```
class MenuFrame extends Frame implements ActionListener {

        Menu Menu1;
        MenuBar Menubar1;
        MenuItem menuitem1, menuitem2, menuitem3;

        TextField text1;

        MenuFrame(String title){
            super(title);
            text1 = new TextField("");
            setLayout(new GridLayout(1, 1));
            add(text1);
            Menubar1 = new MenuBar();

            Menu1 = new Menu("File");
                    .
                    .
                    .

        }
    }
```

The Java `MenuItem` class methods appear in Table 8.3.

TABLE 8.3: The Java `MenuItem` class methods

Method	Does This
`MenuItem()`	Constructs a new `MenuItem` with an empty label and no keyboard shortcut
`MenuItem(String)`	Constructs a new `MenuItem` with the given label and no keyboard shortcut
`MenuItem(String, MenuShortcut)`	Creates a `MenuItem` with an associated keyboard shortcut
`addActionListener(ActionListener)`	Adds the given action listener to receive action events from this menu item
`addNotify()`	Creates the menu item's peer
`deleteShortcut()`	Deletes any MenuShortcut associated with this `MenuItem`
`disable()`	Deprecated. Replaced by setEnabled(boolean)

TABLE 8.3 CONTINUED: The Java MenuItem class methods

Method	Does This
disableEvents(long)	Disables the events defined by the given event mask parameter from being delivered to this menu item
enable()	Deprecated. Replaced by setEnabled(boolean)
enable(boolean)	Deprecated. Replaced by setEnabled(boolean)
enableEvents(long)	Enables the events defined by the given event mask parameter to be delivered to this menu item
getActionCommand()	Returns the command name of the action event fired by this menu item
getLabel()	Gets the label for this menu item
getShortcut()	Returns the MenuShortcut associated with this MenuItem or null if none has been given
isEnabled()	Checks whether the menu item is enabled
paramString()	Returns the String parameter of the menu item
processActionEvent(ActionEvent)	Processes action events occurring on this menu item by dispatching them to any registered ActionListener objects
processEvent(AWTEvent)	Processes events on this menu item
removeActionListener(ActionListener)	Removes the given action listener so it no longer receives action events from this menu item
setActionCommand(String)	Sets the command name of the action event fired by this menu item
setEnabled(boolean)	Sets whether or not this menu item can be chosen
setLabel(String)	Sets the label to be the given label
setShortcut(MenuShortcut)	Sets this MenuItem's MenuShortcut

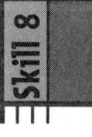

We'll begin with your first menu item: "Hello". Create that item and add it to the menu object this way:

```
class MenuFrame extends Frame {

    Menu Menu1;
    MenuBar Menubar1;
→   MenuItem menuitem1;
```

```
    TextField text1;

    MenuFrame(String title){
         super(title);
         text1 = new TextField("");
         setLayout(new GridLayout(1, 1));
         add(text1);
         Menubar1 = new MenuBar();

         Menu1 = new Menu("File");

➡️       menuitem1 = new MenuItem("Hello");
➡️       Menu1.add(menuitem1);
                .
                .
                .
```

You want to be notified when the user clicks Hello, so install an
ActionListener:

```
➡️class MenuFrame extends Frame implements ActionListener {

    Menu Menu1;
    MenuBar Menubar1;
    MenuItem menuitem1, menuitem2, menuitem3;

    TextField text1;

    MenuFrame(String title){
         super(title);
         text1 = new TextField("");
         setLayout(new GridLayout(1, 1));
         add(text1);
         Menubar1 = new MenuBar();

         Menu1 = new Menu("File");

         menuitem1 = new MenuItem("Hello");
         Menu1.add(menuitem1);
➡️       menuitem1.addActionListener(this);
                .
                .
                .
```

Now you've installed your first menu item. In the same way, install the two remaining items:

```java
class MenuFrame extends Frame implements ActionListener {

    Menu Menu1;
    MenuBar Menubar1;
    MenuItem menuitem1, menuitem2, menuitem3;

    TextField text1;

    MenuFrame(String title){
        super(title);
        text1 = new TextField("");
        setLayout(new GridLayout(1, 1));
        add(text1);
        Menubar1 = new MenuBar();

        Menu1 = new Menu("File");

        menuitem1 = new MenuItem("Hello");
        Menu1.add(menuitem1);
        menuitem1.addActionListener(this);

        menuitem2 = new MenuItem("from");
        Menu1.add(menuitem2);
        menuitem2.addActionListener(this);

        menuitem3 = new MenuItem("Java");
        Menu1.add(menuitem3);
        menuitem3.addActionListener(this);
                .
                .
                .

    }
}
```

Now you've created your File menu. The next step is to add this menu (called menu1) to your menubar, which you do with the add() method this way:

```java
class MenuFrame extends Frame implements ActionListener {

    Menu Menu1;
    MenuBar Menubar1;
    MenuItem menuitem1, menuitem2, menuitem3;

    TextField text1;
```

```
MenuFrame(String title){
     super(title);
     text1 = new TextField("");
     setLayout(new GridLayout(1, 1));
     add(text1);
     Menubar1 = new MenuBar();

     Menu1 = new Menu("File");

     menuitem1 = new MenuItem("Hello");
     Menu1.add(menuitem1);
     menuitem1.addActionListener(this);

     menuitem2 = new MenuItem("from");
     Menu1.add(menuitem2);
     menuitem2.addActionListener(this);

     menuitem3 = new MenuItem("Java");
     Menu1.add(menuitem3);
     menuitem3.addActionListener(this);

➜    Menubar1.add(Menu1);
                 .
                 .
                 .
}

}
```

Now add the menubar to your frame window using the **setMenubar()** method from the Frame Method list described in Table 8.1:

```
class MenuFrame extends Frame implements ActionListener {

     Menu Menu1;
     MenuBar Menubar1;
     MenuItem menuitem1, menuitem2, menuitem3;

     TextField text1;

     MenuFrame(String title){
          super(title);
          text1 = new TextField("");
          setLayout(new GridLayout(1, 1));
          add(text1);
          Menubar1 = new MenuBar();

          Menu1 = new Menu("File");
```

```
        menuitem1 = new MenuItem("Hello");
        Menu1.add(menuitem1);
        menuitem1.addActionListener(this);

        menuitem2 = new MenuItem("from");
        Menu1.add(menuitem2);
        menuitem2.addActionListener(this);

        menuitem3 = new MenuItem("Java");
        Menu1.add(menuitem3);
        menuitem3.addActionListener(this);

        Menubar1.add(Menu1);

➜       setMenuBar(Menubar1);
    }

  }
```

Now your menu system is set up, except for one thing—it doesn't do anything when clicked. To fix that, add an `actionPerformed()` method now to handle menu item clicks:

```
class MenuFrame extends Frame implements ActionListener {

    Menu Menu1;
    MenuBar Menubar1;
    MenuItem menuitem1, menuitem2, menuitem3;

    TextField text1;

    MenuFrame(String title){
        super(title);
        text1 = new TextField("");
        setLayout(new GridLayout(1, 1));
        add(text1);
        Menubar1 = new MenuBar();

        Menu1 = new Menu("File");

        menuitem1 = new MenuItem("Hello");
        Menu1.add(menuitem1);
        menuitem1.addActionListener(this);

        menuitem2 = new MenuItem("from");
        Menu1.add(menuitem2);
        menuitem2.addActionListener(this);
```

```
                menuitem3 = new MenuItem("Java");
                Menu1.add(menuitem3);
                menuitem3.addActionListener(this);

                Menubar1.add(Menu1);

                setMenuBar(Menubar1);
            }

→       public void actionPerformed(ActionEvent event){
                            .
                            .
                            .

→           }
        }
```

You can determine which menu item caused the Java event—menuitem1, menuitem2, or menuitem3—using getSource() in the actionPerformed() method this way:

```
class MenuFrame extends Frame implements ActionListener {

    Menu Menu1;
    MenuBar Menubar1;
    MenuItem menuitem1, menuitem2, menuitem3;

    TextField text1;

    MenuFrame(String title){
        super(title);
        text1 = new TextField("");
        setLayout(new GridLayout(1, 1));
        add(text1);
        Menubar1 = new MenuBar();

        Menu1 = new Menu("File");

        menuitem1 = new MenuItem("Hello");
        Menu1.add(menuitem1);
        menuitem1.addActionListener(this);

        menuitem2 = new MenuItem("from");
        Menu1.add(menuitem2);
        menuitem2.addActionListener(this);

        menuitem3 = new MenuItem("Java");
        Menu1.add(menuitem3);
        menuitem3.addActionListener(this);
```

```
        Menubar1.add(Menu1);

        setMenuBar(Menubar1);
    }

    public void actionPerformed(ActionEvent event){
        if(event.getSource() == menuitem1){
                .
                .
                .

        }
        if(event.getSource() == menuitem2){
                .
                .
                .

        }
        if(event.getSource() == menuitem3){
                .
                .
                .

        }
    }
}
```

If the first menu item caused the click event, you want to place "Hello" in the window's text field, "from" for the second menu item, and "Java" for the third menu item. Install those items in your code now:

```
class MenuFrame extends Frame implements ActionListener {

    Menu Menu1;
    MenuBar Menubar1;
    MenuItem menuitem1, menuitem2, menuitem3;

    TextField text1;

    MenuFrame(String title){
        super(title);
        text1 = new TextField("");
        setLayout(new GridLayout(1, 1));
        add(text1);
        Menubar1 = new MenuBar();

        Menu1 = new Menu("File");

        menuitem1 = new MenuItem("Hello");
        Menu1.add(menuitem1);
```

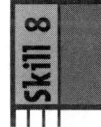

Skill 8

```
        menuitem1.addActionListener(this);
                      .
                      .
                      .
        Menubar1.add(Menu1);

        setMenuBar(Menubar1);
    }

    public void actionPerformed(ActionEvent event){
        if(event.getSource() == menuitem1){
            text1.setText("Hello");
        }
        if(event.getSource() == menuitem2){
            text1.setText("from");
        }
        if(event.getSource() == menuitem3){
            text1.setText("Java");
        }
    }
}
```

The MenuFrame class is complete. Now you have a frame window with your menu set up in it; all that remains is to display that frame window when the user clicks the Show Window button. Start that process by adding the Show Window and Hide Window buttons in your main applet's class:

```
import java.applet.Applet;
import java.awt.*;
import java.awt.event.*;

public class menudemo extends Applet {

    Button button1, button2;
    MenuFrame menuWindow;

    public void init(){

        button1 = new Button("Show window");
        add(button1);

        button2 = new Button("Hide window");
        add(button2);

    }
}
```

Next, set up the ActionListener to handle clicks from those buttons:

```java
import java.applet.Applet;
import java.awt.*;
import java.awt.event.*;

public class menudemo extends Applet implements ActionListener{

    Button button1, button2;
    MenuFrame menuWindow;

    public void init(){

        button1 = new Button("Show window");
        add(button1);
        button1.addActionListener(this);
        button2 = new Button("Hide window");
        add(button2);
        button1.addActionListener(this);

    }
```

Then create and resize the frame window that holds your menu like this:

```java
import java.applet.Applet;
import java.awt.*;
import java.awt.event.*;

public class menudemo extends Applet implements ActionListener {

    Button button1, button2;
    MenuFrame menuWindow;

    public void init(){

        button1 = new Button("Show window");
        add(button1);
        button1.addActionListener(this);
        button2 = new Button("Hide window");
        add(button2);
        button1.addActionListener(this);

        menuWindow = new MenuFrame("Menu Demo");
        menuWindow.setSize(100, 100);
    }
}
```

Skill 8

Next, add your `actionPerformed()` method and check to see which button caused the click event:

```java
import java.applet.Applet;
import java.awt.*;
import java.awt.event.*;

public class menudemo extends Applet implements ActionListener {

    Button button1, button2;
    MenuFrame menuWindow;

    public void init(){

        button1 = new Button("Show window");
        add(button1);
        button1.addActionListener(this);
        button2 = new Button("Hide window");
        add(button2);
        button1.addActionListener(this);

        menuWindow = new MenuFrame("Menu Demo");
        menuWindow.setSize(100, 100);
    }

    public void actionPerformed(ActionEvent event){
        if(event.getSource() == button1){
            .
            .
            .
        }
        if(event.getSource() == button2){
            .
            .
            .
        }
    }
}
```

Finally, place the menu window on the screen when required and hide it when the user wants to dismiss it:

```java
import java.applet.Applet;
import java.awt.*;
import java.awt.event.*;
```

```
public class menudemo extends Applet implements ActionListener {

    Button button1, button2;
    MenuFrame menuWindow;

    public void init(){

        button1 = new Button("Show window");
        add(button1);
        button1.addActionListener(this);
        button2 = new Button("Hide window");
        add(button2);
        button1.addActionListener(this);

        menuWindow = new MenuFrame("Menu Demo");
        menuWindow.setSize(100, 100);
    }

    public void actionPerformed(ActionEvent event){
        if(event.getSource() == button1){
➜           menuWindow.setVisible(true);
        }
        if(event.getSource() == button2){
➜           menuWindow.setVisible(false);
        }
    }
}
```

And that's it—run the menudemo applet now. Click the Show window button, displaying your menu frame, and open the File menu, as shown below.

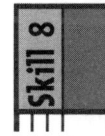

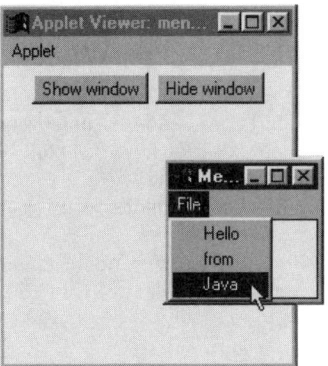

Now click a menu item, such as Java, and you'll see that item appear in the frame window. The listing for this applet appears in menudemo.java.

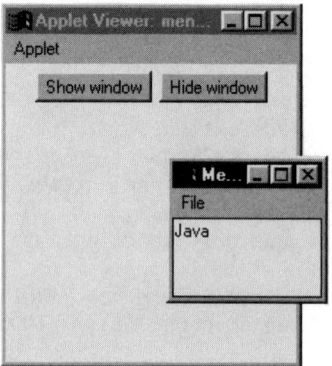

C menudemo.java

```java
import java.applet.Applet;
import java.awt.*;
import java.awt.event.*;

public class menudemo extends Applet implements ActionListener {

    Button button1, button2;
    MenuFrame menuWindow;

    public void init(){

        button1 = new Button("Show window");
        add(button1);
        button1.addActionListener(this);
        button2 = new Button("Hide window");
        add(button2);
        button1.addActionListener(this);

        menuWindow = new MenuFrame("Menu Demo");
        menuWindow.setSize(100, 100);
    }

    public void actionPerformed(ActionEvent event){
        if(event.getSource() == button1){
            menuWindow.setVisible(true);
        }
        if(event.getSource() == button2){
```

```java
                menuWindow.setVisible(false);
            }
        }
}

class MenuFrame extends Frame implements ActionListener {

    Menu Menu1;
    MenuBar Menubar1;
    MenuItem menuitem1, menuitem2, menuitem3;

    TextField text1;

    MenuFrame(String title){
        super(title);
        text1 = new TextField("");
        setLayout(new GridLayout(1, 1));
        add(text1);
        Menubar1 = new MenuBar();

        Menu1 = new Menu("File");

        menuitem1 = new MenuItem("Hello");
        Menu1.add(menuitem1);
        menuitem1.addActionListener(this);

        menuitem2 = new MenuItem("from");
        Menu1.add(menuitem2);
        menuitem2.addActionListener(this);

        menuitem3 = new MenuItem("Java");
        Menu1.add(menuitem3);
        menuitem3.addActionListener(this);

        Menubar1.add(Menu1);

        setMenuBar(Menubar1);
    }

    public void actionPerformed(ActionEvent event){
        if(event.getSource() == menuitem1){
            text1.setText("Hello");
        }
        if(event.getSource() == menuitem2){
            text1.setText("from");
        }
        if(event.getSource() == menuitem3){
            text1.setText("Java");
        }
    }
}
```

And you've completed work on your menudemo applet—now you've got menus working in Java, and you can determine which menu selection the user made. Let's continue by exploring more of the power menus can give us.

Building Full Menus

We'll take a look at what else the Java menu system has to offer us. For example, we might add more menu items to an applet this way—notice that we also use menu separators to separate menu items into groups, as shown in Figure 8.5.

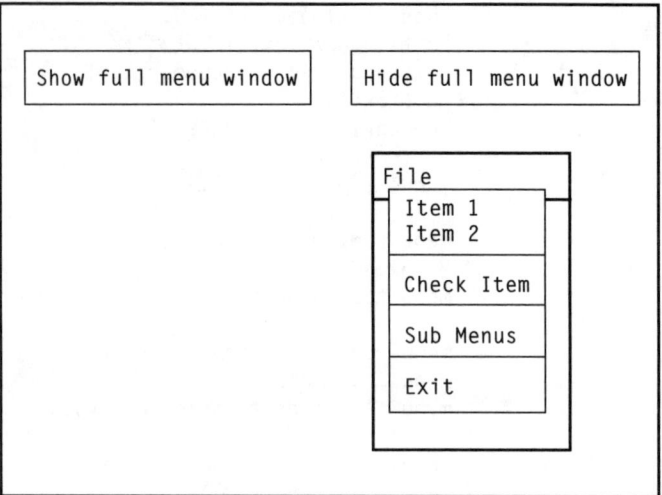

FIGURE 8.5:   Using menu separators to separate menu items into groups

Here, Item 1 is a normal menu item—when you click it, it will display "Item 1" in the frame window. Item 2 will also display its name—"Item 2"—but then will disable itself so that it can't be selected again. In addition, if the user selects the Sub Menus item, a submenu appears, as shown in Figure 8.6. If the user selects the item labeled Check Item, a check mark will appear in front of that item, as shown in Figure 8.7.

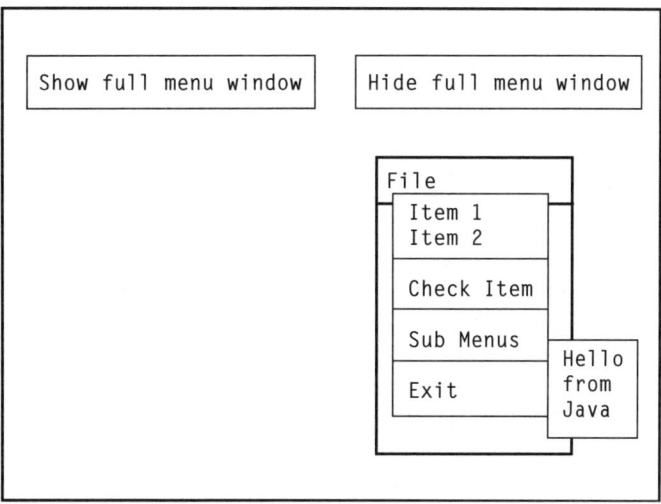

FIGURE 8.6:   When the user selects Sub Menus, a submenu appears.

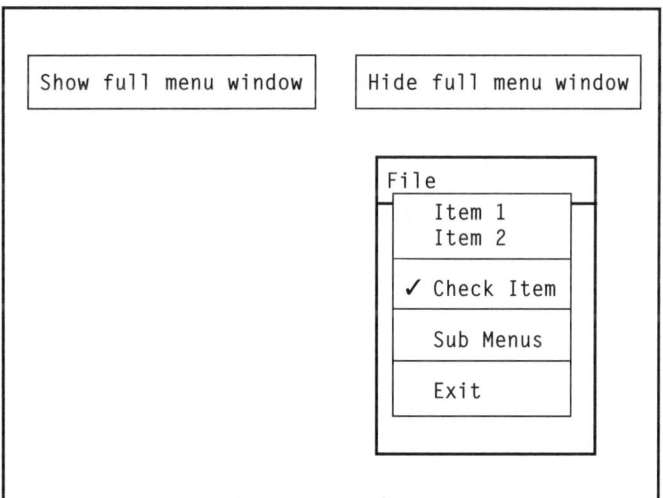

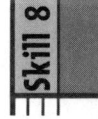

FIGURE 8.7:   When the user selects Check Item, a check mark appears.

Let's start this applet now. To do so, create a file named `fullmenu.java` and add the usual starting code:

```
import java.applet.Applet;
import java.awt.*;
import java.awt.event.*;

public class fullmenu extends Applet {

}
```

As before, create a frame window to support your menu. Here, you can create a new Frame class named `menuFrame` and add two buttons so you can display and hide this frame window as required:

```
import java.applet.Applet;
import java.awt.*;
import java.awt.event.*;

→public class fullmenu extends Applet implements ActionListener{
→      Button button1, button2;
→      MenuFrame fullmenuWindow;
                        .
                        .
                        .
}
```

As before, create the code to implement these two buttons, popping the new frame window with the new menu system on the screen as required:

```
import java.applet.Applet;
import java.awt.*;
import java.awt.event.*;

public class fullmenu extends Applet implements ActionListener
{
      Button button1, button2;
      MenuFrame fullmenuWindow;

→     public void init(){
→          button1 = new Button("Show full menu window");
→          add(button1);
→          button1.addActionListener(this);
→
→          button2 = new Button("Hide full menu window");
→          add(button2);
→          button2.addActionListener(this);
→
→          fullmenuWindow = new menuFrame("Full menus");
→          fullmenuWindow.setSize(100, 100);
```

```
→      }

→      public void actionPerformed(ActionEvent event){
→          if(event.getSource() == button1){
→              fullmenuWindow.setVisible(true);
→          }
→          if(event.getSource() == button2){
→              fullmenuWindow.setVisible(false);
→          }
→      }
   }
```

Now you can create your new menu frame window, menuframe. You will also implement the ActionListener interface so that you can handle menu selections:

```
class menuFrame extends Frame implements ActionListener {

}
```

This is the new frame window you'll attach your full menu system to. Now create a constructor for the window, passing the title of the window back to the Java Frame class:

```
class menuFrame extends Frame implements ActionListener {

→      menuFrame(String title){
→          super(title);
                 .
                 .
                 .
```

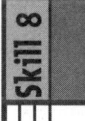

You've created the new window class to which you will attach your menu; now you'll add a text field to this window class so you can report what menu item was selected. This text field will be called text1. You'll also set up a GridLayout manager for the frame:

```
class menuFrame extends Frame implements ActionListener {

→      TextField text1;

       menuFrame(String title){
           super(title);
→          text1 = new TextField("Full menu");
→          setLayout(new GridLayout(1, 1));
→          add(text1);
                 .
                 .
                 .
```

After adding a text field to the window and setting up a GridLayout manager, create your new MenuBar object, giving it one menu, a File menu:

```
class menuFrame extends Frame implements ActionListener {

➜       Menu Menu1;
➜       MenuBar Menubar1;
        TextField text1;

        menuFrame(String title){
             super(title);
             text1 = new TextField("Full menu");
             setLayout(new GridLayout(1, 1));
             add(text1);
➜            Menubar1 = new MenuBar();
➜            Menu1 = new Menu("File");
                    .
                    .
                    .
```

The next step is to add your first two menu items, Item 1 and Item 2, as you've done before:

```
class menuFrame extends Frame implements ActionListener {

        Menu Menu1;
        MenuBar Menubar1;
        TextField text1;
➜       MenuItem menuitem1, menuitem2;

        menuFrame(String title){
             super(title);
             text1 = new TextField("Full menu");
             setLayout(new GridLayout(1, 1));
             add(text1);
             Menubar1 = new MenuBar();
             Menu1 = new Menu("File");

➜            menuitem1 = new MenuItem("Item 1");
➜            menuitem1.addActionListener(this);
➜            Menu1.add(menuitem1);

➜            menuitem2 = new MenuItem("Item 2");
➜            menuitem2.addActionListener(this);
➜            Menu1.add(menuitem2);
                    .
                    .
                    .
```

You've created your menu now and added two of the items you want in it. At this point, you can add a menu separator, the horizontal line that divides menu items into groups.

Adding a Menu Separator

You use menu separators to separate menu items into functional groups. For example, you might place Cut, Paste, and Copy together in a menu by surrounding them with menu separators. To add a menu separator, simply use the Menu class's addSeparator() method:

```
class menuFrame extends Frame implements ActionListener {

    Menu Menu1, SubMenu1;
    MenuBar Menubar1;
    TextField text1;
    MenuItem menuitem1, menuitem2;
    CheckboxMenuItem menuitem3;

    menuFrame(String title){
        super(title);
        text1 = new TextField("Full menu");
        setLayout(new GridLayout(1, 1));
        add(text1);
        Menubar1 = new MenuBar();
        Menu1 = new Menu("File");

        menuitem1 = new MenuItem("Item 1");
        menuitem1.addActionListener(this);
        Menu1.add(menuitem1);

        menuitem2 = new MenuItem("Item 2");
        menuitem2.addActionListener(this);
        Menu1.add(menuitem2);

→       Menu1.addSeparator();
                .
                .
                .
```

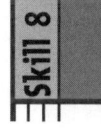

And that's all there is to it—now you've placed a menu separator in your File menu.

You can also put separators in menus by adding a menu item with a hyphen (-) for a caption.

Check Box Menu Items

The next step is to add a check box menu item. You can make this item appear checked or unchecked in the File menu. To create such an item, use the Java class CheckboxMenuItem, giving this item the caption "Check Item", as follows:

```
class menuFrame extends Frame implements ActionListener {

        Menu Menu1;
        MenuBar Menubar1;
        TextField text1;
        MenuItem menuitem1, menuitem2;
→       CheckboxMenuItem menuitem3;

        menuFrame(String title){
            super(title);
            text1 = new TextField("Full menu");
            setLayout(new GridLayout(1, 1));
            add(text1);
            Menubar1 = new MenuBar();
            Menu1 = new Menu("File");

            menuitem1 = new MenuItem("Item 1");
            menuitem1.addActionListener(this);
            Menu1.add(menuitem1);

            menuitem2 = new MenuItem("Item 2");
            menuitem2.addActionListener(this);
            Menu1.add(menuitem2);

            Menu1.addSeparator();

→           menuitem3 = new CheckboxMenuItem("Check Item");
→           menuitem3.addActionListener(this);
→           Menu1.add(menuitem3);
                .
                .
                .
```

Now, because you have a `CheckBoxMenuItem`, you'll be able to place a check mark in front of this item when the user selects it.

Incorporating Submenus

The next step will be to add a *submenu*, or nested menu, which pops up when the user clicks it. What this really means is creating a new `Menu` object—which you'll call `SubMenu1`—and installing it in the File menu just as you would any menu item. Give the new submenu three items, "Hello", "from", and "Java", as follows:

```
class menuFrame extends Frame implements ActionListener {

    Menu Menu1, SubMenu1;
    MenuBar Menubar1;
    TextField text1;
    MenuItem menuitem1, menuitem2;
    CheckboxMenuItem menuitem3;

    menuFrame(String title){
        super(title);
        text1 = new TextField("Full menu");
        setLayout(new GridLayout(1, 1));
        add(text1);
        Menubar1 = new MenuBar();
        Menu1 = new Menu("File");
            .
            .
            .
        menuitem3 = new CheckboxMenuItem("Check Item");
        menuitem3.addActionListener(this);
        Menu1.add(menuitem3);

        Menu1.addSeparator();

        SubMenu1.add(new MenuItem("Hello"));
        SubMenu1.add(new MenuItem("from"));
        SubMenu1.add(new MenuItem("Java"));

        Menu1.add(SubMenu1);
            .
            .
            .
```

That's how a submenu is created: as a menu complete in itself, added to its parent menu as a menu item.

Adding an Exit Item to a Menu

The last menu item will be an Exit item, which every File menu should have. After creating this new menu item, add it to the File menu, and then add that menu to the menubar. Finally, install the menubar in your frame window with the setMenuBar() method:

```
class menuFrame extends Frame implements ActionListener {

    Menu Menu1, SubMenu1;
    MenuBar Menubar1;
    TextField text1;
    MenuItem menuitem1, menuitem2, menuitem4;
    CheckboxMenuItem menuitem3;

    menuFrame(String title){
        super(title);
        text1 = new TextField("Full menu");
        setLayout(new GridLayout(1, 1));
        add(text1);
        Menubar1 = new MenuBar();
        Menu1 = new Menu("File");

        menuitem1 = new MenuItem("Item 1");
        menuitem1.addActionListener(this);
        Menu1.add(menuitem1);

        menuitem2 = new MenuItem("Item 2");
        menuitem2.addActionListener(this);
        Menu1.add(menuitem2);

        Menu1.addSeparator();

        menuitem3 = new CheckboxMenuItem("Check Item");
        menuitem3.addActionListener(this);
        Menu1.add(menuitem3);

        Menu1.addSeparator();

        SubMenu1 = new Menu("Sub menus");
        SubMenu1.add(new MenuItem("Hello"));
        SubMenu1.add(new MenuItem("from"));
        SubMenu1.add(new MenuItem("Java"));
        Menu1.add(SubMenu1);

        Menu1.addSeparator();
```

```
→          menuitem4 = new MenuItem("Exit");
→          menuitem4.addActionListener(this);

→          Menu1.add(menuitem4);
→          Menubar1.add(Menu1);
→          setMenuBar(Menubar1);

       }
```

Activating Our New Menu Items

Now you're ready to make these new menu items active, and you do that in the
`actionPerformed()` method:

```
public void actionPerformed(ActionEvent event){
}
```

First, we activate our standard menu item, Item 1. All this item does is to place
the text "Item 1" in the text field `text1`:

```
    public void actionPerformed(ActionEvent event){
→       if(event.getSource() == menuitem1){
→           text1.setText("Item 1");
    }            .
                 .
                 .
    }
```

When the user selects the next menu item, Item 2, you want to display "Item 2"
in the text field and then disable the item so the user can't select it again. You can
disable and enable menu items with the `setEnabled()` method, passing a value
of true to enable the item and a value of false to disable it:

```
    public void actionPerformed(ActionEvent event){
        if(event.getSource() == menuitem1){
            text1.setText("Item 1");
        }
→       if(event.getSource() == menuitem2){
→           menuitem2.setEnabled(false);
→           text1.setText("Item 2");
→       }            .
                     .
                     .
```

Now that you're using the `setEnabled()` method, you're able to enable and
disable menu items.

Skill 8

The next menu item is the check box menu item. When the user clicks that item, you can place a check mark in front of that item with the **setState( )** method, passing a value of true to make the check mark visible:

```
public void actionPerformed(ActionEvent event){
    if(event.getSource() == menuitem1){
        text1.setText("Item 1");
    }
    if(event.getSource() == menuitem2){
        menuitem2.setEnabled(false);
        text1.setText("Item 2");
    }
→   if(event.getSource() == menuitem3){
→   ((CheckboxMenuItem)event.getSource()).setState(true);
→   }                .
                     .
                     .
}
```

TIP   To get the state of a check box menu item (checked or unchecked) use the getState( ) method.

Finally, enable the last menu item, **menuitem4**, the Exit item. To make this item active, just use the frame window's **setVisible(false)** method:

```
public void actionPerformed(ActionEvent event){
    if(event.getSource() == menuitem1){
        text1.setText("Item 1");
    }
    if(event.getSource() == menuitem2){
        menuitem2.setEnabled(false);
        text1.setText("Item 2");
    }
    if(event.getSource() == menuitem3){
    ((CheckboxMenuItem)event.getSource()).setState(true);
    }
→   if(event.getSource() == menuitem4){
→       setVisible(false);
    }
}
```

And now your full menu system is active. Run it now and click the File menu. As you can see in the graphic below, your menu items are installed, complete with menu separators.

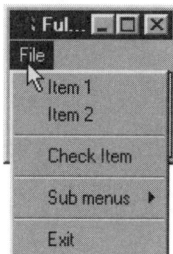

Next, select the check item—when you open the menu again, you'll see a check mark in front of this item, as shown below:

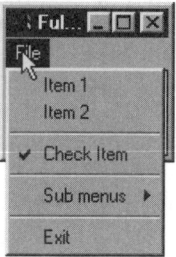

In addition, you can open the Sub Menus item to see the submenu, as shown below. Finally, the Exit item is active as well—use it now to leave the fullmenu applet. The code for this applet appears in fullmenu.java.

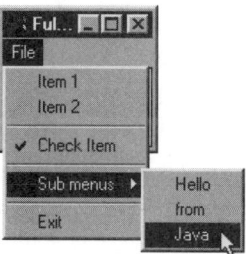

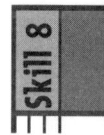

C **fullmenu.java**

```java
import java.applet.Applet;
import java.awt.*;
import java.awt.event.*;

public class fullmenu extends Applet implements ActionListener
{
    Button button1, button2;
    MenuFrame fullmenuWindow;

    public void init(){
        button1 = new Button("Show full menu window");
        add(button1);
        button1.addActionListener(this);

        button2 = new Button("Hide full menu window");
        add(button2);
        button2.addActionListener(this);

        fullmenuWindow = new menuFrame("Full menus");
        fullmenuWindow.setSize(100, 100);
    }

    public void actionPerformed(ActionEvent event){
        if(event.getSource() == button1){
            fullmenuWindow.setVisible(true);
        }
        if(event.getSource() == button2){
            fullmenuWindow.setVisible(false);
        }
    }
}

class menuFrame extends Frame implements ActionListener {

    Menu Menu1, SubMenu1;
    MenuBar Menubar1;
    TextField text1;
    MenuItem menuitem1, menuitem2, menuitem4;
    CheckboxMenuItem menuitem3;

    menuFrame(String title){
        super(title);
        text1 = new TextField("Full menu");
        setLayout(new GridLayout(1, 1));
        add(text1);
        Menubar1 = new MenuBar();
        Menu1 = new Menu("File");
```

```
        menuitem1 = new MenuItem("Item 1");
        menuitem1.addActionListener(this);
        Menu1.add(menuitem1);

        menuitem2 = new MenuItem("Item 2");
        menuitem2.addActionListener(this);
        Menu1.add(menuitem2);

        Menu1.addSeparator();

        menuitem3 = new CheckboxMenuItem("Check Item");
        menuitem3.addActionListener(this);
        Menu1.add(menuitem3);

        Menu1.addSeparator();

        SubMenu1 = new Menu("Sub menus");
        SubMenu1.add(new MenuItem("Hello"));
        SubMenu1.add(new MenuItem("from"));
        SubMenu1.add(new MenuItem("Java"));

        Menu1.add(SubMenu1);
        Menubar1.add(Menu1);
        setMenuBar(Menubar1);

        Menu1.addSeparator();

        menuitem4 = new MenuItem("Exit");
        menuitem4.addActionListener(this);
        Menu1.add(menuitem4);
    }

    public void actionPerformed(ActionEvent event){
        if(event.getSource() == menuitem1){
            text1.setText("Item 1");
        }
        if(event.getSource() == menuitem2){
            menuitem2.setEnabled(false);
            text1.setText("Item 2");
        }
        if(event.getSource() == menuitem3){
        ((CheckboxMenuItem)event.getSource()).setState(true);
        }
        if(event.getSource() == menuitem4){
            setVisible(false);
        }
    }
}
```

Skill 8

You can also add code to create menu items with keyboard shortcuts in Java 1.2. For example, below we add a shortcut of Shift+O to an Open menu item (the boolean parameter in the `MenuShortcut` constructor indicates whether or not this shortcut uses the Shift key):

```
menu.add(new MenuItem("Open", new MenuShortcut('o', true));
```

And, in fact, there is another type of menu that Java 1.2 supports: popup menus.

Popup Menus

You've probably seen popup menus—they are usually triggered by the right mouse button, and can pop up anywhere in a window. A popup menu is shown in Figure 8.8.

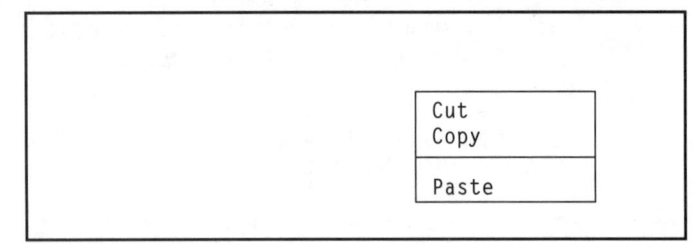

FIGURE 8.8:   A popup menu

Let's put a popup menu to work. Create a new file named `popup.java` and add the usual starting code:

```
import java.applet.Applet;
import java.awt.*;

public class popup extends Applet {
    .
    .
    .
```

You'll add popup menus to this applet now. Add a text field, `text1`, so you can report what menu item was selected. In addition, create a new object of class `PopupMenu` named, say, `popup`, naming this menu "Edit", as follows:

```
import java.applet.Applet;
import java.awt.*;

public class popup extends Applet {

➜      TextField text1;
➜      PopupMenu popup;

        public void init(){

➜              popup = new PopupMenu("Edit");
                        .
                        .
                        .
```

The `PopupMenu` class methods appear in Table 8.4.

TABLE 8.4: The Java PopupMenu Class Methods

Method	Does This
PopupMenu()	Creates a new popup menu
PopupMenu(String)	Creates a new popup menu with the given name
addNotify()	Creates the popup menu's peer
show(Component, int, int)	Shows the popup menu at the x, y position from an origin component

Now add three items to this menu: Cut, Copy, and Paste. Also, add an ActionListener to make these items active:

```
import java.applet.Applet;
import java.awt.*;
import java.awt.event.*;

➜public class popup extends Applet implements ActionListener{

        TextField text1;
        PopupMenu popup;
➜      MenuItem menuitem1, menuitem2, menuitem3;

        public void init(){
```

Skill 8

```
           popup = new PopupMenu("Edit");
→          menuitem1 = new MenuItem("Cut");
→          menuitem1.addActionListener(this);
→          menuitem2 = new MenuItem("Copy");
→          menuitem2.addActionListener(this);
→          menuitem3 = new MenuItem("Paste");
→          menuitem3.addActionListener(this);
                        .
                        .
                        .
```

Then you can add those new menu items to the popup menu, using its **add( )** method:

```
import java.awt.*;
import java.awt.event.*;

public class popup extends Applet implements ActionListener {

    TextField text1;
    PopupMenu popup;
    MenuItem menuitem1, menuitem2, menuitem3;

    public void init(){

        popup = new PopupMenu("Edit");
        menuitem1 = new MenuItem("Cut");
        menuitem1.addActionListener(this);
        menuitem2 = new MenuItem("Copy");
        menuitem2.addActionListener(this);
        menuitem3 = new MenuItem("Paste");
        menuitem3.addActionListener(this);
→       popup.add(menuitem1);
→       popup.add(menuitem2);
→       popup.addSeparator();
→       popup.add(menuitem3);
                    .
                    .
                    .
```

Next, add the popup menu to your applet with the applet's **add( )** method, and create the text field **text1**. In addition, you'll implement the MouseListener interface to handle mouse events—you'll see how this works in Skill 10 (although you can probably figure it out now, given the Listener interfaces you've already worked with); for now, just add the following code:

```
import java.awt.*;
import java.awt.event.*;

public class popup extends Applet implements ActionListener,
MouseListener {

        TextField text1;
        PopupMenu popup;
        MenuItem menuitem1, menuitem2, menuitem3;

        public void init(){

                popup = new PopupMenu("Edit");
                menuitem1 = new MenuItem("Cut");
                menuitem1.addActionListener(this);
                menuitem2 = new MenuItem("Copy");
                menuitem2.addActionListener(this);
                menuitem3 = new MenuItem("Paste");
                menuitem3.addActionListener(this);
                popup.add(menuitem1);
                popup.add(menuitem2);
                popup.addSeparator();
                popup.add(menuitem3);
                add(popup);
                add(text1);
                addMouseListener(this);
        }
```

To implement mouse handling, add five methods: mousePressed(), mouseClicked(), mouseReleased(), mouseEntered(), and mouseExited():

```
        public void mousePressed(MouseEvent e){
        }

        public void mouseClicked(MouseEvent e){
        }

        public void mouseReleased(MouseEvent e){
        }

        public void mouseEntered(MouseEvent e){
        }

        public void mouseExited(MouseEvent e){
        }
```

Skill 8

You'll learn more about these methods in Skill 10—for now, add the following code to the mousePressed() method to check if the right mouse button, the button that brings up the popup menu, was clicked. Here, you can check the modifiers member of the MouseEvent object you are passed in mousePressed() to check on the right mouse button:

```
        public void mousePressed(MouseEvent e){
➜           if(e.getModifiers() != 0){
                    .
                    .
                    .
➜           }
        }
```

If the right mouse button was indeed pressed, show the popup menu with its show() method at the present mouse location, which you get with the getX() and getY() MouseEvent methods, as follows:

```
        public void mousePressed(MouseEvent e){
            if(e.getModifiers() != 0){
➜              popup.show(this, e.getX(), e.getY());
            }
        }
```

At this point, then, the popup menu appears on the screen. Add an action-Performed() method now to handle menu selections:

```
        public void actionPerformed(ActionEvent event){

        }
```

Add standard menu-handling code here to handle menuitem1, menuitem2, and menuitem3 this way, displaying a different text string for each menu item:

```
        public void actionPerformed(ActionEvent event){
            if(event.getSource() == menuitem1){
                text1.setText("Hello");
            }
            if(event.getSource() == menuitem2){
                text1.setText("from");
            }
            if(event.getSource() == menuitem3){
                text1.setText("Java");
            }
        }
```

And you're finished—run the applet now. You can pop up the popup menu now by clicking the right mouse button, as shown in Figure 8.7. When you click an item in that menu, the corresponding string appears in the text field—your popup menu applet is a success. The code for this applet appears in popup.java.

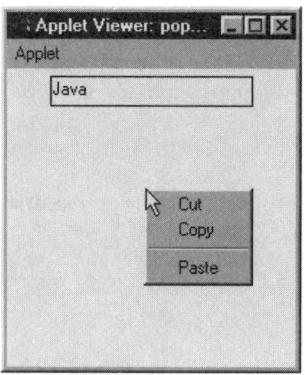

popup.java

```java
import java.applet.Applet;
import java.awt.*;
import java.awt.event.*;

public class popup extends Applet implements ActionListener,
MouseListener {

    TextField text1;
    PopupMenu popup;
    MenuItem menuitem1, menuitem2, menuitem3;

    public void init(){

        popup = new PopupMenu("Edit");
        menuitem1 = new MenuItem("Cut");
        menuitem1.addActionListener(this);
        menuitem2 = new MenuItem("Copy");
        menuitem2.addActionListener(this);
        menuitem3 = new MenuItem("Paste");
        menuitem3.addActionListener(this);
        popup.add(menuitem1);
        popup.add(menuitem2);
        popup.addSeparator();
```

```
                popup.add(menuitem3);
                add(popup);
                text1 = new TextField(20);
                add(text1);
                addMouseListener(this);
            }

        public void mousePressed(MouseEvent e){
                if(e.getModifiers() != 0){
                popup.show(this, e.getX(), e.getY());
            }
            }

        public void mouseClicked(MouseEvent e){
            }

        public void mouseReleased(MouseEvent e){
            }

        public void mouseEntered(MouseEvent e){
            }

        public void mouseExited(MouseEvent e){
            }

        public void actionPerformed(ActionEvent event){
                if(event.getSource() == menuitem1){
                    text1.setText("Hello");
                }
                if(event.getSource() == menuitem2){
                    text1.setText("from");
                }
                if(event.getSource() == menuitem3){
                    text1.setText("Java");
                }
            }

    }
```

That's it for the moment for menu handling and popup menus. As you can see, the menu system in Java is a powerful tool, with a great deal of programming strength. In Skill 9, we will continue our exploration of Java by looking at dialog boxes.

Are You up to Speed?

Now you can. . .

☑ use Java windows to display information outside an application's window or an applet's Web browser

☑ show or hide windows as required

☑ give the user a selection of choices with Java menus

☑ use submenus, check box menu items, and menu separators

☑ use popup menus to give the user additional help

☑ determine which menu items the user selected and take the appropriate action

SKILL 9

Constructing Java Dialog Boxes

- Creating dialog boxes
- Showing and hiding dialog boxes
- Using controls in a dialog box
- Laying out controls in a dialog box
- Retrieving values from a dialog box

In this Skill you'll see how to create and use your own dialog boxes. If you are a Windows user you are familiar with dialog boxes—they're those specialized windows that pop up and give you various controls to choose from, controls such as buttons and text fields. You'll see how to add controls to your Java programs, how to lay out the controls in a dialog box, as well as how to transfer values from controls in a dialog box to controls in an applet.

Using Dialog Boxes

Like menus, dialog classes need to be attached to frame windows. For that reason, you can start this dialog box example as you started the menu example—with an applet that pops a frame window on the screen. When the user clicks a Show Dialog Window button, you can pop a frame window on the screen. You want to let the user pop up a dialog box from this frame window, so you put a File menu in this frame window with a menu item "Dialog Box..." in it, as shown in Figure 9.1. When the user selects Dialog Box..., you will pop up a dialog box with two buttons: OK and Cancel (see Figure 9.2). To remove the dialog box from the screen, the user can just click the OK or Cancel button.

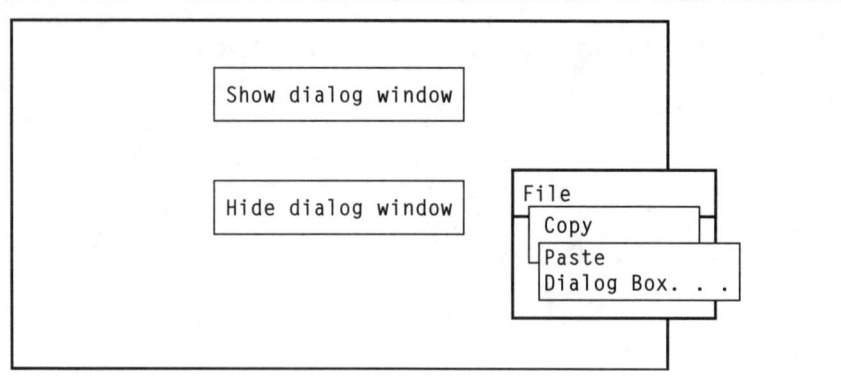

FIGURE 9.1: Your popup window has a File menu in it.

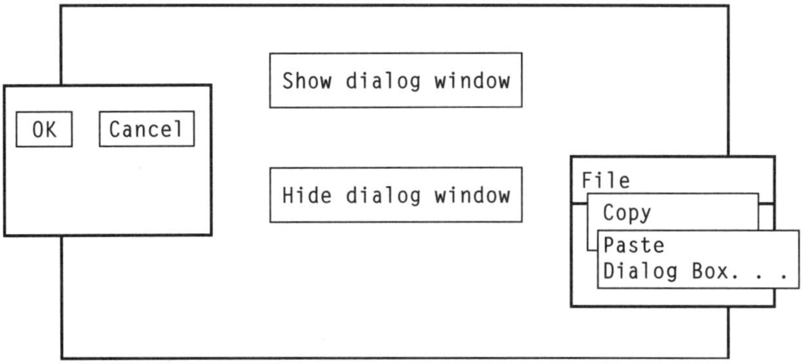

FIGURE 9.2: When the user selects File ➤ Dialog Box..., a dialog box pops up on the screen.

Let's create this applet now. Create a file named `dialogs.java` and add our standard code:

```
import java.applet.Applet;
import java.awt.*;

public class dialogs extends Applet {

}
```

First add the two buttons you'll use to show and hide the frame window you'll need—here, these two buttons will have the captions "Show Dialog Window" and "Hide Dialog Window". You can name your frame window class `dialogframe` and add an object of that class named `frameWindow`, as follows:

```
import java.applet.Applet;
import java.awt.*;
import java.awt.event.*;

public class dialogs extends Applet
{

        Button button1, button2;
➜       dialogframe frameWindow;
                .
                .
                .
```

Skill 9

As before, just connect those buttons and add code to pop the frame window on the screen this way:

```java
import java.applet.Applet;
import java.awt.*;
import java.awt.event.*;

public class dialogs extends Applet implements ActionListener
{

    Button button1, button2;
    dialogframe frameWindow;

    public void init(){
        button1 = new Button("Show dialog window");
        add(button1);
        button1.addActionListener(this);
        button2 = new Button("Hide dialog window");
        add(button2);
        button2.addActionListener(this);

        frameWindow = new dialogframe("Dialogs");
        frameWindow.setSize(100, 100);
    }

    public void actionPerformed(ActionEvent event){
        if(event.getSource() == button1){
            frameWindow.setVisible(true);
        }
        if(event.getSource() == button2){
            frameWindow.setVisible(false);
        }
    }
}
```

Now you can pop the frame window you'll need for your menu onto the screen. The next step is to create the frame window you'll need, `dialogframe`, and implement the ActionListener interface so you can enable the items in your menubar. Add this text to the end of `dialogs.java`:

```java
class dialogframe extends Frame implements ActionListener {
        .
        .
        .
}
```

You start the `dialogframe` class with a constructor:

```
class dialogframe extends Frame implements ActionListener {

        dialogframe(String title){
            super(title);
                .
                .
                .

    }
  }
```

Next, add a text field to your `dialogframe` class to report the menu selections the user has made:

```
class dialogframe extends Frame implements ActionListener {

        TextField text1;

        dialogframe(String title){
            super(title);
            text1 = new TextField("");
            setLayout(new GridLayout(1, 1));
            add(text1);
                .
                .
                .
```

Having added the text field, now add your File menu with three items: Copy, Paste, and Dialog Box..., as follows:

```
class dialogframe extends Frame implements ActionListener {

        Menu Menu1;
        MenuBar Menubar1;
        MenuItem menuitem1, menuitem2, menuitem3;

        TextField text1;

        dialogframe(String title){
            super(title);
            text1 = new TextField("");
            setLayout(new GridLayout(1, 1));
            add(text1);

            Menubar1 = new MenuBar();
            Menu1 = new Menu("File");
```

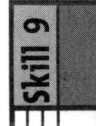

Skill 9

```
➜          menuitem1 = new MenuItem("Copy");
➜          Menu1.add(menuitem1);
➜          menuitem1.addActionListener(this);

➜          menuitem2 = new MenuItem("Paste");
➜          Menu1.add(menuitem2);
➜          menuitem2.addActionListener(this);

➜          menuitem3 = new MenuItem("Dialog box...");
➜          Menu1.add(menuitem3);
➜          menuitem3.addActionListener(this);

➜          Menubar1.add(Menu1);
➜          setMenuBar(Menubar1);
                    .
                    .
                    .
       }
```

To actually display the dialog box when the user selects Dialog Box... in your menu, you will create a new class, extending the Java `Dialog` class. You can call your new class `buttondialog` and call the new object of that class `dialogBox`, as follows:

```
class dialogframe extends Frame implements ActionListener {

    Menu Menu1;
    MenuBar Menubar1;
    MenuItem menuitem1, menuitem2, menuitem3;

    TextField text1;
    buttondialog dialogBox;

    dialogframe(String title){
        super(title);
        text1 = new TextField("");
        setLayout(new GridLayout(1, 1));
        add(text1);
        Menubar1 = new MenuBar();

        Menu1 = new Menu("File");

        menuitem1 = new MenuItem("Copy");
        Menu1.add(menuitem1);
        menuitem1.addActionListener(this);

        menuitem2 = new MenuItem("Paste");
        Menu1.add(menuitem2);
        menuitem2.addActionListener(this);
```

```
        menuitem3 = new MenuItem("Dialog box...");
        Menu1.add(menuitem3);
        menuitem3.addActionListener(this);

        Menubar1.add(Menu1);

        setMenuBar(Menubar1);
➜       dialogBox = new buttondialog(this, "Dialog", true);
    }
```

The Dialog class methods appear in Table 9.1.

TABLE 9.1: The Java Dialog class methods

Method	Does This
Dialog(Dialog)	Constructs an initially invisible Dialog with an empty title
Dialog(Dialog, String)	Constructs an initially invisible Dialog with a title
Dialog(Dialog, String, boolean)	Constructs an initially invisible Dialog with a title
Dialog(Frame)	Constructs an initially invisible Dialog with an empty title
Dialog(Frame, boolean)	Deprecated. Replaced by Dialog(Frame, String, boolean)
Dialog(Frame, String)	Constructs an initially invisible Dialog with a title
Dialog(Frame, String, boolean)	Constructs an initially invisible Dialog with a title
addNotify()	Creates the frame's peer
getTitle()	Gets the title of the Dialog
isModal()	Returns true if the Dialog is modal
isResizable()	Returns true if the user can resize the dialog
paramString()	Returns the parameter String of this Dialog
setModal(boolean)	Specifies whether this Dialog is modal
setResizable(boolean)	Sets the resizable flag
setSize()	Shows the Dialog's size
SetTitle(String)	Sets the title of the Dialog
setVisible()setVisible(true)	Shows or hides the Dialog

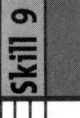

Skill 9

You've allowed the user to pop up a new window with a menu in it on the screen. Now you can make the frame window menu items active. Add an actionPerformed() method to dialogframe:

```
public void actionPerformed(ActionEvent event){

}
```

You can make the first two menu items active by simply having them display text in the applet's text field text1:

```
public void actionPerformed(ActionEvent event){
    if(event.getSource() == menuitem1){
        text1.setText("Copy");
    }
    if(event.getSource() == menuitem2){
        text1.setText("Paste");
    }           .
                .
                .

}
```

When the user selects Dialog Box..., however, they want to display the dialog box object you named dialogBox. Make that happen by using the dialogBox object's setVisible(true) method:

```
public void actionPerformed(ActionEvent event){
    if(event.getSource() == menuitem1){
        text1.setText("Copy");
    }
    if(event.getSource() == menuitem2){
        text1.setText("Paste");
    }
    if(event.getSource() == menuitem3){
        dialogBox.setVisible(true);
    }
}
```

Creating a Dialog Box

The next step is to create the dialog box class itself, buttondialog. This class supports a dialog box with two buttons, OK and Cancel, as shown below.

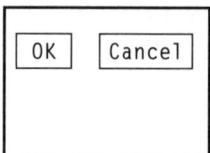

Create the `buttondialog` class now, extending the Java `Dialog` class and implementing the ActionListener interface so you can enable your OK and Cancel buttons (note that you can implement the ActionListener interface with the `Dialog` class):

```
class buttondialog extends Dialog implements ActionListener {

}
```

Go ahead and add those buttons now:

```
class buttondialog extends Dialog implements ActionListener {

➜        Button OKButton, CancelButton;
                 .
                 .
                 .
```

Next, add a constructor for your class. In this case, the constructor is passed these values: the host frame window, a title for the dialog box, and a boolean value indicating whether or not the dialog box is *modal*. (If it's modal, the user can't do anything else in your program until they dismiss the dialog box.) Pass these values back to the `Dialog` class's constructor:

```
class buttondialog extends Dialog implements ActionListener {

        Button OKButton, CancelButton;

        buttondialog(Frame hostFrame, String title, boolean dModal){
➜            super(hostFrame, title, dModal);
                 .
                 .
                 .
```

Next, resize your dialog box to (100, 100) and install a layout manager. You always need to install a layout manager in dialog boxes; here, you can use the FlowLayout manager:

```
class buttondialog extends Dialog implements ActionListener {

        Button OKButton, CancelButton;

        buttondialog(Frame hostFrame, String title, boolean dModal){
            super(hostFrame, title, dModal);
            setSize(100, 100);
            setLayout(new FlowLayout());
                 .
                 .
                 .
```

Skill 9

 **WARNING**   If you don't set the size of a dialog box, many Web browsers won't display it.

You've created the basic dialog box. Now you can just create and add your OK and Cancel buttons:

```java
class buttondialog extends Dialog implements ActionListener {

    Button OKButton, CancelButton;

    buttondialog(Frame hostFrame, String title, boolean dModal){
        super(hostFrame, title, dModal);
        setSize(100, 100);
        setLayout(new FlowLayout());

        OKButton = new Button("OK");
        add(OKButton);
        OKButton.addActionListener((ActionListener)this);

        CancelButton = new Button("Cancel");
        add(CancelButton);
        CancelButton.addActionListener(this);
    }
                    .
                    .
                    .
```

You've added your buttons. Now you just need to connect them to your code in an `actionPerformed()` method:

```java
class buttondialog extends Dialog implements ActionListener {

    Button OKButton, CancelButton;

    buttondialog(Frame hostFrame, String title, boolean dModal){
        super(hostFrame, title, dModal);
        setSize(100, 100);
        setLayout(new FlowLayout());

        OKButton = new Button("OK");
        add(OKButton);
        OKButton.addActionListener((ActionListener)this);

        CancelButton = new Button("Cancel");
        add(CancelButton);
        CancelButton.addActionListener(this);
    }
```

```
        public void actionPerformed(ActionEvent event){
                        .
                        .
                        .
➜       }
     }
```

These are the two buttons that appear in your dialog box. When the user clicks either button in the dialog box, they are indicating that they want you to take an action (such as closing the dialog box). To respond correctly, you need to know which button was pushed. You can determine which button caused an event in actionPerformed, OKButton or CancelButton:

```
    class buttondialog extends Dialog implements ActionListener {

        Button OKButton, CancelButton;

        buttondialog(Frame hostFrame, String title, boolean dModal){
            super(hostFrame, title, dModal);
            setSize(100, 100);
            setLayout(new FlowLayout());

            OKButton = new Button("OK");
            add(OKButton);
            OKButton.addActionListener((ActionListener)this);

            CancelButton = new Button("Cancel");
            add(CancelButton);
            CancelButton.addActionListener(this);
        }

        public void actionPerformed(ActionEvent event){
➜           if(event.getSource() == OKButton){
                        .
                        .
                        .
➜           }
➜           if(event.getSource() == CancelButton){
                        .
                        .
                        .
➜           }
        }
     }
```

If either button is clicked, just hide the dialog box (you'll do more in the next example) using the Dialog class's setVisible(false) method. You can accomplish this as shown on the next page.

```
class buttondialog extends Dialog implements ActionListener {

    Button OKButton, CancelButton;

    buttondialog(Frame hostFrame, String title, boolean dModal){
        super(hostFrame, title, dModal);
        setSize(100, 100);
        setLayout(new FlowLayout());

        OKButton = new Button("OK");
        add(OKButton);
        OKButton.addActionListener((ActionListener)this);

        CancelButton = new Button("Cancel");
        add(CancelButton);
        CancelButton.addActionListener(this);
    }

    public void actionPerformed(ActionEvent event){
        if(event.getSource() == OKButton){
            setVisible(false);
        }
        if(event.getSource() == CancelButton){
            setVisible(false);
        }
    }
}
```

And you're finished—you can run the applet now. When you open the frame window and select File ➤ Dialog Box…, the dialog box appears on the screen, as shown in Figure 9.3. When you click the OK or Cancel button, the dialog box disappears from the screen. The listing for this applet appears in `dialogs.java`.

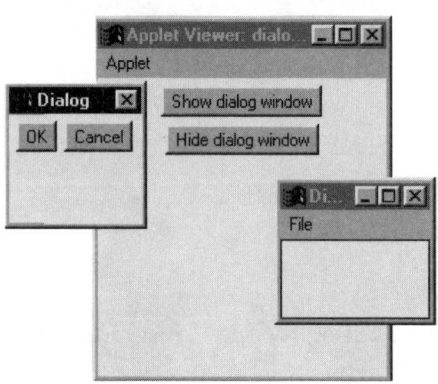

FIGURE 9.3: Your applet supports a dialog box.

dialogs.java

```java
import java.applet.Applet;
import java.awt.*;
import java.awt.event.*;

public class dialogs extends Applet implements ActionListener
{

    Button button1, button2;
    dialogframe frameWindow;

    public void init(){
        button1 = new Button("Show dialog window");
        add(button1);
        button1.addActionListener(this);
        button2 = new Button("Hide dialog window");
        add(button2);
        button2.addActionListener(this);

        frameWindow = new dialogframe("Dialogs");
        frameWindow.setSize(100, 100);
    }

    public void actionPerformed(ActionEvent event){
        if(event.getSource() == button1){
            frameWindow.setVisible(true);
        }
        if(event.getSource() == button2){
            frameWindow.setVisible(false);
        }
    }
}

class dialogframe extends Frame implements ActionListener {

    Menu Menu1;
    MenuBar Menubar1;
    MenuItem menuitem1, menuitem2, menuitem3;

    TextField text1;
    buttondialog dialogBox;

    dialogframe(String title){
        super(title);
        text1 = new TextField("");
        setLayout(new GridLayout(1, 1));
```

```
            add(text1);
            Menubar1 = new MenuBar();

            Menu1 = new Menu("File");

            menuitem1 = new MenuItem("Copy");
            Menu1.add(menuitem1);
            menuitem1.addActionListener(this);

            menuitem2 = new MenuItem("Paste");
            Menu1.add(menuitem2);
            menuitem2.addActionListener(this);

            menuitem3 = new MenuItem("Dialog box...");
            Menu1.add(menuitem3);
            menuitem3.addActionListener(this);

            Menubar1.add(Menu1);

            setMenuBar(Menubar1);
            dialogBox = new buttondialog(this, "Dialog", true);
        }

    public void actionPerformed(ActionEvent event){
            if(event.getSource() == menuitem1){
                text1.setText("Copy");
            }
            if(event.getSource() == menuitem2){
                text1.setText("Paste");
            }
            if(event.getSource() == menuitem3){
                dialogBox.setVisible(true);
            }
        }
}

class buttondialog extends Dialog implements ActionListener {

    Button OKButton, CancelButton;

    buttondialog(Frame hostFrame, String title, boolean dModal){
            super(hostFrame, title, dModal);
            setSize(100, 100);
            setLayout(new FlowLayout());
            OKButton = new Button("OK");
            add(OKButton);

OKButton.addActionListener((ActionListener)this);
            CancelButton = new Button("Cancel");
            add(CancelButton);
```

```
        CancelButton.addActionListener(this);
    }

    public void actionPerformed(ActionEvent event){
        if(event.getSource() == OKButton){
            setVisible(false);
        }
        if(event.getSource() == CancelButton){
            setVisible(false);
        }
    }
}
```

So far, then, you've seen how to build and display a rudimentary dialog box. However, you haven't retrieved any values that the user entered into the dialog box or set up the layout of your dialog box controls in any significant way.

Building a Popup Calculator

It's time to put together a more complete dialog box example now. This time, you'll pop up a window with a File menu that contains one item, Calculator…, as shown in Figure 9.4. When the user clicks that item, you can pop up the layout calculator you developed earlier as a dialog box—with an added Exit button to close the dialog box when not needed (see Figure 9.5). When the calculator is closed, you can read the answer and display it in a text field in the main applet, as shown in Figure 9.6.

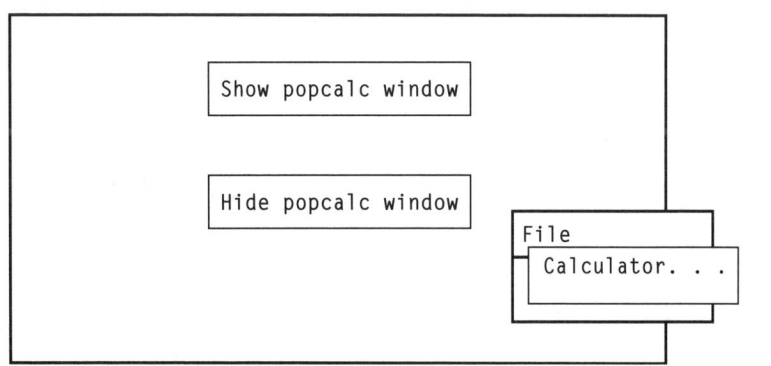

FIGURE 9.4:   You pop up a window with a File menu onto the screen.

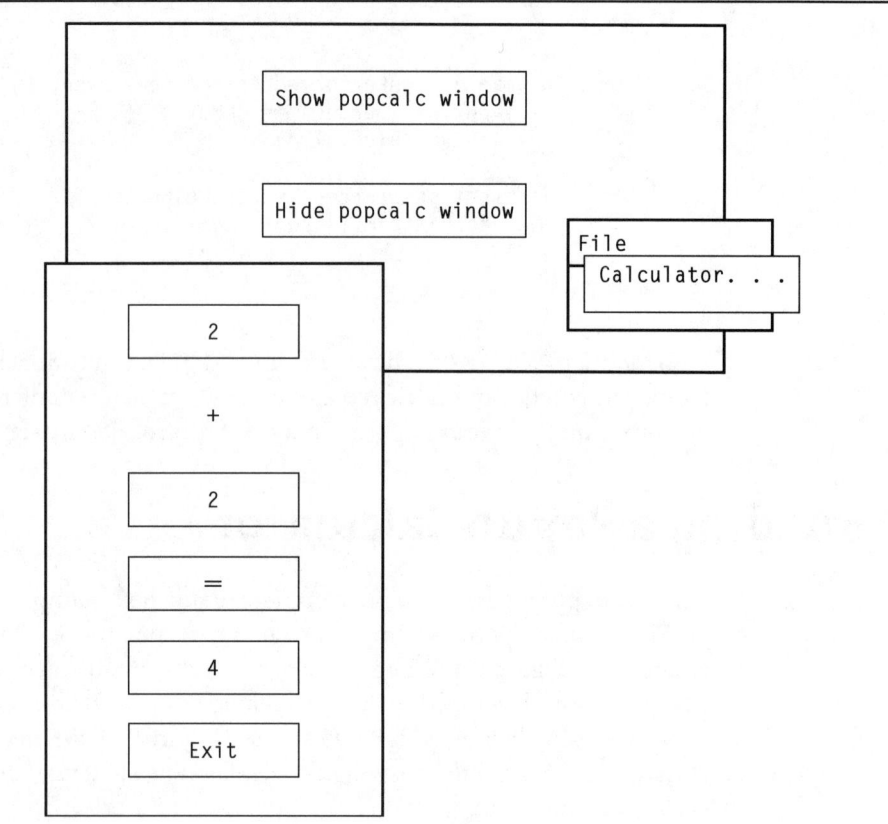

FIGURE 9.5: Your popup calculator allows the user to enter numeric values.

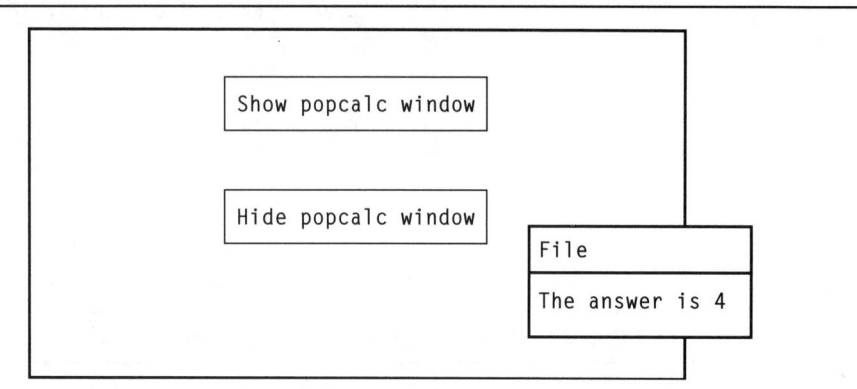

FIGURE 9.6: When the calculator is closed, a text field displays the answer.

Let's develop this example now. Create a new file named popcalc.java. You'll need a frame window to display the File menu with the Calculator item in it, so you need to create a class named MenuFrame. The applet class itself will only be responsible for placing that window on the screen, so write that class as you did above:

```
import java.applet.Applet;
import java.awt.*;
import java.awt.event.*;

public class popcalc extends Applet implements ActionListener
{

    Button button1, button2;
    MenuFrame frameWindow;

    public void init(){
        button1 = new Button("Show popcalc window");
        add(button1);
        button1.addActionListener(this);
        button2 = new Button("Hide popcalc window");
        add(button2);
        button2.addActionListener(this);

        frameWindow = new MenuFrame("Popup Calculator");
        frameWindow.setSize(100, 100);
    }

    public void actionPerformed(ActionEvent event){
        if(event.getSource() == button1){
            frameWindow.setVisible(true);
        }
        if(event.getSource() == button2){
            frameWindow.setVisible(false);
        }
    }
}
```

At this point, the applet is set up to place an object of class MenuFrame on the screen—create that class now:

```
class MenuFrame extends Frame implements ActionListener {

}
```

Here, add the text field in which you'll display the results from the calculator; you can name that text field "text1". Next, add the menu system itself, with one item, Calculator...:

```
class MenuFrame extends Frame implements ActionListener {

        Menu Menu1;
        MenuBar Menubar1;
        MenuItem menuitem1;

        TextField text1;

        MenuFrame(String title){
            super(title);
            text1 = new TextField("");
            setLayout(new GridLayout(1, 1));
            add(text1);
            Menubar1 = new MenuBar();

            Menu1 = new Menu("File");

            menuitem1 = new MenuItem("Calculator...");
            Menu1.add(menuitem1);
            menuitem1.addActionListener(this);

            Menubar1.add(Menu1);
            setMenuBar(Menubar1);
                    .
                    .
    }
```

The popup calculator itself will be a dialog box of the class `calculatordialog`. You'll create an object of that class named `dialogBox` now:

```
class MenuFrame extends Frame implements ActionListener {

        Menu Menu1;
        MenuBar Menubar1;
        MenuItem menuitem1, menuitem2, menuitem3;

        TextField text1;
        calculatordialog dialogBox;

        MenuFrame(String title){
            super(title);
            text1 = new TextField("");
            setLayout(new GridLayout(1, 1));
            add(text1);
            Menubar1 = new MenuBar();
```

```
                    Menu1 = new Menu("File");

                    menuitem1 = new MenuItem("Calculator...");
                    Menu1.add(menuitem1);
                    menuitem1.addActionListener(this);

                    Menubar1.add(Menu1);

                    setMenuBar(Menubar1);
  ➜                 dialogBox = new Calculatordialog(this, "Calculator", true);
                }
            }
```

When the user clicks the Calculator… menu item, you want to pop up the calculator object on the screen. You can do that in an `actionPerformed()` method:

```
    class MenuFrame extends Frame implements ActionListener {

            Menu Menu1;
            MenuBar Menubar1;
            MenuItem menuitem1, menuitem2, menuitem3;

            TextField text1;
            calculatordialog dialogBox;

            MenuFrame(String title){
                    super(title);
                    text1 = new TextField("");
                    setLayout(new GridLayout(1, 1));
                    add(text1);
                    Menubar1 = new MenuBar();

                    Menu1 = new Menu("File");

                    menuitem1 = new MenuItem("Calculator...");
                    Menu1.add(menuitem1);
                    menuitem1.addActionListener(this);

                    Menubar1.add(Menu1);

                    setMenuBar(Menubar1);
                    dialogBox = new calculatordialog(this, "Calculator", true);
            }

            public void actionPerformed(ActionEvent event){
  ➜                 if(event.getSource() == menuitem1){
  ➜                         dialogBox.setVisible(true);
  ➜                 }
  ➜         }
        }
```

All that's left is to create your calculator class, `calculatordialog`. As with the previous dialog box, place a constructor in your calculator dialog and pass back to yourself the parameters passed to the `Dialog` class's constructor:

```
class calculatordialog extends Dialog {

    calculatordialog(Frame hostFrame, String title, boolean dModal){
        super(hostFrame, title, dModal);
        setSize(300, 300);
            .
            .
            .
```

Next, add the controls you'll need for this popup calculator, including the new Exit button at the bottom of the dialog box. The controls you'll use in your calculator are shown in Figure 9.7.

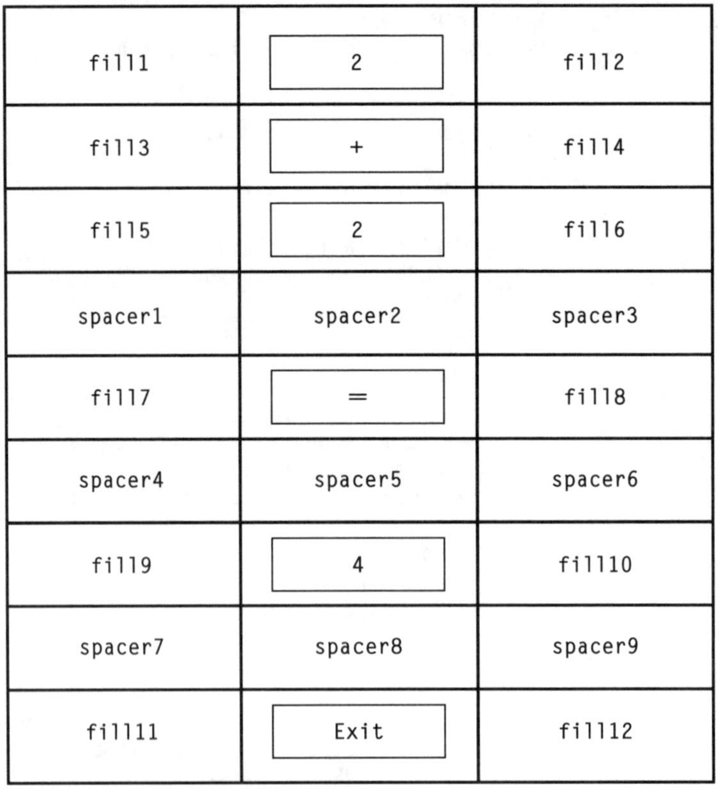

fill1	2	fill2
fill3	+	fill4
fill5	2	fill6
spacer1	spacer2	spacer3
fill7	=	fill8
spacer4	spacer5	spacer6
fill9	4	fill10
spacer7	spacer8	spacer9
fill11	Exit	fill12

FIGURE 9.7: The controls used in your calculator

Add those new controls in a grid layout, as follows:

```
class calculatordialog extends Dialog implements ActionListener {
→       TextField text1, text2, answertext;
→       Label pluslabel, fill1, fill2, fill3, fill4, fill5, fill6, fill7,➡
        fill8, fill9, fill10, fill11, fill12;
→       Label spacer1, spacer2, spacer3, spacer4, spacer5, spacer6,➡
        spacer7, spacer8, spacer9;
→       Button button1, button2;

        calculatordialog(Frame hostFrame, String title, boolean dModal){
            super(hostFrame, title, dModal);
            setSize(300, 300);
→           setLayout(new GridLayout(10, 3));
→
→           fill1 = new Label();
→           add(fill1);
→           text1 = new TextField(10);
→           add(text1);
→           fill2 = new Label();
→           add(fill2);
→
→           fill3 = new Label();
→           add(fill3);
→           pluslabel = new Label("+", Label.CENTER);
→           add(pluslabel);
→           fill4 = new Label();
→           add(fill4);
→
→           fill5 = new Label();
→           add(fill5);
→           text2 = new TextField(10);
→           add(text2);
→           fill6 = new Label();
→           add(fill6);
→
→           spacer1 = new Label();
→           add(spacer1);
→           spacer2 = new Label();
→           add(spacer2);
→           spacer3 = new Label();
→           add(spacer3);

→           fill7 = new Label();
→           add(fill7);
→           button1 = new Button("=");
→           add(button1);
```

```
→          button1.addActionListener(this);
→          fill8 = new Label();
→          add(fill8);
→
→          spacer4 = new Label();
→          add(spacer4);
→          spacer5 = new Label();
→          add(spacer5);
→          spacer6 = new Label();
→          add(spacer6);
→
→          fill9 = new Label();
→          add(fill9);
→          answertext = new TextField(10);
→          add(answertext);
→          fill10 = new Label();
→          add(fill10);
→
→          spacer7 = new Label();
→          add(spacer7);
→          spacer8 = new Label();
→          add(spacer8);
→          spacer9 = new Label();
→          add(spacer9);
→
→          fill11 = new Label();
→          add(fill11);
→          button2 = new Button("Exit");
→          add(button2);
→          button2.addActionListener(this);
→          fill12 = new Label();
→          add(fill12);
       }
```

Now you've added to the calculator dialog box all the controls that you'll need, including the = button (button1) and the Exit button (button2). When the user places an integer in the text1 text field, places another integer in the text2 text field, and clicks the = button, you want to add those two values and display their sum in the text field named answertext. You can do that by adding an actionPerformed() method and placing this code in it:

```
       public void actionPerformed(ActionEvent e){
→          if(e.getSource() == button1){
→              int sum = Integer.parseInt(text1.getText()) + ➡
    Integer.parseInt(text2.getText());
```

```
→                answertext.setText(String.valueOf(sum));
→           }        .
                     .
                     .

        }
  }
```

After the user completes the calculation and clicks Exit (`button2`), you can take the result from the `answertext` text field and place it in the frame window's text field, which you named `text1`. You can do so as follows:

```
public void actionPerformed(ActionEvent event){
    if(event.getSource() == menuitem1){
        dialogBox.setVisible(true);
→       text1.setText("The answer is: " + ➥
.answertext.getText());
    }
}
```

And your applet is finished. Start the applet now and select the Calculator item in the frame window's File menu, as shown in Figure 9.8. When the calculator dialog opens, add two numbers, as shown in Figure 9.9. After you click the Exit button, the sum appears in the frame window, as shown in Figure 9.10.

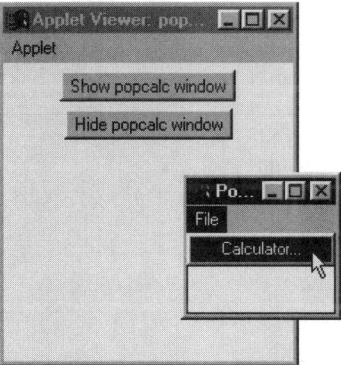
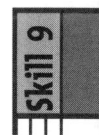

FIGURE 9.8:   Your applet supports a popup calculator.

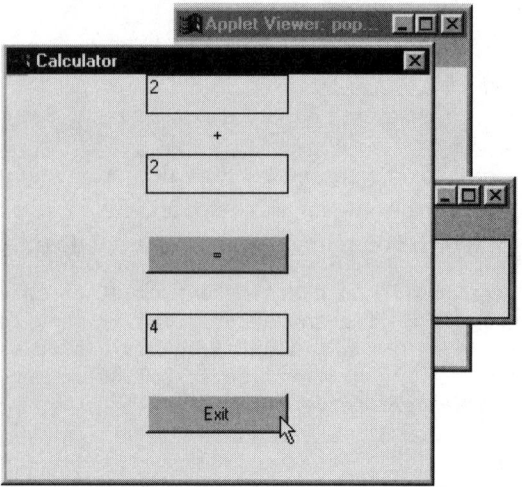

FIGURE 9.9:   You add numbers in your popup calculator.

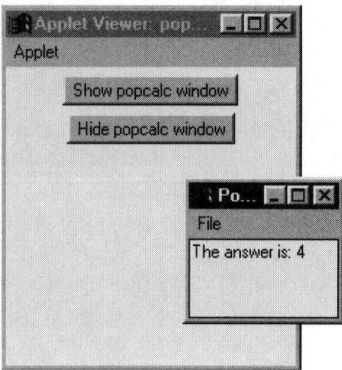

FIGURE 9.10:   The calculator dialog places its answer in the frame window.

Now your popup calculator is finished. You're able to lay out your controls in dialog boxes as you want them, and you're able to retrieve values that the user enters in dialog boxes. The listing for this applet appears in popcalc.java.

C   popcalc.java

```java
import java.applet.Applet;
import java.awt.*;
import java.awt.event.*;

public class popcalc extends Applet implements ActionListener
{

    Button button1, button2;
    MenuFrame frameWindow;

    public void init(){
        button1 = new Button("Show popcalc window");
        add(button1);
        button1.addActionListener(this);
        button2 = new Button("Hide popcalc window");
        add(button2);
        button2.addActionListener(this);

        frameWindow = new MenuFrame("Popup Calculator");
        frameWindow.setSize(100, 100);
    }

    public void actionPerformed(ActionEvent event){
        if(event.getSource() == button1){
            frameWindow.setVisible(true);
        }
        if(event.getSource() == button2){
            frameWindow.setVisible(false);
        }
    }
}

class MenuFrame extends Frame implements ActionListener {

    Menu Menu1;
    MenuBar Menubar1;
    MenuItem menuitem1, menuitem2, menuitem3;

    TextField text1;
    Calculatordialog dialogBox;

    MenuFrame(String title){
        super(title);
        text1 = new TextField("");
        setLayout(new GridLayout(1, 1));
```

```
        add(text1);
        Menubar1 = new MenuBar();

        Menu1 = new Menu("File");

        menuitem1 = new MenuItem("Calculator...");
        Menu1.add(menuitem1);
        menuitem1.addActionListener(this);

        Menubar1.add(Menu1);

        setMenuBar(Menubar1);
        dialogBox = new Calculatordialog(this, "Calculator", true);
    }

    public void actionPerformed(ActionEvent event){
        if(event.getSource() == menuitem1){
            dialogBox.setVisible(true);
            text1.setText("The answer is: " + ➥
dialogBox.answertext.getText());
        }
    }
}

class Calculatordialog extends Dialog implements ActionListener {

    TextField text1, text2, answertext;
    Label pluslabel, fill1, fill2, fill3, fill4, fill5, fill6, fill7,➥
fill8, fill9, fill10, fill11, fill12;
    Label spacer1, spacer2, spacer3, spacer4, spacer5, spacer6, ➥
spacer7, spacer8, spacer9;
    Button button1, button2;

    Calculatordialog(Frame hostFrame, String title, boolean dModal){
        super(hostFrame, title, dModal);
        setSize(300, 300);
        setLayout(new GridLayout(10, 3));

        fill1 = new Label();
        add(fill1);
        text1 = new TextField(10);
        add(text1);
        fill2 = new Label();
        add(fill2);

        fill3 = new Label();
        add(fill3);
```

```
pluslabel = new Label("+", Label.CENTER);
add(pluslabel);
fill4 = new Label();
add(fill4);

fill5 = new Label();
add(fill5);
text2 = new TextField(10);
add(text2);
fill6 = new Label();
add(fill6);

spacer1 = new Label();
add(spacer1);
spacer2 = new Label();
add(spacer2);
spacer3 = new Label();
add(spacer3);

fill7 = new Label();
add(fill7);
button1 = new Button("=");
add(button1);
button1.addActionListener(this);
fill8 = new Label();
add(fill8);

spacer4 = new Label();
add(spacer4);
spacer5 = new Label();
add(spacer5);
spacer6 = new Label();
add(spacer6);

fill9 = new Label();
add(fill9);
answertext = new TextField(10);
add(answertext);
fill10 = new Label();
add(fill10);

spacer7 = new Label();
add(spacer7);
spacer8 = new Label();
add(spacer8);
spacer9 = new Label();
add(spacer9);
```

```
                fill11 = new Label();
                add(fill11);
                button2 = new Button("Exit");
                add(button2);
                button2.addActionListener(this);
                fill12 = new Label();
                add(fill12);
        }

        public void actionPerformed(ActionEvent e){
                if(e.getSource() == button1){
                        int sum = Integer.parseInt(text1.getText())+ ➥
        Integer.parseInt(text2.getText());
                        answertext.setText(String.valueOf(sum));
                }
                if(e.getSource() == button2){
                        setVisible(false);
                }
        }
}
```

You've come far in this Skill, from basic dialog boxes to dialog boxes with layout, from dialog boxes with only the most basic of actions to dialog boxes that report results. In Skill 10, we're going to turn to another favorite with Java and Internet programmers everywhere—graphics programming.

Are You up to Speed?

Now you can...

- ☑ create and use dialog boxes

- ☑ show and hide dialog boxes from code as required

- ☑ lay out controls in a dialog box for more control

- ☑ use controls in a dialog box to activate your controls and respond to the user's actions

- ☑ retrieve and use values from dialog box controls in the rest of the program

SKILL 10

Java Graphics!

- Using the mouse
- Handling mouse events
- Drawing rectangles and rounded rectangles
- Drawing ovals and circles
- Drawing lines
- Drawing freehand with the mouse
- Printing in Java

In this chapter, we're going to start exploring a topic very popular among Java programmers—graphics. We'll see how to work with the elementary graphics methods in Java: drawing lines, rectangles, circles, and ovals. We'll even design and run a graphics applet named "dauber," which will allow the user to draw their own graphics with the mouse. At the end of the chapter, we'll take a look at the Java support for printing. Let's begin now by seeing how to use the mouse so we can add mouse support to our dauber applet.

Using the Mouse

To learn how to use the mouse, set up a new file named `mousedemo.java`. You can add a text field to your mousedemo applet, as shown in Figure 10.1.

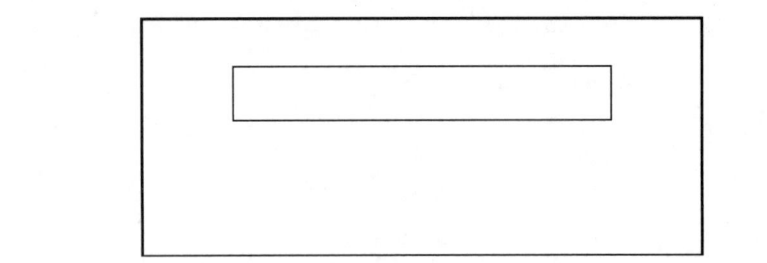

FIGURE 10.1:   Adding a text field to the applet

Then, when a mouse event—such as a mouse button going down or up—occurs, you can report the event in the text field. For example, if the `mouseEntered()` method is called in your applet, you can report that the mouse has entered your applet's boundaries, as shown in Figure 10.2. When the user presses a mouse button, you can report its position in pixels in your applet, as shown in Figure 10.3. You'll also report when the user clicks the mouse (see Figure 10.4) and when the mouse leaves the boundaries of the applet (see Figure 10.5).

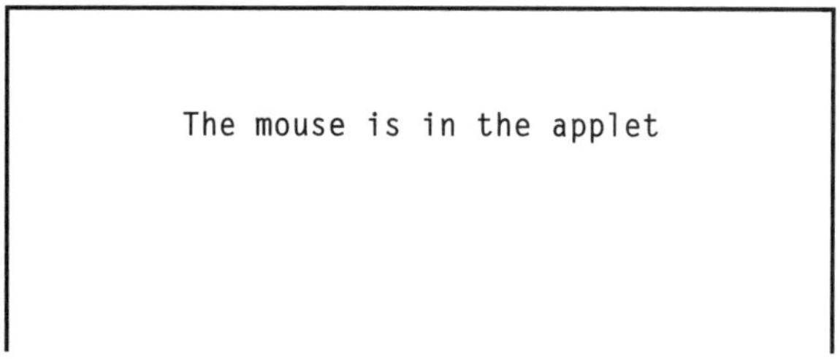

```
                    The mouse is in the applet
```

FIGURE 10.2:   Your message reports that the mouse has entered the applet.

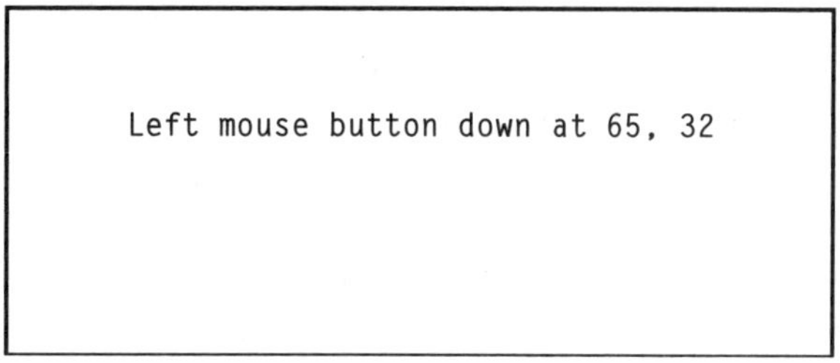

```
                  Left mouse button down at 65, 32
```

FIGURE 10.3:   Reporting the position where the user pressed a mouse button

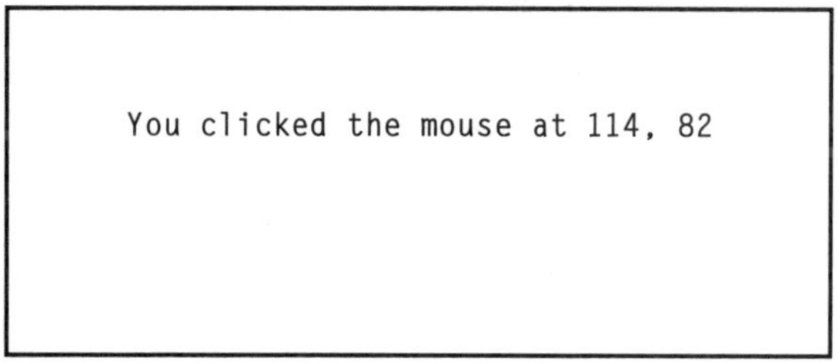

```
                  You clicked the mouse at 114, 82
```

FIGURE 10.4:   Reporting the position of a mouse click

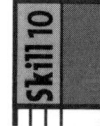

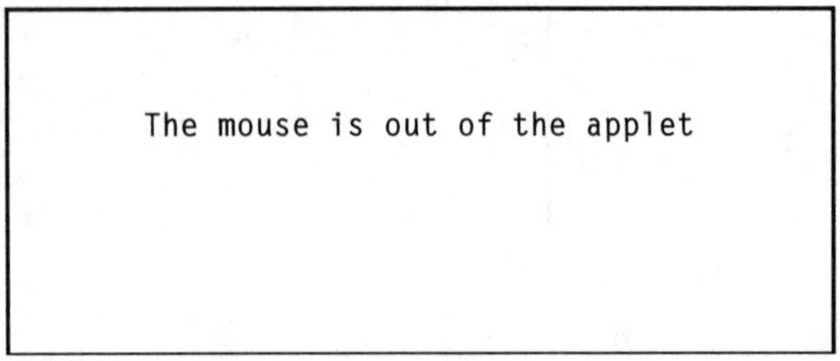

```
                 The mouse is out of the applet
```

FIGURE 10.5:   When the mouse leaves the applet this message appears.

Now it's time to start writing your Java code. Give your text field the name mousetext, and add the declaration of this text field to your applet as follows:

```
import java.applet.Applet;
import java.awt.*;

public class mousedemo extends Applet {

➡       TextField mousetext;

}
```

Next, create this text field in the init() method:

```
import java.applet.Applet;
import java.awt.*;

public class mousedemo extends Applet {

        TextField mousetext;

        public void init(){
➡           mousetext = new TextField(25);
➡           add(mousetext);
                    .
                    .
                    .

        }
```

Using *MouseListener*

Now you can connect the MouseListener interface to your applet so you'll be able to handle mouse events:

```
 import java.applet.Applet;
 import java.awt.*;
➜import java.awt.event.*;

➜public class mousedemo extends Applet implements MouseListener{

     TextField mousetext;

     public void init(){
         mousetext = new TextField(25);
         add(mousetext);
➜        addMouseListener(this);
     }            .
                  .
                  .
```

Now your text field and your applet are ready to go. It's time to examine the mouse support that Java includes for you.

Mouse events like clicking or moving the mouse are handled in mouse event methods. The first mouse event we'll take a look at is the mousePressed event. (this is different from the mousePressed event used in Java 1.0. All of the mouse handling methods have changed in Java 1.2.) If you define a mousePressed() method in your applet, the method will be called when a mouse button is pressed while the mouse is in the boundaries of your applet. Add a mousePressed() method to your applet now.

Using *mousePressed()*

The mousePressed()method looks like this:

```
import java.applet.Applet;
import java.awt.*;
import java.awt.event.*;

public class mousedemo extends Applet implements MouseListener {

     TextField mousetext;

     public void init(){
         mousetext = new TextField(25);
```

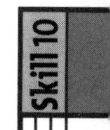

```
                add(mousetext);
                addMouseListener(this);
        }

        public void mousePressed(MouseEvent e){

→       }
    }
```

This method will be called if the mouse button is pressed while the mouse is in your applet. The MouseEvent object holds the position of the mouse when the mouse button was pressed, and you can get that location with the MouseEvent getX() and getY() methods. In addition, the MouseEvent class member named modifiers (which you get with the getModifiers() method) lets us know which mouse button was pressed. You can use that information to display which button was clicked.

 **NOTE**   Java currently handles only two mouse buttons, even though some mice have three buttons.

First, you need to check to see if the modifiers member is 0, which means the left mouse button was clicked:

```
public void mousePressed(MouseEvent e){
                        if((e.getModifiers()& InputEvent.BUTTON1_MASK)
== InputEvent.BUTTON1_MASK){
                            mousetext.setText("Left mouse button down
at " + e.getX() + "," + e.getY());
                        }
                        else{
                            mousetext.setText("Right mouse button down
at " + e.getX() + "," + e.getY());
                        }
                }
]

import java.applet.Applet;
import java.awt.*;
import java.awt.event.*;

public class mousedemo extends Applet implements MouseListener {

    TextField mousetext;
```

```
        public void init(){
            mousetext = new TextField(25);
            add(mousetext);
            addMouseListener(this);
        }

        public void mousePressed(MouseEvent e){
→            if((e.getModifiers()& InputEvent.BUTTON1_MASK) == ➡
    InputEvent.BUTTON1_MASK){
                        .
                        .
                        .
→            }
    }
```

If the modifiers member indicates the left mouse button is down, you report that the left mouse button was pressed. Place the text "Left mouse button down at" and the location of the mouse in your text field named mousetext:

```
    import java.applet.Applet;
    import java.awt.*;
    import java.awt.event.*;

    public class mousedemo extends Applet implements MouseListener {

        TextField mousetext;

        public void init(){
            mousetext = new TextField(25);
            add(mousetext);
            addMouseListener(this);
        }

        public void mousePressed(MouseEvent e){
            if((e.getModifiers()& InputEvent.BUTTON1_MASK) == ➡
    InputEvent.BUTTON1_MASK){
→mousetext.setText("Left mouse button down at " + e.getX() + "," + ➡
    e.getY());
            }    .
                 .
                 .
    }
```

Otherwise, there's only one other possibility, and you indicate that the right mouse button went down in an `else` clause:

```java
import java.applet.Applet;
import java.awt.*;
import java.awt.event.*;

public class mousedemo extends Applet implements MouseListener {

    TextField mousetext;

    public void init(){
        mousetext = new TextField(25);
        add(mousetext);
        addMouseListener(this);
    }

    public void mousePressed(MouseEvent e){
        if((e.getModifiers()& InputEvent.BUTTON1_MASK) == ➥
InputEvent.BUTTON1_MASK){

            mousetext.setText("Left mouse button down at " + ➥
e.getX() + "," + e.getY());
        }
        else{
            mousetext.setText("Right mouse button down at " + ➥
e.getX() + "," + e.getY());
        }
    }
```

NOTE   The general form of the Java `if` statement is:

```java
if(conditional){
[code block 1]
}
else{
[code block 2]
}
```

where the code in code block 1 is executed if the conditional expression evaluates to `true`, and the code in code block 2 is executed otherwise.

And that's it—you've handled the `mousePressed` event. Now let's take a look at the `mouseClicked` event.

Using *mouseClicked()*

The mouseClicked() method is called when the mouse is clicked, and you can add that method to the applet now:

```
import java.applet.Applet;
import java.awt.*;
import java.awt.event.*;

public class mousedemo extends Applet implements MouseListener {

    TextField mousetext;

    public void init(){
        mousetext = new TextField(25);
        add(mousetext);
        addMouseListener(this);
    }

    public void mousePressed(MouseEvent e){
        if((e.getModifiers()& InputEvent.BUTTON1_MASK) == ➥
InputEvent.BUTTON1_MASK){

            mousetext.setText("Left mouse button down at " + ➥
e.getX() + "," + e.getY());
        }
        else{
            mousetext.setText("Right mouse button down at " + ➥
e.getX() + "," + e.getY());
        }
    }

➥   public void mouseClicked(MouseEvent e){
                    .
                    .
                    .

➥      }
    }
```

Here, just report the location of the mouse click, as follows:

```
import java.applet.Applet;
import java.awt.*;
import java.awt.event.*;

public class mousedemo extends Applet implements MouseListener {

    TextField mousetext;
```

Skill 10

```
        public void init(){
            mousetext = new TextField(25);
            add(mousetext);
            addMouseListener(this);
        }

        public void mousePressed(MouseEvent e){
            if(e.getModifiers() == 0){
                mousetext.setText("Left mouse button down at " + ➥
e.getX() + "," + e.getY());
            }
            else{
                mousetext.setText("Right mouse button down at " + ➥
e.getX() + "," + e.getY());
            }
        }

        public void mouseClicked(MouseEvent e){
➤           mousetext.setText("You clicked the mouse at " + e.getX() + ➥
"," + e.getY());
        }
    }
```

That's it—now you've handled the `mousePressed()` and `mouseClicked()`
methods. The next mouse method is `mouseReleased()`.

Using *mouseReleased()*

To identify when a mouse button is released, use the `mouseReleased()` event.
The `mouseReleased` event is handled in the `mouseReleased()` method:

```
import java.applet.Applet;
import java.awt.*;
import java.awt.event.*;

public class mousedemo extends Applet implements MouseListener {

    TextField mousetext;

    public void init(){
        mousetext = new TextField(25);
        add(mousetext);
        addMouseListener(this);
    }

    public void mousePressed(MouseEvent e){
```

```
            if((e.getModifiers()& InputEvent.BUTTON1_MASK) == ➡
InputEvent.BUTTON1_MASK){

                mousetext.setText("Left mouse button down at " + ➡
e.getX() + "," + e.getY());
            }
            else{
                mousetext.setText("Right mouse button down at " + ➡
e.getX() + "," + e.getY());
            }
    }

➡    public void mouseReleased(MouseEvent e){
                    .
                    .
                    .
➡    }
    }
```

That's one way to identify that a mouse button is released. You can also indicate that the mouse button went up using the following method:

```
import java.applet.Applet;
import java.awt.*;
import java.awt.event.*;

public class mousedemo extends Applet implements MouseListener {

    TextField mousetext;

    public void init(){
        mousetext = new TextField(25);
        add(mousetext);
        addMouseListener(this);
    }

    public void mousePressed(MouseEvent e){
        if((e.getModifiers()& InputEvent.BUTTON1_MASK) == ➡
InputEvent.BUTTON1_MASK){

                mousetext.setText("Left mouse button down at " + ➡
e.getX() + "," + e.getY());
        }
        else{
                mousetext.setText("Right mouse button down at " + ➡
e.getX() + "," + e.getY());
        }
    }
```

Skill 10

```
→     public void mouseReleased(MouseEvent e){
→          mousetext.setText("The mouse button is up");
→     }
     }
```

And that's it—you've reported what happened by placing the text, "The mouse button is up", in your text field named mousetext. That takes care of mousePressed(), mouseClicked, and mouseReleased(). Next, we'll take a look at mouseEntered().

Using *mouseEntered()*

The mouseEntered event occurs when the mouse enters the boundaries of your applet on the screen. Place the following code in your applet to handle this event:

```
import java.applet.Applet;
import java.awt.*;
import java.awt.event.*;

public class mousedemo extends Applet implements MouseListener {

     TextField mousetext;

     public void init(){
          mousetext = new TextField(25);
          add(mousetext);
          addMouseListener(this);
     }

     public void mousePressed(MouseEvent e){
          if((e.getModifiers()& InputEvent.BUTTON1_MASK) == ➥
InputEvent.BUTTON1_MASK){

               mousetext.setText("Left mouse button down at " + ➥
e.getX() + "," + e.getY());
          }
          else{
               mousetext.setText("Right mouse button down at " + ➥
e.getX() + "," + e.getY());
          }
     }

     public void mouseClicked(MouseEvent e){
          mousetext.setText("You clicked the mouse at " + e.getX() + ➥
"," + e.getY());
     }

     public void mouseReleased(MouseEvent e){
```

```
                    mousetext.setText("The mouse button is up");
        }

→       public void mouseEntered(MouseEvent e){
                              .
                              .
                              .

→       }

    }
```

Using the mouseEntered() method, you can report that the mouse has entered your applet by placing the message, "The mouse is in the applet", into the mousetext:

```
import java.applet.Applet;
import java.awt.*;
import java.awt.event.*;

public class mousedemo extends Applet implements MouseListener {

    TextField mousetext;

    public void init(){
        mousetext = new TextField(25);
        add(mousetext);
        addMouseListener(this);
    }

    public void mousePressed(MouseEvent e){
        if((e.getModifiers()& InputEvent.BUTTON1_MASK) == ➡
InputEvent.BUTTON1_MASK){

            mousetext.setText("Left mouse button down at " + ➡
e.getX() + "," + e.getY());
        }
        else{
            mousetext.setText("Right mouse button down at " + ➡
e.getX() + "," + e.getY());
        }
    }

    public void mouseClicked(MouseEvent e){
        mousetext.setText("You clicked the mouse at " + e.getX() + ➡
"," + e.getY());
    }

    public void mouseReleased(MouseEvent e){
```

```
                    mousetext.setText("The mouse button is up");
            }

→       public void mouseEntered(MouseEvent e){
→               mousetext.setText("The mouse is in the applet");
→       }
        }
```

 TIP   If you take advantage of the mouseEntered event in a Java frame window, you can change the mouse cursor to whatever you want with the Frame class setCursor() method when the mouse is in your window.

The last of the mouse events is the mouseExited event; we will take a look at that now.

Using *mouseExited()*

As you might expect—having seen the mouseEntered event—the mouseExited event occurs when the mouse leaves your applet. Place the following code in your applet to handle the mouseExited event:

```
import java.applet.Applet;
import java.awt.*;
import java.awt.event.*;

public class mousedemo extends Applet implements MouseListener {

    TextField mousetext;

    public void init(){
        mousetext = new TextField(25);
        add(mousetext);
        addMouseListener(this);
    }

    public void mousePressed(MouseEvent e){
        if((e.getModifiers()& InputEvent.BUTTON1_MASK) == ➡
InputEvent.BUTTON1_MASK){

            mousetext.setText("Left mouse button down at " + ➡
e.getX() + "," + e.getY());
        }
        else{
```

```
                    mousetext.setText("Right mouse button down at " + ➥
        e.getX() + "," + e.getY());
                }
        }

        public void mouseClicked(MouseEvent e){
                mousetext.setText("You clicked the mouse at " + e.getX() + ➥
        "," + e.getY());
            }

        public void mouseReleased(MouseEvent e){
                mousetext.setText("The mouse button is up");
            }

        public void mouseEntered(MouseEvent e){
                mousetext.setText("The mouse is in the applet");
            }

➔       public void mouseExited(MouseEvent e){

                        .
                        .
                        .

➔       }
      }
```

In this example, just report that the mouse left the applet with a message, as follows:

```
import java.applet.Applet;
import java.awt.*;
import java.awt.event.*;

public class mousedemo extends Applet implements MouseListener {

        TextField mousetext;

        public void init(){
                mousetext = new TextField(25);
                add(mousetext);
                addMouseListener(this);
            }

        public void mousePressed(MouseEvent e){
                if((e.getModifiers()& InputEvent.BUTTON1_MASK) == ➥
        InputEvent.BUTTON1_MASK){

                        mousetext.setText("Left mouse button down at " + ➥
        e.getX() + "," + e.getY());
```

```
            }
            else{
                 mousetext.setText("Right mouse button down at " + ➡
    e.getX() + "," + e.getY());
            }
    }

    public void mouseClicked(MouseEvent e){
        mousetext.setText("You clicked the mouse at " + e.getX() + ➡
    "," + e.getY());
    }

    public void mouseReleased(MouseEvent e){
        mousetext.setText("The mouse button is up");
    }

    public void mouseEntered(MouseEvent e){
        mousetext.setText("The mouse is in the applet");
    }

    public void mouseExited(MouseEvent e){
➡       mousetext.setText("The mouse is out of the applet");
    }
}
```

And now your mousedemo applet is ready to use. In the graphic below, the mousedemo applet is indicating that the mouse has entered the applet:

If the user presses the left mouse button, the applet displays the following message.

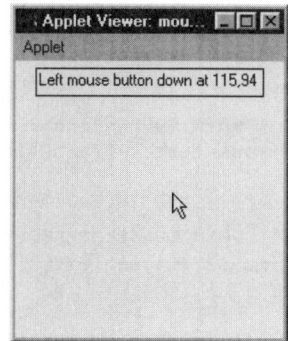

As you can tell by playing around with this applet for a while, all the other mouse events are active as well. The code for this applet appears in mousedemo.java.

mousedemo.java

```java
import java.applet.Applet;
import java.awt.*;
import java.awt.event.*;

public class mousedemo extends Applet implements MouseListener {

    TextField mousetext;

    public void init(){
        mousetext = new TextField(25);
        add(mousetext);
        addMouseListener(this);
    }

    public void mousePressed(MouseEvent e){
        if((e.getModifiers()& InputEvent.BUTTON1_MASK) == ➥
InputEvent.BUTTON1_MASK){

            mousetext.setText("Left mouse button down at " + ➥
e.getX() + "," + e.getY());
        }
        else{
            mousetext.setText("Right mouse button down at " + ➥
e.getX() + "," + e.getY());
        }
    }

    public void mouseClicked(MouseEvent e){
```

```
            mousetext.setText("You clicked the mouse at " + e.getX() + ➡
    "," + e.getY());
        }

    public void mouseReleased(MouseEvent e){
            mousetext.setText("The mouse button is up");
        }

    public void mouseEntered(MouseEvent e){
            mousetext.setText("The mouse is in the applet");
        }

    public void mouseExited(MouseEvent e){
            mousetext.setText("The mouse is out of the applet");
        }
}
```

Now that you've seen how to use the mouse in a Java applet, you're ready to create the dauber applet, which will let the user create graphics like lines, rectangles, and circles with the mouse.

The Dauber Applet

To explore how graphics works in Java, you'll learn to create the dauber applet now. You can present the user with a collection of drawing "tools"—as shown in Figure 10.6, these tools will be buttons the user can select from. After the user selects a drawing tool (i.e., by clicking a drawing tool button), they can draw the figure they chose with the mouse.

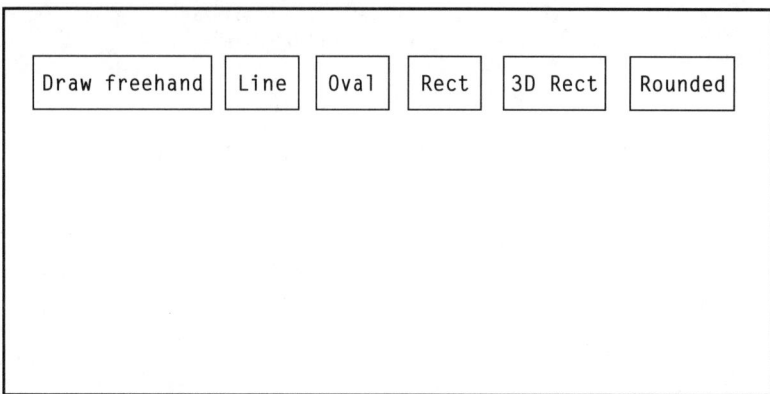

FIGURE 10.6: You can present the user with a collection of drawing tools.

To draw a rectangle, the user clicks the Rect button, moves the mouse to the place where they'd like their new graphics figure to begin, presses and holds the mouse button, drags the mouse to the other end of the graphics figure, and releases the mouse button. When the mouse button goes up, the applet draws the figure the user has described.

Let's see drawing in action. Create a new file named dauber.java now. Open the file and add the new dauber class now:

```
public class dauber extends Applet
{            .
             .
             .
```

Creating Dauber's Drawing Tools

You can add drawing tools now as buttons—let's examine six types of graphics here: lines, ovals (including circles), rectangles, 3D rectangles, rounded rectangles, and freehand drawing. You'll need six buttons, which you can set up as follows:

```
     public class dauber extends Applet
     {
→         Button buttonDraw, buttonLine, buttonOval, buttonRect,
     button3DRect, buttonRounded;
     7
                   .
                   .
```

Next, add the six buttons and create them in the init() method:

```
     public class dauber extends Applet {

          Button buttonDraw, buttonLine, buttonOval, buttonRect, →
     button3DRect, buttonRounded;

→         public void init() {
→
→             buttonDraw = new Button("Draw Freehand");
→             buttonLine = new Button("Line");
→             buttonOval = new Button("Oval");
→             buttonRect = new Button("Rect");
→             button3DRect = new Button("3D Rect");
→             buttonRounded = new Button("Round");
                    .
                    .
                    .
          }
```

To arrange those buttons, use the default FlowLayout manager here. Just add the buttons to that layout now, as well as adding an ActionListener for each button as follows:

```
→public class dauber extends Applet implements ActionListener{

        Button buttonDraw, buttonLine, buttonOval, buttonRect, ➡
    button3DRect;
        Button buttonRounded;

        public void init() {

                buttonDraw = new Button("Draw Freehand");
                buttonLine = new Button("Line");
                buttonOval = new Button("Oval");
                buttonRect = new Button("Rect");
                button3DRect = new Button("3D Rect");
                buttonRounded = new Button("Round");

→               add(buttonDraw);
→               buttonDraw.addActionListener(this);
→               add(buttonLine);
→               buttonLine.addActionListener(this);
→               add(buttonOval);
→               buttonOval.addActionListener(this);
                add(buttonRect);
→               buttonRect.addActionListener(this);
→               add(button3DRect);
→               button3DRect.addActionListener(this);
→               add(buttonRounded);
→               buttonRounded.addActionListener(this);
                         .
                         .
                         .

        }
```

Now that your buttons have been installed, you can make them active. Note that the drawing does not take place when the user clicks a drawing tool—it takes place when the user releases the mouse button. That is, the applet draws the required figure in the mouseReleased() method.

How will the applet know what figure to draw? The applet will have to know which button the user clicked, so it will set some *boolean* flags, one for each drawing tool, when the user clicks one of the drawing tools.

NOTE
A boolean flag is just a boolean variable used to indicate the state (true or false) of some option in a program. For example, windowvisibleboolean may be a boolean flag, which, if true, indicates that a particular window is visible.

Creating Dauber's Boolean Flags

You will learn to create and initialize your boolean flags now. If the user clicks the line drawing tool, set the flag named bLineFlag to true; if they click the rectangle drawing tool, set the flag named bRectFlag to true, and so on. Your flags will be: bDrawFlag, bLineFlag, bOvalFlag, bRectFlag, b3DRectFlag, and bRoundedFlag, and you should start out with all of them set to false:

```
public class dauber extends Applet implements ActionListener {

        Button buttonDraw, buttonLine, buttonOval, buttonRect,
    button3DRect, buttonRounded;

➜       boolean bMouseDownFlag = false;
➜       boolean bMouseUpFlag = false;
➜       boolean bDrawFlag = false;
➜       boolean bLineFlag = false;
➜       boolean bOvalFlag = false;
➜       boolean bRectFlag = false;
➜       boolean b3DRectFlag = false;
➜       boolean bRoundedFlag = false;
                .
                .
                .
```

Keep track of the mouse in your dauber applet because dauber draws the graphics figures after the mouse button goes up, so you need to add two new flags, bMouseDownFlag and bMouseUpFlag as follows:

```
public class dauber extends Applet implements ActionListener {

        Button buttonDraw, buttonLine, buttonOval, buttonRect, ➡
    button3DRect, buttonRounded;

➜       boolean bMouseDownFlag = false;
➜       boolean bMouseUpFlag = false;
➜       boolean bDrawFlag = false;
```

```
→      boolean bLineFlag = false;
→      boolean bOvalFlag = false;
→      boolean bRectFlag = false;
→      boolean b3DRectFlag = false;
→      boolean bRoundedFlag = false;
              .
              .
              .
```

After you make these flags active, you'll know in any method of the applet which drawing tool the user has selected and what the mouse state is. That's what's important to know—what you're being asked to draw and when you can draw it. Connect the buttons you've installed to these flags, and then you won't need to think about the buttons any more.

 TIP   In this example, you're dividing your program into a user interface part (using buttons) and a separate drawing part (using flags). Dividing the parts of a program into self-contained (and therefore easily debugged) parts is usually a good programming practice. Long, monolithic programs get to be unwieldy very quickly.

You make the drawing tool buttons active in an `actionPerformed()` method that you can add to your applet now:

```
public void actionPerformed(ActionEvent e){
              .
              .
              .

}
```

First, check whether the user clicked the Draw Freehand button to start freehand drawing. The name of this button is `buttonDraw`, and you can check whether it was clicked this way:

```
public void actionPerformed(ActionEvent e){
    if(e.getSource() == buttonDraw){
              .
              .
              .

    }
}
```

If so, you can toggle the setting of the freehand drawing flag, bDrawFlag, using the Java exclamation point (!) operator, which reverses boolean values (a value of true becomes false, and a value of false becomes true):

```
public void actionPerformed(ActionEvent e){
    if(e.getSource() == buttonDraw){
→       bDrawFlag = !bDrawFlag;
                .
                .
                .

    }
```

In addition, now that the user has clicked the Draw Freehand button, you should set the other button's flags to false:

```
public void actionPerformed(ActionEvent e){
    if(e.getSource() == buttonDraw){
        bDrawFlag = !bDrawFlag;
→       bLineFlag = false;
→       bOvalFlag = false;
→       bRectFlag = false;
→       b3DRectFlag = false;
→       bRoundedFlag = false;
    }           .
                .
                .

    }
```

You can connect the other buttons to their boolean flags as follows:

```
public void actionPerformed(ActionEvent e){
    if(e.getSource() == buttonDraw){
        bDrawFlag = !bDrawFlag;
        bLineFlag = false;
        bOvalFlag = false;
        bRectFlag = false;
        b3DRectFlag = false;
        bRoundedFlag = false;
    }
→   if(e.getSource() == buttonLine){
→       bLineFlag = !bLineFlag;
→       bDrawFlag = false;
→       bOvalFlag = false;
→       bRectFlag = false;
→       b3DRectFlag = false;
→       bRoundedFlag = false;
→   }
→   if(e.getSource() == buttonOval){
```

```
→               bOvalFlag = !bOvalFlag;
→               bLineFlag = false;
→               bDrawFlag = false;
→               bRectFlag = false;
→               b3DRectFlag = false;
→               bRoundedFlag = false;
→            }
→            if(e.getSource() == buttonRect){
→               bRectFlag = !bRectFlag;
→               bLineFlag = false;
→               bOvalFlag = false;
→               bDrawFlag = false;
→               b3DRectFlag = false;
→               bRoundedFlag = false;
→            }
→            if(e.getSource() == button3DRect){
→               b3DRectFlag = !b3DRectFlag;
→               bLineFlag = false;
→               bOvalFlag = false;
→               bRectFlag = false;
→               bDrawFlag = false;
→               bRoundedFlag = false;
→            }
→            if(e.getSource() == buttonRounded){
→               bRoundedFlag = !bRoundedFlag;
→               bLineFlag = false;
→               bOvalFlag = false;
→               bRectFlag = false;
→               b3DRectFlag = false;
→               bDrawFlag = false;
→            }
→         }
```

And so, you've connected your buttons to the settings of associated boolean flags. You don't have to worry about the buttons anymore; from now on you can just check the boolean flags you set up.

Drawing in the Dauber Applet

Now the user turns from the drawing tool buttons to using the mouse to outline the graphics figure they want to draw. They will press the mouse button at some location in your applet that you can call the *anchor point*, and then they will move the mouse to a new location, which you can call the *drawto* point. When they release the mouse button, your applet will draw the graphics figure, as bounded by the anchor and drawto points:

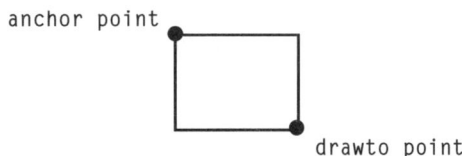

anchor point

drawto point

That's how you'll proceed, then—record the location at which the mouse went down in the mousePressed() method and start the drawing process in the mouseReleased() method. Let's look at the mousePressed() method now.

Using *mousePressed()* in Dauber

In the mousePressed event, you want to record the beginning point of the graphics figure, the point called the anchor point. You can store points in Java using the Java Point class, which has two data members: x and y. You'll declare two Point objects, ptAnchor and ptDrawTo in your applet as follows:

```
public class dauber extends Applet implements ActionListener {

    Button buttonDraw, buttonLine, buttonOval, buttonRect, ➡
    button3DRect, buttonRounded;

➜   Point ptAnchor, ptDrawTo;

    boolean bMouseDownFlag = false;
    boolean bMouseUpFlag = false;
    boolean bDrawFlag = false;
    boolean bLineFlag = false;
    boolean bOvalFlag = false;
    boolean bRectFlag = false;
    boolean b3DRectFlag = false;
    boolean bRoundedFlag = false;
                    .
                    .
                    .
```

The x coordinate of a point like ptAnchor can be reached as ptAnchor.x and the y coordinate as prAnchor.y.

Adding MouseListener Support to Dauber

Now you'll learn how to add the mouse support you need. You'll implement the MouseListener interface for mousePressed() and mouseReleased(). In addition, you'll use the mouseDragged() method when you draw freehand with the mouse. To use mouseDragged(), you need a new listener—MouseMotionListener—and you add that as follows:

```
→public class dauber extends Applet implements ActionListener,
  MouseListener, MouseMotionListener {
```

Next, you'll install your new listeners:

```
public class dauber extends Applet implements ActionListener,
  MouseListener, MouseMotionListener {

     Button buttonDraw, buttonLine, buttonOval, buttonRect, ➡
     button3DRect, buttonRounded;

     Point ptAnchor, ptDrawTo;

     boolean bMouseDownFlag = false;
     boolean bMouseUpFlag = false;
     boolean bDrawFlag = false;
     boolean bLineFlag = false;
     boolean bOvalFlag = false;
     boolean bRectFlag = false;
     boolean b3DRectFlag = false;
     boolean bRoundedFlag = false;

     public void init() {

          buttonDraw = new Button("Draw Freehand");
          buttonLine = new Button("Line");
          buttonOval = new Button("Oval");
          buttonRect = new Button("Rect");
          button3DRect = new Button("3D Rect");
          buttonRounded = new Button("Round");
                 .
                 .
                 .
          button3DRect.addActionListener(this);
          add(buttonRounded);
          buttonRounded.addActionListener(this);
  →       addMouseListener(this);
  →       addMouseMotionListener(this);
     }
                 .
                 .
                 .
```

Having added the MouseMotionListener, next add the mouse methods you'll use `mousePressed()`, `mouseReleased()`, and `mouseDragged()`.

```
public void mousePressed(MouseEvent e){
        .
        .
        .
}

public void mouseReleased(MouseEvent e){
        .
        .
        .
}

public void mouseDragged(MouseEvent e){
        .
        .
        .
}

public void mouseClicked(MouseEvent e){}

public void mouseEntered(MouseEvent e){}

public void mouseExited(MouseEvent e){}

public void mouseMoved(MouseEvent e){}
```

The location at which the mouse went down is passed to you with the `e.getX()` and `e.getY()` methods, and you want to store that location in the anchor point object, `ptAnchor`. You can do so by creating a new object of the `Point` class, passing the x and y coordinates as arguments to the `Point` class's constructor:

```
    public void mousePressed(MouseEvent e){
➡         ptAnchor = new Point(e.getX(), e.getY());
           .
           .
           .
    }
```

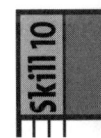

Skill 10

DO EXTRA ANCHOR POINTS WASTE MEMORY?

Memory-frugal C++ programmers may worry about lines of code like

```
ptAnchor = new Point(x, y);
```

because the user may click the mouse button several times while using your applet and so execute this line each time. What happens to the old anchor points—do those objects just remain in memory, taking up space? Should you delete them?

It turns out there is not a delete operator in Java like the one in C++. But that's not a big problem, because when no object variables refer to a particular object, Java deallocates that object's memory automatically (a process called *automatic garbage collection*). If you want to save memory space by getting rid of objects that are no longer needed, simply set their variables to null, for example:

```
framewindow = null;
```

Now that the mouse button is down, set the mouse boolean flags, bMouseDownFlag and bMouseUpFlag to indicate the following:

```
    public void mousePressed(MouseEvent e){
➜       bMouseDownFlag = true;
➜       bMouseUpFlag = false;
        ptAnchor = new Point(e.getX(), e.getY());
    }
```

You'll set the same flags when the mouse button goes back up in the mouseReleased() method.

Using *mouseReleased()* in Dauber

You can set the mouse boolean flags like this in the mouseReleased() method:

```
    public void mouseReleased(MouseEvent e){
➜       bMouseDownFlag = false;
➜       bMouseUpFlag = true;
            .
            .
            .
    }
```

Note that when the mouse button goes up the user is indicating the end point of the graphics figure—the drawto point. You can record the drawto point as follows, using the x and y location of the mouse.

```
public void mouseReleased(MouseEvent e){
    bMouseDownFlag = false;
    bMouseUpFlag = true;

    ptDrawTo = new Point(e.getX(), e.getY());
        .
        .
        .
}
```

→ (arrow pointing to `ptDrawTo = new Point(e.getX(), e.getY());` line)

Now you have the two points you'll need to draw your figure, ptAnchor and ptDrawTo. The actual drawing should be done in the paint() method—that is where you are passed an object of the Graphics class to use in painting your applet. To force the paint event to occur, call repaint() in the mouseReleased() method as follows:

```
public void mouseReleased(MouseEvent e){
    bMouseDownFlag = false;
    bMouseUpFlag = true;

    ptDrawTo = new Point(e.getX(), e.getY());
    repaint();
}
```

→ (arrow pointing to `repaint();` line)

Now you're ready to draw. So let's start with one of the most common graphics figures—the line.

Drawing Lines in Dauber

When the user clicks the Line button, they can draw lines in the applet, stretching from the point you called ptAnchor to the point you called ptDrawTo, as shown in Figure 10.7.

Now that the mouse button has been released, the paint() method is called, and you can draw the line. Add the paint() method now:

```
public void paint (Graphics g) {
        .
        .
        .
}
```

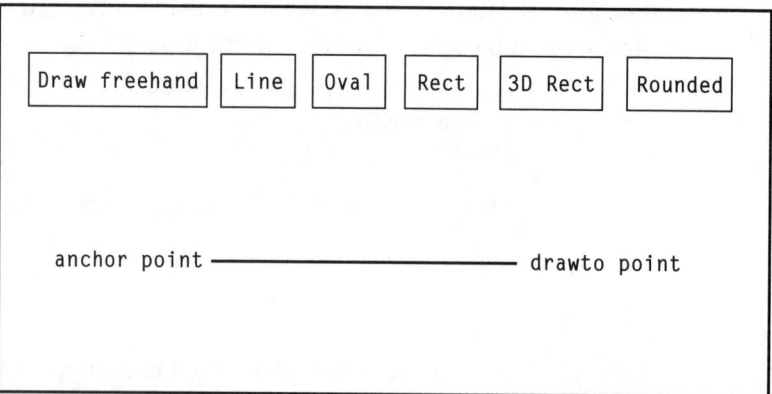

FIGURE 10.7: The line extends from the anchor point to the drawto point.

Because there can be many causes for the paint event, first check to make sure that the mouse button went up—by checking the variables bMouseUpFlag and bLineFlag to make sure you are supposed to be drawing a line. If so, you should draw your figure as follows:

```
public void paint (Graphics g) {

➤       if(bLineFlag && bMouseUpFlag){
                .
                .
                .
        }
}
```

If you are expected to draw a line, the line is to stretch from the anchor point to the drawto point. Use the Graphics class's drawLine() method to draw this line, and pass it the start and end coordinates of the line as follows:

```
public void paint (Graphics g) {

        if(bLineFlag && bMouseUpFlag){
➤               g.drawLine(ptAnchor.x, ptAnchor.y, ptDrawTo.x, ➡
ptDrawTo.y);
        }
}
```

And now your line appears in the applet, as shown in Figure 10.8. The drawLine() method is just one of the methods of the Graphics class—that class's methods appear in Table 10.1.

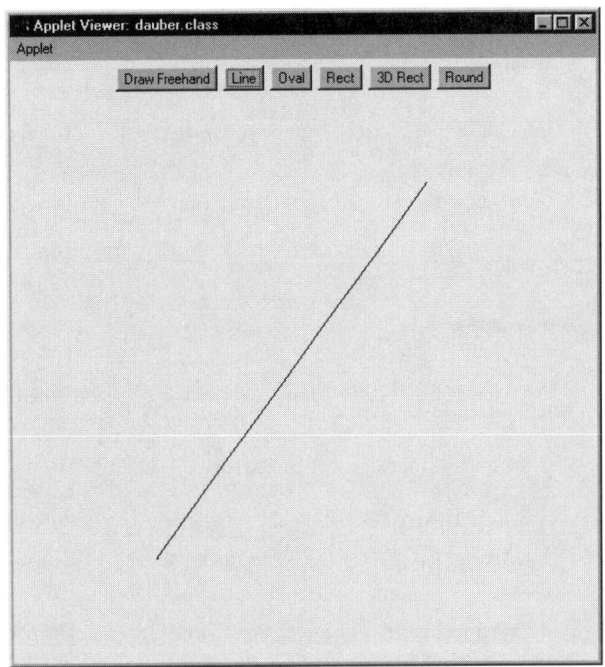

FIGURE 10.8: Drawing lines in the dauber applet

TABLE 10.1: The methods of the Graphics class

Method	Does This
Graphics()	Constructs a new Graphics object
clearRect(int, int, int, int)	Clears the given rectangle by filling it with the current background color
clipRect(int, int, int, int)	Intersects the current clip with the given rectangle
copyArea(int, int, int, int, int, int)	Copies an area of the Component
create()	Creates a new Graphics object that is a copy of this Graphics object

Skill 10

TABLE 10.1 CONTINUED: The methods of the Graphics class

Method	Does This
create(int, int, int, int)	Creates a new Graphics object based on this Graphics object but with a new translation and clip area
dispose()	Disposes of the system resources used by this graphics context
draw3DRect(int, int, int, int, boolean),	Draws a 3D highlighted outline of the given rectangle
drawArc(int, int, int, int, int, int)	Draws the outline of an arc covering the given rectangle, starting at startAngle and extending for arcAngle degrees, using the current color
drawBytes(byte[], int, int, int, int)	Draws the given bytes using the current font and color
drawChars(char[], int, int, int, int)	Draws the given characters using the current font and color
drawImage(Image, int, int, Color, ImageObserver)	Draws as much of the given image as is currently available at the given coordinate with the given solid background
drawImage(Image, int, int, ImageObserver)	Draws as much of the given image as is currently available at the given coordinate (x, y)
drawImage(Image, int, int, int, int, Color, ImageObserver)	Draws as much of the given image as has already been scaled to fit inside the given rectangle with the given solid background color
drawImage(Image, int, int, int, int,) ImageObserver	Draws as much of the given image as has already been scaled to fit inside the given rectangle
drawImage(Image, int, int, int, int, int, int, int, int, Color, ImageObserver)	Draws as much of the given area of the given image as is currently available, scaling it to fit inside the given area of destination drawable surface with the given solid the background color
drawImage(Image, int, int, int, int, int, int, int, int, ImageObserver)	Draws as much of the given area of the given image as is available, scaling it to fit inside the given area of the destination drawable surface
drawLine(int, int, int, int)	Draws a line between the coordinates (x1,y1) and (x2,y2) using the current color

TABLE 10.1 CONTINUED: The methods of the Graphics class

Method	Does This
`drawOval(int, int, int, int)`	Draws the outline of an oval covering the given rectangle using the current color
`drawPolygon(int[], int[], int)`	Draws the outline of a polygon defined by arrays of x coordinates and y coordinates using the current color
`drawPolygon(Polygon)`	Draws the outline of a polygon defined by the given Polygon object using the current color
`drawPolyline(int[], int[], int)`	Draws a sequence of connected lines defined by arrays of x coordinates and y coordinates using the current color
`drawRect(int, int, int, int)`	Draws the outline of the given rectangle using the current color
`drawRoundRect(int, int, int, int, int, int)`	Draws the outline of the given rounded corner rectangle using the current color
`drawString(String, int, int)`	Draws the given String using the current font and color
`fill3DRect(int, int, int, int, boolean)`	Paints a 3D highlighted rectangle filled with the current color
`fillArc(int, int, int, int, int, int)`	Fills an arc bounded by the given rectangle, starting at startAngle and extending for arcAngle degrees, with the current color
`fillOval(int, int, int, int)`	Fills an oval bounded by the given rectangle with the current color
`fillPolygon(int[], int[], int)`	Fills a polygon defined by arrays of coordinates and y coordinates with the current color using an even-odd fill rule
`fillPolygon(Polygon)`	Fills the polygon defined by the given Polygon object with the current color using an even-odd fill rule
`fillRect(int, int, int, int)`	Fills the given rectangle with the current color
`fillRoundRect(int, int, int, int, int, int)`	Fills the given rounded corner rectangle with the current color
`finalize()`	Disposes of this graphics context once it is no longer referenced

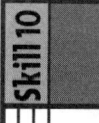
Skill 10

TABLE 10.1 CONTINUED: The methods of the Graphics class

Method	Does This
getClip()	Returns a Shape object representing the current clipping area
getClipBounds()	Returns the bounding rectangle of the current clipping area
getClipRect()	Deprecated. Replaced by getClipBounds()
getColor()	Gets the current color
getFont()	Gets the current font
getFontMetrics()	Gets the font metrics of the current font
getFontMetrics(Font)	Gets the font metrics for the given font
setClip(int, int, int, int)	Sets the current clip to the rectangle given by the given coordinates
setClip(Shape)	Set the current clipping area to an arbitrary clip shape
setColor(Color)	Sets the current color to the given color
setFont(Font)	Sets the font for all subsequent text rendering operations
setPaintMode()	Sets the logical pixel operation function to the Paint, or overwrite mode
setXORMode(Color)	Sets the logical pixel operation function to the XOR mode, which alternates pixels between the current color and a new given XOR color
toString()	Returns a String object representing this Graphics object's value
translate(int, int)	Translates the origin of the graphics context to a point in the current coordinate system

Now that you've learned how to create lines, it's time to move on to creating circles and ovals.

Creating Circles and Ovals in Dauber

When the user clicks the Oval tool button, they can draw circles and ovals, as shown in Figure 10.9.

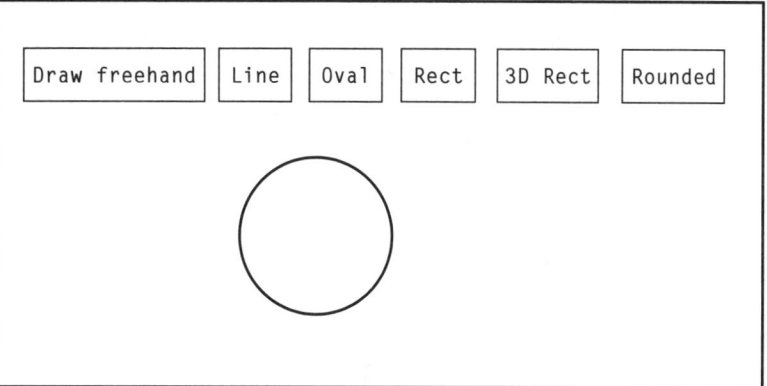

FIGURE 10.9:   Drawing a circle

Let's work on creating circles now. You can do that with the Graphics class's drawOval() method (with which you can draw both ovals and circles). This method—like the other graphics methods you'll see in this chapter—works slightly differently from the drawLine() method you just used. In drawLine(), you only needed to pass the (x, y) coordinates of the beginning and end of the line. With other graphics methods like drawOval() and drawRect(), you need to pass the upper-left corner of the figure's bounding rectangle and its width and height:

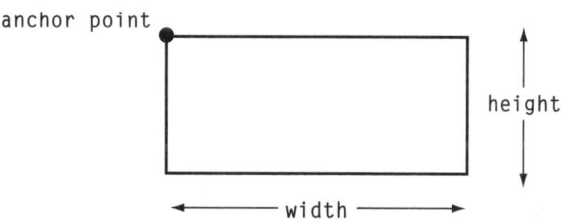

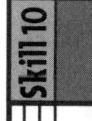

It looks as if you can pass the anchor point as the upper-left corner of the figure's bounding rectangle. However, there is no special reason that the user would have placed the anchor point at the upper left—in fact, the anchor point may even be at the lower right. Therefore, reorder the anchor point and the drawto point to make sure that the anchor point is at the upper left and the drawto point is at the lower right. (The Java graphics methods require that you pass them the point you know to be the upper left of the image you want to draw.)

You can reorder these points in the mouseReleased() method, just before you paint the graphics figure the user has requested in your applet. As mentioned, you won't need to rearrange the two bounding points for the drawLine() method, but you will for the other graphics methods. For that reason, first make sure you are not drawing a line by checking the bLineFlag variable in an if statement, as follows:

```
        public void mouseReleased(MouseEvent e){
            bMouseDownFlag = false;
            bMouseUpFlag = true;
            ptDrawTo = new Point(e.getX(), e.getY());
→           if(!bLineFlag){
                        .
                        .
                        .
            }
            repaint();
        }
```

If you are not drawing a line, you can continue on, rearranging the point named ptAnchor to be the top left of your figure's bounding rectangle and the ptDrawTo point to be the bottom left of the bounding rectangle. You can do that simply by numerically comparing values in each of these points.

You can use the Java Math class's min() and max() methods to compare values. The min() method takes two values and returns the lesser; the max() method takes two values and returns the greater. That means that you can sort the anchor and drawto points as follows:

```
        public void mouseReleased(MouseEvent e){
            bMouseDownFlag = false;
            bMouseUpFlag = true;
            ptDrawTo = new Point(e.getX(), e.getY());
            If(!bLineFlag){
→           ptDrawTo = new Point(Math.max(e.getX(), ptAnchor.x), ➡
    Math.max(e.getY(), ptAnchor.y));
→               ptAnchor = new Point(Math.min(e.getX(), ptAnchor.x), ➡
    Math.min(e.getY(), ptAnchor.y));
            }
            repaint();
        }
```

Here you are using the Java Math class, and that class is part of the java.lang package. You need to import that class in the beginning of your applet as follows so Java can find the min() and max() methods:

```
 import java.awt.Graphics;
 import java.awt.*;
 import java.awt.event.*;
→import java.lang.Math;
 import java.applet.Applet;

 public class dauber extends Applet implements ActionListener, ➡
 MouseListener, MouseMotionListener {

      Button buttonDraw, buttonLine, buttonOval, buttonRect, ➡
 button3DRect, buttonRounded;
            .
            .
            .
```

Now you're ready to draw ovals and circles with the drawOval() method. Place the code to draw these figures in the paint() method, which currently looks like this:

```
        public void paint (Graphics g) {
              int loop_index;
              int drawWidth, drawHeight;

              if(bLineFlag && bMouseUpFlag){
                   g.drawLine(ptAnchor.x, ptAnchor.y, ptDrawTo.x, ➡
    ptDrawTo.y);
                   }
→             if(bOvalFlag && bMouseUpFlag){
→                  drawWidth = ptDrawTo.x - ptAnchor.x;
→                  drawHeight = ptDrawTo.y - ptAnchor.y;
→                  g.drawOval(ptAnchor.x, ptAnchor.y, drawWidth, ➡
    drawHeight);
                        .
                        .
                        .

          }
```

Here, by examining the boolean flag bMouseUpFlag, check to make sure that the user has released the mouse button and that you should draw the oval or

circle. If the flag is set, you are supposed to draw a figure. Next, check the
bOvalFlag boolean flag to see if you are supposed to be drawing an oval:

```
public void paint (Graphics g) {
        int loop_index;
        int drawWidth, drawHeight;

        if(bLineFlag && bMouseUpFlag){
                g.drawLine(ptAnchor.x, ptAnchor.y, ptDrawTo.x, ➡
    ptDrawTo.y);
        }
➡        if(bOvalFlag && bMouseUpFlag){
                .
                .
                .
➡        }
```

To draw the oval or circle, you'll need the width and height of the figure. Now
that you've ordered your drawto and anchor points, you can find those dimensions by simple subtraction, as follows:

```
public void paint (Graphics g) {
        int loop_index;
        int drawWidth, drawHeight;

        if(bLineFlag && bMouseUpFlag){
                g.drawLine(ptAnchor.x, ptAnchor.y, ptDrawTo.x, ➡
    ptDrawTo.y);
        }
        if(bOvalFlag && bMouseUpFlag){
➡                drawWidth = ptDrawTo.x - ptAnchor.x;
➡                drawHeight = ptDrawTo.y - ptAnchor.y;
                .
                .
                .

        }
```

You can use the Graphics class drawOval() method to draw the oval or circle.
Pass it the coordinates of the upper-left point of the figure's bounding rectangle—
that is, your anchor point—and the figure's width and height:

```
public void paint (Graphics g) {
        int loop_index;
        int drawWidth, drawHeight;

        if(bLineFlag && bMouseUpFlag){
```

```
                g.drawLine(ptAnchor.x, ptAnchor.y, ptDrawTo.x, ➡
      ptDrawTo.y);
              }
          if(bOvalFlag && bMouseUpFlag){
              drawWidth = ptDrawTo.x - ptAnchor.x;
              drawHeight = ptDrawTo.y - ptAnchor.y;
➡             g.drawOval(ptAnchor.x, ptAnchor.y, drawWidth, ➡
      drawHeight);
                    .
                    .
                    .

      }
```

Now you have drawn ovals and circles. The circles and ovals appear on the screen, as shown in Figure 10.10.

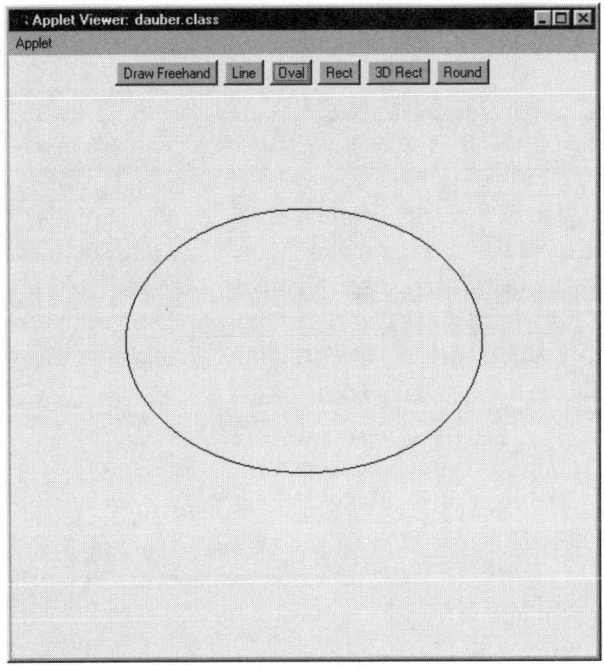

FIGURE 10.10:   Your dauber applet can draw ovals.

Using Dauber to Draw Rectangles

The next step is to draw rectangles. The user can draw rectangles by clicking the Rect button and using the mouse, as shown in Figure 10.11.

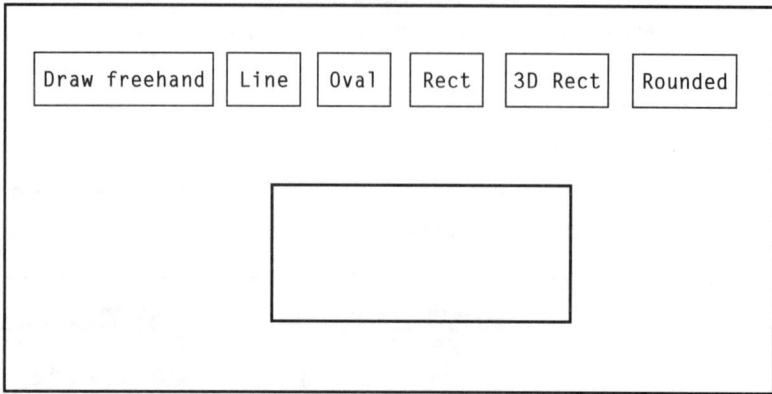

FIGURE 10.11:   Drawing a rectangle in dauber

You've already included all the mouse support that you'll need to draw rectangles. The Graphics method you'll use to draw rectangles is drawRect(), and you'll use that method in your applet's paint() method. You'll need to pass the upper-left point of your rectangle and its width and height. First, make sure that you are supposed to be drawing rectangles by checking the bRectFlag boolean flag (set when the user clicks the Rect button):

```
        public void paint (Graphics g) {
              int loop_index;
              int drawWidth, drawHeight;

              if(bLineFlag && bMouseUpFlag){
                    g.drawLine(ptAnchor.x, ptAnchor.y, ptDrawTo.x, ➥
        ptDrawTo.y);
              }
              if(bOvalFlag && bMouseUpFlag){
                    drawWidth = ptDrawTo.x - ptAnchor.x;
                    drawHeight = ptDrawTo.y - ptAnchor.y;
                    g.drawOval(ptAnchor.x, ptAnchor.y, drawWidth, ➥
        drawHeight);
              }
➜             if(bRectFlag && bMouseUpFlag){
                          .
                          .
                          .
➜             }
```

If you are indeed drawing rectangles, use the `drawRect()` method, passing it the four parameters it needs: the upper-left point of the rectangle's x and y coordinates, as well as the rectangle's width and height:

```
public void paint (Graphics g) {
    int loop_index;
    int drawWidth, drawHeight;

    if(bLineFlag && bMouseUpFlag){
        g.drawLine(ptAnchor.x, ptAnchor.y, ptDrawTo.x, ➥
ptDrawTo.y);
    }
    if(bOvalFlag && bMouseUpFlag){
        drawWidth = ptDrawTo.x - ptAnchor.x;
        drawHeight = ptDrawTo.y - ptAnchor.y;
        g.drawOval(ptAnchor.x, ptAnchor.y, drawWidth, ➥
drawHeight);
    }
    if(bRectFlag && bMouseUpFlag){
➜       drawWidth = ptDrawTo.x - ptAnchor.x;
➜       drawHeight = ptDrawTo.y - ptAnchor.y;
➜       g.drawRect(ptAnchor.x, ptAnchor.y, drawWidth, ➥
drawHeight);
    }
```

Now the user can draw rectangles in your dauber applet, as shown in Figure 10.12.

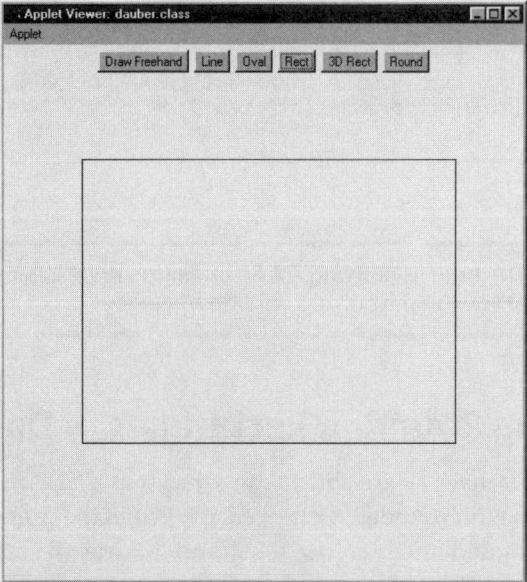

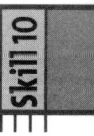

FIGURE 10.12:   Your dauber applet can draw rectangles.

Drawing 3D Rectangles in Dauber

It's also theoretically possible to draw 3D rectangles in dauber; that process works just as it did for drawing rectangles, except that you use the `draw3DRect()` method (adding a final parameter set to true is supposed to make the rectangle appear 3D, or raised):

```
public void paint (Graphics g) {
        int loop_index;
        int drawWidth, drawHeight;

        if(bLineFlag && bMouseUpFlag){
            g.drawLine(ptAnchor.x, ptAnchor.y, ptDrawTo.x, ➡
ptDrawTo.y);
        }
        if(bOvalFlag && bMouseUpFlag){
            drawWidth = ptDrawTo.x - ptAnchor.x;
            drawHeight = ptDrawTo.y - ptAnchor.y;
            g.drawOval(ptAnchor.x, ptAnchor.y, drawWidth, ➡
drawHeight);
        }
        if(bRectFlag && bMouseUpFlag){
            drawWidth = ptDrawTo.x - ptAnchor.x;
            drawHeight = ptDrawTo.y - ptAnchor.y;
            g.drawRect(ptAnchor.x, ptAnchor.y, drawWidth, ➡
drawHeight);
        }
➡       if(b3DRectFlag && bMouseUpFlag){
➡           drawWidth = ptDrawTo.x - ptAnchor.x;
➡           drawHeight = ptDrawTo.y - ptAnchor.y;
➡           g.draw3DRect(ptAnchor.x, ptAnchor.y, ➡
drawWidth,drawHeight, true);
                .
                .
                .
```

NOTE The truth is, drawing a 3D rectangle is impossible; it results in simply a rectangle—at least in the current version of Java.

Drawing Rounded Rectangles in Dauber

Now that you are able to draw rectangles, it turns out that you can draw rectangles with rounded corners easily. When the user clicks the button you've labeled Rounded, they can use the mouse to draw rounded rectangles, as shown in Figure 10.13.

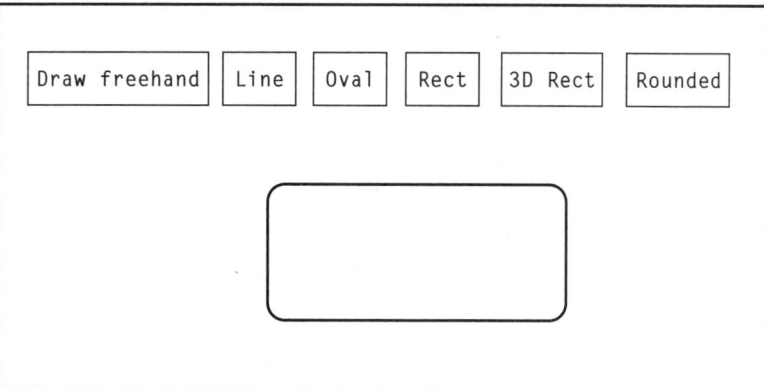

FIGURE 10.13:   Drawing a rectangle with rounded corners

Because you've stored the anchor and drawto points already, all the mouse handling has already been done when it comes time to draw your new rounded rectangle—you can determine the rectangle's width and height, and you already know the location of its upper-left corner. All you have to do in the paint() method is check if you are supposed to draw a rounded rectangle by examining the bRoundedFlag boolean flag:

```
public void paint (Graphics g) {
      int loop_index;
      int drawWidth, drawHeight;

      if(bLineFlag && bMouseUpFlag){
            g.drawLine(ptAnchor.x, ptAnchor.y, ptDrawTo.x, ➥
ptDrawTo.y);
      }
      if(bOvalFlag && bMouseUpFlag){
            drawWidth = ptDrawTo.x - ptAnchor.x;
            drawHeight = ptDrawTo.y - ptAnchor.y;
            g.drawOval(ptAnchor.x, ptAnchor.y, drawWidth, ➥
drawHeight);
                           .
                           .
                           .

➔          if(bRoundedFlag && bMouseUpFlag){
                           .
                           .
                           .

➔          }
```

Skill 10

If you are supposed to draw rounded rectangles, you can call the `Graphics` method `drawRoundRect()`. This method takes the usual parameters—the coordinates of the upper left of the rectangle, as well as its height and width—and two new parameters as well. These new parameters control the rounding of the corners. The first parameter is the width of the rounding arc (in pixels) and the second parameter is the height of the rounding arc. In this example, give both of these parameters the value of 10:

```
public void paint (Graphics g) {
    int loop_index;
    int drawWidth, drawHeight;

    if(bLineFlag && bMouseUpFlag){
        g.drawLine(ptAnchor.x, ptAnchor.y, ptDrawTo.x, ➡
    ptDrawTo.y);
    }
    if(bOvalFlag && bMouseUpFlag){
        drawWidth = ptDrawTo.x - ptAnchor.x;
        drawHeight = ptDrawTo.y - ptAnchor.y;
        g.drawOval(ptAnchor.x, ptAnchor.y, drawWidth, ➡
    drawHeight);

                            .
                            .
                            .

    if(bRoundedFlag && bMouseUpFlag){
➜       drawWidth = ptDrawTo.x - ptAnchor.x;
➜       drawHeight = ptDrawTo.y - ptAnchor.y;
➜       g.drawRoundRect(ptAnchor.x, ptAnchor.y, drawWidth, ➡
    drawHeight, 10, 10);
    }
```

And now the user can draw rounded rectangles, as shown in Figure 10.14.

That's it for the standard graphics figures: lines, circles, ovals, rectangles, and rounded rectangles. However, you can go one better—you can support freehand drawing in your dauber applet, letting the user draw with the mouse. You'll learn all about that that next.

Dauber and Freehand Drawing

After the user clicks the freehand drawing tool—the button labeled Draw Freehand—they can draw with the mouse, as shown in Figure 10.15.

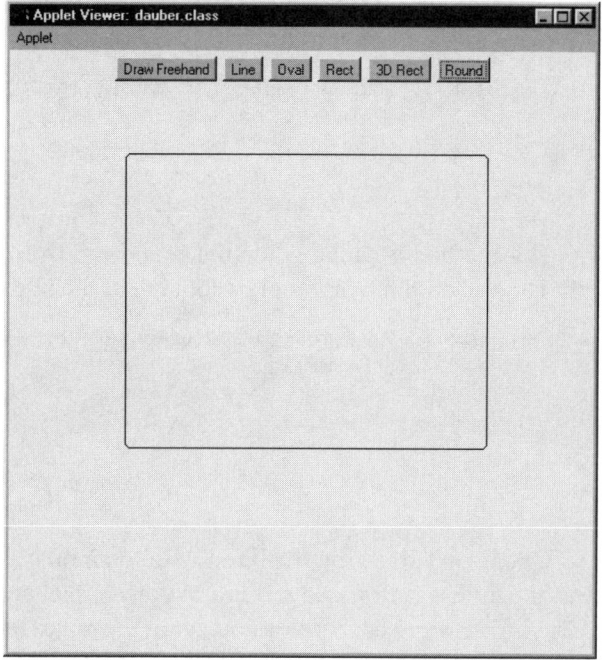

FIGURE 10.14: Your dauber applet can draw rounded rectangles.

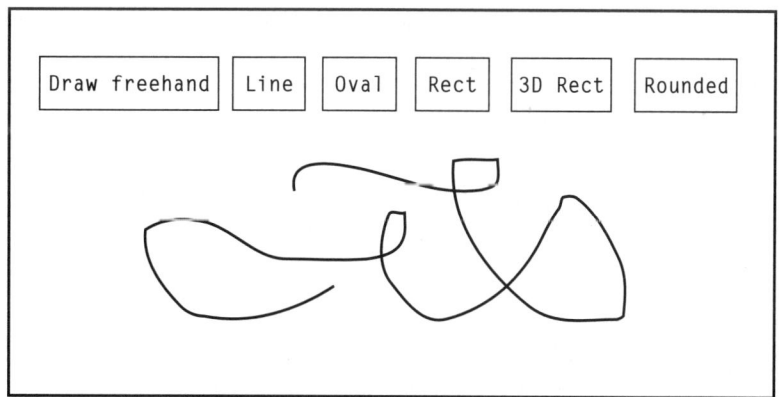

FIGURE 10.15: A freehand drawing

The user can do this by pressing the mouse button at some starting location in your applet and dragging the mouse. To handle this new capability, you can use the mouseDrag() method:

```
public void mouseDragged(MouseEvent e){
       .
       .
       .

}
```

This method is called when the user drags the mouse. You can check if they have selected the Draw tool by looking at the bDrawFlag boolean flag:

```
public void mouseDragged(MouseEvent e){
     if(bDrawFlag){
         .
         .
         .

     }
}
```

One way of drawing freehand with the mouse is to record the mouse locations as the mouse is dragged around in your applet and then "connect the dots." That is, you can store each point you get in the mouseDrag event and then draw from point to point in the paint() method.

Start that process by storing the points you get in the mouseDrag event in an array of Point objects named, say, pts[]. You can declare an array of, say, 1000 Point objects. The syntax of declaring an array in Java is like this: Type name[] = new Type[number]. This means you can declare your array of points as follows:

```
import java.awt.Graphics;
import java.awt.*;
import java.awt.event.*;
import java.lang.Math;
import java.applet.Applet;

public class dauber extends Applet implements ActionListener, ➥
MouseListener, MouseMotionListener {

     Button buttonDraw, buttonLine, buttonOval, buttonRect, ➥
button3DRect, buttonRounded;

➜    Point pts[] = new Point[1000];
     Point ptAnchor, ptDrawTo;
         .
         .
         .
```

> **NOTE** Technically, Java only supports one-dimensional arrays. Two-dimensional arrays are really arrays of one-dimensional arrays. For example, here is how you declare and initialize a 3 x 3 two-dimensional array of String objects:
>
> ```
> String stringarray[][] =
> {
>     {"Hello", "there", "USA"},
>     {"Hello", "there", "Asia"},
>     {"Hello", "there", "World!"},
>
> };
> ```

Now you've set up the array of points to store the mouse locations as the user moves the mouse. In addition, you will need an index value in that array so that you will be able to tell where to add the next point and how many points there are to draw. You can call that array index ptindex:

```
import java.awt.Graphics;
import java.awt.*;
import java.awt.event.*;
import java.lang.Math;
import java.applet.Applet;

public class dauber extends Applet implements ActionListener, ➡
MouseListener, MouseMotionListener {

    Button buttonDraw, buttonLine, buttonOval, buttonRect,
button3DRect, buttonRounded;

    Point pts[] = new Point[1000];
    Point ptAnchor, ptDrawTo;
➡   int ptindex = 0;
          .
          .
          .
```

Now your point array is set up, and you can add points to it in the mouseDrag() method. The point passed to you is the current location of the mouse, so add that to your points[] array this way, incrementing ptindex after you have done so:

```
    public void mouseDragged(MouseEvent e){
        if(bDrawFlag){
➡           pts[ptindex] = new Point(e.getX(), e.getY());
➡           ptindex++;
                .
                .
                .

        }
    }
```

 **NOTE**

The C++ operator ++ simply increments a variable. Used this way, as a postfix operator: pts[ptindex++] = new Point(x, y);, it adds 1 to the variable ptindex after the whole statement is executed. Used as a prefix operator: pts[++ptindex] = new Point(x, y);, it adds 1 to ptindex before the rest of the statement is executed, and so you use that new, incremented value as the array index. The operator ++ is an operator that may be overloaded, so you should not assume that it always adds 1 when used—it may have been redefined for a certain class to add, say, 1000, or even the characters "abc".

Add a new point made from the x and y parameters passed to you, store it in the pts[] array, and then increment the array index named ptindex. After you have stored the point, call repaint() to draw the points in the array on the screen:

```
public void mouseDragged(MouseEvent e){
        if(bDrawFlag){
            pts[ptindex] = new Point(e.getX(), e.getY());
            ptindex++;
➡           repaint();
        }
    }
```

All that remains is to add code to the paint() method to draw the points in the pts[] array. First, in the paint() method, check to make sure you are supposed to be drawing freehand by examining the bDrawFlag boolean flag:

```
        public void paint (Graphics g) {
            int loop_index;
            int drawWidth, drawHeight;

            if(bLineFlag && bMouseUpFlag){
                g.drawLine(ptAnchor.x, ptAnchor.y, ptDrawTo.x, ➡
ptDrawTo.y);
            }
            if(bOvalFlag && bMouseUpFlag){
                drawWidth = ptDrawTo.x - ptAnchor.x;
                drawHeight = ptDrawTo.y - ptAnchor.y;
                g.drawOval(ptAnchor.x, ptAnchor.y, drawWidth, ➡
drawHeight);
                        .
                        .
                        .
➡           if(bDrawFlag){
                        .
                        .
                        .
➡           }
        }
```

If the user is to draw freehand, that means you will draw the points in the `pts[]` array. You can loop over all those points, from 0 to the value in `ptindex` with a `for` loop. In general, this loop looks just like it would in C or C++:

```
for(initial statement; conditional test; increment statement){
        loop body
}
```

You use the initial statement to set up a loop index, the conditional test to see if you have looped enough, and the increment statement to increment (or decrement) your loop index. In this case, you can loop over all the points in the `points[]` array as follows:

```
        public void paint (Graphics g) {
                int loop_index;
                int drawWidth, drawHeight;

                if(bLineFlag && bMouseUpFlag){
                        g.drawLine(ptAnchor.x, ptAnchor.y, ptDrawTo.x, ➥
ptDrawTo.y);
                }
                if(bOvalFlag && bMouseUpFlag){
                        drawWidth = ptDrawTo.x - ptAnchor.x;
                        drawHeight = ptDrawTo.y - ptAnchor.y;
                        g.drawOval(ptAnchor.x, ptAnchor.y, drawWidth, ➥
drawHeight);
                            .
                            .
                            .
                if(bRoundedFlag && bMouseUpFlag){
                        drawWidth = ptDrawTo.x - ptAnchor.x;
                        drawHeight = ptDrawTo.y - ptAnchor.y;
                        g.drawRoundRect(ptAnchor.x, ptAnchor.y, drawWidth, ➥
drawHeight, 10, 10);
                }
                if(bDrawFlag){
➥for(loop_index = 0; loop_index < ptindex - 1; loop_index++){
                            .
                            .
                            .
➥               }
                }
        }
```

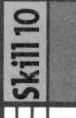

NOTE   There are three types of loops in Java—for, while, and do loops. Their syntax looks like this:

```
for(initial statement; conditional test; increment statement){
        loop body
}

while(conditional test){
        loop body
}

do{
        loop body
}while(conditional test(/)[/]
```

You will then connect the dots, drawing a line from one point to the next, which will display a continuous freehand drawing on the screen. You can draw all these line segments with the Graphics drawLine() method:

```
public void paint (Graphics g) {
        int loop_index;
        int drawWidth, drawHeight;

        if(bLineFlag && bMouseUpFlag){
                g.drawLine(ptAnchor.x, ptAnchor.y, ptDrawTo.x, ➡
ptDrawTo.y);
        }
        if(bOvalFlag && bMouseUpFlag){
                drawWidth = ptDrawTo.x - ptAnchor.x;
                drawHeight = ptDrawTo.y - ptAnchor.y;
                g.drawOval(ptAnchor.x, ptAnchor.y, drawWidth, ➡
drawHeight);
                            .
                            .
                            .
        if(bDrawFlag){
                for(loop_index = 0; loop_index < ptindex - 1; ➡
loop_index++){
➡                       g.drawLine(pts[loop_index].x, pts[loop_index].y, ➡
pts[loop_index + 1].x, pts[loop_index + 1].y);
                }
        }
}
```

NOTE
You may wonder why you used lines to connect the points you stored when the mouse moved across our applet, instead of just drawing the points themselves. The reason is that the mouseDrag() method is not called for each pixel the mouse moves over—there are only a limited number of mouse events generated each second, and if you just drew the individual points you got, you'd end up with a series of unconnected points trailing over the screen.

That's all there is to it—now run the dauber applet, and click the Draw button. When you do, you can draw freehand with the mouse, as shown in Figure 10.16. That's it for freehand drawing—and that's it for the dauber applet. You've come far in this applet—from handling the mouse to drawing graphics like lines, circles, ovals, rectangles, and more. You've gotten a good start in graphics handling. You can find the code for this applet in dauber.java.

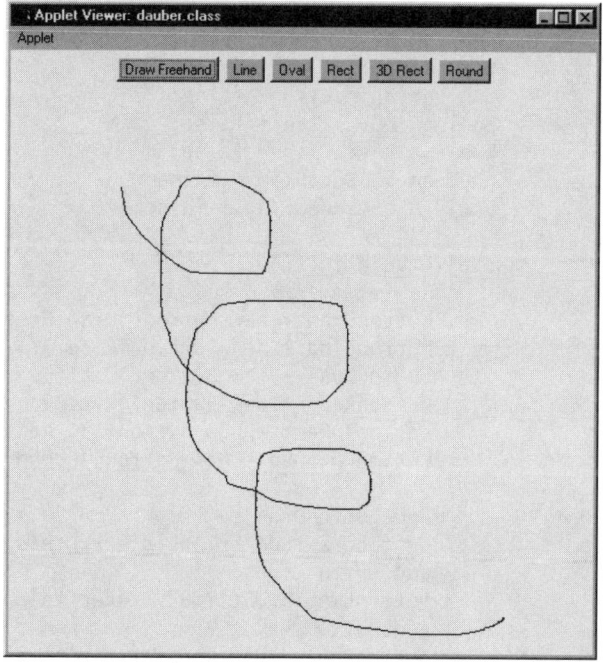

FIGURE 10.16: Your dauber applet supports freehand drawing.

C **dauber.java**

```java
import java.awt.Graphics;
import java.awt.*;
import java.awt.event.*;
import java.lang.Math;
import java.applet.Applet;

public class dauber extends Applet implements ActionListener, ➥
MouseListener, MouseMotionListener {

    Button buttonDraw, buttonLine, buttonOval, buttonRect, ➥
button3DRect, buttonRounded;

    Point pts[] = new Point[1000];
    Point ptAnchor, ptDrawTo;
    int ptindex = 0;

    boolean bMouseDownFlag = false;
    boolean bMouseUpFlag = false;
    boolean bDrawFlag = false;
    boolean bLineFlag = false;
    boolean bOvalFlag = false;
    boolean bRectFlag = false;
    boolean b3DRectFlag = false;
    boolean bRoundedFlag = false;

    public void init() {

        buttonDraw = new Button("Draw Freehand");
        buttonLine = new Button("Line");
        buttonOval = new Button("Oval");
        buttonRect = new Button("Rect");
        button3DRect = new Button("3D Rect");
        buttonRounded = new Button("Round");

        add(buttonDraw);
        buttonDraw.addActionListener(this);
        add(buttonLine);
        buttonLine.addActionListener(this);
        add(buttonOval);
        buttonOval.addActionListener(this);
        add(buttonRect);
        buttonRect.addActionListener(this);
        add(button3DRect);
        button3DRect.addActionListener(this);
        add(buttonRounded);
```

```
            buttonRounded.addActionListener(this);
            addMouseListener(this);
            addMouseMotionListener(this);
        }

    public void mousePressed(MouseEvent e){
        bMouseDownFlag = true;
        bMouseUpFlag = false;
        ptAnchor = new Point(e.getX(), e.getY());
    }

    public void mouseReleased(MouseEvent e){
        bMouseDownFlag = false;
        bMouseUpFlag = true;
        ptDrawTo = new Point(e.getX(), e.getY());
            if(!bLineFlag){
            ptDrawTo = new Point(Math.max(e.getX(), ptAnchor.x), ➥
Math.max(e.getY(), ptAnchor.y));
            ptAnchor = new Point(Math.min(e.getX(), ptAnchor.x), ➥
Math.min(e.getY(), ptAnchor.y));
        }
        repaint();
    }

    public void mouseDragged(MouseEvent e){
        if(bDrawFlag){
            pts[ptindex] = new Point(e.getX(), e.getY());
            ptindex++;
            repaint();
        }
    }

    public void mouseClicked(MouseEvent e){}

    public void mouseEntered(MouseEvent e){}

    public void mouseExited(MouseEvent e){}

    public void mouseMoved(MouseEvent e){}

    public void paint (Graphics g) {
        int loop_index;
        int drawWidth, drawHeight;

        if(bLineFlag && bMouseUpFlag){
            g.drawLine(ptAnchor.x, ptAnchor.y, ptDrawTo.x, ➥
ptDrawTo.y);
        }
```

```
            if(bOvalFlag && bMouseUpFlag){
                 drawWidth = ptDrawTo.x - ptAnchor.x;
                 drawHeight = ptDrawTo.y - ptAnchor.y;
                 g.drawOval(ptAnchor.x, ptAnchor.y, drawWidth, ➥
drawHeight);
            }
            if(bRectFlag && bMouseUpFlag){
                 drawWidth = ptDrawTo.x - ptAnchor.x;
                 drawHeight = ptDrawTo.y - ptAnchor.y;
                 g.drawRect(ptAnchor.x, ptAnchor.y, drawWidth, ➥
drawHeight);
            }
            if(b3DRectFlag && bMouseUpFlag){
                 drawWidth = ptDrawTo.x - ptAnchor.x;
                 drawHeight = ptDrawTo.y - ptAnchor.y;
                 g.draw3DRect(ptAnchor.x, ptAnchor.y, drawWidth, ➥
drawHeight, true);
            }
            if(bRoundedFlag && bMouseUpFlag){
                 drawWidth = ptDrawTo.x - ptAnchor.x;
                 drawHeight = ptDrawTo.y - ptAnchor.y;
                 g.drawRoundRect(ptAnchor.x, ptAnchor.y, drawWidth, ➥
drawHeight, 10, 10);
            }
            if(bDrawFlag){
                 for(loop_index = 0; loop_index < ptindex - 1; ➥
loop_index++){
                      g.drawLine(pts[loop_index].x, pts[loop_index].y, ➥
pts[loop_index + 1].x, pts[loop_index + 1].y);
                 }
            }
        }

    public void actionPerformed(ActionEvent e){
            if(e.getSource() == buttonDraw){
                 bDrawFlag = !bDrawFlag;
                 bLineFlag = false;
                 bOvalFlag = false;
                 bRectFlag = false;
                 b3DRectFlag = false;
                 bRoundedFlag = false;
            }
            if(e.getSource() == buttonLine){
                 bLineFlag = !bLineFlag;
                 bDrawFlag = false;
                 bOvalFlag = false;
                 bRectFlag = false;
                 b3DRectFlag = false;
```

```
                    bRoundedFlag = false;
            }
            if(e.getSource() == buttonOval){
                bOvalFlag = !bOvalFlag;
                bLineFlag = false;
                bDrawFlag = false;
                bRectFlag = false;
                b3DRectFlag = false;
                bRoundedFlag = false;
            }
            if(e.getSource() == buttonRect){
                bRectFlag = !bRectFlag;
                bLineFlag = false;
                bOvalFlag = false;
                bDrawFlag = false;
                b3DRectFlag = false;
                bRoundedFlag = false;
            }
            if(e.getSource() == button3DRect){
                b3DRectFlag = !b3DRectFlag;
                bLineFlag = false;
                bOvalFlag = false;
                bRectFlag = false;
                bDrawFlag = false;
                bRoundedFlag = false;
            }
            if(e.getSource() == buttonRounded){
                bRoundedFlag = !bRoundedFlag;
                bLineFlag = false;
                bOvalFlag = false;
                bRectFlag = false;
                b3DRectFlag = false;
                bDrawFlag = false;
            }
        }
    }
```

You've gotten your dauber applet working. You're able to use the mouse to receive input and draw lines, rectangles, 3D rectangles, ovals, circles, and rounded rectangles. You've added quite a few new talents to your Java arsenal in this skill. There's one more ability we're going to add in this chapter—printing.

Printing from Java

It is possible to print graphics from Java 1.1 and Java 1.2 programs, and we'll take a look at that here. In this case, our goal might be to print a simple graphics figure—just a box with a diagonal line.

You'll need the getToolkit() method here, so start by deriving a class named printgraphics from the Frame class because that class includes the getToolkit() method:

```
class printgraphics extends Frame {
                .
                .
                .
}
```

Java Security

You may ask why we don't derive the class from the Applet class (the Applet class also contains the getToolkit() method). The answer is that in Java 1.1 and Java 1.2, security is currently set up so that applets can't print to a printer. However, Java *applications* can, and you'll learn how to install this new printgraphics class in a Java application in a minute. Next, you'll add a constructor to the new printgraphics class like this:

```
  class printgraphics extends Frame {
→     printgraphics() {
                .
                .
                .
→     }
  }
```

Here in the printgraphics constructor, create an object of class PrintJob, indicating what object you want the print job for, the name you want to give the print job, and a reference to a Properties object, which you will set to null:

```
  class printgraphics extends Frame {
      printgraphics() {
→PrintJob p = getToolkit().getPrintJob(this, "Print graphics", null);
                .
                .
                .
      }
  }
```

Now you have a print job, and the next step is to get a `Graphics` object for this print job so you can actually create the graphics you want to print. You can do that with the `getGraphics()` method:

```
class printgraphics extends Frame {
    printgraphics() {
        PrintJob p = getToolkit().getPrintJob(this, ➡
"Print graphics", null);
➡        Graphics g = p.getGraphics();
                 .
                 .
                 .

    }
}
```

Now you can draw the graphics you want in the new `Graphics` object, just as you did in the dauber applet:

```
class printgraphics extends Frame {
    printgraphics() {
        PrintJob p = getToolkit().getPrintJob(this, "Print graphics",
        ➡ null);
        Graphics g = p.getGraphics();
➡        g.drawRect(1, 1, 40, 40);
➡        g.drawLine(1, 1, 40, 40);
                 .
                 .
                 .

    }
}
```

To start the printing, you have to dispose of the `Graphics` object, which you do with its `dispose()` method:

```
class printgraphics extends Frame {
    printgraphics() {
        PrintJob p = getToolkit().getPrintJob(this, "Print graphics",
        ➡ null);
        Graphics g = p.getGraphics();
        g.drawRect(1, 1, 40, 40);
        g.drawLine(1, 1, 40, 40);
➡        g.dispose();
                 .
                 .
                 .

    }
}
```

And finally, end the print job with the **end( )** method this way:

```
class printgraphics extends Frame {
    printgraphics() {
        PrintJob p = getToolkit().getPrintJob(this, ➡
"Print graphics", null);
        Graphics g = p.getGraphics();
        g.drawRect(1, 1, 40, 40);
        g.drawLine(1, 1, 40, 40);
        g.dispose();
➜       p.end();
    }
}
```

At this point, then, the graphics image you have drawn is printed. However, this class only does the printing—you still need to set up your application itself, and you'll learn to do that now.

Java Applications

You've only used applets in this book so far, because they are still the most popular type of Java programs, but Java can also create applications, which are not intended to be embedded in a Web page (although you can run applications as applets). To create an application, you just set up a public class, as you would for an applet. You can name this class **app**, and put it in a file named **app.java**:

```
public class app {
         .
         .
         .
}
```

What distinguishes applications from applets is that applications have a **main( )** method, where code is executed first (note that having a **main( )** method does not stop a program from being executed as an applet):

```
public class app {
➜    public static void main(String[] argv) {
              .
              .
              .
➜    }
}
```

The `String` array passed to the application holds the command-line arguments pass to the application. In this first, small application, you might just display "Hello from Java" on the screen, and you can do that with the `System.out.println()` method:

```java
public class app {
    public static void main(String[] argv) {
        System.out.println("Hello from Java");
    }
}
```

When you run this application, you'll see "Hello from Java" appear. To do that, compile the application by typing **javac app**. To run the application, use the `java.exe` interpreter which comes with the JDK 1.2 like this at the command line (i.e., in DOS):

```
c:\java1-2\app>java app
```

When you do, you'll see the "Hello from Java" message:

```
c:\java1-2\app>java app
Hello from Java
```

Now run the code in your `printgraphics` class. To do that, just create a new application class named `printer` that creates an object of the `printgraphics` class—when you do that, the `printgraphics` constructor will start the printing job, printing the graphics you want printed:

```java
import java.awt.*;
import java.awt.event.*;

public class printer {
    public static void main(String[] argv) {
        printgraphics w = new printgraphics();
    }
}
```

And that's it—create `printer.class` now and run it with the Java interpreter to see the graphics printed out. A standard Print dialog box will appear (as with any Windows program that prints) where you can select how many copies you want to print, and so on. After clicking the OK button, your graphics image is printed. Your printer application is a success, and the code for this application appears in `printer.java`.

Skill 10

TIP   You can also show the Frame window in your application, if you like–just resize the window (with `resize()`) to give it a size, and use the window's `show()` method.

C printer.java

```
import java.awt.*;
import java.awt.event.*;

public class printer {
    public static void main(String[] argv) {
        printgraphics w = new printgraphics();
    }
}

class printgraphics extends Frame {
    printgraphics() {
        PrintJob p = getToolkit().getPrintJob(this, ➡
        "Print graphics", null);
        Graphics g = p.getGraphics();
        g.drawRect(1, 1, 40, 40);
        g.drawLine(1, 1, 40, 40);
        g.dispose();
        p.end();
    }
}
```

You've gotten a good introduction to the mouse, graphics handling, and printing in Java 1.2. Let's turn now to another powerful graphics topic—handling images. In the Skill 11, you'll learn how to read images in and how to work with them.

Are You up to Speed?

Now you can...

☑ **use the mouse and handle mouse events**

☑ **draw lines, rectangles, ovals, circles, and 3D rectangles in Java**

☑ **let the user draw freehand with the mouse**

☑ **print from Java applications using the *getPrintJob()* method**

Displaying and Stretching Images

- Loading images into an applet
- Manipulating images
- Displaying images
- Creating a clickable image map
- Navigating a Web browser to a new URL

n Skill 11, we're going to examine the ins and outs of Java image handling. As you can imagine, image handling is a very popular topic. In this skill, we'll see how to read images into our applet, display them, and stretch them to new shapes. We'll also see how to support *image maps*—those clickable images you see on the Web. Let's start at once with our first example, which will read an image and stretch it as we direct.

The Imagesizer Applet

Let's start off the image handling discussion with a simple applet that reads an image. Then, the user can press the mouse in one location and drag it to another. When they release the mouse button, you can draw the image in the coordinates they've given, as shown in Figure 11.1. If the user selects a different size, you can draw the image again, using the new coordinates, as shown in Figure 11.2. This process can continue as many times as the user likes:

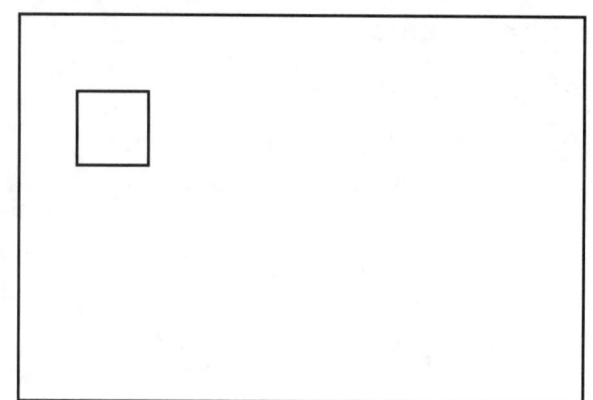

FIGURE 11.1: You can let the user specify coordinates for an image.

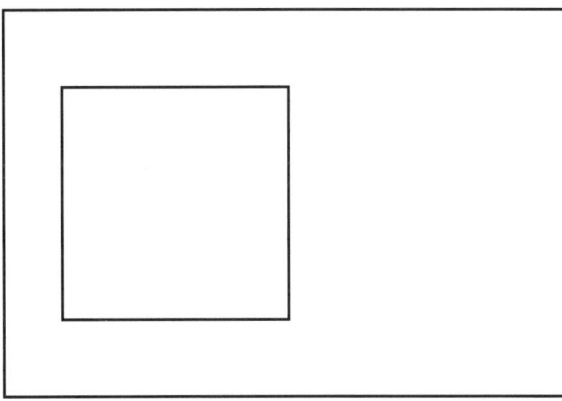

FIGURE 11.2:   The user can change the size of the image.

Let's see how this works now. Create a new file named, say, "imagesizer.java." In this applet, you'll read in a graphics figure and allow the user to resize it. You might use an image like the one shown below. We can name that image "figure.jpg."

TIP   You can read both .jpg and .gif files into your applets.

Create the `imagesizer` class now:

```
import java.awt.*;
import java.awt.event.*;
import java.applet.Applet;

public class imagesizer extends Applet {
        .
        .
        .
}
```

Skill 11

You'll need to store the image after you read it in, and you can do that in a Java Image object that you can name "image":

```
import java.awt.*;
import java.awt.event.*;
import java.applet.Applet;

public class imagesizer extends Applet {
```

➡   `Image image;`
                 .
                 .
                 .

The Image class is the class that you'll be using throughout this skill, because it provides Java's support for image handling. The Image class's methods appear in Table 11.1.

T A B L E 1 1 . 1 : The Image class methods

Method	Does This
Image()	Constructs a new Image object
flush()	Flushes resources of this Image object
getGraphics()	Gets a graphics object for this image
getHeight(ImageObserver)	Gets the height of image in pixels
getProperty(String, ImageObserver)	Gets a property of image
getScaledInstance(int, int, int)	Creates a scaled version of this image
getSource()	Gets object that actually produces image's pixels
getWidth(ImageObserver)	Get the width of image in pixels

Now you have the file you want to read, `figure.jpg`, and you've declared the Image object you'll store that image in, `image`. The next step is to read in that image, and you can do that with the Java Applet class method `getImage()`. One way to use `getImage()` is to pass an object of the Java URL class to `getImage()`, which specifies the URL of the image to read.

The URL class just holds URLs; its methods appear in Table 11.2. If you know the absolute URL of an image, you can create a URL object like this: `url = new URL("http://www.javasoft.com");`.

TABLE 11.2: The URL class methods

Method	Does This
URL(String)	Creates a URL from the unparsed absolute URL
URL(String, String, int, String)	Creates an absolute URL from the given protocol, host, port, and file
URL(String, String, String)	Creates an absolute URL from the given protocol, host, and file
URL(URL, String)	Creates a URL from the unparsed URL in the given context. If spec is an absolute URL it is used as is
CompareTo(Object)	Compares a URL to another URL
equals(Object)	Compares two URLs
getContent()	Gets the contents from this opened connection
getFile()	Gets the file name
getHost()	Gets the host name, if applicable
getPort()	Gets the port number
getProtocol()	Gets the protocol name
getRef()	Gets the ref
hashCode()	Creates an integer suitable for hash table indexing
OpenConnection()	Creates (if not already in existence) a URLConnection object that contains a connection to the remote object referred to by the URL
OpenStream()	Opens an input stream
sameFile(URL)	Compares two URLs
set(String, String, int, String, String)	Sets the fields of the URL
SetURLStreamHandlerFactory (URLStreamHandlerFactory)	Sets the URLStreamHandler factory
toExternalForm()	Reverses the parsing of the URL
toString()	Converts to a human-readable form

Another way to use the getImage() method is to pass the URL of the directory containing the image and the name of the image file like this: getImage(url, "figure.jpg");. In this case, you can assume the figure is in the same directory as the file figure.jpg, and you can use the handy Applet method getCodeBase().

This method returns the URL of the `.class` file you are executing, and that means you can read your image in the applet's `init()` method as follows:

```
import java.awt.*;
import java.awt.event.*;
import java.applet.Applet;

public class imagesizer extends Applet {

    Image image;

    public void init() {
➜           image = getImage(getCodeBase(), "figure.jpg");
                .
                .
                .

    }
```

The line of code marked above reads the image into your applet and stores it in the `Image` object, `image`. In addition, you can add a MouseListener to your applet in `init()`:

```
import java.awt.*;
import java.awt.event.*;
import java.applet.Applet;

➜   public class imagesizer extends Applet implements MouseListener{

    Image image;
    boolean bMouseDownFlag = false;
    boolean bMouseUpFlag = false;
    Point ptAnchor, ptDrawTo;

    public void init() {
        image = getImage(getCodeBase(), "figure.jpg");
➜          addMouseListener(this);
    }
```

You'll set up your applet much like the dauber applet was set up: when the user presses the mouse button, you can set the anchor point, and when they release it, you can draw your image in the given rectangle:

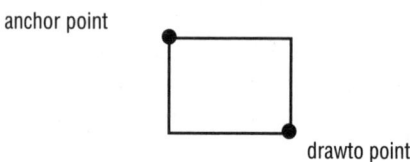

Add those points to your applet now:

```
import java.awt.*;
import java.awt.event.*;
import java.applet.Applet;

public class imagesizer extends Applet implements MouseListener {

      Image image;
→         Point ptAnchor, ptDrawTo;
                .
                .
                .
```

In addition, you can keep track of the mouse state with two flags, bMouseUpFlag and bMouseDownFlag, as you did in the dauber applet. You should add those flags to your applet now:

```
import java.awt.*;
import java.awt.event.*;
import java.applet.Applet;

public class imagesizer extends Applet implements MouseListener {

      Image image;
→         boolean bMouseDownFlag = false;
→         boolean bMouseUpFlag = false;
      Point ptAnchor, ptDrawTo;
                .
                .
                .
```

When the user presses the mouse button, you can store the location at which they did so (the anchor point) and set the mouse flags in the mousePressed() method:

```
→         public void mousePressed(MouseEvent e){
→             bMouseDownFlag = true;
→             bMouseUpFlag = false;
→             ptAnchor = new Point(e.getX(), e.getY());
→         }
```

Next, add the mouseReleased() method:

```
      public void mouseReleased(MouseEvent e){
                .
                .
                .
      }
```

Here you first set the mouse flags:

```
    public void mouseReleased(MouseEvent e){
→           bMouseDownFlag = false;
→           bMouseUpFlag = true;
            .
            .
            .

    }
```

When the user releases the mouse button, you can set the DrawTo point. In fact, you should order the Anchor and DrawTo points as you did in the dauber applet, so the Anchor point is at upper left and the DrawTo point is at lower right:

```
    public void mouseReleased(MouseEvent e){
        bMouseDownFlag = false;
        bMouseUpFlag = true;

        ptDrawTo = new Point(Math.max(e.getX(), ptAnchor.x),
Math.max(e.getY(), ptAnchor.y));
        ptAnchor = new Point(Math.min(e.getX(), ptAnchor.x),
Math.min(e.getY(), ptAnchor.y));
            .
            .
            .

    }
```

Now you're ready to draw the image. You do that in the paint() method, so call repaint() here to make sure paint() is called:

```
    public void mouseReleased(MouseEvent e){
        bMouseDownFlag = false;
        bMouseUpFlag = true;

        ptDrawTo = new Point(Math.max(e.getX(), ptAnchor.x),
Math.max(e.getY(), ptAnchor.y));
        ptAnchor = new Point(Math.min(e.getX(), ptAnchor.x),
Math.min(e.getY(), ptAnchor.y));
        repaint();
    }
```

Displaying Images in Java

Because you have the image in the image object, and the coordinates in which to draw it, you can now draw your image. Add the paint() method below.

```
    public void paint (Graphics g) {
```

```
                .
                .
                .
        }
```

First, check to make sure you should be drawing your image by making sure the mouse is up:

```
public void paint (Graphics g) {

        if(bMouseUpFlag){
                .
                .
                .
        }
}
```

If the mouse is up, you will use the drawImage() method to draw your image in the given coordinates. To do that, you'll need the width and height of your image, and you get those measurements as follows:

```
public void paint (Graphics g) {
        int drawWidth, drawHeight;

        if(bMouseUpFlag){
→               drawWidth = ptDrawTo.x - ptAnchor.x;
→               drawHeight = ptDrawTo.y - ptAnchor.y;
                        .
                        .
                        .

        }
}
```

Next, draw a rectangle to surround your image:

```
public void paint (Graphics g) {
        int drawWidth, drawHeight;

        if(bMouseUpFlag){
                drawWidth = ptDrawTo.x - ptAnchor.x;
                drawHeight = ptDrawTo.y - ptAnchor.y;
→                       g.drawRect(ptAnchor.x, ptAnchor.y, drawWidth,
        drawHeight);
                        .
                        .
                        .

        }
}
```

Skill 11

Now draw the image with `drawImage()`. All you have to do is to pass the image and the coordinates you want it drawn in—`drawImage()` will stretch the image as required—and a reference to an `ImageObserver` object. This object watches the process of drawing images, and in this case, you'll just pass a reference to your `applet` object with a `this` keyword:

```
    public void paint (Graphics g) {
        int drawWidth, drawHeight;

        if(bMouseUpFlag){
            drawWidth = ptDrawTo.x - ptAnchor.x;
            drawHeight = ptDrawTo.y - ptAnchor.y;
            g.drawRect(ptAnchor.x, ptAnchor.y, drawWidth,
drawHeight);
➜                g.drawImage(image, ptAnchor.x, ptAnchor.y,
drawWidth, drawHeight, this);
            }
        }
```

And that's all there is to drawing images—now the user can draw an image using the mouse, as shown below. The code for this applet appears in `imagesizer.java`.

---

imagesizer.java

```
import java.awt.*;
import java.awt.event.*;
import java.lang.Math;
import java.applet.Applet;
```

```java
public class imagesizer extends Applet implements MouseListener {

    Image image;
    boolean bMouseDownFlag = false;
    boolean bMouseUpFlag = false;
    Point ptAnchor, ptDrawTo;

    public void init() {
        image = getImage(getCodeBase(), "figure.jpg");
        addMouseListener(this);
    }

    public void mousePressed(MouseEvent e){
        bMouseDownFlag = true;
        bMouseUpFlag = false;
        ptAnchor = new Point(e.getX(), e.getY());
    }

    public void mouseReleased(MouseEvent e){
        bMouseDownFlag = false;
        bMouseUpFlag = true;

        ptDrawTo = new Point(Math.max(e.getX(), ptAnchor.x), ➥
Math.max(e.getY(), ptAnchor.y));
        ptAnchor = new Point(Math.min(e.getX(), ptAnchor.x), ➥
Math.min(e.getY(), ptAnchor.y));
        repaint();
    }

    public void mouseClicked(MouseEvent e){}

    public void mouseEntered(MouseEvent e){}

    public void mouseExited(MouseEvent e){}

    public void paint (Graphics g) {
        int drawWidth, drawHeight;

        if(bMouseUpFlag){
            drawWidth = ptDrawTo.x - ptAnchor.x;
            drawHeight = ptDrawTo.y - ptAnchor.y;
            g.drawRect(ptAnchor.x, ptAnchor.y, drawWidth, ➥
drawHeight);
            g.drawImage(image, ptAnchor.x, ptAnchor.y, drawWidth, ➥
drawHeight, this);
        }
    }
}
```

Skill 11

Now that you've seen how to load an image in, let's take a look at how to "interact" with an image. In this case, you'll see how to support image maps, those clickable maps you see on the World Wide Web.

Using Image Maps

An image map is an image you can click in a Web browser to move to a new URL. An image map might have several active areas, as shown in Figure 11.3.

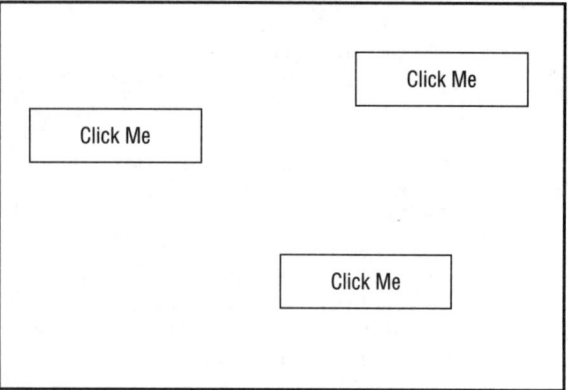

FIGURE 11.3: An image map with three active areas

When the user clicks one of these areas, the Web browser takes them to a new URL. The image map we'll use in this example, `imap.gif`, appears below, where we have hyperlinks to Sun and to Sybex. When the user clicks one of those labeled rectangles, the Web browser will open the appropriate URL.

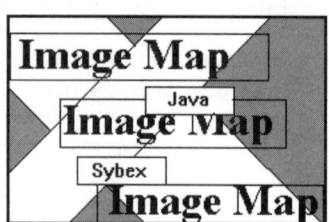

Let's begin this example now. Create a new file called imap.java. You'll need a place to store your image after you load it in and before displaying it, so you can create a new Image object named "image":

```
public class imap extends Applet
{
→          Image image;
         .
         .
         .
```

You can load your image map in from the file imap.gif and store it in the object named image in the init() method, as follows:

```
public class imap extends Applet {

    Image image;

    public void init(){
→          image = getImage(getCodeBase(), "imap.gif");
    }
```

Next, display the image in your applet by adding a paint() method:

```
public void paint (Graphics g) {
    g.drawImage(image, 10, 10, 240, 155, this);
}
```

Although the image is displayed, it's still just a part of your applet, so the normal mousePressed and mouseReleased events will occur even when you click the image. That's the key to Java image maps—you just find the location that the user clicked in your applet to see if they have clicked an active area.

You can add mouse support to your applet now by adding a MouseListener and the mouse methods as follows:

```
import java.applet.Applet;
import java.awt.*;
→    import java.awt.event.*;

→    public class imap extends Applet implements MouseListener{

    Image Imap;

    public void init(){
        Imap = getImage(getCodeBase(), "imap.gif");
        addMouseListener(this);
    }
```

```
➜            public void mousePressed(MouseEvent e){
                 .
                 .
                 .
➜            }

➜            public void mouseClicked(MouseEvent e){}

➜            public void mouseReleased(MouseEvent e){}

➜            public void mouseEntered(MouseEvent e){}

➜            public void mouseExited(MouseEvent e){}
```

Open the mousePressed() method now:

```
        public void mousePressed(MouseEvent e){
             .
             .
             .
        }
```

First, you need to get the location of the mouse and store it in the variables x and y:

```
        public void mousePressed(MouseEvent e){
➜               int x = e.getX();
➜               int y = e.getY();
                 .
                 .
                 .
        }
```

Checking an Image Map's Hotspots

Now you need to determine the location in your image of the *hotspots*—the locations that cause the browser to do something when clicked—once you do that, you can check if the mouse went down in one of them.

TIP   To determine the location of the hotspots in your image map, you can use the Windows Paint program; as you move the mouse, the Paint program indicates the current mouse location (in pixels). The Paint program only uses .BMP files. However, many Web browsers, such as the free Microsoft Internet Explorer, can convert image files for you.

You can check to see if the mouse was clicked in the first of these areas, the Java hyperlink, in the `mousePressed()` method, where you can compare the mouse location passed to us in the x and y parameters with the Java hyperlink's coordinates, as follows:

```
public void mousePressed(MouseEvent e){
     int x = e.getX();
     int y = e.getY();
         if( x > 104 && x < 171 && y > 53 && y < 75){
             .
             .
             .

}
```

Here, && is the Java logical AND operator, which means that we are requiring x > 104 AND x < 171 AND y > 53 AND y < 75 to be true.

> **TIP** There are other logical operators like && in Java. The || operator ORs a number of boolean values together, and the result is true if any of the values are true. There are also the binary (i.e., bit-by-bit numeric) operators &, |, and ^ (XOR). The other common boolean operator is the NOT operator, !, which toggles a boolean—if `booleanvalue` is true, then `!booleanvalue` is false.

In fact, the lines of code you just added are not quite right because these are the coordinates of the Sybex hyperlink in the image map, but you started the image map at the location (10, 10) in the `paint()` method:

```
public void paint (Graphics g) {
         g.drawImage(Imap, 10, 10, 240, 155, this);
}
```

That means you have to add 10 to each coordinate measurement as follows:

```
public void mousePressed(MouseEvent e){
     int x = e.getX();
     int y = e.getY();
     if( x > 104 + 10 && x < 171 + 10 && y > 53 + 10 && y < 75 + 10){
             .
             .
             .

         }
     }
```

If the user did, in fact, click inside the Java hyperlink, you can navigate the Web browser to the Java Web site, `http://www.javasoft.com`.

The Java *URL* Class

To do that, you'll need a new URL class object representing this URL. You can declare a new URL object named `url` and set it to `http://www.javasoft.com` as follows (note that to use the URL class, you have to import the `java.net.*` package):

```
      public void mousePressed(MouseEvent e){
→             URL newURL = null;
          int x = e.getX();
          int y = e.getY();
          if( x > 104 + 10 && x < 171 + 10 && y > 53 + 10 && y < 75 + ➡
  10){
→                  try { newURL = new URL("http://www.javasoft.com");
  }
→                  catch (MalformedURLException e1) {}
                              .
                              .
                              .

          }
      }
```

Note the `try` and `catch` keywords here. These keywords are used to catch Java *exceptions*, which represent error conditions (you'll learn more about Java exceptions later). Because loading in a new URL is an operation that is subject to many errors, Java requires that you enclose this operation in a `try...catch` block like you just did.

Now that you have your new URL object, you can navigate the Web browser to that URL. You can do so by working with the Web browser itself, which is called the applet's *context*. Here, you'll use the `Applet` class's `getAppletContext()` method to reach the Web browser and the context's `showDocument()` method to open the new URL:

```
      public void mousePressed(MouseEvent e){
          URL newURL = null;
          int x = e.getX();
          int y = e.getY();
          if( x > 104 + 10 && x < 171 + 10 && y > 53 + 10 && y < 75 + ➡
  10){
                  try { newURL = new URL("http://www.javasoft.com"); }
                  catch (MalformedURLException e1) {}
→                      getAppletContext().showDocument(newURL);
          }        .
                   .
                   .

      }
```

And you've opened the new URL. You can check for the other active spots in your image map, adding them to your applet as follows:

```java
public void mousePressed(MouseEvent e){
        URL newURL = null;
        int x = e.getX();
        int y = e.getY();
        if( x > 104 + 10 && x < 171 + 10 && y > 53 + 10 && y < 75 + ➥
 10){
                try { newURL = new URL("http://www.javasoft.com"); }
                catch (MalformedURLException e1) {}
                getAppletContext().showDocument(newURL);
        }
➥       if( x > 54 + 10 && x < 118 + 10 && y > 105 + 10 && y < ➥
 125 + 10){
➥               try {newURL = new URL("http://www.sybex.com");}
➥               catch (MalformedURLException e2) {}
➥               getAppletContext().showDocument(newURL);
➥       }
        }
```

And now the imap applet is ready to go, as shown below. When you open the applet in a Web browser that supports Java 1.2, the Web browser will navigate to the corresponding URL. The imap applet is a success. The code for this applet appears in imap.java.

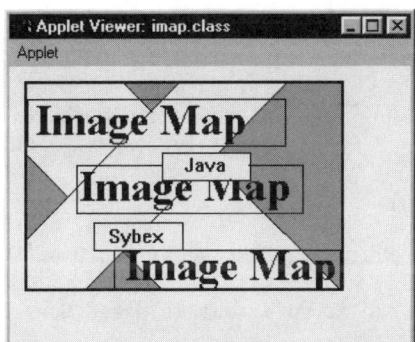

 **TIP**   If you want to show the user what hyperlink the mouse cursor is over in your image map, you can use the mouseMoved() method to track the mouse movements, reporting back to the user in a Label control.

C imap.java

```java
import java.applet.Applet;
import java.awt.*;
import java.awt.event.*;
import java.net.*;

public class imap extends Applet implements MouseListener {

    Image Imap;

    public void init(){
        Imap = getImage(getCodeBase(), "imap.gif");
        addMouseListener(this);
    }

    public void mousePressed(MouseEvent e){
        URL newURL = null;
        int x = e.getX();
        int y = e.getY();
        if( x > 104 + 10 && x < 171 + 10 && y > 53 + 10 && y ➥
< 75 + 10){
            try {newURL = new URL("http://www.javasoft.com");}
            catch (MalformedURLException e1) {}
            getAppletContext().showDocument(newURL);
        }
        if( x > 54 + 10 && x < 118 + 10 && y > 105 + 10 && y ➥
< 125 + 10){
            try {newURL = new URL("http://www.sybex.com");}
            catch (MalformedURLException e2) {}
            getAppletContext().showDocument(newURL);
        }
    }

    public void mouseClicked(MouseEvent e){}

    public void mouseReleased(MouseEvent e){}

    public void mouseEntered(MouseEvent e){}

    public void mouseExited(MouseEvent e){}

    public void paint (Graphics g) {
        g.drawImage(Imap, 10, 10, 240, 155, this);
    }
}
```

You've learned a lot about image maps, from loading images to displaying them, from stretching images to creating a clickable image map. In Skill 12, we'll turn to another popular Java topic: font handling.

Are You up to Speed?

Now you can. . .

- ☑ load images into an applet using *getImage()*
- ☑ stretch images to the size you want, zooming in or out as you like
- ☑ create one of the most popular aspects of the Java-enabled Web page, the clickable image map
- ☑ use the Java *URL* class to navigate a Web browser to a new URL

SKILL 12

Swing and Java 2D

- Using the Java Swing package
- Using the Java 2D graphics rendering system
- Adding images to buttons and other controls
- Putting combo boxes to work
- Adding sliders to Java programs
- Programming toolbars
- Working with graphics in Java 2D

In Skill 11 we worked with images, and in this chapter we'll continue our graphical work with the Java Swing and Java 2D packages. Using the Swing package, we'll see how to create buttons with images in them, slider controls, combo boxes, and toolbars. The Java 2D package provides us with the means of creating high-quality rendered images; we can design and overlay graphics images with this package, as we'll see in this skill.

Let's start by looking at some of the new controls available to us in the Swing package.

The Swing Package

Swing is the part of the Java Foundation Classes (JFC), and it includes a new set of components with a "pluggable" look and feel. The pluggable look and feel lets you design components that have the look and feel of any platform such as Windows, Solaris, or the Macintosh OS. Swing components include both the existing AWT components like buttons and scrollbars, and many higher-level components.

The Swing package offers us new controls as well as enhanced versions of the standard AWT controls. Here are the controls available to us in Swing: buttons, check boxes, labels, borders, combo boxes, progress bars, bordered panes, tool tips, tree views, split panes, scroll panes, menus, toolbars, list boxes, internal frames, table views, HTML text controls, radio buttons, labels, and others.

Let's start our exploration of Swing controls with a simple one: Swing buttons. Let's turn to that now.

Using Swing Buttons

In this first Swing example, you will learn to use a Swing button to display an image like this:

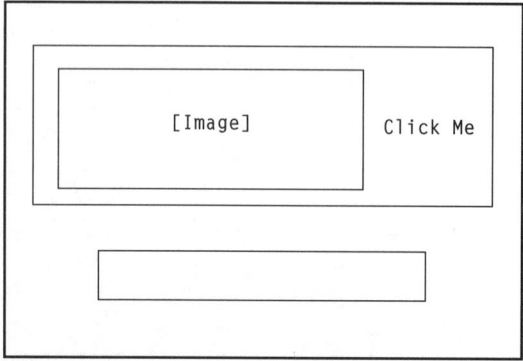

When the user clicks the button, you can display an acknowledging message in a text field:

```
┌──────────────────────────────────────────┐
│  ┌───────────────────────────┐            │
│  │                           │            │
│  │         [Image]           │  Click Me  │
│  │                           │            │
│  └───────────────────────────┘            │
│                                            │
│        ┌─────────────────────────┐        │
│        │  Button pressed.        │        │
│        └─────────────────────────┘        │
└──────────────────────────────────────────┘
```

The image you will use in the button appears in Figure 12.1.

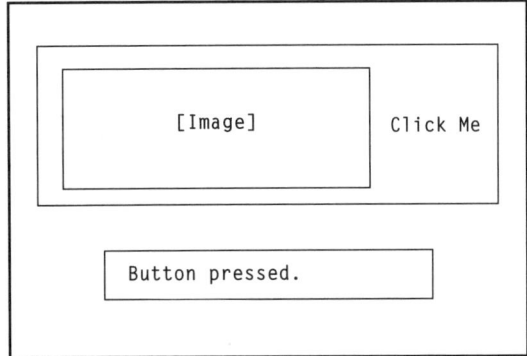

FIGURE 12.1:   The image in the Swing button

You can start this applet now. Swing is implemented as part of the AWT package in Java, so you can start by including the Swing package this way in your applet, SwingButton.java:

```
import com.sun.java.swing.*;
    .
    .
    .
```

Next, include the text field and Swing button you'll need. The Swing button class is JButton, and you can call your new button control simply "button," so setting up the button and text field looks like this:

```
import com.sun.java.swing.*;

import java.awt.*;
import java.awt.event.*;
import java.applet.*;
```

```
public class SwingButton extends Applet implements ActionListener {
```
→   `TextField text;`
→   `JButton button;`
          .
          .
          .

Now you've declared your first Swing button. The `JButton` class methods appear in Table 12.1.

TABLE 12.1: The `JButton` class methods

Method	Does This
getAccessibleContext()	Get the AccessibleContext associated with this JComponent
isDefaultButton()	Returns whether or not this button is the default button on the RootPane
JButton()	Creates a button with no set text or icon
JButton(Icon icon)	Creates a button with an icon
JButton(String text)	Creates a button with text
JButton(String text, Icon icon)	Creates a button
updateUI()	Notification from the UIFactory that the look and feel has changed
getUIClassID()	Returns a string that specifies the name of the look and feel class that renders this component

Now you have to get the image you want in your button into the button. You can start by loading that image into your applet. You can load the image, `image.jpg`, into a Java `ImageIcon` object this way:

```
import com.sun.java.swing.*;

import java.awt.*;
import java.awt.event.*;
import java.applet.*;

public class SwingButton extends Applet implements ActionListener {

    TextField text;
    JButton button;
```

```
    public void init() {

→        ImageIcon buttonIcon = new ImageIcon("image.jpg");
         .
         .
         .
```

Now you can create the new button:

```
import com.sun.java.swing.*;

import java.awt.*;
import java.awt.event.*;
import java.applet.*;

public class SwingButton extends Applet implements ActionListener {

    TextField text;
    JButton button;

    public void init() {

        ImageIcon buttonIcon = new ImageIcon("image.jpg");

→        button = new JButton("Click Me", buttonIcon);
         .
         .
         .
```

Here you can give this new button the image you want by passing the ImageIcon object you just created to the button's constructor. Now you've created an image button.

Then, you position the text "Click Me" as you want it in the button with the setVerticalTextPosition() and setHorizontalTextPosition() methods and add the button and text field to the applet:

```
import com.sun.java.swing.*;

import java.awt.*;
import java.awt.event.*;
import java.applet.*;

public class SwingButton extends Applet implements ActionListener {

    TextField text;
    JButton button;

    public void init() {
```

Skill 12

```
            ImageIcon buttonIcon = new ImageIcon("image.jpg");

            button = new JButton("Click Me", buttonIcon);
➜           button.setVerticalTextPosition(AbstractButton.CENTER);
➜           button.setHorizontalTextPosition(AbstractButton.RIGHT);
➜
➜           button.addActionListener(this);
➜           add(button);
➜
➜           text = new TextField(20);
➜           add(text);
        }
```

When the user clicks the button, you simply display the message "Button pressed." in the text field. You can do this with code in `actionPerformed()`:

```
        public void actionPerformed(java.awt.event.ActionEvent e) {
            if (e.getSource() == button) {
➜               text.setText("Button pressed.");
            }
        }
```

That's it— now run the applet as shown in Figure 12.2. As you can see, the image appears in your image button. When the user clicks the button, you display your message, as also shown in Figure 12.2. Your first Swing button example is a success!

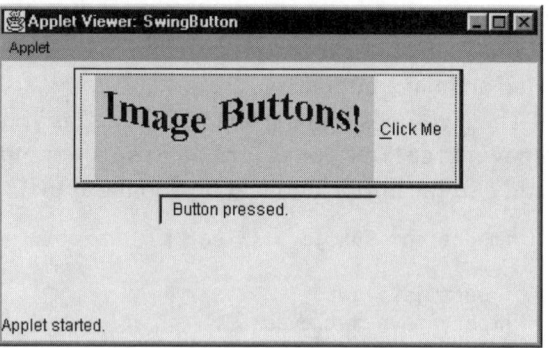

FIGURE 12.2:   A Swing button with an image

The code for this applet appears in `SwingButton.java`.

SwingButton.java

```java
import com.sun.java.swing.*;

import java.awt.*;
import java.awt.event.*;
import java.applet.*;

public class SwingButton extends Applet implements ActionListener {

    TextField text;
    JButton button;

    public void init() {

        ImageIcon buttonIcon = new ImageIcon("image.jpg");

        button = new JButton("Click Me", buttonIcon);
        button.setVerticalTextPosition(AbstractButton.CENTER);
        button.setHorizontalTextPosition(AbstractButton.RIGHT);
        button.setActionCommand("disable");

        button.addActionListener(this);
        add(button);

        text = new TextField(20);
        add(text);
    }

    public void actionPerformed(java.awt.event.ActionEvent e) {
        if (e.getSource() == button) {
            text.setText("Button pressed.");
        }
    }
}
```

Now that you've gotten your start with Swing controls, we'll move on to the next Swing control: *combo boxes*.

Using Swing Combo Boxes

Combo boxes work much like the choice controls you've already seen, but they integrate an editable text field in with the choice control. In this way, the user can change the combo box's selected item simply by typing into the text field.

Now, you'll learn to put together a Swing combo box example, `SwingCombo`
`.java`. Start by including the Swing package and creating a combo box of the Swing class `JComboBox`:

```
import com.sun.java.swing.*;

import java.awt.*;
import java.awt.event.*;
import java.applet.*;

public class SwingCombo extends Applet implements ActionListener {
```

→   `TextField text;`
→   `JComboBox combo;`
       `.`
       `.`
       `.`

The methods of the Java `JComboBox` class appear in Table 12.2.

TABLE 12.2: The JCombBox class methods

Method	Does This
JComboBox()	Creates a combo box
JComboBox(ComboBoxModel aModel)	Creates a combo box
JComboBox(Object[] items)	Creates a JComboBox that contains the elements in the specified array
JComboBox(Vector items)	Creates a JComboBox that contains the elements in the specified vector
actionPerformed(ActionEvent e)	This method is public as an implementation side effect. Do not call or override
addActionListener(ActionListener l)	Adds an ActionListener. The listener will receive an Action event when the selected item changes
addItem(Object anObject)	Adds an item in the item list

TABLE 12.2 CONTINUED: The JCombBox class methods

Method	Does This
addItemListener(ItemListener aListener)	Adds an ItemListener. aListener will receive an event when the selected item changes
configureEditor(ComboBoxEditor anEditor, Object anItem)processKeyEvent(KeyEvent e)	Overrides processKeyEvent to process events
contentsChanged(ListDataEvent e)	This method is public as an implementation side effect. Do not call or override
createDefaultKeySelectionManager()	Creates a default key selection manager
fireActionEvent()	Fires the Action event
fireItemStateChanged(ItemEvent e)	Fires the ItemStateChanged event
getAccessibleContext()	Gets the AccessibleContext associated with this JComponent
getActionCommand()	Returns the action command that is included in the event sent to action listeners
getEditor()	Gets the editor
getItemAt(int index)	Returns the item with a specific index
getItemCount()	Returns the number of items
getKeySelectionManager()	Gets the key selection manager
getMaximumRowCount()	Gets the maximum row count
getModel()	Gets the model
getRenderer()	Gets the renderer
getSelectedIndex()	Gets the selected item's index
getSelectedItem()	Gets the selected item
getSelectedObjects()	Returns an array containing the selected item
getUI()	Gets the UI
getUIClassID()	Returns the UI class ID
hidePopup()	Causes the combo box to hide its popup
insertItemAt(Object anObject, int index)	Inserts an item in the item list at a given index
intervalAdded(ListDataEvent e)	Invoked when items have been added to the internal data model

Skill 12

TABLE 12.2 CONTINUED: The JCombBox class methods

Method	Does This
intervalRemoved(ListDataEvent e)	Invoked when values have been removed from the data model
isEditable()	Returns true if editable
isFocusTraversable()	Identifies whether or not this component can receive the focus
isLightWeightPopupEnabled()	Returns true if lightweight popups are in use. Returns false if heavyweight (native peer) popups are in use
isOpaque()	Returns true if this component is completely opaque
removeActionListener(ActionListener l)	Removes an ActionListener
removeAllItems()	Removes all items
removeItem(Object anObject)	Removes an item from the item list
removeItemAt(int anIndex)	Removes the item at anIndex
removeItemListener(ItemListener aListener)	Removes an ItemListener
selectedItemChanged()	Is called when the selected item changes. Its default implementation notifies the item listeners
selectWithKeyChar(char keyChar)	Selects an item with a key
setActionCommand(String aCommand)	Sets the action command that should be included into the event sent to the action listeners
setEditable(boolean aFlag)	Makes the combo box editable
setEditor(ComboBoxEditor anEditor)	Sets the editor
setEnabled(boolean b)	Enables or disables this component, depending on the value of the parameter b
setKeySelectionManager(JComboBox.Key SelectionManager aManager)	Sets the key selection manager
setLightWeightPopupEnabled(boolean aFlag)	When displaying the popup, JComboBox chooses to use a lightweight popup if it fits
setMaximumRowCount(int count)	Sets the maximum row count
setModel(ComboBoxModel aModel)	Sets the model
setRenderer(ListCellRenderer aRenderer)	Sets the renderer

TABLE 12.2 CONTINUED: The JCombBox class methods

Method	Does This
setSelectedIndex(int anIndex)	Sets the selected item's index
setSelectedItem(Object anObject)	Sets the receiving JComboBox selected item. If anObject is in the list of items, the list will display anObject as selected
setUI(ComboBoxUI ui)	Sets the UI
showPopup()	Causes the combo box to show its popup
updateUI()	Overridden from JComponent to change the UI according to the default factory

Next, create the new combo box and make the text field in it editable with the setEditable() method:

```
import com.sun.java.swing.*;

import java.awt.*;
import java.awt.event.*;
import java.applet.*;

public class SwingCombo extends Applet implements ActionListener {

    TextField text;
    JComboBox combo;

    public void init() {

        combo = new JComboBox();
        combo.setEditable(true);
        .
        .
        .
```

The combo box is ready. You will use the addItem() method to add items 1 to 9 to this combo box this way:

```
import com.sun.java.swing.*;

import java.awt.*;
import java.awt.event.*;
import java.applet.*;

public class SwingCombo extends Applet implements ActionListener {
```

Skill 12

```
    TextField text;
    JComboBox combo;

    public void init() {

        combo = new JComboBox();
        combo.setEditable(true);
➜       combo.addItem("Item 1");
➜       combo.addItem("Item 2");
➜       combo.addItem("Item 3");
➜       combo.addItem("Item 4");
➜       combo.addItem("Item 5");
➜       combo.addItem("Item 6");
➜       combo.addItem("Item 7");
➜       combo.addItem("Item 8");
➜       combo.addItem("Item 9");
                    .
                    .
                    .
```

You can also set the initially-selected item in the combo box with
`setSelectedItem()`. You do that and add the combo box and a text field
to your applet like this:

```
import com.sun.java.swing.*;

import java.awt.*;
import java.awt.event.*;
import java.applet.*;

public class SwingCombo extends Applet implements ActionListener {

    TextField text;
    JComboBox combo;

    public void init() {

        combo = new JComboBox();
        combo.setEditable(true);
        combo.addItem("Item 1");
        combo.addItem("Item 2");
        combo.addItem("Item 3");
        combo.addItem("Item 4");
        combo.addItem("Item 5");
        combo.addItem("Item 6");
        combo.addItem("Item 7");
```

```
        combo.addItem("Item 8");
        combo.addItem("Item 9");
→       combo.setSelectedItem("Item 5");
→
→       combo.addActionListener(this);
→       add(combo);
→
→       text = new TextField(20);
→       add(text);

    }
```

Finally, you can set up the actionPerformed() method to display which item in the combo box the user has selected. You can determine which item is selected with the getSelectedItem() method:

```
    public void actionPerformed(java.awt.event.ActionEvent e) {
→       text.setText("You chose: " + (String) combo.getSelectedItem());
    }
```

That's it—open the SwingCombo applet in the applet viewer now, as shown in Figure 12.3. Using the mouse, you can make selections from the combo box, as also shown in Figure 12.3.

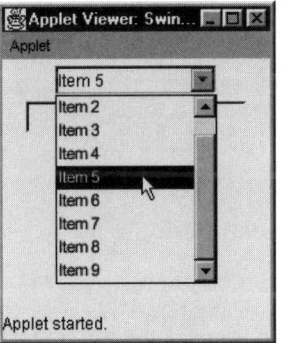

FIGURE 12.3: A Swing combo box

When the user does make a selection, you can indicate which item they selected in the text field, as shown in Figure 12.4. Now you're able to use combo boxes in your applets and applications.

Skill 12

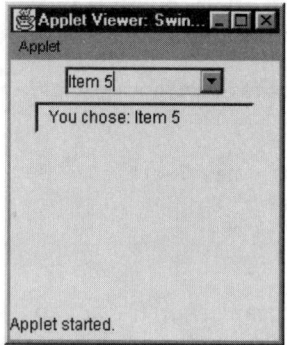

FIGURE 12.4: Making a selection in the Swing combo box

The code for this applet appears in SwingCombo.java.

SwingCombo.java

```
import com.sun.java.swing.*;

import java.awt.*;
import java.awt.event.*;
import java.applet.*;

public class SwingCombo extends Applet implements ActionListener {

    TextField text;
    JComboBox combo;

    public void init() {

        combo = new JComboBox();
        combo.setEditable(true);
        combo.addItem("Item 1");
        combo.addItem("Item 2");
        combo.addItem("Item 3");
        combo.addItem("Item 4");
        combo.addItem("Item 5");
        combo.addItem("Item 6");
        combo.addItem("Item 7");
        combo.addItem("Item 8");
        combo.addItem("Item 9");
        combo.setSelectedItem("Item 5");
```

```
combo.addActionListener(this);
add(combo);

text = new TextField(20);
add(text);

}

public void actionPerformed(java.awt.event.ActionEvent e) {
    text.setText("You chose: " + (String) combo.getSelectedItem());
}
}
```

As you can see, working with Swing combo boxes can provide a lot of power in Java applications and applets. We'll turn to another Swing control next, *sliders*.

Using Swing Sliders

A slider control works much like the controls on a stereo, providing the user with a knob that they can move in a grooved track to specify a setting. You'll see how this works in an example, SwingSlider.java.

In this example, start by adding a new slider of the Swing JSlider class to your applet, as well as a text field. You can make the slider horizontal, give it a range from 0 to 100, and give it an initial value of 50, this way:

```
import com.sun.java.swing.*;
import com.sun.java.swing.event.*;

import java.awt.*;
import java.awt.event.*;
import java.applet.*;

public class SwingSlider extends Applet implements ChangeListener {

    JSlider slider;
    TextField text;

    public void init() {

        slider = new JSlider(JSlider.HORIZONTAL, 0, 100, 50);
        .
        .
        .
```

The JSlider class methods appear in Table 12.3.

Skill 12

TABLE 12.3: The JSlider class methods

Method	Does This
addChangeListener(ChangeListener l)	Adds a ChangeListener to the slider
createChangeListener()	Subclasses that want to handle model ChangeEvents differently can override this method to return their own ChangeListener implementation
createStandardLabels(int increment)	Creates a hash table that will draw text labels starting at the slider minimum using the increment specified
fireStateChanged()	Sends a ChangeEvent, whose source is this slider, to each listener
getAccessibleContext()	Gets the AccessibleContext associated with this JComponent
getExtent()	Gets extent of the control
getInverted()	Returns true if the value range shown for the slider is reversed, with the maximum value at the left end of a horizontal slider or at the bottom of a vertical one
getLabelTable()	Returns the dictionary of what labels to draw at which values
getMajorTickSpacing()	Gets the major tick spacing
getMaximum()	Returns the maximum value supported by the slider
getMinimum()	Returns the minimum value supported by the slider
getMinorTickSpacing()	Gets the minor tick spacing
getModel()	Returns data model that handles the slider's three fundamental properties: minimum, maximum, and value
getOrientation()	Gets the slider's orientation
getPaintLabels()	Gets the paint labels
getPaintTicks()	Gets the paint ticks
getSnapToTicks()	Returns true if the knob (and the data value it represents) resolves to the closest tick mark next to where the user positioned the knob
getUIClassID()	Returns the name of the class that renders this component

TABLE 12.3 CONTINUED: The JSlider class methods

Method	Does This
getValue()	Returns the slider's value
getValueIsAdjusting()	Returns true if the slider knob is being dragged
JSlider()	Creates a horizontal slider with the range 0 to 100 and an initial value of 50
JSlider(int orientation, int min, int max, int value)	Creates a slider with the specified orientation and the specified minimum, maximum, and initial values
removeChangeListener(ChangeListener l)	Removes a ChangeListener from the slider
setExtent(int extent)	Sets the size of the range "covered" by the knob
setInverted(boolean b)	Specifies true to reverse the value range shown for the slider so that the maximum value is at the left end of a horizontal slider or at the bottom of a vertical one
setLabelTable(Dictionary labels)	Specifies what label will be drawn at any given value
setMajorTickSpacing(int n)	Sets the number of pixels between major tick marks
setMaximum(int maximum)	Sets the model's maximum property
setMinimum(int minimum)	Sets the model's minimum property
setMinorTickSpacing(int n)	Sets the number of pixels between minor tick marks
setModel(BoundedRangeModel newModel)	Sets the model that handles the slider's three fundamental properties: minimum, maximum, and value
setOrientation(int orientation)	Sets the scroll bars orientation to either vertical or horizontal
setPaintLabels(boolean b)	Determines whether labels are painted on the slider
setPaintTicks(boolean b)	Determines whether tick marks are painted on the slider
setSnapToTicks(boolean b)	Specifying true makes the knob (and the data value it represents) resolve to the closest tick mark next to where the user positioned the knob

Skill 12

TABLE 12.3 CONTINUED: The JSlider class methods

Method	Does This
setUI(com.sun.java.swing.plaf.SliderUI ui)	Sets the UI object, which implements the look and feel for this component
setValue(int n)	Sets the slider's current value
setValueIsAdjusting(boolean b)	Sets the model's valueIsAdjusting property
toString()	Returns a string that displays and identifies this object's properties
updateLabelUIs()	Called internally to replace the label UIs with the latest versions from the UIFactory when the UIFactory gives notification via updateUI that the look and feel has changed
updateUI()	Notification from the UIFactory that the look and feel has changed

Next, you need to indicate that you want tick marks to appear on the slider, using the setPaintTicks() method. In this case, you'll set a major (i.e., long) tick every 20 units and a minor tick (i.e., small) tick every five units this way:

```
import com.sun.java.swing.*;
import com.sun.java.swing.event.*;

import java.awt.*;
import java.awt.event.*;
import java.applet.*;

public class SwingSlider extends Applet implements ChangeListener {

    JSlider slider;
    TextField text;

    public void init() {

        slider = new JSlider(JSlider.HORIZONTAL, 0, 100, 50);
→       slider.setPaintTicks(true);
→       slider.setMajorTickSpacing(20);
→       slider.setMinorTickSpacing(5);
        .
        .
        .
```

Now add the listener you'll use for the slider; in this case, that's a ChangeListener, not an ActionListener. Finally, add your controls to the applet:

```
import com.sun.java.swing.*;
import com.sun.java.swing.event.*;

import java.awt.*;
import java.awt.event.*;
import java.applet.*;

public class SwingSlider extends Applet implements ChangeListener {

    JSlider slider;
    TextField text;

    public void init() {

        slider = new JSlider(JSlider.HORIZONTAL, 0, 100, 50);
        slider.setPaintTicks(true);
        slider.setMajorTickSpacing(20);
        slider.setMinorTickSpacing(5);
        slider.addChangeListener(this);
        add(slider);

        text = new TextField(20);
        add(text);
    }
```

You're almost done. When the user moves the slider, the program calls the stateChanged() method, so add that method now, and create an object corresponding to the slider this way in that method:

```
    public void stateChanged(ChangeEvent e) {
        JSlider slider = (JSlider)e.getSource();
            .
            .
            .
    }
```

Finally, you need to indicate the new setting of the slider, which you get from the slider's getValue() method, in the text field this way:

```
    public void stateChanged(ChangeEvent e) {
        JSlider slider = (JSlider)e.getSource();
        text.setText("The slider is at: " + slider.getValue());
    }
```

Skill 12

And that's it. Open the applet now in the applet viewer, as shown in Figure 12.5. As you can see in that figure, the applet reports the movements of the slider's knob—your Swing slider applet is a success. At this point, you've used Java Swing to add several new controls to your programs.

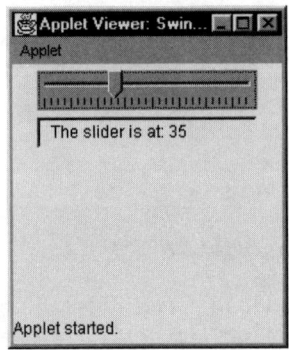

FIGURE 12.5:   Using a Swing slider

The code for this applet appears in `SwingSlider.java`.

 SwingSlider.java

```java
import com.sun.java.swing.*;
import com.sun.java.swing.event.*;

import java.awt.*;
import java.awt.event.*;
import java.applet.*;

public class SwingSlider extends Applet implements ChangeListener {

    JSlider slider;
    TextField text;

    public void init() {

        slider = new JSlider(JSlider.HORIZONTAL, 0, 100, 50);
        slider.setPaintTicks(true);
        slider.setMajorTickSpacing(20);
        slider.setMinorTickSpacing(5);
        slider.addChangeListener(this);
        add(slider);
```

```
        text = new TextField(20);
        add(text);
    }

    public void stateChanged(ChangeEvent e) {
        JSlider slider = (JSlider)e.getSource();
        text.setText("The slider is at: " + slider.getValue());
    }
}
```

Now that you've seen Swing sliders at work, let's continue on with Swing toolbars.

Using Swing Toolbars

One of the most attractive Swing controls is the toolbar control. This control lets you install buttons in it, just as the standard toolbars you might be familiar with in Windows or other operating systems.

 TIP   In fact, you can make Swing toolbars *dockable*, which means they can attach or detach themselves to your main Java application.

If you use Swing buttons, you can install images in the tools in your toolbar, and the result is just as professional as you'll see in any application. Let's take a look at the process of using toolbars now with an example, SwingToolbar.java.

Start this new applet by adding a toolbar of the JToolBar class, as well as three Swing buttons and a text field:

```
import com.sun.java.swing.*;
import com.sun.java.swing.event.*;

import java.awt.*;
import java.awt.event.*;
import java.applet.*;

public class SwingToolbar extends Applet {

➡       JToolBar toolbar;
➡       JButton button1, button2, button3;
➡       TextField text;
        .
        .
        .
```

Skill 12

The JToolBar class methods appear in Table 12.4.

TABLE 12.4: The JToolbar class methods

Method	Does This
JToolBar()	Creates a toolbar
add(Action a)	Adds a new JButton that dispatches the action
addSeparator()	Adds a separator to the toolbar
createActionChangeListener(JButton b)	Creates an ActionChangeListener
getAccessibleContext()	Gets the role of this object
getComponentAtIndex(int i)	Gets the ComponentAt specified index
getComponentIndex(Component c)	Gets the index of a component
getMargin()	Returns the margin between the toolbar's border and its buttons
getUI()	Returns the toolbar's current UI
getUIClassID()	Gets the UI class
isBorderPainted()	Checks whether the border should be painted
isFloatable()	Returns true if the toolbar can be dragged out by the user
paintBorder(Graphics g)	Paints the toolbar's border if the BorderPainted property is true
setBorderPainted(boolean b)	Sets whether the border should be painted
setFloatable(boolean b)	Sets whether the toolbar can be made to float
setMargin(Insets m)	Sets the margin between the toolbar's border and its buttons
setUI(ToolBarUI ui)	Sets the toolbar's UI
updateUI()	Gets a new UI object from the default UIFactory

Now you need to create the new controls you'll need in the init() method, starting with the toolbar:

```
public void init() {

→       JToolBar toolBar = new JToolBar();
           .
           .
           .
```

Next, create the first button, button1; you'll give the three buttons you'll use in a smaller version of the image you used in the Swing button example above:

```
public void init() {

    JToolBar toolBar = new JToolBar();

➡       JButton button1 = new JButton("Button 1", new ➡
    ImageIcon("image.jpg"));
        .
        .
        .
```

Plan to add three buttons to your toolbar, and that raises a problem. Because the toolbar is a composite of controls, calling e.getSource() in an actionPerformed() method does *not* return the button that was clicked. How can you determine which button was clicked? You can do that by setting up a separate action listener for each button.

You can call your new action listener class Command, and pass an ID value for the current button (1 for the first button, 2 for the second, and so on) to Command's constructor, as well as a this keyword, so you can reach the applet object from the Command class (you need to reach the applet object so you can place text into the applet's text field):

```
public void init() {

    JToolBar toolBar = new JToolBar();

    JButton button1 = new JButton("Button 1", new ➡
    ImageIcon("image.jpg"));
➡       Command command1 = new Command(1, this);
        .
        .
        .
```

Having created the new action listener object for the first button, add that object to that button, then add the button to the toolbar itself this way:

```
public void init() {

    JToolBar toolBar = new JToolBar();

    JButton button1 = new JButton("Button 1", new ➡
    ImageIcon("image.jpg"));
        Command command1 = new Command(1, this);
➡       button1.addActionListener(command1);
```

Skill 12

```
➜          toolBar.add(button1);
                  .
                  .
                  .
```

Then we do the same for the second and third buttons, finally adding the prepared toolbar to the applet as well as the text field:

```
public void init() {

    JToolBar toolBar = new JToolBar();

    JButton button1 = new JButton("Button 1", new
ImageIcon("image.jpg"));
    Command command1 = new Command(1, this);
    button1.addActionListener(command1);
    toolBar.add(button1);

➜   JButton button2 = new JButton("Button 2", new ➥
ImageIcon("image.jpg"));
➜   Command command2 = new Command(2, this);
➜   button2.addActionListener(command2);
➜   toolBar.add(button2);
➜
➜   JButton button3 = new JButton("Button 3", new ➥
ImageIcon("image.jpg"));
➜   Command command3 = new Command(3, this);
➜   button3.addActionListener(command3);
➜   toolBar.add(button3);
➜
➜   add(toolBar);
➜
➜   text = new TextField(20);
➜   add(text);
}
```

Now you're ready to design your Command action listener class.

Designing the Command Action Listener Class

You need to take two parameters in the Command class's constructor: the ID for the current button and a this keyword pointing to the applet object. You store those items this way in the Command object:

```
class Command implements ActionListener {

➜   int commandID;
```

➡   ```
     SwingToolbar toolbarApplet;
     ```

➡
➡    ```
     public Command(int commandID, SwingToolbar toolbarApplet){
         this.commandID = commandID;
         this.toolbarApplet = toolbarApplet;
     }
     ```

Now that you've given each button its own ID value, you can check that ID with a `switch` statement in `Command`'s `actionPerformed()` method:

```
class Command implements ActionListener {

int commandID;
SwingToolbar toolbarApplet;

public Command(int commandID, SwingToolbar toolbarApplet){
    this.commandID = commandID;
    this.toolbarApplet = toolbarApplet;
}

public void actionPerformed(ActionEvent e){
```
➡
➡
```
    switch(commandID) {
        case 1:
            .
            .
            .
```
➡
```
        case 2:
            .
            .
            .
```
➡
```
        case 3:
            .
            .
            .

    }
}
```

After you identify the button's ID, you can place the matching message, "Button 1 clicked.", "Button 2 clicked.", and so on, into the applet's text box. You reach the applet object this way, placing the correct message in the text field there:

```
public void actionPerformed(ActionEvent e){
    switch(commandID) {
        case 1:
```

```
→            toolbarApplet.text.setText("Button 1 clicked.");
→            break;
        case 2:
→            toolbarApplet.text.setText("Button 2 clicked.");
→            break;
        case 3:
→            toolbarApplet.text.setText("Button 3 clicked.");
→            break;
        }
    }
```

And that's it—open the applet in the applet viewer now, as shown in Figure 12.6. As you can see in that figure, your three buttons appear with their images in the toolbar. Clicking one of the buttons displays the appropriate message, as also shown in Figure 12.6. Your toolbar example is a success.

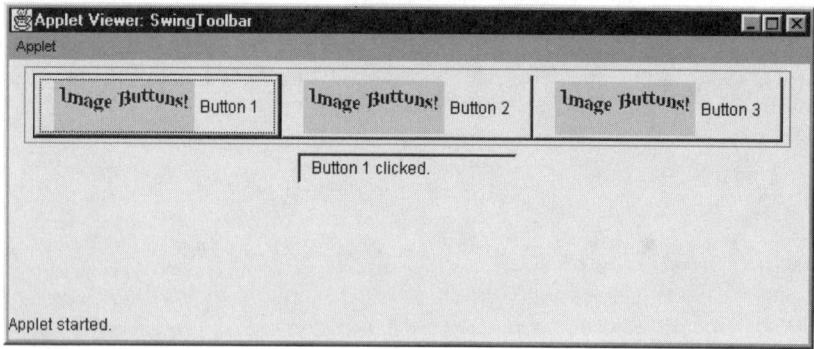

FIGURE 12.6:   Using a Swing toolbar

The code for this applet appears in SwingToolbar.java.

SwingToolbar.java

```java
import com.sun.java.swing.*;
import com.sun.java.swing.event.*;

import java.awt.*;
import java.awt.event.*;
import java.applet.*;

public class SwingToolbar extends Applet {

    JToolBar toolbar;
    JButton button1, button2, button3;
```

```
    TextField text;

    public void init() {

        JToolBar toolBar = new JToolBar();

        JButton button1 = new JButton("Button 1", new ➥
ImageIcon("image.jpg"));
        Command command1 = new Command(1, this);
        button1.addActionListener(command1);
        toolBar.add(button1);

        JButton button2 = new JButton("Button 2", new ➥
ImageIcon("image.jpg"));
        Command command2 = new Command(2, this);
        button2.addActionListener(command2);
        toolBar.add(button2);

        JButton button3 = new JButton("Button 3", new ➥
ImageIcon("image.jpg"));
        Command command3 = new Command(3, this);
        button3.addActionListener(command3);
        toolBar.add(button3);

        add(toolBar);

        text = new TextField(20);
        add(text);
    }
}

class Command implements ActionListener {

    int commandID;
    SwingToolbar toolbarApplet;

    public Command(int commandID, SwingToolbar toolbarApplet){
        this.commandID = commandID;
        this.toolbarApplet = toolbarApplet;
    }

    public void actionPerformed(ActionEvent e){
        switch(commandID) {
            case 1:
                toolbarApplet.text.setText("Button 1 clicked.");
                break;
            case 2:
                toolbarApplet.text.setText("Button 2 clicked.");
```

Skill 12

```
                            break;
                    case 3:
                        toolbarApplet.text.setText("Button 3 clicked.");
                        break;
                }
            }
        }
```

Now you've gotten an overview of the Swing package and some of its most important controls. Next we'll to take a look at using the Java 2D package for rendering high-quality graphics. Let's turn to that now.

Using Java 2D

Java 2D is a set of classes for advanced two-dimensional graphics and imaging. It includes support for line art, text, and images. Java 2D also provides support for compositing images and alpha channel images, as well as a full set of display-oriented image operators. These classes are additions to the `java.awt` and `java.awt.image` packages.

Java 2D is an extensive package, full of professional capabilities. To see how all this works, let's put together a Java 2D example now. In this example, `Box2D.java`, you'll draw two boxes, one green and one blue, at right angles to each other.

You use Java 2D by creating a `Graphics2D` object in an applet or application's `paint()` method, and you'll create that object from a standard graphics object, like the one you're passed in the `paint()` method:

```
import java.awt.*;
import java.awt.geom.*;

public class Box2D extends java.applet.Applet
{

    public void paint(Graphics g) {

➔       Graphics2D graphics2D = (Graphics2D) g;
        .
        .
        .
```

The `Graphics2D` methods appear in Table 12.5.

TABLE 12.5: The Graphics2D class methods

Method	Does This
clip(Shape s)	Intersects the current clip with the interior of the specified shape and sets the current clip to the resulting intersection
draw(Shape s)	Strokes the outline of a shape using the settings of the current graphics state
drawImage(BufferedImage img, BufferedImageOp op, int x, int y)	Draws a BufferedImage that is filtered with a BufferedImageOp
drawImage(Image img, AffineTransform xform, ImageObserver obs)	Draws an image, applying a transform
drawRenderableImage(RenderableImage img, AffineTransform xfrom, Hashtable renderHints, Hashtable renderHintsObserved)	Draws an image
drawRenderedImage(RenderedImage img, AffineTransform xform)	Draws an image, applying a transform
drawString(GlyphSet g, float x, float y)	Draws a glyph set
drawString(String s, float x, float y)	Draws a string of text
drawString(StyledString s, float x, float y)	Draws a styled string
drawString(TextLayout text, float x, float y)	Draws a string of text
fill(Shape s)	Fills the interior of a shape using the settings of the current graphics state
getBackground()	Returns the background color used for clearing a region
getComposite()	Returns the current composite in the Graphics2D state
getDeviceConfiguration()	Returns the device configuration associated with this Graphics2D
getPaint()	Returns the current paint in the Graphics2D state
getRenderingHints(int hintCategory)	Returns the preferences for the rendering algorithms

TABLE 12.5 CONTINUED: The Graphics2D class methods

Method	Does This
getStroke()	Returns the current stroke in the Graphics2D state
getTransform()	Returns the current transform in the Graphics2D state
Graphics2D()	Constructs a new Graphics2D object
hit(Rectangle rect, Shape s, boolean onStroke)	Checks to see if the outline of a shape intersects the specified rectangle in device space
hitString(Rectangle rect, StyledString s, float x, float y)	Checks to see if the styled string intersects the specified rectangle in device space
rotate(double theta)	Concatenates the current transform of this Graphics2D with a rotation transformation
rotate(double theta, double x, double y)	Concatenates the current transform of this Graphics2D with a translated rotation transformation
scale(double sx, double sy)	Concatenates the current transform of this Graphics2D with a scaling transformation
setBackground(Color color)	Sets the background color in this context used for clearing a region
setComposite(Composite comp)	Sets the composite in the current graphics state
setPaint(Paint paint)	Sets the paint in the current graphics state
setRenderingHints(int hintCategory, int hintValue)	Sets the preferences for the rendering algorithms
setStroke(Stroke s)	Sets the stroke in the current graphics state
setTransform(AffineTransform Tx)	Sets the transform in the current graphics state
shear(double shx, double shy)	Concatenates the current transform of this Graphics2D with a shearing transformation
transform(AffineTransform Tx)	Composes an AffineTransform object with the transform in this Graphics2D according to the rule last-specified-first-applied
translate(double tx, double ty)	Concatenates the current transform of this Graphics2D with a translation transformation
translate(int x, int y)	Translates the origin of the graphics context to the point (x, y) in the current coordinate system

Next, you can set the drawing color in the `Graphics2D` object to green:

```
import java.awt.*;
import java.awt.geom.*;

public class Box2D extends java.applet.Applet
{

    public void paint(Graphics g) {

        Graphics2D graphics2D = (Graphics2D) g;

➜        graphics2D.setColor(Color.green);
         .
         .
         .
```

All that remains is to draw the first rectangle and fill it in. You can draw shapes in Java 2D with the `GeneralPath` class, and we'll do that now.

Defining Shapes with GeneralPath

You can use the `GeneralPath` class to define shapes in Java 2D. To draw a rectangle, create a new `GeneralPath` object named `rectangle`:

```
import java.awt.*;
import java.awt.geom.*;

public class Box2D extends java.applet.Applet
{

    public void paint(Graphics g) {

        Graphics2D graphics2D = (Graphics2D) g;

        graphics2D.setColor(Color.green);

➜        GeneralPath rectangle = new GeneralPath();
          .
          .
          .
```

Use the `GeneralPath` class's `moveTo()` method to start at a particular location, `lineTo()`, to draw a line to a new location, and `closePath()` to finish the

Skill 12

figure you're drawing. Using these methods, you can draw the rectangle you want this way:

```
import java.awt.*;
import java.awt.geom.*;

public class Box2D extends java.applet.Applet
{

    public void paint(Graphics g) {

        Graphics2D graphics2D = (Graphics2D) g;

        graphics2D.setColor(Color.green);

        GeneralPath rectangle = new GeneralPath();

        rectangle.moveTo(0, 0);
        rectangle.lineTo(-100, 0);
        rectangle.lineTo(-100, 50);
        rectangle.lineTo(0, 50);
        rectangle.closePath();
            .
            .
            .
```

Now that you've drawn your rectangle, you will move it to a new location by setting up a *transform*.

Moving and Rotating with Transforms

You can move or rotate the graphics environment using Graphics2D *affine transforms*. For example, to translate your rectangle, you can create a new transform object and apply it with the transform() method this way:

```
    public void paint(Graphics g) {

        Graphics2D graphics2D = (Graphics2D) g;

        graphics2D.setColor(Color.green);

        GeneralPath rectangle = new GeneralPath();

        rectangle.moveTo(0, 0);
        rectangle.lineTo(-100, 0);
        rectangle.lineTo(-100, 50);
        rectangle.lineTo(0, 50);
        rectangle.closePath();
```

```
➜          AffineTransform transform = new AffineTransform();
➜          transform.setToTranslation(100, 100);
➜          graphics2D.transform(transform);
                  .
                  .
                  .
```

Finally, you can fill in the rectangle with the fill() method:

```
public void paint(Graphics g) {

    Graphics2D graphics2D = (Graphics2D) g;

    graphics2D.setColor(Color.green);

    GeneralPath rectangle = new GeneralPath();

    rectangle.moveTo(0, 0);
    rectangle.lineTo(-100, 0);
    rectangle.lineTo(-100, 50);
    rectangle.lineTo(0, 50);
    rectangle.closePath();

    AffineTransform transform = new AffineTransform();
    transform.setToTranslation(100, 100);
    graphics2D.transform(transform);

➜  graphics2D.fill(rectangle);
                  .
                  .
                  .
```

Now you've completed your first rectangle. You can draw another rectangle at right angles to the first and make this one blue:

```
public void paint(Graphics g) {

    Graphics2D graphics2D = (Graphics2D) g;

    graphics2D.setColor(Color.green);

    GeneralPath rectangle = new GeneralPath();
              .
              .
              .
    graphics2D.fill(rectangle);
```

```
➜        graphics2D.setColor(Color.blue);
                 .
                 .
                 .
```

You can move this rectangle to a new location; and you can also rotate it at right angles to the first one by creating a rotation transform with the setToRotation() method and applying that new transform to the Graphics2D object:

```
public void paint(Graphics g) {

    Graphics2D graphics2D = (Graphics2D) g;

    graphics2D.setColor(Color.green);

    GeneralPath rectangle = new GeneralPath();
            .
            .
            .
    graphics2D.fill(rectangle);

    graphics2D.setColor(Color.blue);
```
```
➜        transform.setToTranslation(50.0, 0.0);
➜        graphics2D.transform(transform);

➜        transform.setToRotation(Math.PI/2.0);
➜        graphics2D.transform(transform);
            .
            .
            .
```

Finally, fill in the second rectangle this way:

```
public void paint(Graphics g) {

    Graphics2D graphics2D = (Graphics2D) g;

    graphics2D.setColor(Color.green);

    GeneralPath rectangle = new GeneralPath();
            .
            .
            .
    graphics2D.fill(rectangle);
```

```
        graphics2D.setColor(Color.blue);

        transform.setToTranslation(50.0, 0.0);
        graphics2D.transform(transform);

        transform.setToRotation(Math.PI/2.0);
        graphics2D.transform(transform);

➜       graphics2D.fill(rectangle);
    }
```

That completes the Box2D applet. Run it now, as shown in Figure 12.7. As you can see in that figure, you've drawn two rectangles, one green and one blue, and set them at right angles to each other. Your Java 2D example is a success.

 **NOTE**

There is a great deal more to Java 2D—too much to cover here. For example, not only can you draw images, but you can also blend and overlap them in varying degrees of transparency. It takes a good amount of work to become proficient in Java 2D, but if you're after professional graphics, it can be worth it.

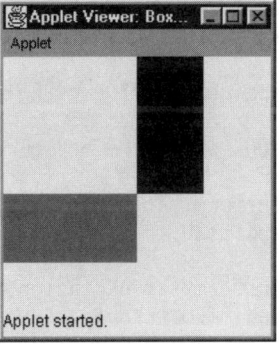

FIGURE 12.7: Drawing with Java 2D

The code for this applet appears in Box2D.java.

Box2D.java

```java
import java.awt.*;
import java.awt.geom.*;

public class Box2D extends java.applet.Applet
{

    public void paint(Graphics g) {

        Graphics2D graphics2D = (Graphics2D) g;

        graphics2D.setColor(Color.green);

        GeneralPath rectangle = new GeneralPath();

        rectangle.moveTo(0, 0);
        rectangle.lineTo(-100, 0);
        rectangle.lineTo(-100, 50);
        rectangle.lineTo(0, 50);
        rectangle.closePath();

        AffineTransform transform = new AffineTransform();
        transform.setToTranslation(100, 100);
        graphics2D.transform(transform);

        graphics2D.fill(rectangle);

        graphics2D.setColor(Color.blue);

        transform.setToTranslation(50.0, 0.0);
        graphics2D.transform(transform);

        transform.setToRotation(Math.PI/2.0);
        graphics2D.transform(transform);

        graphics2D.fill(rectangle);
    }
}
```

That finishes our chapter on Swing and Java 2D. You've seen how Swing introduces a whole new set of controls for you to use in Java and gotten an introduction to the creation of high-quality graphics with Java 2D. All in all, these two parts of Java provide you with a great deal of control over graphics and Java.

In the next skill you'll see how to work with another popular topic: text and fonts. Let's turn to that now.

Are You up to Speed?

Now you can. . .

- ☑ use Swing controls, combo boxes, toolbars, and sliders
- ☑ use button accelerators
- ☑ display images in buttons
- ☑ understand the basics of Java 2D

Setting and Modifying Text and Fonts

- Setting a program's font
- Using the system clipboard
- Making text bold and italic
- Reading keyboard input
- Determining a text string's length on the screen
- Centering text
- Using the *FontMetric* class

In Skill 12, we worked with graphics. In this skill, we'll work on the presentation of text in Java. So far, we've used text in text fields and labels, but now we'll take over the process directly as we display text in our programs without those controls. Text is just another type of graphic; we'll see how to determine a text string's length and height as it appears on the screen so we can place it as we want it. We'll also see how to switch to various fonts, such as Times New Roman or Courier, and how to make text italic or bold. Finally, we'll see the new techniques of using the system clipboard.

Creating the Scribbler Applet

You'll write an applet called "scribbler," which will present the user with a series of buttons representing various font options, such as italics, bold, Roman, and Courier, as shown in Figure 13.1. After the user selects the font options they want, they can type text, which you'll read directly from the keyboard (in the keyPressed( ) method) and display in your applet. The text will appear as a centered string in the font, with the font options the user wants.

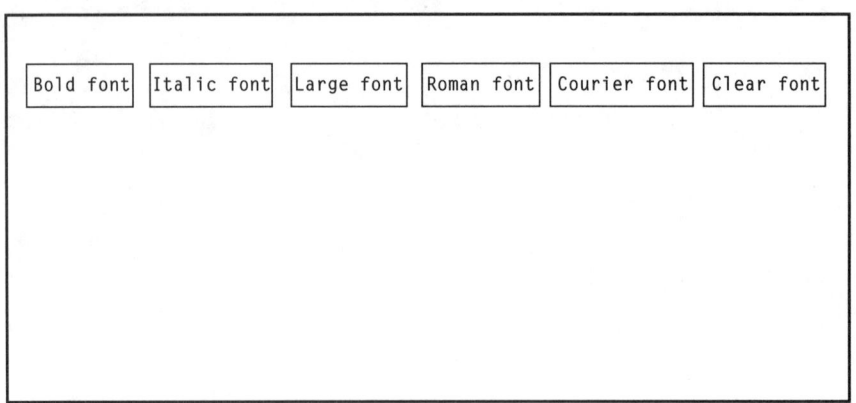

FIGURE 13.1:   Buttons representing font options

Start this applet now. To do that, create the new file named `scribbler.java`, and create the new `scribbler` class now. Then you can start by setting up the buttons in your applet. There are six buttons, and you should name the buttons after their functions: `boldbutton` (makes text bold), `italicbutton` (makes text italic), largebutton (sets the font to a large type size), romanbutton (switches to the Roman font), courierbutton (switches to the Courier font), and clearbutton (clears the text string). Add these buttons now:

```
     public class scribbler extends Applet{
➜        Button boldbutton, italicbutton, largebutton;
➜        Button romanbutton, courierbutton, clearbutton;
                    .
                    .
                    .
```

Next, create these buttons in the init() method and add them to your applet's layout:

```
     public class scribbler extends Applet {

         Button boldbutton, italicbutton, largebutton;
         Button romanbutton, courierbutton, clearbutton;

         public void init()
         {
➜            boldbutton = new Button("Bold font");

➜            italicbutton = new Button("Italic font");

➜            largebutton = new Button("Large font");

➜            romanbutton = new Button("Roman font");

➜            courierbutton = new Button("Courier font");

             clearbutton = new Button("Clear text");

➜            add(boldbutton);
➜            add(italicbutton);
➜            add(largebutton);
➜            add(romanbutton);
➜            add(courierbutton);
➜            add(clearbutton);
         }        .
                  .
                  .
```

In addition, add an ActionListener to each button in your applet as follows:

```
➜public class scribbler extends Applet implements ActionListener{

         Button boldbutton, italicbutton, largebutton;
```

```
        Button romanbutton, courierbutton, clearbutton;

        public void init()
        {
            boldbutton = new Button("Bold font");
→           boldbutton.addActionListener(this);

            italicbutton = new Button("Italic font");
→           italicbutton.addActionListener(this);

            largebutton = new Button("Large font");
→           largebutton.addActionListener(this);

            romanbutton = new Button("Roman font");
→           romanbutton.addActionListener(this);

            courierbutton = new Button("Courier font");
→           courierbutton.addActionListener(this);

            clearbutton = new Button("Clear text");
→           clearbutton.addActionListener(this);

            add(boldbutton);
            add(italicbutton);
            add(largebutton);
            add(romanbutton);
            add(courierbutton);
            add(clearbutton);
                    .
                    .
                    .
        }
```

As in the artist applet, set up a boolean flag for each of the buttons, except for the clear button (the clear button can clear the text string as soon as it is clicked—you do not have to wait for the paint() method to be executed):

```
    public class scribbler extends Applet implements ActionListener {

        Button boldbutton, italicbutton, largebutton;
        Button romanbutton, courierbutton, clearbutton;
→       boolean bBoldFlag = false;
→       boolean bItalicFlag = false;
→       boolean bLargeFlag = false;
→       boolean bRomanFlag = true;
→       boolean bCourierFlag = false;

        public void init()
```

```
        {
                boldbutton = new Button("Bold font");
                boldbutton.addActionListener(this);

                italicbutton = new Button("Italic font");
                italicbutton.addActionListener(this);

                largebutton = new Button("Large font");
                largebutton.addActionListener(this);

                romanbutton = new Button("Roman font");
                romanbutton.addActionListener(this);

                courierbutton = new Button("Courier font");
                courierbutton.addActionListener(this);

                clearbutton = new Button("Clear text");
                clearbutton.addActionListener(this);

                add(boldbutton);
                add(italicbutton);
                add(largebutton);
                add(romanbutton);
                add(courierbutton);
                add(clearbutton);
                        .
                        .
                        .

        }
```

All of your boolean flags are set to false initially, except the flag bRomanFlag, since you will use Roman as your default font. To make these boolean flags active, set up an actionPerformed() method in the scribbler class:

```
public void actionPerformed(ActionEvent event){
                        .
                        .
                        .

        }
```

You will handle the first of the buttons—the one with the caption "Bold font"—now. When the user clicks this button, they want to make the text they will type boldface, so you could set the boolean flag bBoldFlag to true. But this way, how can the user turn off boldface typing? It's better to *toggle* the bold setting on and off, and you can do that with the negation operator (!) as follows, where you just reverse the setting of the bBoldFlag flag:

```
public void actionPerformed(ActionEvent event){
    if(event.getSource() == boldbutton){
        bBoldFlag = !bBoldFlag;
    }             .
                  .
                  .
}
```

When the Bold button is clicked, that gives the *input focus*—the target of keyboard strokes in Windows—to the button itself. When the user types again, no further text will appear, as the applet itself lost the focus when the button gained it. (The button has the focus, and buttons don't display keystrokes.) For that reason, after you have handled the button click, have the applet request the focus back again as follows using the requestFocus() method:

```
public void actionPerformed(ActionEvent event){
    if(event.getSource() == boldbutton){
        bBoldFlag = !bBoldFlag;
➜       requestFocus();
    }             .
                  .
                  .
}
```

The first three font settings can be toggled on and off: boldface, italics, and large (versus normal) text, and you can set them up as follows:

```
    public void actionPerformed(ActionEvent event){
        if(event.getSource() == boldbutton){
➜          bBoldFlag = !bBoldFlag;
➜          requestFocus();
➜      }
➜      if(event.getSource() == italicbutton){
➜          bItalicFlag = !bItalicFlag;
➜          requestFocus();
➜      }
➜      if(event.getSource() == largebutton){
➜          bLargeFlag = !bLargeFlag;
➜          requestFocus();
➜      }             .
                     .
                     .

    }
```

Skill 13

If, however, the user clicks a button with the caption "Roman font" or "Courier font", you can't just toggle a boolean flag. There are two font name flags: bRomanFlag and bCourierFlag; because only one can be true at a time, when you set one to true, you must set the other one to false:

```java
public void actionPerformed(ActionEvent event){
    if(event.getSource() == boldbutton){
        bBoldFlag = !bBoldFlag;
        requestFocus();
    }
    if(event.getSource() == italicbutton){
        bItalicFlag = !bItalicFlag;
        requestFocus();
    }
    if(event.getSource() == largebutton){
        bLargeFlag = !bLargeFlag;
        requestFocus();
    }
    if(event.getSource() == romanbutton){
        bRomanFlag = true;
        bCourierFlag = false;
        requestFocus();
    }
    if(event.getSource() == courierbutton){
        bCourierFlag = true;
        bRomanFlag = false;
        requestFocus();
    }            .
                 .
                 .
}
```

So far, then, you've made your Bold, Italic, Large, Roman, and Courier buttons active. All that remains is to activate the Clear Text button, which the user clicks when they want to clear the text they've typed. You can store that text in a String object named text:

```java
import java.applet.Applet;
import java.awt.*;
import java.awt.event.*;

public class scribbler extends Applet implements ActionListener {

    String text = "";

    Button boldbutton, italicbutton, largebutton;
    Button romanbutton, courierbutton, clearbutton;
```

```
boolean bBoldFlag = false;
boolean bItalicFlag = false;
boolean bLargeFlag = false;
boolean bRomanFlag = true;
boolean bCourierFlag = false;

         .
         .
         .
```

And now you should clear the text object by simply setting it to a null or empty string when the user clicks the Clear button:

```
public void actionPerformed(ActionEvent event){
    if(event.getSource() == boldbutton){
        bBoldFlag = !bBoldFlag;
        requestFocus();
    }
    if(event.getSource() == italicbutton){
        bItalicFlag = !bItalicFlag;
        requestFocus();
    }
    if(event.getSource() == largebutton){
        bLargeFlag = !bLargeFlag;
        requestFocus();
    }
    if(event.getSource() == romanbutton){
        bRomanFlag = true;
        bCourierFlag = false;
        requestFocus();
    }
    if(event.getSource() == courierbutton){
        bCourierFlag = true;
        bRomanFlag = false;
        requestFocus();
    }
    if(event.getSource() == clearbutton){
        text = "";
        requestFocus();
    }
    repaint();
}
```

Note that you also include a call to repaint() at the end of the action method. This is so the user can see the result of clicking a button immediately, without having to wait for the new key to be struck. And that brings us to the question, just how do we read direct keyboard input in Java?

Working with the Keyboard

So far, you've used text fields and text areas to handle all of your keyboard input. It is possible, however, to read keys directly in Java using the `keyTyped()` method. To use this method, you have to implement the KeyListener interface, and you do that as follows:

```java
import java.applet.Applet;
import java.awt.*;
import java.awt.event.*;

public class scribbler extends Applet implements ActionListener,
KeyListener {

    String text = "";

    Button boldbutton, italicbutton, largebutton;
    Button romanbutton, courierbutton, clearbutton;
    boolean bBoldFlag = false;
    boolean bItalicFlag = false;
    boolean bLargeFlag = false;
    boolean bRomanFlag = true;
    boolean bCourierFlag = false;

    public void init()
    {
        boldbutton = new Button("Bold font");
        boldbutton.addActionListener(this);

        italicbutton = new Button("Italic font");
        italicbutton.addActionListener(this);

        largebutton = new Button("Large font");
        largebutton.addActionListener(this);

        romanbutton = new Button("Roman font");
        romanbutton.addActionListener(this);

        courierbutton = new Button("Courier font");
        courierbutton.addActionListener(this);

        clearbutton = new Button("Clear text");
        clearbutton.addActionListener(this);

        add(boldbutton);
        add(italicbutton);
```

```
            add(largebutton);
            add(romanbutton);
            add(courierbutton);
            add(clearbutton);

➔           addKeyListener(this);
            requestFocus();
    }
```

Now you're ready to add the three key-handling methods of the KeyListener interface, keyTyped(), keyPressed(), and keyReleased(), each of which is passed a KeyEvent object:

```
    public void keyTyped(KeyEvent e) {}

    public void keyPressed(KeyEvent e) {}

    public void keyReleased(KeyEvent e) {}
```

We'll use the keyTyped() method here:

```
    public void keyTyped(KeyEvent e) {
                        .
                        .
                        .
    }
```

Here, you want to add the just-typed key to the string of text you already have in memory: the String object named text. You get that key by using the KeyEvent getKeyChar() method, and you add it to the text string the user has already typed as follows:

```
    public void keyTyped(KeyEvent e) {
➔       text = text + e.getKeyChar();
                        .
                        .
                        .
    }
```

The real work of the applet is done in the paint() method, and you can force a paint event now with the repaint() method:

```
    public void keyTyped(KeyEvent e) {
        text = text + e.getKeyChar();
➔       repaint();
    }
```

> **NOTE** Unless you are familiar with C++, you may be surprised to see a line like
>
> ```
> text = text + e.getKeyChar();
> ```
>
> because text is an object of the Java String class. However, in Java and in C++, operators like the + operator can be overloaded to work with objects of various classes. The + operator is overloaded to work with String objects.

Let's write the paint() method now; that's where the guts of this applet are.

Working with Fonts

When you enter the paint() method, you already have a string of text—that is, the String object named text—to display. Your goal is to display that text using the font settings the user has indicated (which are now mirrored in the settings of your boolean flags) so that the text appears centered in your applet, as shown in Figure 13.2.

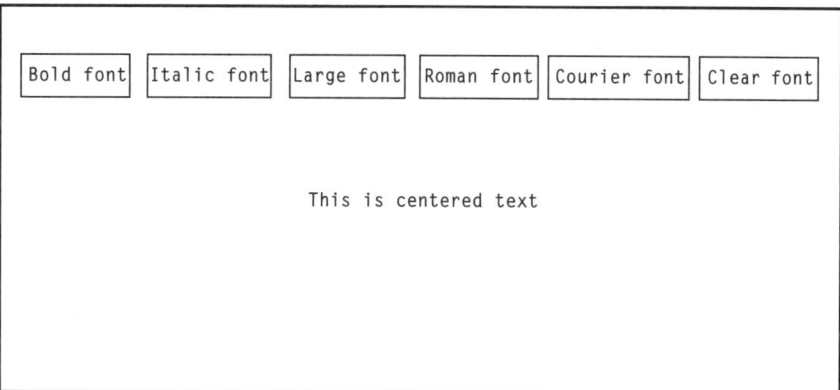

FIGURE 13.2:   The applet centers the text.

In the paint() method, you'll set up the type, the size, and the actual typeface of the font you will use to display the characters in the text object, and you'll set up an object of class Font with this information. Then you'll simply install that Font object in the Graphics object passed to you in paint() and draw your string.

You should start your `paint()` method by setting up the variables you'll need and setting the font type to default values. For example, the name of the font you'll use is stored as a string, like "Roman" or "Courier", and your default will be Roman:

```
public void paint(Graphics g)
{
    String fontname = "Roman";
        .
        .
        .
```

TIP   If you don't know what fonts are installed on your system, you can check in the Windows 95 registry with the Windows REGEDIT tool, `regedit.exe`, which Windows 95 places in the `c:\windows` directory. You can also see what fonts are available by using a word processing program like Microsoft Word. Another option is to look in the Control Panel and click the Fonts icon.

The type of font—plain, bold, or italic—is set up in an integer variable that can take one of these pre-defined Font class constants: `Font.PLAIN`, `Font.BOLD`, or `Font.ITALIC`. Make your default plain text, `Font.PLAIN`:

```
public void paint(Graphics g)
{
    String fontname = "Roman";
    int type = Font.PLAIN;
        .
        .
        .
```

The point size of the font is also stored as an integer. Make your default font size 24 point:

```
public void paint(Graphics g)
{
    String fontname = "Roman";
    int type = Font.PLAIN;
    int size = 24;
        .
        .
        .
```

You've set up the default values for your font. Next, you need to create the Font object itself—which you should name font—that you will load into the Graphics object passed to you in the paint() method:

```
public void paint(Graphics g)
{
    String fontname = "Roman";
    int type = Font.PLAIN;
    int size = 24;
→   Font font;
        .
        .
        .
```

The methods of the Java Font class appear in Table 13.1.

TABLE 13.1: The Font class methods

Method	Does This
Font(AttributeSet)	Creates a new font with the specified attributes
Font(FontObject)	Creates a new font from the specified Font object
Font(String, int, int)	Creates a new font from the specified name, style, and point size
canDisplay(char)	Checks if this font has a glyph for the specified character
canDisplayUpTo(char[], int, int)	Is a convenience overload
canDisplayUpTo(CharacterIterator, int, int)	Indicates whether a string is displayable by this Font
canDisplayUpTo(String)	Indicates whether a string is displayable by this Font
decode(String)	Returns the specified font using the name passed in
deriveFont(AffineTransform)	Creates a new Font object by replicating the current Font object with a new transform associated with it
deriveFont(float)	Creates a new Font object by replicating the current Font object with a new size
deriveFont(int)	Creates a new Font object by replicating the current Font object with a new style associated with it
deriveFont(int, AffineTransform)	Creates a new Font object by replicating the current Font object with a new style, transform, and font attributes

TABLE 13.1 CONTINUED: The Font class methods

Method	Does This
deriveFont(int, float)	Creates a new Font object by replicating the current Font object with a new style, size, and font attributes associated with it
deriveFont(TextAttributeSet)	Creates a new Font object by replicating the current Font object with a new set of font attributes associated with it
equals(Object)	Compares this object to the specified object
finalize()	Called by the garbage collector on an object when garbage collection determines that there are no more references to the object
getAdvance(char)	Gets the advance
getAscent()	Returns the ascent of the font above the roman baseline
getAttributes()	Returns an array of font attributes available in this font
getAvailableAttributes()	Returns the names of all the attributes supported by this font
getBaselineFor(char)	Returns the baseline appropriate for displaying this character
getBaselineOffset(byte)	Returns the offset from the roman baseline of the font to the specified baseline
getBaselineOffsetsFor(char)	Returns a list of relative offsets for the different baselines
getBestFontFor(Attributed-CharacterIterator)	Resolves styles on the character at start into an instance of Font that can best render the text between start and limit
getBestFontFor(Attributed-CharacterIterator, int, int)	Resolves styles on the character at start into an instance of Font that can best render the text between start and limit
getDescent()	Returns the descent of the font above the roman baseline
getFamily()	Returns the family name of the font (for example, Helvetica)
getFamily(Locale)	Returns the family name of the font (for example, Helvetica), localized for the given locale
getFont(AttributeSet)	Returns a font appropriate to this attribute set

TABLE 13.1 CONTINUED: The Font class methods

Method	Does This
getFont(String)	Returns a font from the system properties list
getFont(String, Font)	Returns the specified font from the system properties list
getFontName()	Returns the font face name of the font (for example, Helvetica Bold)
getFontName(Locale)	Returns the font face name of the font (for example, Helvetica Fett) localized for the specified locale
getGlyphJustificationInfo(int)	Returns justification info for the glyph specified by glyphCode
getGlyphMetrics(int)	Returns the metrics information for a glyph specified by a glyph code
getGlyphOutline(int, float, float)	Returns the outline description of a glyph specified by a glyph code
getGlyphSet(char[], int, int, byte, int[], byte[])	Constructs a glyph set for the text between start and limit
getGlyphSet(CharacterIterator, int, int, byte, int[], byte[])	Creates a glyph set for the text between start and limit
getGlyphSet(String)	Converts all characters in the String Object to font glyph codes
getItalicAngle()	Returns the italic angle of this font
getLeading()	Returns the leading for this font
getMaxAdvance()	Returns the maximum advance of any glyph in this font
getMaxBounds2D()	Returns the maximum bounding box of this font
getMetrics(GlyphSet, AffineTransform)	getMissingGlyphCode()
getName()	Returns the logical name of the font
getNumGlyphs()	Returns number of glyphs in the font
getOutline(GlyphSet, AffineTransform, float, float)	Gets the font outline
getPeer()	Gets the peer of the font
getPSName()	Returns the postscript name of the font
getRequestedAttributes()	Returns the attribute set used to create this font

Skill 13

TABLE 13.1 CONTINUED: The Font class methods

Method	Does This
getSize()	Returns the point size of the font, rounded to an integer
getSize2D()	Returns the point size of the font in float
getStrikethroughOffsetFor(char)	Returns the strikethrough offset from the roman baseline for this character
getStrikethroughThicknessFor(char)	Returns the strikethrough thickness for this character
getStyle()	Returns the style of the font
getTransform()	Returns the transform associated with this font
getUnderlineOffsetFor(char)	Returns the underline offset from the roman baseline for this character
getUnderlineThicknessFor(char)	Returns the underline thickness for this character
hashCode()	Returns a hashcode for this font
isBold()	Indicates whether the font's style is bold
isItalic()	Indicates whether the font's style is italic
isPlain()	Returns true if the font is plain
isUniformBaseline()	Returns true if this font places all glyphs on a single baseline
isVerticalBaseline()	Returns true if vertical baseline is used
sameBaselineUpTo(char[], int, int)	Returns the index of the first character with a different baseline from the character at start, or the limit if all characters between start and limit have the same baseline
sameBaselineUpTo(CharacterIterator)	Returns the index of the first character with a different baseline from the first character in the range
toString()	Converts this object to a String representation

The next step is to set up the variables fontname, type, and size according to how the user wants them so that you can use them to set up the Font object. To do so, just check the various boolean flags you have set up and set these three variables accordingly:

```
public void paint(Graphics g)
{
```

Skill 13

```
          String fontname = "Roman";
          int type = Font.PLAIN;
          int size = 24;
          Font font;

→         if(bBoldFlag){
               type = type | Font.BOLD;
→         }
→         if(bItalicFlag){
→              type = type | Font.ITALIC;
→         }
→         if(bLargeFlag){
→              size = 48;
→         }
→         if(bRomanFlag){
→              fontname = "Roman";
→         }
→         if(bCourierFlag){
→              fontname = "Courier";
→         }            .
                       .
                       .
```

TIP   Because text can be italic and bold at the same time, you can use the bitwise OR
operator (|) to combine font types. For example, valid font types include:
Font.PLAIN | Font.ITALIC or Font.BOLD | Font.ITALIC.

At this point, then, you have the font's name, its size, and its type (i.e., plain or
bold, italic or not). Now create the Font object, and install it in your Graphics
object using the setFont() method as follows:

```
public void paint(Graphics g)
{
     String fontname = "Roman";
     int type = Font.PLAIN;
     int size = 24;
     Font font;

     if(bBoldFlag){
          type = type | Font.BOLD;
     }            .
                  .
                  .
→    font = new Font(fontname, type, size);
→    g.setFont(font);
}
```

And now the font the user selected, in the font style they want, is installed. When you draw text in the Graphics object with drawString(), the text will appear in this new font.

However, suppose you want to do more—suppose you want to make sure the text appears centered in the applet. You can do that with a FontMetrics object, which you'll learn about next.

Working with the *FontMetrics* Class

To make sure your text string is centered in the applet, you have to know how much space the string will take up on the screen, both horizontally and vertically. You can do that with a FontMetrics object (in addition, you'll have to find out how wide and how tall your applet is in pixels). First, add a new FontMetrics object to your applet:

```
→import java.applet.Applet;
 import java.awt.*;
 import java.awt.event.*;

 public class scribbler extends Applet implements ActionListener,
 KeyListener {

     String text = "";
     int x = 0;
     int y = 0;

     Button boldbutton, italicbutton, largebutton;
     Button romanbutton, courierbutton, clearbutton;
     boolean bBoldFlag = false;
     boolean bItalicFlag = false;
     boolean bLargeFlag = false;
     boolean bRomanFlag = true;
     boolean bCourierFlag = false;
→    FontMetrics fontmetrics;
                .
                .
                .
```

Then create this FontMetrics object, passing it the font object you set up so it will be able to return information about strings displayed in that font:

```
     public void paint(Graphics g)
     {
         String fontname = "Roman";
         int type = Font.PLAIN;
```

```
        int size = 24;
        Font font;

        if(bBoldFlag){
             type = type | Font.BOLD;
        }
        if(bItalicFlag){
             type = type | Font.ITALIC;
        }
        if(bLargeFlag){
             size = 48;
        }
        if(bRomanFlag){
             fontname = "Roman";
        }
        if(bCourierFlag){
             fontname = "Courier";
        }

        font = new Font(fontname, type, size);
        g.setFont(font);

➡        fontmetrics = getFontMetrics(font);
             .
             .
             .
```

The FontMetric class methods appear in Table 13.2.

TABLE 13.2: The FontMetric class methods

Method	Does This
FontMetrics(Font)	Creates a FontMetrics object using given font
bytesWidth(byte[], int, int)	Returns the width of a byte array
charWidth(int)	Gets the width of a given character
charWidth(char)	Gets the width of a given character
charsWidth(char[], int, int)	Gets the width of the character array
getAscent()	Gets the font ascent
getDescent()	Gets the font descent
getFont()	Gets the font
getHeight()	Gets the total height of this font
getLeading()	Gets the standard line spacing for this font
getMaxAdvance()	Gets the maximum advance width of any character

TABLE 13.2 CONTINUED: The FontMetric class methods

Method	Does This
getMaxAscent()	Gets the maximum ascent of characters
getMaxDescent()	Gets the maximum descent of characters
getWidths()	Gets the widths of the first 256 characters
stringWidth(String)	Gets the width of a given string
toString()	Gets the string representation for an object

Getting the Width of a Text String

Now you can retrieve the width of the text this way:

```
width = fontmetrics.stringWidth(text);
```

and the height this way:

```
height = fontmetrics.getHeight();
```

 **NOTE**   The height of the line of text is a constant—it's not dependent on the string length—so you don't have to pass the line of text itself to the getHeight() method.

You'll also need the height and width of your applet, and you'll find those values with the Applet method size(), which returns an object of the Java Dimension class. The width and height members of this Dimension object will give you the width and height of your applet.

The last thing to keep in mind is that when you pass the location of a string to drawString() so that it can appear on the screen, the location you pass is actually the bottom left of the string on the screen—*not* the top left as many Windows programmers expect.

Centering Displayed Text

Putting together all you've learned in this skill means that you find the x and y location at which to print your string as follows, making sure it is centered in the applet's display:

```
public void paint(Graphics g)
{
```

```
String fontname = "Roman";
int type = Font.PLAIN;
int size = 24;
Font font;

if(bBoldFlag){
    type = type | Font.BOLD;
}
if(bItalicFlag){
    type = type | Font.ITALIC;
}
if(bLargeFlag){
    size = 48;
}
if(bRomanFlag){
    fontname = "Roman";
}
if(bCourierFlag){
    fontname = "Courier";
}

font = new Font(fontname, type, size);
g.setFont(font);

fontmetrics = getFontMetrics(font);
x =(size().width - fontmetrics.stringWidth(text)) / 2;
y = (size().height + fontmetrics.getHeight()) / 2;
                .
                .
                .

}
```

You may also need to declare the new integer variables x and y, which hold the location of the text string in the applet:

```
import java.applet.Applet;
import java.awt.*;
import java.awt.event.*;

public class scribbler extends Applet implements ActionListener,
KeyListener {

    String text = "";
    int x = 0;
    int y = 0;

    Button boldbutton, italicbutton, largebutton;
    Button romanbutton, courierbutton, clearbutton;
```

```
boolean bBoldFlag = false;
boolean bItalicFlag = false;
boolean bLargeFlag = false;
boolean bRomanFlag = true;
boolean bCourierFlag = false;
FontMetrics fontmetrics;
        .
        .
        .
```

All that remains now is to display the text string itself, and you can do that with drawString():

```
public void paint(Graphics g)
{
        String fontname = "Roman";
        int type = Font.PLAIN;
        int size = 24;
        Font font;

        if(bBoldFlag){
            type = type | Font.BOLD;
        }
        if(bItalicFlag){
            type = type | Font.ITALIC;
        }
        if(bLargeFlag){
            size = 48;
        }
        if(bRomanFlag){
            fontname = "Roman";
        }
        if(bCourierFlag){
            fontname = "Courier";
        }

        font = new Font(fontname, type, size);
        g.setFont(font);

        fontmetrics = getFontMetrics(font);
        x =(size().width - fontmetrics.stringWidth(text)) / 2;
        y = (size().height + fontmetrics.getHeight()) / 2;

➜       g.drawString(text, x, y);
}
```

Select a few font options–in Figure 13.3, a bold italic font is selected and a few characters have been typed. As you can see, you "scribbler" applet is a success. The code for this applet appears in `scribbler.java`.

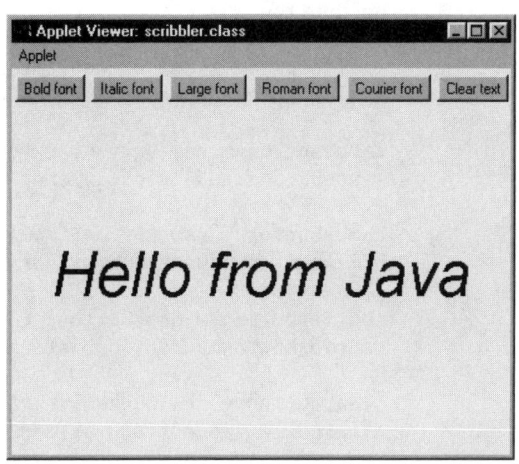

FIGURE 13.3:   The scribbler applet lets the user specify various font options.

scribbler.java

```java
import java.applet.Applet;
import java.awt.*;
import java.awt.event.*;

public class scribbler extends Applet implements ActionListener,
KeyListener {

    String text = "";
    int x = 0;
    int y = 0;

    Button boldbutton, italicbutton, largebutton;
    Button romanbutton, courierbutton, clearbutton;
    boolean bBoldFlag = false;
    boolean bItalicFlag = false;
    boolean bLargeFlag = false;
    boolean bRomanFlag = true;
    boolean bCourierFlag = false;
```

```
FontMetrics fontmetrics;

public void init()
{
    boldbutton = new Button("Bold font");
    boldbutton.addActionListener(this);

    italicbutton = new Button("Italic font");
    italicbutton.addActionListener(this);

    largebutton = new Button("Large font");
    largebutton.addActionListener(this);

    romanbutton = new Button("Roman font");
    romanbutton.addActionListener(this);

    courierbutton = new Button("Courier font");
    courierbutton.addActionListener(this);

    clearbutton = new Button("Clear text");
    clearbutton.addActionListener(this);

    add(boldbutton);
    add(italicbutton);
    add(largebutton);
    add(romanbutton);
    add(courierbutton);
    add(clearbutton);

    addKeyListener(this);
    requestFocus();
}

public void actionPerformed(ActionEvent event){
    if(event.getSource() == boldbutton){
        bBoldFlag = !bBoldFlag;
        requestFocus();
    }
    if(event.getSource() == italicbutton){
        bItalicFlag = !bItalicFlag;
        requestFocus();
    }
    if(event.getSource() == largebutton){
        bLargeFlag = !bLargeFlag;
        requestFocus();
    }
    if(event.getSource() == romanbutton){
        bRomanFlag = true;
```

```
              bCourierFlag = false;
              requestFocus();
          }
      if(event.getSource() == courierbutton){
              bCourierFlag = true;
              bRomanFlag = false;
              requestFocus();
          }
      if(event.getSource() == clearbutton){
              text = "";
              requestFocus();
          }
      repaint();
  }


public void paint(Graphics g)
{
      String fontname = "Roman";
      int type = Font.PLAIN;
      int size = 24;
      Font font;

      if(bBoldFlag){
          type = type | Font.BOLD;
      }
      if(bItalicFlag){
          type = type | Font.ITALIC;
      }
      if(bLargeFlag){
          size = 48;
      }
      if(bRomanFlag){
          fontname = "Roman";
      }
      if(bCourierFlag){
          fontname = "Courier";
      }

      font = new Font(fontname, type, size);
      g.setFont(font);

      fontmetrics = getFontMetrics(font);
      x =(size().width - fontmetrics.stringWidth(text)) / 2;
      y = (size().height + fontmetrics.getHeight()) / 2;

      g.drawString(text, x, y);
  }
```

```
public void keyTyped(KeyEvent e) {
    text = text + e.getKeyChar();
    repaint();
}

public void keyPressed(KeyEvent e) {}

public void keyReleased(KeyEvent e) {}

}
```

And now you're displaying text the user typed in with the font options they've picked.

While we're working with text in Java, let's take a look at one more way of handling text—using the clipboard.

Using the Clipboard from Java

To see how to use the clipboard in Java, place a small text string, "Hello from Java", into the clipboard. Then you'll be able to paste that text string into other programs, like Microsoft Word (using Word's Paste menu item). Create a new file named clipboarder.java now. This program will be a Java application because, as is the case with printing, applets cannot access the clipboard for security reasons. Add the application's main class to clipboarder.java now:

```
public class clipboarder {
        .
        .
        .
}
```

Because this is a Java application, add a main() method:

```
public class clipboarder {
    public static void main(String[] argv) {
          .
          .
          .
    }
}
```

Here you can simply create a new object of the class you'll name `writetext`, which will write to the clipboard. You create that object this way:

```
public class clipboarder {
    public static void main(String[] argv) {
        writetext w = new writetext();
    }
}
```

Next, write the `writetext` class. You'll need a frame window to implement the ClipboardOwner interface, so you can start with the following code:

```
class writetext extends Frame {
        .
        .
        .
}
```

To handle clipboard operations, add the ClipboardOwner interface this way:

```
→class writetext extends Frame implements ClipboardOwner {
        .
        .
        .
}
```

Now create the `writetext` class's constructor and the `lostOwnership()` method, which is required to implement this interface:

```
class writetext extends Frame implements ClipboardOwner {
→        writetext() {
        }

→        public void lostOwnership(Clipboard clipboard, Transferable ➡
    contents){}
}
```

You can get an object of the `Clipboard` class as follows:

```
class writetext extends Frame implements ClipboardOwner {
    writetext() {
→        Clipboard clipboard = getToolkit().getSystemClipboard();
        .
        .
        .
    }

    public void lostOwnership(Clipboard clipboard, Transferable ➡
    contents){}
}
```

The Java `Clipboard` class's methods appear in Table 13.3—you can place text in the clipboard with `setContents()`, and you can retrieve it with `getContents()`.

TABLE 13.3: The `Clipboard` class methods

Method	Does This
`Clipboard(String)`	Creates a clipboard object
`getContents(Object)`	Returns a transferable object representing the current contents of the clipboard
`getName()`	Returns the name of this clipboard object
`setContents(Transferable, ClipboardOwner)`	Sets the current contents of the clipboard to the specified transferable object and registers the specified clipboard owner as the owner of the new contents

Next, create the string of text you want to place in the clipboard with the Java `StringSelection` class; in this case, that string is simply "Hello from Java."

```
class writetext extends Frame implements ClipboardOwner {
     writetext() {
          Clipboard clipboard = getToolkit().getSystemClipboard();
➡         StringSelection contents = new StringSelection("Hello from ➡
     Java");

                         .
                         .
                         .

     }

     public void lostOwnership(Clipboard clipboard, Transferable ➡
  contents){}
  }
```

Finally, place the string into the clipboard with the `Clipboard` class's `setContents()` method:

```
class writetext extends Frame implements ClipboardOwner {
     writetext() {
          Clipboard clipboard = getToolkit().getSystemClipboard();
          StringSelection contents = new StringSelection("Hello from ➡
     Java");
➡          clipboard.setContents(contents, this);
     }

     public void lostOwnership(Clipboard clipboard, Transferable ➡
  contents){}
  }
```

Use `javac.exe` to compile `clipboarder.java` and `java.exe` to run it. When the application runs, the string "Hello from Java" is placed in the clipboard, and you can paste it into other applications, like Microsoft Word, as shown in Figure 13.4. The code for this application appears in `clipboarder.java`.

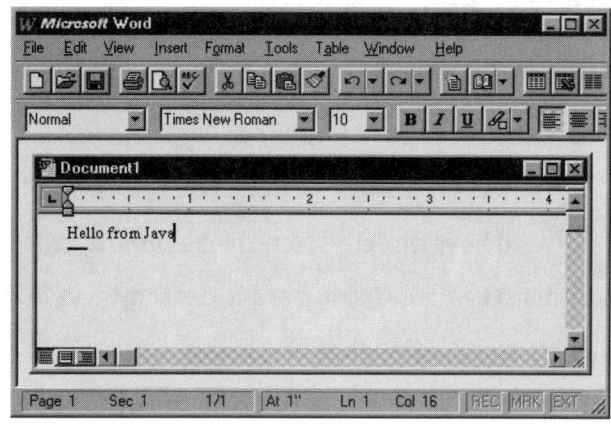

FIGURE 13.4:   You can place text into the Clipboard and paste it into other applications such as Microsoft Word.

clipboarder.java

```
public class clipboarder {
    public static void main(String[] argv) {
        writetext w = new writetext();
    }
}

class writetext extends Frame implements ClipboardOwner {
    writetext() {
        Clipboard clipboard = getToolkit().getSystemClipboard();
        StringSelection contents = new StringSelection("Hello from ➥
Java");
        clipboard.setContents(contents, this);
    }

    public void lostOwnership(Clipboard clipboard, Transferable ➥
contents){}
}
```

As you can see, working with fonts can be an indispensable technique, allowing you to display text in Java in a wide variety of formats. In Skill 14, you'll turn to an important and very popular Java topic: graphics animation.

Are You up to Speed?

Now you can. . .

- ☑ set a program's font by using *setFont()*
- ☑ make text bold or italic as you require
- ☑ read keys directly from the keyboard, using the *KeyListener* methods
- ☑ use the *FontMetric* class to determine a text string's length
- ☑ center displayed text
- ☑ copy and paste text to and from other applications with the system Clipboard

SKILL 14

Understanding Graphics Animation

- Creating animated programs
- Using *Canvas* controls
- Using the *Animator* class
- Examining how animation works
- Reducing screen flicker
- Customizing an animation applet

In Skill 13, we saw how to work with text and fonts. Here, we'll take a guided tour of a very popular Java topic: graphics animation. For a long time, Web pages were static things of images and text. Java brought animation to Web pages, and that was one of the chief reasons for its popularity. There are other ways to animate Web pages now: embedding video files like .avi files, using looping .gif images (which hold a number of internal images), or using other packages like Visual Basic Script. However, Java remains the animation tool of choice for most Web programmers.

The fundamentals of animation are simply placing a series of images on the screen in rapid succession to give the impression of movement. You can start with one image, as shown in Figure 14.1, and then rapidly move on to the next, as shown in Figure 14.2.

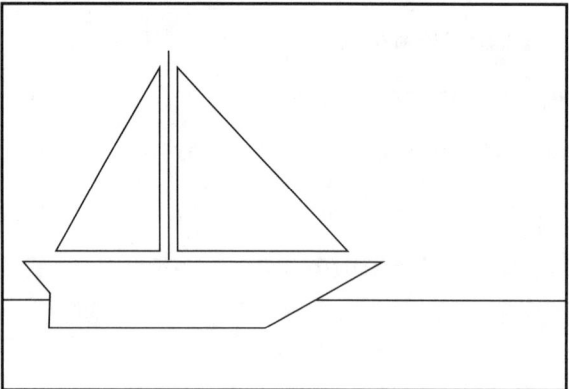

FIGURE 14.1: The first image is on the left.

Flipping quickly through images this way, like you would do with a flip book, creates the animation. Graphics animation was one of the biggest reasons that Java took the Internet by storm. Let's start now with our first animation applet.

If you were to add more images like this and cycle through them quickly, the boat would appear to move.

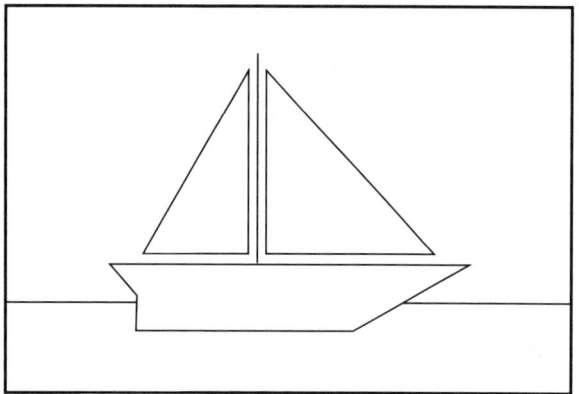

FIGURE 14.2:   The second image is closer to the center.

Creating Basic Animation

In this first animation example, you will draw a graphics image and move it across the screen. For this purpose, you'll use a Canvas *control*. Canvas controls are very useful Java controls that you can draw in; you'll draw an image in a Canvas control and use that control's setLocation() method to animate the image. Let's put this to work now. Create a new file named canvaser.java and add the standard starting code:

```
import java.applet.Applet;
import java.awt.*;

public class canvaser extendsApplet {
        .
        .
        .
}
```

You'll create a new class derived from the Java Canvas class and place your image in that new control. Here, you can draw a small box in your Canvas control and call this new Canvas control class BoxCanvas. You can create an object of that class in your applet as follows. (You'll create the BoxCanvas class in a minute.)

```
import java.applet.Applet;
import java.awt.*;

public class canvaser extends Applet {
```
→   BoxCanvas boxcanvas;
          .
          .
          .

The Canvas class methods appear in Table 14.1.

TABLE 14.1: The Java Canvas class methods

Method	Does This
Canvas()	Constructs a new canvas
Canvas(GraphicsConfiguration config)	Constructs a new Canvas given a GraphicsConfiguration object
addNotify()	Creates the peer of the canvas
paint(Graphics)	Paints the canvas in the default background color

You can create and add the boxcanvas control to your applet in the init() method as follows:

```
import java.applet.Applet;
import java.awt.*;

public class canvaser extends Applet {
```
→   BoxCanvas boxcanvas;

          public void init(){
→   boxcanvas = new BoxCanvas();
→   boxcanvas.resize(100, 100);
→   add(boxcanvas);
                  .
                  .
                  .

Add a button with the caption "Move Rectangle" to your applet. When the user clicks the button, you can move the box across the screen. Add that button, button1, this way:

```
 import java.applet.Applet;
 import java.awt.*;
→import java.awt.event.*;

→public class canvaser extends Applet implements ActionListener {

     BoxCanvas boxcanvas;
→    Button button1;

     public void init(){
         boxcanvas = new BoxCanvas();
         boxcanvas.resize(100, 100);
         add(boxcanvas);
→        button1 = new Button("Move Rectangle");
→        add(button1);
→        button1.addActionListener(this);
     }            .
                  .
                  .
```

To make your new button active, add an actionPerformed() method:

```
 import java.applet.Applet;
 import java.awt.*;
 import java.awt.event.*;

 public class canvaser extends Applet implements ActionListener {

     BoxCanvas boxcanvas;
     Button button1;

     public void init(){
         boxcanvas = new BoxCanvas();
         boxcanvas.resize(100, 100);
         add(boxcanvas);
         button1 = new Button("Move Rectangle");
         add(button1);
         button1.addActionListener(this);
     }

→    public void actionPerformed(ActionEvent event){
                  .
                  .
                  .
→    }
 }
```

You can check to make sure your button was the control that caused this event:

```java
import java.applet.Applet;
import java.awt.*;
import java.awt.event.*;

public class canvaser extends Applet implements ActionListener {

    BoxCanvas boxcanvas;
    Button button1;

    public void init(){
        boxcanvas = new BoxCanvas();
        boxcanvas.resize(100, 100);
        add(boxcanvas);
        button1 = new Button("Move Rectangle");
        add(button1);
        button1.addActionListener(this);
    }

    public void actionPerformed(ActionEvent event){
        if(event.getSource() == button1){
            .
            .
            .
        }
    }
}
```

If the button has indeed been clicked, set up a **for** loop, using a loop index named `loop_index`, that will loop 150 times:

```java
import java.applet.Applet;
import java.awt.*;
import java.awt.event.*;

public class canvaser extends Applet implements ActionListener {

    BoxCanvas boxcanvas;
    Button button1;

    public void init(){
        boxcanvas = new BoxCanvas();
        boxcanvas.resize(100, 100);
        add(boxcanvas);
        button1 = new Button("Move Rectangle");
        add(button1);
        button1.addActionListener(this);
    }
```

```
      public void actionPerformed(ActionEvent event){
            if(event.getSource() == button1){
➜for(loop_index = 0; loop_index < 150; loop_index++){
                         .
                         .
                         .
                  }
            }
      }
}
```

And you use the Canvas control's setLocation() method (all controls have this method built in to move the Canvas control across the screen):

```
import java.applet.Applet;
import java.awt.*;
import java.awt.event.*;

public class canvaser extends Applet implements ActionListener {

      BoxCanvas boxcanvas;
      Button button1;

      public void init(){
            boxcanvas = new BoxCanvas();
            boxcanvas.resize(100, 100);
            add(boxcanvas);
            button1 = new Button("Move Rectangle");
            add(button1);
            button1.addActionListener(this);
      }

      public void actionPerformed(ActionEvent event){
            if(event.getSource() == button1){
                  for(loop_index = 0; loop_index < 150; loop_index++){
➜                       boxcanvas.setLocation(loop_index, 0);
                  }
            }
      }
}
```

All that remains now is to create the BoxCanvas class. You can create that class now, extending the Java Canvas class. Add the following code to the end of the canvaser.java file:

```
class BoxCanvas extends java.awt.Canvas {
                  .
                  .
                  .
}
```

Here, you want to draw a box in the control, so override the `paint()` method and draw that box with the `drawRect()` method:

```
class BoxCanvas extends java.awt.Canvas {

    public void paint (Graphics g) {
➜        g.drawRect(10, 50, 40, 40);
    }
}
```

You can run the applet now, as shown below. When you click the button, the box moves across the screen, from left to right. Your first animation—created simply by moving a Canvas control—is a success. The code for this applet appears in `canvaser.java`.

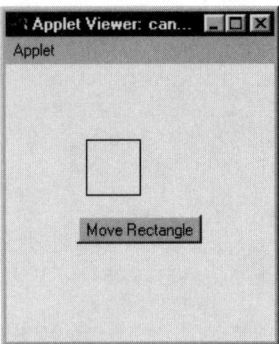

canvaser.java

```
import java.applet.Applet;
import java.awt.*;
import java.awt.event.*;

public class canvaser extends java.applet.Applet implements
ActionListener {

    BoxCanvas boxcanvas;
    Button button1;

    public void init(){
        boxcanvas = new BoxCanvas();
        boxcanvas.resize(100, 100);
        add(boxcanvas);
        button1 = new Button("Move Rectangle");
```

```
            add(button1);
            button1.addActionListener(this);
        }

        public void actionPerformed(ActionEvent event){
            if(event.getSource() == button1){
                for(loop_index = 0; loop_index < 150; loop_index++){
                    boxcanvas.setLocation(loop_index, 0);
                }
            }
        }
    }

    class BoxCanvas extends java.awt.Canvas {

        public void paint (Graphics g) {
            g.drawRect(10, 50, 40, 40);
        }
    }
```

The "canvaser" example showed you a quick and easy method of animation, but of course moving an image around is relatively crude. Java offers a great deal more animation power. Let's explore the other standard Java animation techniques now.

Your First True Animation

A *thread* is an execution stream; so far, all the programs you've learned to create have only had one thread. But Java programs can have a number of threads, each executing code in the same program, and each running at the same time. This is called *multi-threading*, and it's one of the reasons that Java animation is so powerful. With multi-threading, you can run the animation at the same time as the rest of your applet, without interference. Let's take a look at this now.

 NOTE   You'll see a great deal more about threads in Skill 15.

You can create an example of an animation applet with a circular image in it, as shown in Figure 14.3. When the applet runs, you can have your graphics image appear to spin. You'll use four images to create the illusion of motion in this applet, flashing these images on the screen, one at a time.

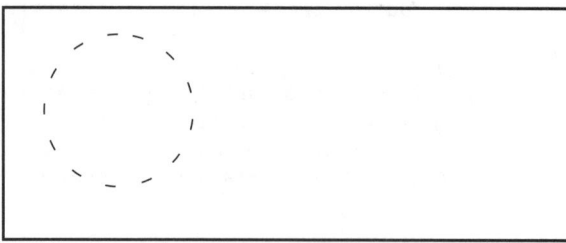

FIGURE 14.3:   An applet with a circular image

These four images appear below. You can use a small colored disk and animate it to give the impression that it is spinning.

Let's put this technique to work now. Create a new file named `spinner.java` and install the usual starting code there:

```
import java.awt.*;
import java.applet.Applet;

public class spinner extends Applet {
        .
        .
        .
}
```

You can start your new applet by reading in the four images, which you might save in the four files `spin1.gif` through `spin4.gif`. First, set up an `Image` array named `spinImages[]` to hold those images:

```
import java.awt.*;
import java.applet.Applet;
```

```
    public class spinner extends Applet {

➜       Image spinImages[] = new Image[4];
                    .
                    .
                    .
```

Next, load the images themselves in the init() method:

```
import java.awt.*;
import java.applet.Applet;

public class spinner extends Applet{

    Image spinImages[] = new Image[4];

➜   public void init() {
➜       spinImages[0] = getImage(getCodeBase(), "spin1.gif");
➜       spinImages[1] = getImage(getCodeBase(), "spin2.gif");
➜       spinImages[2] = getImage(getCodeBase(), "spin3.gif");
➜       spinImages[3] = getImage(getCodeBase(), "spin4.gif");
➜   }
```

Now your images are ready to go, and you're ready to introduce multi-threading to your applet.

Working with Multi-Threading

As we'll see in Skill 15, the basis of multi-threading in Java is the three methods, start(), run(), and stop():

```
start()
{
}

run()
{
}

stop()
{
}
```

Usually, Java programs have one thread, the main thread, running. However, you can start a new thread in the start() method. The code that you want this thread to run appears in the run() method. This means that the code in that method will be run automatically as the main thread continues on with the rest of the applet. You can stop the thread in the `stop()` method, which is called when the applet is unloaded or the application finishes.

 **NOTE**   It's important to stop the thread in the `stop()` method, or your applet will continue to run in a Web browser, even when the user goes on to other pages.

Let's install the code you'll need for your animation applet now. You'll create a new thread named `spinThread` to handle your animation. You'll start the new thread in the `start()` method, run your animation in the `run()` method, and stop the thread in the `stop()` method.

Handling the *start()* Method

Add the new thread, `spinThread`, to your applet now:

```
import java.awt.*;
import java.applet.Applet;

public class spinner extends Applet {

    Image spinImages[] = new Image[4];
→   Thread spinThread;
         .
         .
         .
```

The Java Thread class methods appear in Table 14.2

TABLE 14.2: The Java Thread class methods

Method	Does This
Thread()	Constructs a new thread
Thread(Runnable)	Constructs a new thread that applies the run() method of the given target
Thread(Runnable, String)	Constructs a new thread with the given name and applies the run() method of the given target
Thread(String)	Constructs a new thread with the given name
Thread(ThreadGroup, Runnable)	Constructs a new thread in the given thread group that applies the run() method of the given target

TABLE 14.2 CONTINUED: The Java Thread class methods

Method	Does This
`Thread(ThreadGroup, Runnable, String)`	Constructs a new thread in the given thread group with the given name and applies the run() method of the given target
`Thread(ThreadGroup, String)`	Constructs a new thread in the given thread group with the given name
`activeCount()`	Returns the current number of active threads in this thread group
`checkAccess()`	Checks whether the current thread is allowed to modify this thread
`countStackFrames()`	Returns the number of stack frames in this thread
`currentThread()`	Returns a reference to the currently executing thread object
`destroy()`	Destroys a thread, without any cleanup
`dumpStack()`	Is a debugging procedure to print a stack trace for the current thread
`enumerate(Thread[])`	Copies into the given array references to every active thread in this thread's group
`getContextClassLoader()`	Gets the context classloader for this thread
`getName()`	Gets and returns this thread's name
`getPriority()`	Gets and returns the thread's priority
`getThreadGroup()`	Gets and returns this thread's group
`interrupt()`	Sends an interrupt to a thread
`interrupted()`	Asks if the thread is interrupted
`isAlive()`	Returns a boolean indicating if the thread is active
`isDaemon()`	Returns the daemon flag of the thread
`isInterrupted()`	Asks if some thread (not necessarily self) has been interrupted
`join()`	Waits forever for this thread to die
`join(long)`	Waits for this thread to die
`join(long, int)`	Waits for the thread to die with more precise time
`resume()`	Deprecated. Resumes this thread execution

TABLE 14.2 CONTINUED: The Java Thread class methods

Method	Does This
run()	Is the actual body of this thread
setContextClassLoader(ClassLoader)	Sets the context classloader for this thread
setDaemon(boolean)	Marks this thread as a daemon thread or a user thread
setName(String)	Sets the thread's name
setPriority(int)	Sets the thread's priority
sleep(long)	Causes the currently executing thread to sleep for the given number of milliseconds
sleep(long, int)	Causes the thread to sleep, in milliseconds and additional nanoseconds
start()	Starts this thread
stop()	Deprecated. Stops a thread by tossing an object
stop(Throwable)	Deprecated. Stops a thread by tossing an object
suspend()	Deprecated. Suspends this thread's execution
toString()	Returns a string representation of the thread, including the thread's name, priority, and thread group
yield()	Causes the currently executing thread object to yield

To handle multi-threading, you have to implement the Runnable interface, which you can do as follows. (You'll see more about this interface later.)

```
import java.awt.*;
import java.applet.Applet;

public class spinner extends Applet implements Runnable{

    Image spinImages[] = new Image[4];
    Thread spinThread;
        .
        .
        .
```

Now add the start() method:

```
import java.awt.*;
import java.applet.Applet;
```

```
public class spinner extends Applet implements Runnable{

    Image spinImages[] = new Image[4];
    Thread spinThread;

    public void init() {
        spinImages[0] = getImage(getCodeBase(), "spin1.gif");
        spinImages[1] = getImage(getCodeBase(), "spin2.gif");
        spinImages[2] = getImage(getCodeBase(), "spin3.gif");
        spinImages[3] = getImage(getCodeBase(), "spin4.gif");
    }

➜   public void start() {
                .
                .
                .
➜   }
```

Now create your new **thread** object as follows:

```
import java.awt.*;
import java.applet.Applet;

public class spinner extends Applet implements Runnable{

    Image spinImages[] = new Image[4];
    Thread spinThread;

    public void init() {
        spinImages[0] = getImage(getCodeBase(), "spin1.gif");
        spinImages[1] = getImage(getCodeBase(), "spin2.gif");
        spinImages[2] = getImage(getCodeBase(), "spin3.gif");
        spinImages[3] = getImage(getCodeBase(), "spin4.gif");
    }

    public void start() {
➜       spinThread = new Thread(this);
                .
                .
                .
    }
```

Next, start that thread running with its start() method. That is, start executing the code in the run() method as follows:

```
import java.awt.*;
import java.applet.Applet;
```

```
public class spinner extends Applet implements Runnable{

    Image spinImages[] = new Image[4];
    Thread spinThread;

    public void init() {
        spinImages[0] = getImage(getCodeBase(), "spin1.gif");
        spinImages[1] = getImage(getCodeBase(), "spin2.gif");
        spinImages[2] = getImage(getCodeBase(), "spin3.gif");
        spinImages[3] = getImage(getCodeBase(), "spin4.gif");
    }

    public void start() {
        spinThread = new Thread(this);
➜       spinThread.start();
    }
```

The start() method is ready to go, so now let's turn to the stop() method.

Handling the *stop()* Method

You've started your new thread, but you have to be able to stop it. You can do that in the stop() method, as follows:

```
public void start() {
        spinThread = new Thread(this);
        spinThread.start();
    }

➜   public void stop() {
            .
            .
            .

➜       }
```

When the stop() method is called, you should stop your thread. You used to do that with the Thread class's stop() method, however, this method is now deprecated in Java 1.2, because Sun considers it unsafe.

Instead of using the Thread class's Stop() method, then, set a boolean flag named animateFlag to false when you should stop the thread:

```
➜boolean animateFlag = true;
  public void start() {
          spinThread = new Thread(this);
          spinThread.start();
      }
```

```
      public void stop() {
➜         animateFlag = false;
      }
```

And the `stop()` method is all set. Now we'll turn to the `run()` method, where the real work takes place, and you'll make use of your new flag, `animateFlag`.

Handling the *run()* Method

Now the thread enters the `run()` method. Here, you'll set up a loop that runs until the `stop()` method is called, terminating the thread. You'll use a Java `while` loop here, which keeps executing while its conditional statement is true. That conditional statement will simply be your variable `animateFlag`, which is set to `true` until you should stop the animation:

```
public void start() {
        spinThread = new Thread(this);
        spinThread.start();
}

public void stop() {
        spinThread.stop();
}

public void run() {
➜       while(animateFlag){
                     .
                     .
                     .
➜       }
}
```

Here's where you'll perform your animation. To do so, simply keep flashing a new image on the screen continually. You'll set up an index named `spinIndex` that you can loop over; this will be your index into your array of images, `spinImages[]`. You'll also load the current image to display now in an `Image` object named `nowImage`:

```
import java.awt.*;
import java.applet.Applet;

public class spinner extends Applet implements Runnable{

        Image spinImages[] = new Image[4];
➜       Image nowImage;
```

➜
```
       int spinIndex = 0;
       Thread spinThread;
```

You can keep loading a new image into nowImage each time the loop is exe-cuted this way, as follows:

```
       public void run() {
           while(animateFlag){
➜              nowImage = spinImages[spinIndex++];
               if(spinIndex > 3)spinIndex = 0;
                         .
                         .
                         .

           }
       }
```

At this point, the image in nowImage is continually updated, and the next step is to display it on the screen. You can do that in the paint() method (where you'll find a Graphics object to draw with), so you can force a paint event now by calling repaint():

```
       public void run() {
           while(animateFlag){
               nowImage = spinImages[spinIndex++];
               if(spinIndex > 3)spinIndex = 0;
➜              repaint();
                         .
                         .
                         .
```

In the paint() method, simply draw the image nowImage on the screen:

```
       public void run() {
           while(animateFlag){
               nowImage = spinImages[spinIndex++];
               if(spinIndex > 3)spinIndex = 0;
               repaint();
                         .
                         .
                         .

           }
       }

       public void paint (Graphics g) {
➜          if(nowImage != null) g.drawImage(nowImage, 10, 10, this);
           }
       }
```

> **NOTE**   Make sure nowImage is not null before drawing it. You do so to make sure that the images are loaded in before you try to display them.

Using the *sleep* Method

Drawing images like this is fine, but this approach flashes the images on the screen with great rapidity—as fast as the computer can do it. You want the user to have time to view each image, not just a blur of action, so you slow things down with the Thread class's sleep() method. This method puts the thread to "sleep" for the number of milliseconds (thousandths of a second) that you pass to it. You can make each image appear for .2 seconds by passing a value of 200 milliseconds to sleep() as follows:

```
        public void run() {
            while(animateFlag){
                nowImage = spinImages[spinIndex++];
                if(spinIndex > 3)spinIndex = 0;
                repaint();
➔               Thread.sleep(200);
            }
        }


        public void paint (Graphics g) {
            if(nowImage != null) g.drawImage(nowImage, 10, 10, this);
        }
    }
```

Actually, Java insists that you place that statement in a try{} block, with an accompanying catch{} block in case there is an error, and so instead of the code listed above, enter the following:

```
        public void run() {
            while(animateFlag){
                nowImage = spinImages[spinIndex++];
                if(spinIndex > 3)spinIndex = 0;
                repaint();
➔               try {Thread.sleep(200);}
➔               catch(InterruptedException e) { }
            }
        }
```

```
        public void paint (Graphics g) {
            if(nowImage != null) g.drawImage(nowImage, 10, 10, this);
        }
    }
```

You can run the applet now, as shown below. The image spins around and around, as it should. The code for this applet appears in `spinner.java`.

spinner.java

```
import java.awt.*;
import java.applet.Applet;

public class spinner extends Applet implements Runnable{

    Image spinImages[] = new Image[4];
    Image nowImage;
    int spinIndex = 0;
    Thread spinThread;
    boolean animateFlag = true;

    public void init() {
        spinImages[0] = getImage(getCodeBase(), "spin1.gif");
        spinImages[1] = getImage(getCodeBase(), "spin2.gif");
        spinImages[2] = getImage(getCodeBase(), "spin3.gif");
        spinImages[3] = getImage(getCodeBase(), "spin4.gif");
    }

    public void start() {
        spinThread = new Thread(this);
        spinThread.start();
    }
```

```
public void stop() {
    animateFlag = false;
}

public void run() {
    while(animateFlag){
        nowImage = spinImages[spinIndex++];
        if(spinIndex > 3)spinIndex = 0;
        repaint();
        try {Thread.sleep(200);}
        catch(InterruptedException e) { }
    }
}

public void paint (Graphics g) {
    if(nowImage != null) g.drawImage(nowImage, 10, 10, this);
}
}
```

If you watch the "spinner" applet, you'll see that it flickers occasionally. If you make the spinner spin faster, there will be even more flicker. There is a way to get rid of screen flicker, for the most part anyway, and we'll take a look at that now.

Eliminating Screen Flicker

One of the main reasons that the applet flickers is that each time the paint() method is called, the update() method is called first, which clears the entire applet display. That means that between successive images, your applet's display is entirely repainted with the background color. There is no need for this repainting—the spinner images are all the same size, each one exactly covers the previous one, and so there is no need to clear the whole applet between images. Let's stop the flickering now.

Stopping Java from Clearing an Applet's Display

Here, you will discover how to stop the update() method from clearing the applet each time you place a new image on the screen. You can do that by overriding the update() method yourself:

```
public class spinner extends Applet implements Runnable{

    Image spinImages[] = new Image[4];
    Image nowImage;
```

```
int spinIndex = 0;
Thread spinThread;

public void init() {
    spinImages[0] = getImage(getCodeBase(), "spin1.gif");
    spinImages[1] = getImage(getCodeBase(), "spin2.gif");
    spinImages[2] = getImage(getCodeBase(), "spin3.gif");
    spinImages[3] = getImage(getCodeBase(), "spin4.gif");
}
         .
         .
         .
public void run() {
    while(animateFlag){
        nowImage = spinImages[spinIndex++];
        if(spinIndex > 3)spinIndex = 0;
        repaint();
        try {Thread.sleep(200);}
        catch(InterruptedException e) { }
    }
}

public void paint (Graphics g) {
    if(nowImage != null) g.drawImage(nowImage, 10, 10, this);
}

public void update(Graphics g) {
        .
        .
        .

}
}
```

Here, you can skip the step of clearing the applet's display entirely and simply call the paint() method as follows:

```
import java.awt.*;
import java.applet.Applet;

public class spinner extends Applet implements Runnable{

    Image spinImages[] = new Image[4];
    Image nowImage;
    int spinIndex = 0;
    Thread spinThread;

    public void init() {
```

```
            spinImages[0] = getImage(getCodeBase(), "spin1.gif");
            spinImages[1] = getImage(getCodeBase(), "spin2.gif");
            spinImages[2] = getImage(getCodeBase(), "spin3.gif");
            spinImages[3] = getImage(getCodeBase(), "spin4.gif");
        }         .
                  .
                  .
        public void run() {
            while(animateFlag){
                nowImage = spinImages[spinIndex++];
                if(spinIndex > 3)spinIndex = 0;
                repaint();
                try {Thread.sleep(200);}
                catch(InterruptedException e) { }
            }
        }

        public void paint (Graphics g) {
            if(nowImage != null) g.drawImage(nowImage, 10, 10, this);
        }

        public void update(Graphics g) {
→           paint(g);
        }
    }
```

You've done a lot of good—now the applet isn't cleared between images. However, you can do more. The paint() method still paints the entire applet display each time it is called. It turns out you can restrict the drawing operations to just part of the applet's display, and in this case, that means you can restrict drawing to just the space in which your images appear. This saves time and reduces flicker.

Restricting Drawing to a Section of the Applet

To restrict drawing operations to a specific region of the display, you can use the Graphics class's clipRect() method. Using this method means that drawing operations will only take place in the rectangle given; you can make that rectangle correspond to the location of your images this way:

```
        public void update(Graphics g) {
→           g.clipRect(10, 10, 100, 100);
            paint(g);
        }
```

Your new version of the spinner applet works just as the first one did, but without the screen flicker. The new version of spinner is a success. The code for this applet appears in `spinner.java, version 2` (Version 2 of the `spinner.java` file can be found in the `spinner2` directory where you installed the example source code.)

spinner.java, version 2

```java
import java.awt.*;
import java.applet.Applet;

public class spinner extends Applet implements Runnable{

    Image spinImages[] = new Image[4];
    Image nowImage;
    int spinIndex = 0;
    Thread spinThread;
    boolean animateFlag = true;

    public void init() {
        spinImages[0] = getImage(getCodeBase(), "spin1.gif");
        spinImages[1] = getImage(getCodeBase(), "spin2.gif");
        spinImages[2] = getImage(getCodeBase(), "spin3.gif");
        spinImages[3] = getImage(getCodeBase(), "spin4.gif");
    }

    public void start() {
        spinThread = new Thread(this);
        spinThread.start();
    }

    public void stop() {
        animateFlag = false;
    }

    public void run() {
        while(animateFlag){
            nowImage = spinImages[spinIndex++];
            if(spinIndex > 3)spinIndex = 0;
            repaint();
            try {Thread.sleep(200);}
            catch(InterruptedException e) { }
        }
    }

    public void paint (Graphics g) {
```

```
            if(nowImage != null) g.drawImage(nowImage, 10, 10, this);
        }

        public void update(Graphics g) {
            g.clipRect(10, 10, 100, 100);
            paint(g);
        }
    }
```

So far, you've seen several ways of creating graphics animation in Java. It turns out that Sun has created a class that it distributes as an example to support animation, so let's explore that now.

The *Animator* Class

You can use the `Animator` class to create motion in your applets. The `Animator` class comes with the JDK 1.2 as an example. To use this class, you pass various parameters to the `Animator` class as parameters in your Web page. Here is Sun's own documentation for the `Animator` class:

`<APPLET CODE="Animator.class"`	
`WIDTH = "aNumber"`	the width (in pixels) of the widest frame
`HEIGHT = "aNumber">`	the height (in pixels) of the tallest frame
`<PARAM NAME="IMAGESOURCE"`	
`VALUE="aDirectory">`	the directory that has the animation frames (a series of pictures in GIF or JPEG format, by default named T1.gif, T2.gif, ...)
`<PARAM NAME="STARTUP"`	
`VALUE="aFile">`	an image to display at load time
`<PARAM NAME="BACKGROUND"`	
`VALUE="aFile">`	an image to paint the frames against
`<PARAM NAME="STARTIMAGE"`	
`VALUE="aNumber">`	number of the starting frame (1..n)
`<PARAM NAME="ENDIMAGE"`	
`VALUE="aNumber">`	number of the end frame (1..n)
`<PARAM NAME="NAMEPATTERN"`	
`VALUE="dir/prefix%N.suffix"`	a pattern to use for generating names based on STARTIMAGE and ENDIMAGE (See below.)

```
<PARAM NAME="PAUSE"
VALUE="100">                              milliseconds to pause
                                          between images
                                          default (can be overriden
                                          by PAUSES)

<PARAM NAME="PAUSES"
VALUE="300|200||400|200">                 millisecond delay per
                                          frame. Blank
                                          uses default PAUSE value

<PARAM NAME="REPEAT"
VALUE="true">                             repeat the sequence?
<PARAM NAME="POSITIONS"
VALUE="100@200||200@100||200@200|100@100|105@105">
                                          positions (X@Y) for each
                                          frame. Blank means use previous
                                          frame's position

<PARAM NAME="IMAGES"
VALUE="3|3|2|1|2|3|17">                   explicit order for frames
                                          (see below)

<PARAM NAME="SOUNDSOURCE"
VALUE="aDirectory">                       the directory that has the
                                          audio files

<PARAM NAME="SOUNDTRACK"
VALUE="aFile">                            an audio file to play
                                          throughout

<PARAM NAME="SOUNDS"
SOUNDS="aFile.au|||||bFile.au">           audio files keyed to
                                          individual frames

</APPLET>
```

To use the `Animator` class, all you have to do is name your images `T1.gif`, `T2.gif`, `T3.gif`, and so on, and then set the `endimage` parameter to the number of images you have. For example, here's how you would set up your spinner images with the `Animator` class:

```
<HTML>
<BODY>

<CENTER>
<H1>Our animation example</H1>
<APPLET CODE = Animator.class WIDTH = 300 HEIGHT = 200>
<PARAM NAME = endimage VALUE = 4>
<PARAM NAME = pause VALUE = 200>
<PARAM NAME = repeat VALUE = true>
</APPLET>
</CENTER>

</HTML>
</BODY>
```

Copy the classes in the `Animator` example folder to the folder with this Web page, and copy over the `spin1.gif` to `spin4.gif` files as `T1.gif` to `T4.gif`, placing them in the same folder. Then use the Applet Viewer to take a look at this Web page. This displays the spinner on the screen.

You've gotten your start in graphics animation, and thanks to Java, it's been easy. There are more animation techniques available in Java. One of them is *double buffering*, which lets you handle complex animation images. We'll explore that technique and more in Skill 15.

Are You up to Speed?

Now you can. . .

☑ **create animated graphics programs**

☑ **support an easy method of animation in Java by using the *Canvas* control**

☑ **reduce screen flicker by overriding the *update()* method**

☑ **use the *Animator* class**

More Graphics Animation Power

- Using double buffering for faster animation updating
- Using the card layout to animate panels of controls
- Updating the dauber applet to include animation
- Creating graphic images in memory

In Skill 14, you got your start in animation. Here, we're going to continue that work by examining some popular animation techniques. One of those is *double-buffering*, which is a method that allows you to construct complicated graphics images in memory and then flash them on the screen, rather than having to construct them on the screen as the user watches. We'll also see how to update the dauber painting program in this skill. Finally, we'll look at one more Java layout: the *card* layout, which lets you flash panels of controls or images onto the screen as you like, animating them. We'll start at once with the double-buffering technique now.

Working with Double Buffering

Double buffering allows you to develop complex graphics images off-screen and then flash them on the screen when they are complete. You wouldn't want to create the graphics you want to animate on the screen, in front of the user, frame by frame, as the user watches. It is far better to create each image in memory first and display it only when ready. This technique, double buffering, is a powerful Java technique that you'll learn how to use now.

For this example, the graphics images won't be all that complex. You'll develop just a series of white boxes, as shown in Figure 15.1. In succeeding frames, the innermost rectangle becomes larger, so as you work through all 20 images in an animation example, it looks as though the rectangle is growing from upper left to the lower right, as shown in Figure 15.2. None of these images will exist on disk. You'll create them in memory and then display them on the screen.

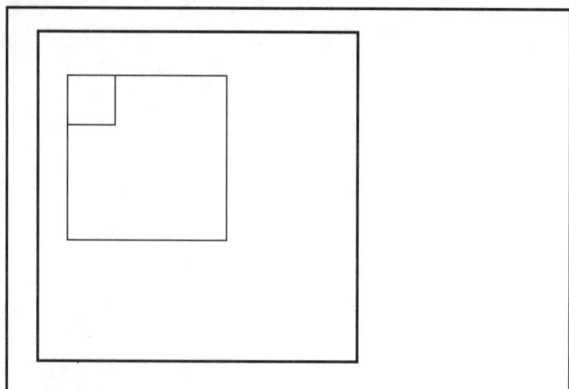

FIGURE 15.1:   You'll develop simple graphics images for this example.

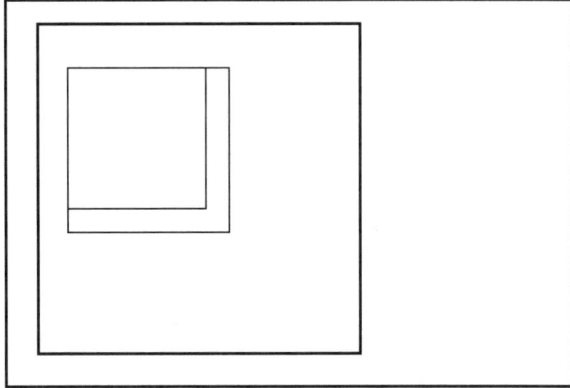

FIGURE 15.2:   Over the course of our example, the innermost rectangle will get larger.

Create a new file named `doublebuffer.java`. You will need an image object in memory that you can draw in—this will be your "buffer" image. Create this image object as an object of the `Image` class, calling it `memoryimage`:

```
import java.awt.*;
import java.applet.Applet;

public class doublebuffer extends Applet {

→       Image memoryimage;
            .
            .
            .
```

The `Image` class methods appear in Table 15.1.

TABLE 15.1: The Java Image class methods

Method	Does This
`Image()`	Creates a new Image object
`createScaledImage(int, int, int)`	Creates a scaled version of this image
`flush()`	Flushes all resources being used by this Image object
`getGraphics()`	Gets a graphics object to draw into this image

TABLE 15.1 CONTINUED: The Java Image class methods

Method	Does This
getHeight(ImageObserver)	Gets the actual height of the image
getProperty(String, ImageObserver)	Gets a property of the image by name
getSource()	Gets the object that produces the pixels for the image
getWidth(ImageObserver)	Gets the actual width of the image

You can create that new object in the init() method as follows, giving your image a size (in pixels) of 100 x 100:

```
import java.awt.*;
import java.applet.Applet;

public class doublebuffer extends Applet {

    Image memoryimage;

    public void init() {
        memoryimage = createImage(100, 100);
    }
        .
        .
        .
```

Drawing in Images Stored in Memory

To actually draw in your image in memory, you will need a Graphics object. You can get a Graphics object for your memory image, naming that object memorygraphics:

```
import java.awt.*;
import java.applet.Applet;

public class doublebuffer extends Applet {

    Image memoryimage;
    Graphics memorygraphics;

    public void init() {
        memoryimage = createImage(100, 100);
        memorygraphics = memoryimage.getGraphics();
    }
        .
        .
        .

}
```

Now you can start your new thread, which will perform the actual animation. In this case, give the new thread the name `doublebufferthread`:

```java
import java.awt.*;
import java.applet.Applet;

public class doublebuffer extends Applet {

    Image memoryimage;
    Graphics memorygraphics;
→   Thread doublebufferthread;

    public void init() {
        memoryimage = createImage(100, 100);
        memorygraphics = memoryimage.getGraphics();
    }            .
                 .
                 .
```

Now create and start that new thread in the `start()` method and implement the Runnable interface as well:

```java
import java.awt.*;
import java.applet.Applet;

→public class doublebuffer extends Applet implements Runnable{

    Image memoryimage;
    Graphics memorygraphics;
    Thread doublebufferthread;

    public void init() {
        memoryimage = createImage(100, 100);
        memorygraphics = memoryimage.getGraphics();
    }

→   public void start() {
→       doublebufferthread = new Thread(this);
→       doublebufferthread.start();
→   }        .
                 .
                 .

}
```

In addition, add code to stop the new thread in the `stop()` method, as follows:

```java
import java.awt.*;
import java.applet.Applet;
```

Skill 15

```
        public class doublebuffer extends Applet implements Runnable{

            Image memoryimage;
            Graphics memorygraphics;
            Thread doublebufferthread;
   →        boolean animateFlag = true;

            public void init() {
                memoryimage = createImage(100, 100);
                memorygraphics = memoryimage.getGraphics();
            }

            public void start() {
                doublebufferthread = new Thread(this);
                doublebufferthread.start();
            }

   →        public void stop() {
   →            animateFlag = false;
   →        }           .
                        .
                        .
                        .
        }
```

Implementing the *run()* Method

Now that you've drawn your images, it's time to create the run() method. In
this case, simply cause the paint() method to be called repeatedly by calling
repaint() every .2 seconds:

```
import java.awt.*;
import java.applet.Applet;

public class doublebuffer extends Applet implements Runnable{

    Image memoryimage;
    Graphics memorygraphics;
    Thread doublebufferthread;

    public void init() {
        memoryimage = createImage(100, 100);
        memorygraphics = memoryimage.getGraphics();
    }

    public void start() {
        doublebufferthread = new Thread(this);
        doublebufferthread.start();
```

```
        }

        public void stop() {
            doublebufferthread.stop();
        }

➜       public void run() {
➜           while(animateFlag){
➜               repaint();
➜               try {Thread.sleep(200);}
➜               catch(InterruptedException e) { }
➜           }
➜       }
```

You'll put the real code in the paint() method, so open that method now:

```
        public void paint (Graphics g) {
                    .
                    .
                    .

    }
```

You will need a loop index to keep track of the current size of your rectangle. Call the index loop_index and add it to your applet as follows:

```
import java.awt.*;
import java.applet.Applet;

public class doublebuffer extends Applet implements Runnable{

        Image memoryimage;
        Graphics memorygraphics;
        Thread doublebufferthread;
        boolean animateFlag = true;
➜       int loop_index = 0;
                .
                .
                .
```

In this example, you'll make each box five pixels larger than the last, so you'll increment the loop_index variable by five each time the paint() method is called:

```
        public void paint (Graphics g) {

            loop_index += 5;
                    .
                    .
                    .

    }
```

And if that loop index exceeds 100 pixels (the size of the image), you can set it back to 5:

```
public void paint (Graphics g) {

        loop_index += 5;
➡       if(loop_index >= 100) loop_index = 5;
                .
                .
                .

    }
```

Now you can draw the box itself in your memorygraphics object. Because you also want to draw over any previous boxes, you'll start by drawing a white rectangle to clear the display. To do that, first set the drawing color in the applet to white (with red, green, and blue color values of 255, 255, and 255) with the Graphics setColor() method, which you can use with your memory graphics object, memorygraphics:

```
public void paint (Graphics g) {

        loop_index += 5;
        if(loop_index >= 100) loop_index = 5;

➡       memorygraphics.setColor(new Color(255, 255, 255));
                .
                .
                .

    }
```

Next, draw your filled-in rectangle with the fillRect() method to erase any previous rectangles:

```
public void paint (Graphics g) {

        loop_index += 5;
        if(loop_index >= 100) loop_index = 5;

        memorygraphics.setColor(new Color(255, 255, 255));
➡       memorygraphics.fillRect(0, 0, 100, 100);
                .
                .
                .

    }
```

At this point, you are ready to draw your box in the memory image, so set the drawing color back to black (color values 0, 0, 0):

```
public void paint (Graphics g) {

        loop_index += 5;
        if(loop_index >= 100) loop_index = 5;

        memorygraphics.setColor(new Color(255, 255, 255));
        memorygraphics.fillRect(0, 0, 100, 100);
➜       memorygraphics.setColor(new Color(0, 0, 0));
                        .
                        .
                        .

    }
```

Then draw the box itself using the `loop_index` (incremented by 5 each time you draw an image) as the extent of the box:

```
public void paint (Graphics g) {

        loop_index += 5;
        if(loop_index >= 100) loop_index = 5;

        memorygraphics.setColor(new Col .,or(255, 255, 255));
        memorygraphics.fillRect(0, 0, 100, 100);
        memorygraphics.setColor(new Color(0, 0, 0));
➜       memorygraphics.drawRect(0, 0, loop_index, loop_index);
                        .
                        .
                        .

    }
```

And finally, draw the new image with the `Graphics` class's `drawImage()` method:

```
public void paint (Graphics g) {

        loop_index += 5;
        if(loop_index >= 100) loop_index = 5;

        memorygraphics.setColor(new Color(255, 255, 255));
        memorygraphics.fillRect(0, 0, 100, 100);
        memorygraphics.setColor(new Color(0, 0, 0));
        memorygraphics.drawRect(0, 0, loop_index, loop_index);

➜       g.drawImage(memoryimage, 10, 10, this);
    }
```

You can run the applet now, as shown below. The boxes appear to grow steadily from the upper left, and then they disappear and start out small again, repeating the process over and over. The code for this applet appears in doublebuffer.java.

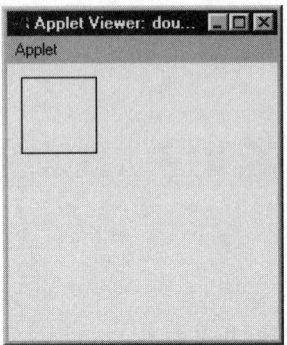

doublebuffer.java

```java
import java.awt.*;
import java.applet.Applet;

public class doublebuffer extends Applet implements Runnable{

    Image memoryimage;
    Graphics memorygraphics;
    Thread doublebufferthread;
    boolean animateFlag = true;
    int loop_index = 0;

    public void init() {
        memoryimage = createImage(100, 100);
        memorygraphics = memoryimage.getGraphics();
    }

    public void start() {
        doublebufferthread = new Thread(this);
        doublebufferthread.start();
    }

    public void stop() {
        animateFlag = false;
    }

    public void run() {
```

```
        while(animateFlag){
            repaint();
            try {Thread.sleep(200);}
            catch(InterruptedException e) { }
        }
    }

    public void paint (Graphics g) {

        loop_index += 5;
        if(loop_index >= 100) loop_index = 5;

        memorygraphics.setColor(new Color(255, 255, 255));
        memorygraphics.fillRect(0, 0, 100, 100);
        memorygraphics.setColor(new Color(0, 0, 0));
        memorygraphics.drawRect(0, 0, loop_index, loop_index);

        g.drawImage(memoryimage, 10, 10, this);
    }
}
```

Using double-buffering techniques, then, you can prepare graphics "off screen" and pop them up on the screen as needed. This is very useful if you want to support and draw complex images.

Updating the Dauber Applet

Another method of animation involves dynamically stretching images on the screen in reaction to the user's mouse movements. This method doesn't use the start(), stop(), and run() methods, but nonetheless, it gives the impression of movement, this time in response to the user's direction. This technique involves several new drawing methods, and we'll look into that now as you update your dauber painting applet to allow the user to stretch images as they draw them.

When the user draws using your dauber applet, they press the mouse at one location, move the mouse to another location, and release the mouse button. When they do, the image appears. But in between those two actions, there is nothing to be seen on the screen. However, popular paint programs animate this process by displaying an image that the user can stretch as they like with the mouse. You can incorporate this feature in the dauber applet. This feature is an example of user-driven animation—the process will be the same in essence as the animation techniques we have explored so far: drawing a figure, erasing it, and drawing a new figure, but this time, the user directs the action. This technique involves a new drawing technique, *XOR* drawing, which you'll learn now. When you're done, the user will be able to draw a line like the one shown in Figure 15.3. As the user draws, the line will stretch to match the mouse movements, as shown in Figure 15.4.

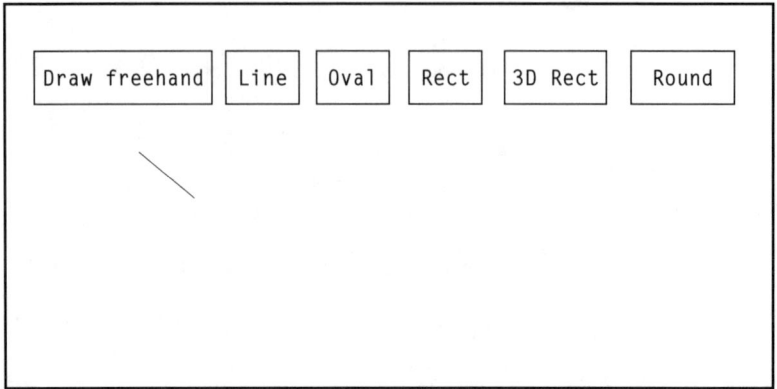

FIGURE 15.3:   The user can draw a line.

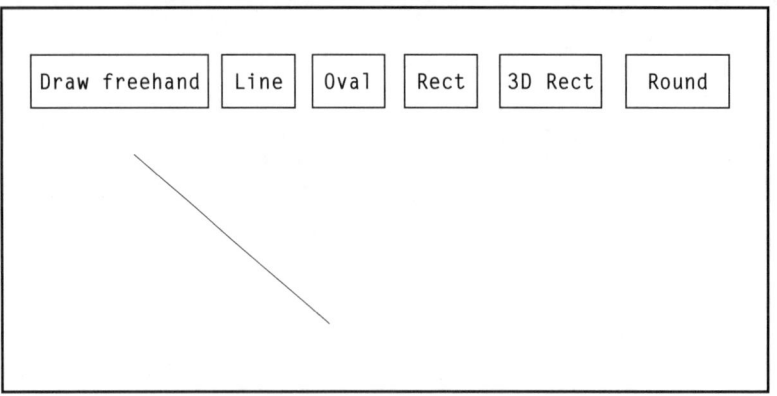

FIGURE 15.4:   The line stretches as the user draws.

Let's put this idea to work now. Here's how it works: the user starts by pressing the mouse to establish the anchor point, and then moves the mouse to a new point, the drawto point, as shown below:

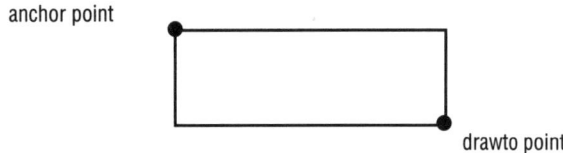

Next, the user moves on as they drag the mouse, stretching the figure to a new drawto point, past the old drawto point, as shown below:

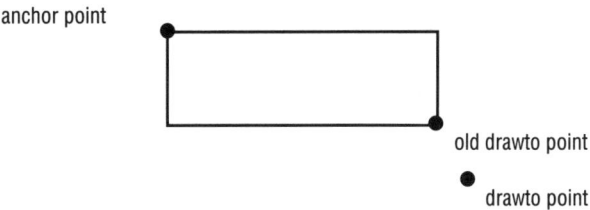

To give the impression that the user has stretched the graphics figure, erase the old graphics figure:

Then, draw the new graphics figure, stretching from the anchor point to the new drawto point:

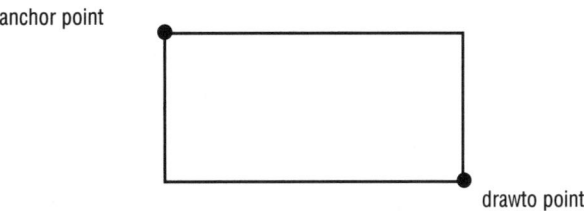

And the process continues in this manner—drawing to a new drawto point, then a new one, and a new one, and so on. Each time, you have to erase the old figure and draw a new one.

Let's start writing code now. First, you have to keep track of the old drawto point, and you can do that by adding a new point, ptOldDrawTo, to the dauber applet:

```java
import java.awt.Graphics;
import java.awt.*;
import java.awt.event.*;
import java.lang.Math;
import java.applet.Applet;

public class dauber extends Applet implements ActionListener,
MouseListener, MouseMotionListener {

    Button buttonDraw, buttonLine, buttonOval, buttonRect,
button3DRect;
    Button buttonRounded;

    Point pts[] = new Point[1000];
    Point ptAnchor, ptDrawTo, ptOldDrawTo;
    int ptindex = 0;

    boolean bMouseDownFlag = false;
    boolean bMouseUpFlag = false;
    boolean bDrawFlag = false;
    boolean bLineFlag = false;
    boolean bOvalFlag = false;
    boolean bRectFlag = false;
    boolean b3DRectFlag = false;
    boolean bRoundedFlag = false;
                    .
                    .
                    .
```

Next, set the old drawto point when the user presses the mouse in the mousePressed() method:

```java
    public void mousePressed(MouseEvent e){
        bMouseDownFlag = true;
        bMouseUpFlag = false;
        ptOldDrawTo = new Point(e.getX(), e.getY());
        ptDrawTo = new Point(e.getX(), e.getY());
        ptAnchor = new Point(e.getX(), e.getY());
    }
```

In addition, when the user drags the mouse, you need to update the drawto point. You will copy the old drawto point to the `ptOldDrawTo` point and update the new `ptDrawTo` point. Then, in the `paint()` method, you can erase the old figure, drawn from the anchor point to the old drawto point, and draw the new figure, from the anchor point to the new drawto point. Start in the `mouseDragged()` method by making the current drawto point the old drawto point (so the current graphics figure can be drawn over):

```
        public void mouseDragged(MouseEvent e){
            if(bDrawFlag){
                pts[ptindex] = new Point(e.getX(), e.getY());
                ptindex++;
            }
→           else{
→               ptOldDrawTo = ptDrawTo;
                        .
                        .
                        .
→           }
            repaint();
        }
```

Next, update the drawto point itself to the current location of the mouse, and call `repaint()`:

```
        public void mouseDragged(MouseEvent e){
            if(bDrawFlag){
                pts[ptindex] = new Point(e.getX(), e.getY());
                ptindex++;
            }
            else{
                ptOldDrawTo = ptDrawTo;
                ptDrawTo = new Point(e.getX(), e.getY());
            }
→           repaint();
        }
```

In the `paint()` method, erase the old figure (stretching from `ptAnchor` to `ptOldDrawTo`) and draw the new figure (stretching from `ptAnchor` to `ptDrawTo`).

In addition, when the user releases the mouse button, do the same thing so the screen is updated one last time and the figure is drawn in its final state:

```
        public void mouseReleased(MouseEvent e){
                bMouseDownFlag = false;
                bMouseUpFlag = true;
→               ptOldDrawTo = ptDrawTo;
```

```
→          ptDrawTo = new Point(e.getX(), e.getY());
           if(!bLineFlag){
                ptDrawTo = new Point(Math.max(ptAnchor.x, ptDrawTo.x), ➥
       Math.max(ptAnchor.y, ptDrawTo.y));
                ptAnchor = new Point(Math.min(ptDrawTo.x, ptAnchor.x), ➥
       Math.min(ptDrawTo.y, ptAnchor.y));
           }
           repaint();
       }
```

Now you will update the paint() method to make use of these changes.

Updating the Dauber *paint()* Method

Here, in the paint() method, you want to erase the current graphics figure, which stretches from ptAnchor to ptOldDrawTo, and draw the new graphics figure, which stretches from ptAnchor to ptDrawTo.

You'll use XOR drawing to do this. The XOR exclusive OR operator is a unique one. It operates much like the OR operator. The OR operator takes binary values like 0 and 1, and it combines them. In all cases but 0 ORed with 0, the result is 1:

```
            OR
            0     1
       ____
  0    |    0     1
  1    |    1     1
```

The XOR operator is a little different. Here, when you XOR 1 and 1, you do not get 1, but 0. For all other cases, XOR works just like OR.

```
            XOR
            0     1
       ____
   0   |    0     1
 →1    |    1     0
```

What this means in practice is that when you XOR a number with itself, you get 0. The interesting thing is that when you XOR number A with number B, you get a certain result, number C. However, when you XOR C with B again, you get A back. This property is useful for, among other things, placing mouse cursors on the screen. When you place the mouse cursor on the screen, you can XOR the pixels in the cursor's image with the pixels on the screen, pixel by pixel. The cursor appears. When you want to get rid of it, you just repeat the same process again—XORing the cursor with the screen at the same location again—and the screen is restored. There is no need to store the screen before placing the mouse cursor on the screen.

Let's put XOR to work. Your first task will be to erase the old figure, stretching from ptAnchor to ptOldDrawTo. Your drawing color is black, so install that now in your Graphics object:

```
        public void paint (Graphics g) {
              int loop_index;
              int figureWidth, figureHeight;
              Point topLeft;

              if(bDrawFlag){
                    for(loop_index = 0; loop_index < ptindex - 1; ➡
loop_index++){
                    g.drawLine(pts[loop_index].x, pts[loop_index].y, ➡
pts[loop_index + 1].x, pts[loop_index + 1].y);
                    }
                    return;
              }

➡            g.setColor(new Color(0, 0, 0));
                    .
                    .
                    .
```

Next, set the XOR drawing mode with the Graphics setXORMode() method.

Setting the XOR Mode

Here, you'll set the XOR drawing mode with the background color. This means that when you draw over black pixels (black is the current drawing color) on the screen, they will be changed to the background color:

```
public void paint (Graphics g) {
        int loop_index;

        if(bDrawFlag){
              for(loop_index - 0; loop_index < ptindex - 1; ➡
loop_index++){
              g.drawLine(pts[loop_index].x, pts[loop_index].y,➡
                pts[loop_index + 1].x, pts[loop_index + 1].y);
              }
              return;
        }

        g.setColor(new Color(0, 0, 0));
```

```
→              g.setXORMode(getBackground());
                          .
                          .
                          .
```

Now the XOR mode is set. Next, find the top left point of the graphics figure you want to erase, as well as its width and height:

```
public void paint (Graphics g) {
            int loop_index;
→           int figureWidth, figureHeight;
→           Point topLeft;

            if(bDrawFlag){
                 for(loop_index = 0; loop_index < ptindex - 1;
loop_index++){
                 g.drawLine(pts[loop_index].x, pts[loop_index].y,
pts[loop_index + 1].x, pts[loop_index + 1].y);
                 }
                 return;
            }

            g.setColor(new Color(0, 0, 0));
            g.setXORMode(getBackground());

→           topLeft = new Point(Math.min(ptAnchor.x, ptOldDrawTo.x), ➥
             Math.min(ptAnchor.y, ptOldDrawTo.y));
            figureWidth = Math.abs(ptOldDrawTo.x - ptAnchor.x);
            figureHeight = Math.abs(ptOldDrawTo.y - ptAnchor.y);
                          .
                          .
                          .
```

At this point, you are ready to erase the figure itself, and you can do that simply by drawing over it now that you have set the XOR mode correctly:

```
public void paint (Graphics g) {
            int loop_index;
            int figureWidth, figureHeight;
            Point topLeft;

            if(bDrawFlag){
                 for(loop_index = 0; loop_index < ptindex - 1; ➥
loop_index++){
                 g.drawLine(pts[loop_index].x, pts[loop_index].y, ➥
pts[loop_index + 1].x, pts[loop_index + 1].y);
                 }
                 return;
            }
```

```
            g.setColor(new Color(0, 0, 0));
            g.setXORMode(getBackground());

            topLeft = new Point(Math.min(ptAnchor.x, ptOldDrawTo.x),
    Math.min(ptAnchor.y, ptOldDrawTo.y));
            figureWidth = Math.abs(ptOldDrawTo.x - ptAnchor.x);
            figureHeight = Math.abs(ptOldDrawTo.y - ptAnchor.y);

➡            if(bLineFlag){
➡                g.drawLine(ptAnchor.x, ptAnchor.y, ptOldDrawTo.x, ➡
    ptOldDrawTo.y);
➡            }
➡            if(bOvalFlag){
➡                g.drawOval(topLeft.x, topLeft.y, figureWidth, ➡
    figureHeight);
➡            }
➡            if(bRectFlag){
➡                g.drawRect(topLeft.x, topLeft.y, figureWidth, ➡
    figureHeight);
➡            }
➡            if(b3DRectFlag){
➡                g.draw3DRect(topLeft.x, topLeft.y, figureWidth, ➡
    figureHeight, true);
➡            }
➡            if(bRoundedFlag){
➡                g.drawRoundRect(topLeft.x, topLeft.y, figureWidth, ➡
    figureHeight, 10, 10);
➡            }       .
                    .
                    .
```

This erases the old graphics figure, which is obsolete now that the user has moved the mouse. You've made considerable progress.

The next step is to draw the new figure, which stretches from ptAnchor to ptDrawTo. To do that, now that the XOR mode is set, simply set the drawing color to the background color itself. In this way, you'll end up drawing in the current drawing color. Now that you are not drawing to ptOldDrawTo anymore, but to ptDrawTo instead, you have to recalculate the width and height as well, and you do that this way:

```
public void paint (Graphics g) {
        int loop_index;
        int figureWidth, figureHeight;
        Point topLeft;

        if(bDrawFlag){
```

```
                    for(loop_index = 0; loop_index < ptindex - 1; ➥
        loop_index++){
                        g.drawLine(pts[loop_index].x, pts[loop_index].y, ➥
        pts[loop_index + 1].x, pts[loop_index + 1].y);
                    }
                    return;
                }

            g.setColor(new Color(0, 0, 0));
            g.setXORMode(getBackground());
                        .
                        .
                        .

            if(bRoundedFlag){
                    g.drawRoundRect(topLeft.x, topLeft.y, figureWidth, ➥
        figureHeight, 10, 10);
                }

➔           g.setColor(getBackground());
➔           topLeft = new Point(Math.min(ptAnchor.x, ptDrawTo.x), ➥
        Math.min(ptAnchor.y, ptDrawTo.y));

➔           figureWidth = Math.abs(ptDrawTo.x - ptAnchor.x);
➔           figureHeight = Math.abs(ptDrawTo.y - ptAnchor.y);
                    .
                    .
                    .
```

Finally, draw the new figure, making it appear on the screen:

```
public void paint (Graphics g) {
        int loop_index;
        int figureWidth, figureHeight;
        Point topLeft;

        if(bDrawFlag){
                for(loop_index = 0; loop_index < ptindex - 1; ➥
        loop_index++){
                        g.drawLine(pts[loop_index].x, pts[loop_index].y, ➥
        pts[loop_index + 1].x, pts[loop_index + 1].y);
                    }
                    return;
                }

            g.setColor(new Color(0, 0, 0));
            g.setXORMode(getBackground());
                        .
                        .
```

```
                .
            if(bRoundedFlag){
                 g.drawRoundRect(topLeft.x, topLeft.y, figureWidth, ➥
        figureHeight, 10, 10);
            }

            g.setColor(getBackground());
            topLeft = new Point(Math.min(ptAnchor.x, ptDrawTo.x), ➥
        Math.min(ptAnchor.y, ptDrawTo.y));

            figureWidth = Math.abs(ptDrawTo.x - ptAnchor.x);
            figureHeight = Math.abs(ptDrawTo.y - ptAnchor.y);

➜           if(bLineFlag){
➜                g.drawLine(ptAnchor.x, ptAnchor.y, ptDrawTo.x,
        ptDrawTo.y);
➜           }
➜           if(bOvalFlag){
➜                g.drawOval(topLeft.x, topLeft.y, figureWidth, ➥
        figureHeight);
➜           }
➜           if(bRectFlag){
➜                g.drawRect(topLeft.x, topLeft.y, figureWidth, ➥
        figureHeight);
➜           }
➜           if(b3DRectFlag){
➜                g.draw3DRect(topLeft.x, topLeft.y, figureWidth, ➥
        figureHeight true);
➜           }
➜           if(bRoundedFlag){
➜                g.drawRoundRect(topLeft.x, topLeft.y, figureWidth, ➥
        figureHeight, 10, 10);
➜           }
➜       }
```

And the new version of dauber is ready to run. Run the applet now, as shown in Figure 15.5. When you draw a new figure, that figure stretches until you release the mouse button. The code for this applet appears in dauber.java, version 2.

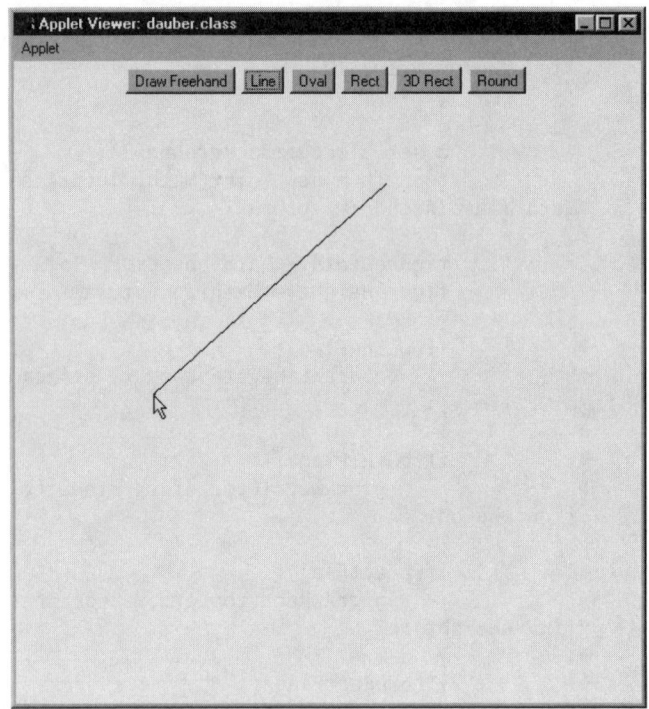

FIGURE 15.5: Now you can stretch figures in dauber, implementing user-driven animation.

dauber.java, version 2

```java
import java.awt.Graphics;
import java.awt.*;
import java.awt.event.*;
import java.lang.Math;
import java.applet.Applet;

public class dauber extends Applet implements ActionListener, MouseListener
MouseMotionListener {

    Button buttonDraw, buttonLine, buttonOval, buttonRect, button3DRect;
    Button buttonRounded;

    Point pts[] = new Point[1000];
```

```
Point ptAnchor, ptDrawTo, ptOldDrawTo;
int ptindex = 0;

boolean bMouseDownFlag = false;
boolean bMouseUpFlag = false;
boolean bDrawFlag = false;
boolean bLineFlag = false;
boolean bOvalFlag = false;
boolean bRectFlag = false;
boolean b3DRectFlag = false;
boolean bRoundedFlag = false;

public void init() {

    buttonDraw = new Button("Draw Freehand");
    buttonLine = new Button("Line");
    buttonOval = new Button("Oval");
    buttonRect = new Button("Rect");
    button3DRect = new Button("3D Rect");
    buttonRounded = new Button("Round");

    add(buttonDraw);
    buttonDraw.addActionListener(this);
    add(buttonLine);
    buttonLine.addActionListener(this);
    add(buttonOval);
    buttonOval.addActionListener(this);
    add(buttonRect);
    buttonRect.addActionListener(this);
    add(button3DRect);
    button3DRect.addActionListener(this);
    add(buttonRounded);
    buttonRounded.addActionListener(this);
    addMouseListener(this);
    addMouseMotionListener(this);
    ptAnchor = new Point(0, 0);
    ptOldDrawTo = new Point(0, 0);
    ptDrawTo = new Point(0, 0);
}

public void mousePressed(MouseEvent e){
    bMouseDownFlag = true;
    bMouseUpFlag = false;
    ptOldDrawTo = new Point(e.getX(), e.getY());
    ptDrawTo = new Point(e.getX(), e.getY());
    ptAnchor = new Point(e.getX(), e.getY());
}
```

```
    public void mouseReleased(MouseEvent e){
        bMouseDownFlag = false;
        bMouseUpFlag = true;
        ptOldDrawTo = ptDrawTo;
        ptDrawTo = new Point(e.getX(), e.getY());
        if(!bLineFlag){
            ptDrawTo = new Point(Math.max(ptAnchor.x, ptDrawTo.x), ➥
Math.max(ptAnchor.y, ptDrawTo.y));
            ptAnchor = new Point(Math.min(ptDrawTo.x, ptAnchor.x), ➥
Math.min(ptDrawTo.y, ptAnchor.y));
        }
        repaint();
    }

    public void mouseDragged(MouseEvent e){
        if(bDrawFlag){
            pts[ptindex] = new Point(e.getX(), e.getY());
            ptindex++;
        }
        else{
            ptOldDrawTo = ptDrawTo;
            ptDrawTo = new Point(e.getX(), e.getY());
        }
        repaint();
    }

    public void mouseClicked(MouseEvent e){}

    public void mouseEntered(MouseEvent e){}

    public void mouseExited(MouseEvent e){}

    public void mouseMoved(MouseEvent e){}

    public void paint (Graphics g) {
        int loop_index;
        int figureWidth, figureHeight;
        Point topLeft;

        if(bDrawFlag){
            for(loop_index = 0; loop_index < ptindex - 1; loop_index++){
            g.drawLine(pts[loop_index].x, pts[loop_index].y, ➥
pts[loop_index + 1].x, pts[loop_index + 1].y);
            }
            return;
        }

        g.setColor(new Color(0, 0, 0));
```

```
        g.setXORMode(getBackground());

        topLeft = new Point(Math.min(ptAnchor.x, ptOldDrawTo.x), ➥
Math.min(ptAnchor.y, ptOldDrawTo.y));
        figureWidth = Math.abs(ptOldDrawTo.x - ptAnchor.x);
        figureHeight = Math.abs(ptOldDrawTo.y - ptAnchor.y);

        if(bLineFlag){
            g.drawLine(ptAnchor.x, ptAnchor.y, ptOldDrawTo.x, ➥
ptOldDrawTo.y);
        }
        if(bOvalFlag){
            g.drawOval(topLeft.x, topLeft.y, figureWidth, figureHeight);
        }
        if(bRectFlag){
            g.drawRect(topLeft.x, topLeft.y, figureWidth, figureHeight);
        }
        if(b3DRectFlag){
            g.draw3DRect(topLeft.x, topLeft.y, figureWidth, ➥
FigureHeight  true);
        }
        if(bRoundedFlag){
            g.drawRoundRect(topLeft.x, topLeft.y, figureWidth, ➥
figureHeight, 10, 10);
        }

        g.setColor(getBackground());
        topLeft = new Point(Math.min(ptAnchor.x, ptDrawTo.x), ➥
Math.min(ptAnchor.y, ptDrawTo.y));

        figureWidth = Math.abs(ptDrawTo.x - ptAnchor.x);
        figureHeight = Math.abs(ptDrawTo.y - ptAnchor.y);

        if(bLineFlag){
            g.drawLine(ptAnchor.x, ptAnchor.y, ptDrawTo.x, ptDrawTo.y);
        }
        if(bOvalFlag){
            g.drawOval(topLeft.x, topLeft.y, figureWidth, figureHeight);
        }
        if(bRectFlag){
            g.drawRect(topLeft.x, topLeft.y, figureWidth, figureHeight);
        }
        if(b3DRectFlag){
            g.draw3DRect(topLeft.x, topLeft.y, figureWidth, ➥
figureHeight, true);
        }
        if(bRoundedFlag){
```

```
                    g.drawRoundRect(topLeft.x, topLeft.y, figureWidth, ➥
figureHeight, 10, 10);
            }
        }

    public void actionPerformed(ActionEvent e){
        if(e.getSource() == buttonDraw){
            bDrawFlag = !bDrawFlag;
            bLineFlag = false;
            bOvalFlag = false;
            bRectFlag = false;
            b3DRectFlag = false;
            bRoundedFlag = false;
        }
        if(e.getSource() == buttonLine){
            bLineFlag = !bLineFlag;
            bDrawFlag = false;
            bOvalFlag = false;
            bRectFlag = false;
            b3DRectFlag = false;
            bRoundedFlag = false;
        }
        if(e.getSource() == buttonOval){
            bOvalFlag = !bOvalFlag;
            bLineFlag = false;
            bDrawFlag = false;
            bRectFlag = false;
            b3DRectFlag = false;
            bRoundedFlag = false;
        }
        if(e.getSource() == buttonRect){
            bRectFlag = !bRectFlag;
            bLineFlag = false;
            bOvalFlag = false;
            bDrawFlag = false;
            b3DRectFlag = false;
            bRoundedFlag = false;
        }
        if(e.getSource() == button3DRect){
            b3DRectFlag = !b3DRectFlag;
            bLineFlag = false;
            bOvalFlag = false;
            bRectFlag = false;
            bDrawFlag = false;
            bRoundedFlag = false;
        }
        if(e.getSource() == buttonRounded){
            bRoundedFlag = !bRoundedFlag;
```

```
            bLineFlag = false;
            bOvalFlag = false;
            bRectFlag = false;
            b3DRectFlag = false;
            bDrawFlag = false;
        }
    }
}
```

Your improved dauber applet is complete, and it's pretty powerful, thanks to the Java `Graphics` class.

The last animation topic we'll take up in this skill is using the card layout manager. With this new layout manager, you can animate not just images, but whole panels complete with controls. Let's look at that now.

Using the Card Layout for Animation

If you want to animate things other than images in Java, there is a Java layout manager that can handle many of the details. For example, if you have a panel filled with label controls (as shown in Figure 15.6), you can use the card layout manager to flash another panel onto the screen (as shown in Figure 15.7).

```
          Welcome to Java


             This is


            Card One
```

FIGURE 15.6:   A panel with label controls

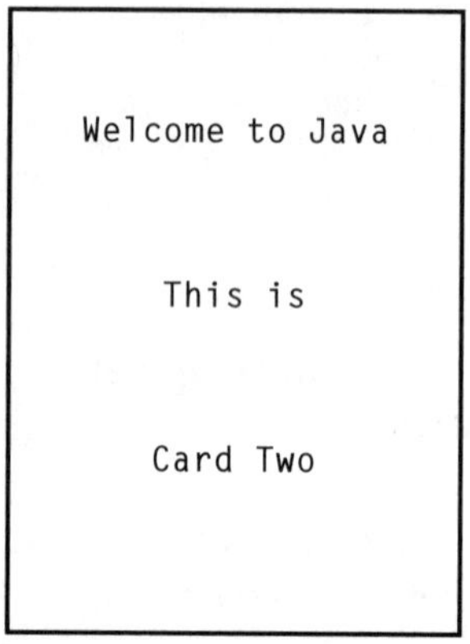

```




                    Welcome to Java


                        This is



                       Card Two



```

FIGURE 15.7: A second panel

And you could keep going, cycling panel after panel as long as you liked. In this way, the card layout manager supports animation—not animation of images, but of controls and panels. You'll take a look at this layout manager now, developing the example above.

Create a new file named `carder.java` and place your standard code in it:

```
import java.awt.*;
import java.applet.Applet;

public class carder extends Applet {
          .
          .
          .
```

In addition to the above code, you'll need a thread in this applet to animate your card layout, so implement the Runnable interface now:

```
import java.awt.*;
import java.applet.Applet;

→public class carder extends Applet implements Runnable{
          .
          .
          .
```

You'll set up three cards in your card layout, of class `cardPanel`. Call those objects `panel1`, `panel2`, and `panel3`. Add those objects to the applet now (you'll create the `cardPanel` class in a minute):

```
import java.awt.*;
import java.applet.Applet;

public class carder extends Applet implements Runnable{

➡       cardPanel panel1, panel2, panel3;
              .
              .
              .
```

Now you are ready to add your new card layout to the applet. You can do that with a new `CardLayout` object, and you can create that object in the `init()` method:

```
import java.awt.*;
import java.applet.Applet;

public class carder extends Applet implements Runnable{

        cardPanel panel1, panel2, panel3;

        int cardindex = 0;
        Thread cardThread;
➡       CardLayout cardlayout;

        public void init() {
➡           cardlayout = new CardLayout();
                  .
                  .
                  .
```

Next, install the new layout manager:

```
import java.awt.*;
import java.applet.Applet;

public class carder extends Applet implements Runnable{

        cardPanel panel1, panel2, panel3;

        CardLayout cardlayout;

        public void init() {
            cardlayout = new CardLayout();
```

```
➔                setLayout(cardlayout);
                       .
                       .
                       .
```

At this point, you can create the three card panels to install in the card layout. You'll give your `cardpanel` class a constructor that will take a string, so you can label each panel (e.g., "Panel One" or "Panel Two"). You'll create your three new panels as follows, passing an appropriate string to each:

```
import java.awt.*;
import java.applet.Applet;

public class carder extends Applet implements Runnable{

     cardPanel panel1, panel2, panel3;

     CardLayout cardlayout;

     public void init() {
          cardlayout = new CardLayout();
          setLayout(cardlayout);
➔         panel1 = new cardPanel("One");
➔         panel2 = new cardPanel("Two");
➔         panel3 = new cardPanel("Three");
                       .
                       .
                       .
```

You can install these new panels in the Java card layout manager with its **add()** method. When you use the card layout manager, you need a string for each new panel that you add: "first" for the first card, "second" for the second card, and so forth. In code, the strings look like this:

```
import java.awt.*;
import java.applet.Applet;

public class carder extends Applet implements Runnable{

     cardPanel panel1, panel2, panel3;

     int cardindex = 0;
     Thread cardThread;
     CardLayout cardlayout;

     public void init() {
          cardlayout = new CardLayout();
          setLayout(cardlayout);
```

```
        panel1 = new cardPanel("One");
        panel2 = new cardPanel("Two");
        panel3 = new cardPanel("Three");
→       add("first", panel1);
→       add("second", panel2);
→       add("third", panel3);
            .
            .
            .
```

Now we'll explore the process of using the card layout manager to actually show one of the cards you've installed.

Showing a Card with the Card Layout Manager

To actually show a card—the first card, for example, use the card layout's show() method, passing the placement strings "first", "second", and so on. To show the first card, execute the following statement:

```
import java.awt.*;
import java.applet.Applet;

public class carder extends Applet implements Runnable{

    cardPanel panel1, panel2, panel3;

    int cardindex = 0;
    Thread cardThread;
    CardLayout cardlayout;

    public void init() {
        cardlayout = new CardLayout();
        setLayout(cardlayout);
        panel1 = new cardPanel("One");
        panel2 = new cardPanel("Two");
        panel3 = new cardPanel("Three");
        add("first", panel1);
        add("second", panel2);
        add("third", panel3);
→       cardlayout.show(this, "first");
    }
```

That's how you'll show cards in your applet, with the show() method. Now you can implement animation itself.

Animating Control Panels

You can animate your panels by setting up a new thread, so call that thread cardThread:

```
import java.awt.*;
import java.applet.Applet;

public class carder extends Applet implements Runnable{

    cardPanel panel1, panel2, panel3;

➜   Thread cardThread;
    CardLayout cardlayout;

    public void init() {
        cardlayout = new CardLayout();
        setLayout(cardlayout);
        panel1 = new cardPanel("One");
        panel2 = new cardPanel("Two");
        panel3 = new cardPanel("Three");
        add("first", panel1);
        add("second", panel2);
        add("third", panel3);
        cardlayout.show(this, "first");
    }
```

Create and start cardThread in the start() method, as follows:

```
    public void start() {
        cardThread = new Thread(this);
        cardThread.start();
    }
```

And stop it in the stop() method as you have before:

```
    public void stop() {
➜       animateFlag = false;
    }
```

In the run() method, you'll cycle between all three cards, showing them one after the other. Add the run() method now, as follows:

```
    public void run() {
        .
        .
        .
    }
```

First, set up your infinite loop for the animation:

```
public void run() {
    while(animateFlag){
        .
        .
        .

    }
}
```

Next, set up an index—cardindex—to keep track of what panel you are currently showing:

```
import java.awt.*;
import java.applet.Applet;

public class carder extends Applet implements Runnable{

    cardPanel panel1, panel2, panel3;

    int cardindex = 0;
    Thread cardThread;
    boolean animateFlag = true;
    CardLayout cardlayout;

    public void init() {
        cardlayout = new CardLayout();
        setLayout(cardlayout);
        panel1 = new cardPanel("One");
        panel2 = new cardPanel("Two");
        panel3 = new cardPanel("Three");
        add("first", panel1);
        add("second", panel2);
        add("third", panel3);
        cardlayout.show(this, "first");
    }
```

You can increment that index and use a switch statement to place the correct panel on the screen. You use a switch statement because you can't pass your cardindex directly to the card layout manager. Instead of passing your cardindex directly to the card layout manager, you need to pass String objects like first and second. To do so, you'll use a switch statement that looks like this:

```
switch(++cardindex){
    case 1:
        [code 1]
        .
        .
        .
```

Skill 15

```
                              break;
                    case 2:
                        [code 2]
                            .
                            .
                            .
                        break;
                    case 3:
                        [code 3]
                            .
                            .
                            .
                        break;
                    case 4:
                        [code 4]
                            .
                            .
                            .
                        break;
              }
```

Here, increment cardindex and then execute code in the case that matches the new value in that variable. For example, if cardindex holds 3 after being incremented, the code labeled [code 3] above will be executed up to the break statement. When execution reaches the break statement, it leaves the switch statement.

 NOTE   If you do not put a break statement at the end of a case, execution "falls through" to the following case in a switch statement. In addition, instead of a case statement, the default statement—usually placed at the end of a list of case statements—handles all remaining cases.

In code, your switch statement looks like this:

```
public void run() {
    while(animateFlag){
        switch(++cardindex){
            case 1:

            case 2:

            case 3:

            case 4:
                .
                .
                .
    }
```

You'll handle `case 1` now. Here, you want to show the first card and also pause for 300 milliseconds:

```
public void run() {
        while(animateFlag){
            switch(++cardindex){
                case 1:
                    cardlayout.show(this, "first");
                    try {Thread.sleep(300);}
                    catch(InterruptedException e) { }
                    break;
                case 2:

                case 3:

                case 4:

            }
```

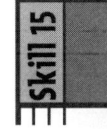

That shows the first card. Now you can do the same for the other cards, as follows:

```
public void run() {
        while(animateFlag){
            switch(++cardindex){
                case 1:
                    cardlayout.show(this, "first");
                    try {Thread.sleep(300);}
                    catch(InterruptedException e) { }
                    break;
                case 2:
                    cardlayout.show(this, "second");
                    try {Thread.sleep(300);}
                    catch(InterruptedException e) { }
                    break;
                case 3:
                    cardlayout.show(this, "third");
                    try {Thread.sleep(300);}
                    catch(InterruptedException e) { }
                    break;
                case 4:

            }
            repaint();
        }
    }
}
```

When the `cardindex` variable reaches a value of 4, you can reset it to 0 again in the fourth case, starting the animation over, as follows:

```
public void run() {
        while(animateFlag){
            switch(++cardindex){
                case 1:
                    cardlayout.show(this, "first");
                    try {Thread.sleep(300);}
                    catch(InterruptedException e) { }
                    break;
                case 2:
                    cardlayout.show(this, "second");
                    try {Thread.sleep(300);}
                    catch(InterruptedException e) { }
                    break;
                case 3:
                    cardlayout.show(this, "third");
                    try {Thread.sleep(300);}
                    catch(InterruptedException e) { }
                    break;
                case 4:
➜                    cardindex = 0;
➜                    break;
            }

            repaint();
        }
    }
}
```

And you're almost finished; all that remains is to create the `cardPanel` class, which is based on the `Panel` class:

```
class cardPanel extends Panel {
        .
        .
        .
}
```

Add a constructor to your `cardPanel` class, which can take a single parameter, `settext`, the label of the panel (the label will hold the text "One," "Two," and so on):

```
class cardPanel extends Panel {

    cardPanel(String settext){

    }
}
```

Next, install three labels in the panel, as follows:

```
class cardPanel extends Panel {
➜      Label label1, label2, label3;

       cardPanel(String settext){
          .
          .
          .
       }
}
```

And create those labels, placing the correct text in each of them, including the text you were passed in the settext string:

```
class cardPanel extends Panel {
       Label label1, label2, label3;

       cardPanel(String settext){
➜          label1 = new Label("Welcome to Java");
➜          add(label1);
➜          label2 = new Label("This is");
➜          add(label2);
➜          label3 = new Label("Card " + settext);
➜          add(label3);
       }
}
```

Your carder applet is ready to go. Run it now and you will see the panels appear and disappear in succession, as shown below. The code for this applet appears in carder.java.

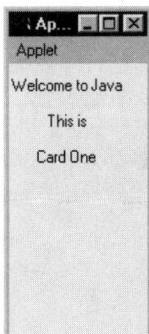

carder.java

```java
import java.awt.*;
import java.applet.Applet;

public class carder extends Applet implements Runnable{

    cardPanel panel1, panel2, panel3;

    int cardindex = 0;
    Thread cardThread;
    boolean animateFlag = true;
    CardLayout cardlayout;

    public void init() {
        cardlayout = new CardLayout();
        setLayout(cardlayout);
        panel1 = new cardPanel("One");
        panel2 = new cardPanel("Two");
        panel3 = new cardPanel("Three");
        add("first", panel1);
        add("second", panel2);
        add("third", panel3);
        cardlayout.show(this, "first");
    }

    public void start() {
        cardThread = new Thread(this);
        cardThread.start();
    }

    public void stop() {
        animateFlag = false;
    }

    public void run() {
        while(animateFlag){
            switch(++cardindex){
                case 1:
                    cardlayout.show(this, "first");
                    try {Thread.sleep(300);}
                    catch(InterruptedException e) { }
                    break;
                case 2:
                    cardlayout.show(this, "second");
                    try {Thread.sleep(300);}
                    catch(InterruptedException e) { }
```

```
                            break;
                    case 3:
                            cardlayout.show(this, "third");
                            try {Thread.sleep(300);}
                            catch(InterruptedException e) { }
                            break;
                    case 4:
                            cardindex = 0;
                            break;
                }
            repaint();
        }
    }
}

class cardPanel extends Panel {
    Label label1, label2, label3;

    cardPanel(String settext){
        label1 = new Label("Welcome to Java");
        add(label1);
        label2 = new Label("This is");
        add(label2);
        label3 = new Label("Card " + settext);
        add(label3);
    }
}
```

You've seen a lot in this skill, including double-buffering, user-directed animation, and using the card layout manager. You've also been introduced to a very powerful Java technique: multi-threading. We'll explore multi-threading further in Skill 16.

Are You up to Speed?

Now you can . . .

☑ **develop complex graphics off-screen, rather than in front of the user, and display the graphics when they are ready**

☑ **use the card layout to animate panels of controls, flashing the card panel you want onto the screen as required**

☑ **create user-directed animation**

☑ **use XOR drawing techniques**

Working with Multi-Threaded Programs and JAR Files

- Understanding the Runnable Interface
- Synchronizing threads
- Protecting data when working with multiple threads
- Creating and using JAR files

In this skill, we're going to explore an aspect of Java that we touched on in Skills 14 and 15—multi-threading. Animation gave you a good introduction to this topic; you learned that the way animation works in Java is to have a thread (that is, an independent stream of execution) endlessly place animation frames in an applet while the applet's main thread is able to do other work.

In this skill, we'll see how to set the priority of the different threads in an applet, how to coordinate threads at work, and how to use multiple threads. Let's start by working through the process of creating a threaded applet.

Creating Thread Objects

To begin exploring threads, you'll create an applet with a thread object that repeatedly prints the message "Hello from Java" on the screen. You'll give your applet two buttons, one to start the thread printing its message, and one to stop it, as shown in Figure 16.1.

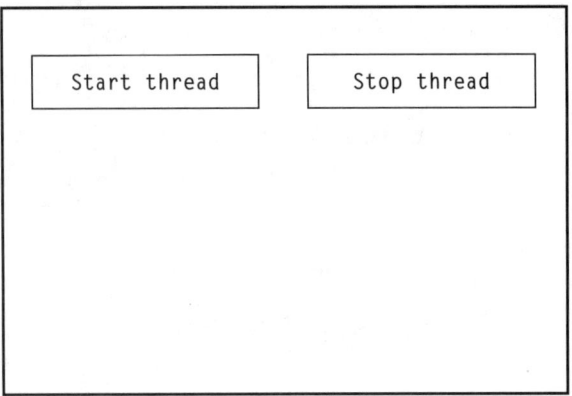

FIGURE 16.1:   Your applet's two buttons

Create a new file named threads.java now. Then start with the usual code, and implement the ActionListener interface for the buttons you'll use:

```
import java.applet.Applet;
import java.awt.*;
import java.awt.event.*;
```

```
→public class threads extends Applet implements ActionListener {
                    .
                    .
                    .
    }
```

Next, add the Start Thread button and the Stop Thread button. Connect them up to your code by installing ActionListeners in each button object:

```
import java.applet.Applet;
import java.awt.*;
import java.awt.event.*;

public class threads extends Applet implements ActionListener {

→       Button button1, button2;

→       public void init(){
→           button1 = new Button("Start thread");
→           add(button1);
→           button1.addActionListener(this);
→           button2 = new Button("Stop thread");
→           add(button2);
→           button2.addActionListener(this);
                    .
                    .
                    .
    }
```

Now you're ready to add your new thread to your applet.

Using the Java *Thread* Class

Threads in Java are supported by the Thread class; add a new thread that you'll name printingThread. You will create the printingThread class soon.

 **NOTE** It is intentional that you aren't implementing the Runnable interface in this example; you will make use of the Runnable interface in the next example.

```
import java.applet.Applet;
import java.awt.*;
import java.awt.event.*;

public class threads extends Applet implements ActionListener {
```

```
      Button button1, button2;
➜     printingThread Thread1;

      public void init(){
          button1 = new Button("Start thread");
          add(button1);
          button1.addActionListener(this);
          button2 = new Button("Stop thread");
          add(button2);
          button2.addActionListener(this);
➜         Thread1 = new printingThread();
      }               .
                      .
                      .
```

To start this new thread, use the Thread class's start() method, and to stop it, use a flag as you have in the last two skills. This way you connect those methods up to your buttons in the actionPerformed() method:

```
import java.applet.Applet;
import java.awt.*;
import java.awt.event.*;

public class threads extends Applet implements ActionListener {

      Button button1, button2;
      printingThread Thread1;

      public void init(){
          button1 = new Button("Start thread");
          add(button1);
          button1.addActionListener(this);
          button2 = new Button("Stop thread");
          add(button2);
          button2.addActionListener(this);
          Thread1 = new printingThread();
      }

➜     public void actionPerformed(ActionEvent e){
➜         if(e.getSource() == button1){
➜             Thread1.start();
➜         }
➜         if(e.getSource() == button2){
➜             Thread1.animateFlag = false;
➜         }
      }
  }
```

> **NOTE** Note this time the reference to the thread's animation flag as `Thread1`
> `.animateFlag`, not just `animateFlag`. We did that because the thread checks that
> flag in its `run()` method—and that method will be part of the `printingThread`
> class, not the main applet class. To make sure `run()` has access to the
> `animateFlag` variable, then, you will make that variable a member of the
> `printingThread` class, and so refer to it as `Thread1.animateFlag`.

Now you can create the `printing Thread` class. This class extends the Java
`Thread` class as follows:

```
public class threads extends Applet implements ActionListener {

    Button button1, button2;
    printingThread Thread1;

    public void init(){
        button1 = new Button("Start thread");
        add(button1);
        button1.addActionListener(this);
        button2 = new Button("Stop thread");
        add(button2);
        button2.addActionListener(this);
        Thread1 = new printingThread();
    }           .
                .
                .

}

→class printingThread extends Thread {
                .
                .
                .
→}
```

Because this new class extends the `Thread` class and not the `Applet` class, you
can't reach the screen (using the `Applet` class's methods) to work with the new
class directly. You also can't extend *both* the `Thread` and `Applet` classes at the
same time because Java doesn't allow multiple inheritance yet. The Runnable
interface was introduced to allow applet classes to be multi-threaded. (Using
interfaces is as close to multiple inheritance as Java gets.) In this case, you'll use
`System.out.println()` to print your message on the screen in a loop that checks
`animateFlag` this way (recall that when the user clicks the Stop button, the applet
object sets `animateFlag` to `false`).

```
class printingThread extends Thread {
    boolean animateFlag = true;

➜   public void run(){
➜       while(animateFlag){
➜           System.out.println("Hello from Java");
➜       }
➜   }
}
```

Running the thread applet produces the following display in the DOS window:

```
Hello from Java
Hello from Java
Hello from Java
Hello from Java
Hello from Java
Hello from Java
Hello from Java
Hello from Java
Hello from Java
Hello from Java
Hello from Java
        .
        .
        .
```

Of course, thread objects like the one introduced above usually perform more useful tasks in the background. For example, they can perform large-scale mathematical operations, setting flags that the rest of the program can check when the operation is complete. In fact, it's worth noting that the I/O here has been restricted to the println() method, which is very restricted indeed. Let's explore how to reach the screen more directly

Working with the Runnable Interface

You've learned how to create Thread objects in Java, but you've also learned that if you want to work with graphics on the screen, you'll need something more. That something more is the Runnable interface. For example, in your spinner applet, you implemented the Runnable interface as follows:

```
import java.awt.*;
import java.applet.Applet;
```

```
→public class spinner extends Applet implements Runnable{
              .
              .
              .
```

Then you were able to add a thread object, `spinThread`, in your applet, as follows:

```
import java.awt.*;
import java.applet.Applet;

public class spinner extends Applet implements Runnable{

      Image spinImages[] = new Image[4];
      Image nowImage;
      int spinIndex = 0;
→     Thread spinThread;

      public void init() {
          spinImages[0] = getImage(getCodeBase(), "spin1.gif");
          spinImages[1] = getImage(getCodeBase(), "spin2.gif");
          spinImages[2] = getImage(getCodeBase(), "spin3.gif");
          spinImages[3] = getImage(getCodeBase(), "spin4.gif");
      }
```

Implementing the Runnable interface means that you can now override the `start()`, `stop()`, and `run()` methods, which you can do as follows:

```
→     public void start() {
→         spinThread = new Thread(this);
→         spinThread.start();
→     }

→     public void stop() {
→         animateFlag = false;
→     }

→     public void run() {
→         while(animateFlag){
→             nowImage = spinImages[spinIndex++];
→             if(spinIndex > 3)spinIndex = 0;
→             repaint();
→             try {Thread.sleep(200);}
→             catch(InterruptedException e) { }
→         }
→     }
```

In this way, you have all the advantages of a thread object without having to create a new thread class. You can see how useful the Runnable interface is and why it was created.

Let's continue on now to explore some of the power of these thread techniques—you'll rewrite the spinner applet soon.

Controlling Threads and Setting Priority

So far, then, you've set up a new thread and let it run, but you can get far more control over threads than that. For example, you can set the *priority* of a thread with the Thread class's setPriority() method. You can give three priorities to threads, using the predefined constants in the Thread class: Thread.MIN_PRIORITY, Thread.NORM_PRIORITY (this is the default), and Thread.MAX_PRIORITY. Minimum priority threads are used to execute tasks in the background, and maximum priority threads are used for urgent tasks. For example, if you wanted to give your m_random thread in the last example the maximum priority, you would do so as follows:

```
public void start()
{
    if (m_random == null)
    {
        m_random = new Thread(this);
        m_random.setPriority(Thread.MAX_PRIORITY);
        m_random.start();
    }
}
```

In this way, you have some control over thread execution and can relegate background tasks to the background. For example, you can perform some time-consuming task named, say, bigTask(), as follows in a thread's run() method after that thread has been set to minimum priority:

```
boolean taskCompleted;

    public void run() {

        taskCompletedFlag = false;

        bigTask();

        taskCompletedFlag = true;
    }
```

 **NOTE** Note that a global flag, taskCompleted, was set to false before starting the task and set to true afterwards. In this way, the rest of the program can check on your progress.

This technique gives you some control over the use of threads, but Java gives you more: you can suspend and resume threads at any time. Let's look into that now.

Suspending and Resuming Threads

To see how to suspend and resume threads, you can modify your spinner applet (which spins a colored disk) so that it includes a Suspend button and a Resume button, as shown in Figure 16.2.

FIGURE 16.2: Adding Suspend and Resume buttons to the spinner applet

When the user clicks the Suspend button, you will suspend the animation thread and the disk will stop rotating. When the user clicks the Resume button, you will resume the thread, and the disk will start rotating again. Let's put this idea to work now. Start by adding the two buttons you'll need, **suspendButton** and **resumeButton**, to the spinner applet and by implementing the ActionListener interface:

```
import java.awt.*;
```

```
    import java.awt.event.*;
    import java.applet.Applet;

➜public class spinner extends Applet implements ActionListener, Runnable
    {

        Image spinImages[] = new Image[4];
        Image nowImage;
        int spinIndex = 0;
        Thread spinThread;
➜       Button suspendButton, resumeButton;
                    .
                    .
                    .
```

Next, add the buttons to your layout:

```
    import java.awt.*;
    import java.awt.event.*;
    import java.applet.Applet;

    public class spinner extends Applet implements ActionListener, Runnable
    {

        Image spinImages[] = new Image[4];
        Image nowImage;
        int spinIndex = 0;
        Thread spinThread;
➜       Button suspendButton, resumeButton;

        public void init() {
            spinImages[0] = getImage(getCodeBase(), "spin1.gif");
            spinImages[1] = getImage(getCodeBase(), "spin2.gif");
            spinImages[2] = getImage(getCodeBase(), "spin3.gif");
            spinImages[3] = getImage(getCodeBase(), "spin4.gif");
➜           suspendButton = new Button("Suspend");
➜           add(suspendButton);
➜           suspendButton.addActionListener(this);
➜           resumeButton = new Button("Resume");
➜           add(resumeButton);
➜           resumeButton.addActionListener(this);
        }
```

At this point, you can add the actionPerformed() method and check which button was clicked:

```
    import java.awt.*;
    import java.awt.event.*;
```

```
import java.applet.Applet;

public class spinner extends Applet implements ActionListener, Runnable
{

    Image spinImages[] = new Image[4];
    Image nowImage;
    int spinIndex = 0;
    Thread spinThread;
    Button suspendButton, resumeButton;

    public void init() {
        spinImages[0] = getImage(getCodeBase(), "spin1.gif");
        spinImages[1] = getImage(getCodeBase(), "spin2.gif");
        spinImages[2] = getImage(getCodeBase(), "spin3.gif");
        spinImages[3] = getImage(getCodeBase(), "spin4.gif");
        suspendButton = new Button("Suspend");
        add(suspendButton);
        suspendButton.addActionListener(this);
        resumeButton = new Button("Resume");
        add(resumeButton);
        resumeButton.addActionListener(this);
    }

    public void actionPerformed(ActionEvent e){
        if(e.getSource() == suspendButton){
                    .
                    .
                    .
        }
        if(e.getSource() == resumeButton){
                    .
                    .
                    .
        }
    }
```

If the user has clicked the Suspend button, you want to suspend the animation thread. In Java 1.0 and 1.1, that meant using the Thread class's suspend() method—but not anymore, since that method is now deprecated (Sun considers the suspend() method inherently deadlock-prone).

Instead, you can now handle thread suspension in a way much like the way you stop threads— by using flags to coordinate your actions. Here, you'll introduce a new flag, goFlag; when you set this flag to false, you'll place your animation thread in a *wait* state. When you place a thread in a wait state, it suspends execution until you *notify* it that it should start again.

Here's how you set that flag when the user clicks the Suspend button:

```java
public class spinner extends Applet implements ActionListener, Runnable
{

    Image spinImages[] = new Image[4];
    Image nowImage;
    int spinIndex = 0;
    Thread spinThread;
    Button suspendButton, resumeButton;
    boolean goFlag = true;

    public void init() {
        spinImages[0] = getImage(getCodeBase(), "spin1.gif");
        spinImages[1] = getImage(getCodeBase(), "spin2.gif");
        spinImages[2] = getImage(getCodeBase(), "spin3.gif");
        spinImages[3] = getImage(getCodeBase(), "spin4.gif");
        suspendButton = new Button("Suspend");
        add(suspendButton);
        suspendButton.addActionListener(this);
        resumeButton = new Button("Resume");
        add(resumeButton);
        resumeButton.addActionListener(this);
    }

    public synchronized void actionPerformed(ActionEvent e){
        if(e.getSource() == suspendButton){
            goFlag = false;
        }
```

Note that here you declare the `actionPerformed()` method as *synchronized*. You'll see more about synchronization in a few pages; when you synchronize your thread actions, you make sure you deal with the same thread in the various parts of your program, which means you'll avoid deadlock situations.

If the user clicks the Resume button, you want to resume thread execution, which means setting `goFlag` to `true` this way:

```java
    public synchronized void actionPerformed(ActionEvent e){
        if(e.getSource() == suspendButton){
            goFlag = false;
        }
        if(e.getSource() == resumeButton){
            goFlag = true;
        }
    }
```

You also must notify the thread to start again, which you can do with the `notify()` method:

```
public synchronized void actionPerformed(ActionEvent e){
    if(e.getSource() == suspendButton){
        goFlag = false;
    }
    if(e.getSource() == resumeButton){
        goFlag = true;
        notify();
    }
}
```

Now you will add the code to the `run()` method to put the thread into a wait state if `goFlag` is `false`. Use the *synchronized* keyword to synchronize your thread actions, and check the flag this way:

```
public void run() {
    while(animateFlag){
        nowImage = spinImages[spinIndex++];
        if(spinIndex > 3)spinIndex = 0;
        repaint();
        try {
            Thread.sleep(200);
            synchronized(this){
                while(!goFlag)
                    wait();
            }
        }
        catch(InterruptedException e) { }
    }
}
```

That's all you need to do—when the user clicks the Suspend button, you put the thread into a wait state, and when they click the Resume button, you notify the thread that it should leave the wait state.

Start the applet, as shown below. Clicking the Suspend button suspends the animation thread and thus the animation itself; clicking the Resume button resumes thread execution and makes the colored disk spin around again. The code for this new version of the spinner applet appears in `spinner.java`, version 3.

spinner.java, version 3

```java
import java.awt.*;
import java.awt.event.*;
import java.applet.Applet;

public class spinner extends Applet implements ActionListener, Runnable
{

    Image spinImages[] = new Image[4];
    Image nowImage;
    int spinIndex = 0;
    Thread spinThread;
    Button suspendButton, resumeButton;
    boolean animateFlag = true;
    boolean goFlag = true;

    public void init() {
        spinImages[0] = getImage(getCodeBase(), "spin1.gif");
        spinImages[1] = getImage(getCodeBase(), "spin2.gif");
        spinImages[2] = getImage(getCodeBase(), "spin3.gif");
        spinImages[3] = getImage(getCodeBase(), "spin4.gif");
        suspendButton = new Button("Suspend");
        add(suspendButton);
        suspendButton.addActionListener(this);
        resumeButton = new Button("Resume");
        add(resumeButton);
        resumeButton.addActionListener(this);
    }

    public synchronized void actionPerformed(ActionEvent e){
        if(e.getSource() == suspendButton){
```

```
                goFlag = false;
            }
        if(e.getSource() == resumeButton){
                goFlag = true;
                notify();
            }
    }

    public void start() {
        spinThread = new Thread(this);
        spinThread.start();
    }

    public void stop() {
        animateFlag = false;
    }

    public void run() {
        while(animateFlag){
            nowImage = spinImages[spinIndex++];
            if(spinIndex > 3)spinIndex = 0;
            repaint();
            try {
                Thread.sleep(200);
                synchronized(this){
                    while(!goFlag)
                        wait();
                }
            }
            catch(InterruptedException e) { }
        }
    }

    public void paint (Graphics g) {
        if(nowImage != null) g.drawImage(nowImage, 100, 100, this);
    }

    public void update(Graphics g) {
        g.clipRect(100, 100, 200, 200);
        paint(g);
    }
}
```

Skill 16

You've taken strides toward controlling your threads. Note however, that so far you have worked with only a single thread. What if your applet starts and works with multiple threads? How do you keep them straight? Let's look into this problem now.

Handling Multiple Threads

If you have multiple threads, each of which is supposed to be performing a different task, all these threads execute the same run() method. How do you keep these simultaneously-executing threads separate? You can do so by *naming* them.

You'll create a new applet now with two text fields and a button with the caption "Start threads," as shown in Figure 16.3. You can have two threads in this applet, each of which writes incrementing numbers to a text field, as shown in Figure 16.4, after the user clicks the Start Threads button.

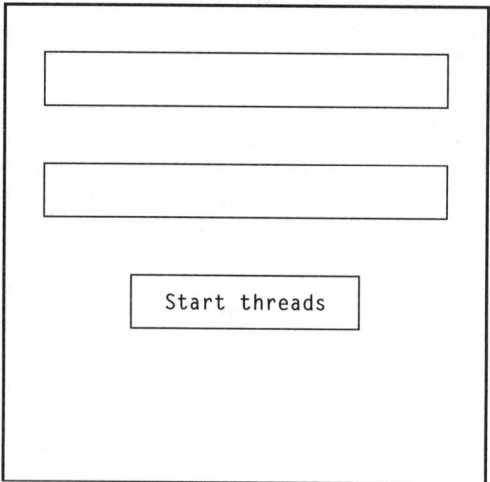

Start threads

FIGURE 16.3:   Your new applet has two text fields and a button.

You'll have only one run() method, but each thread will write to a different text field. You'll have to keep the two threads straight. Create a new file named numbers.java now and place the standard starting code in it:

```
import java.awt.*;
import java.applet.Applet;

public class numbers extends Applet {
    .
    .
    .
}
```

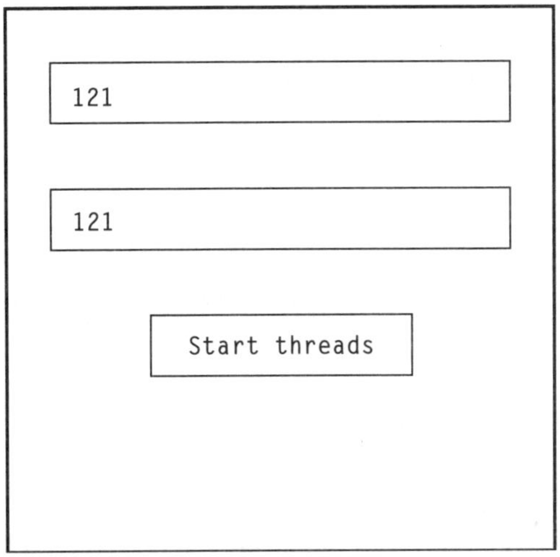

FIGURE 16.4:   Each thread writes numbers in a text field.

Add the two threads you'll use, naming them Thread1 and Thread2, and implement the Runnable interface:

```
import java.awt.*;
import java.awt.event.*; import java.applet.Applet;

→public class numbers extends Applet implements Runnable {

→        Thread Thread1, Thread2;
                    .
                    .
                    .

    }
```

You can add your two text fields and the Start Threads button, as well as implementing the ActionListener interface for the button:

```
import java.awt.*;
import java.awt.event.*;
import java.applet.Applet;

public class numbers extends Applet implements Runnable,
→ActionListener {

        Thread Thread1, Thread2;
```

```
→        TextField text1, text2;
→        Button button1;

→        public void init() {
→              text1 = new TextField(20);
→              text2 = new TextField(20);
→              add(text1);
→              add(text2);
→              button1 = new Button("Start threads");
→              add(button1);
→              button1.addActionListener(this);
→        }
    }
```

Next, you can arrange for the two threads to start when the user clicks the Start Threads button:

```
import java.awt.*;
import java.awt.event.*;
import java.applet.Applet;

public class numbers extends Applet implements Runnable,
ActionListener {

        Thread Thread1, Thread2;
        TextField text1, text2;
        Button button1;

        public void init() {
              text1 = new TextField(20);
              text2 = new TextField(20);
              add(text1);
              add(text2);
              button1 = new Button("Start threads");
              add(button1);
              button1.addActionListener(this);
        }
```

```
→        public void actionPerformed(ActionEvent e){
→              if(e.getSource() == button1){
→                    Thread1 = new Thread(this);
→                    Thread1.start();
→                    Thread2 = new Thread(this);
→                    Thread2.start();
→              }
→        }
```

Now let's work on the run( ) method.

Implementing the *run()* Method

Both of your threads execute the same run() method. You'll have to distinguish them somehow as they are supposed to write to different text fields. Add the run() method now:

```
public void run() {
        .
        .
        .
}
```

You'll have each thread print out, say, 1000 integers by setting up a for loop:

```
public void run() {
→       int loop_index;
→       for(loop_index = 1; loop_index < 1000; loop_index++){
                .
                .
                .
→       }
}
```

Now you will place the ascending integers into the appropriate text fields: text1 for Thread1 and text2 for Thread2. To do so, you have to know which thread is executing in this copy of the run() method. You can keep track by *naming* the threads.

Naming Java Threads

You can give names to threads when you create them. Open the actionPerformed() method now:

```
public void actionPerformed(ActionEvent e){
    if(e.getSource() == button1){
        Thread1 = new Thread(this);
        Thread1.start();
        Thread2 = new Thread(this);
        Thread2.start();
    }
}
```

Give the threads the names "threadname1" and "threadname2" by passing those strings to the thread's constructors:

```
public void actionPerformed(ActionEvent e){
```

Skill 16

```
        if(e.getSource() == button1){
➜               Thread1 = new Thread(this, "threadname1");
                Thread1.start();
➜               Thread2 = new Thread(this, "threadname2");
                Thread2.start();
        }
    }
```

Now in the `run()` method, you can test which thread is executing by using the `getName()` method. But how do you refer to the current thread so that you can use that method? You do that with the `Thread` class's `currentThread()` method. This means that you can test if `Thread1` is executing the `run()` method as follows:

```
    public void run() {
        int loop_index;
        for(loop_index = 1; loop_index < 1000; loop_index++){
➜           if(((Thread.currentThread()). getName()).equals ➡
    ("threadname1")){
                       .
                       .
                       .
            }
        }
    }
```

If `Thread1` *is* executing the `run()` method, you can display the thread's output in the text field **text1** as follows:

```
    public void run() {
➜       String out_string;
        int loop_index;
➜       out_string = new String();
        for(loop_index = 1; loop_index < 1000; loop_index++){
            if(((Thread.currentThread()). getName()).equals ➡
    ("threadname1")){
➜                  text1.setText(out_string. valueOf(loop_index));
                       .
                       .
                       .
            }
        }
    }
```

Now you can do the same for `Thread2`, testing for the thread name "threadname2" as follows:

```
    public void run() {
        String out_string;
        int loop_index;
        out_string = new String();
```

```
        for(loop_index = 1; loop_index < 1000; loop_index++){
                if(((Thread.currentThread()). getName()).equals ➠
  ("threadname1")){
                        text1.setText(out_string. valueOf(loop_index));
                }
→                if(((Thread.currentThread()). getName()).equals ➠
  ("threadname2")){
                              .
                              .
                              .
                }
        }
    }
```

If the current thread is Thread2, you can display its output in the text field
text2 this way:

```
    public void run() {
        String out_string;
        int loop_index;
        out_string = new String();
        for(loop_index = 1; loop_index < 1000; loop_index++){
                if(((Thread.currentThread()). getName()).equals ➠
  ("threadname1")){
                        text1.setText(out_string. valueOf(loop_index));
                }
→                if(((Thread.currentThread()). getName()).equals➠
  ("threadname2")){
→                        text2.setText(out_string. valueOf(loop_index));
→                }
        }
    }
```

You can now run the numbers applet, as shown below. The code for this applet
appears in numbers.java.

numbers.java

```java
import java.awt.*;
import java.awt.event.*;
import java.applet.Applet;

public class numbers extends Applet implements Runnable,
ActionListener {

    Thread Thread1, Thread2;
    TextField text1, text2;
    Button button1;

    public void init() {
        text1 = new TextField(20);
        text2 = new TextField(20);
        add(text1);
        add(text2);
        button1 = new Button("Start threads");
        add(button1);
        button1.addActionListener(this);
    }

    public void actionPerformed(ActionEvent e){
        if(e.getSource() == button1){
            Thread1 = new Thread(this, "threadname1");
            Thread1.start();
            Thread2 = new Thread(this, "threadname2");
            Thread2.start();
        }
    }

    public void run() {
        String out_string;
        int loop_index;
        out_string = new String();
        for(loop_index = 1; loop_index < 1000; loop_index++){
            if(((Thread.currentThread()). getName()).equals ➡
("threadname1")){
                text1.setText(out_string. valueOf(loop_index));
            }
            if(((Thread.currentThread()). getName()).equals ➡
("threadname2")){
                text2.setText(out_string. valueOf(loop_index));
            }
        }
    }
}
```

You've seen how to handle two threads now, but that raises a new issue—what if you want the two threads to work with the same data? For example, if both threads were to work with the same data but execute at different rates (which is determined by the operating system), how would you make sure they didn't interfere with each other?

Setting Up Thread Synchronization

You've gotten a brief introduction to thread synchronization above, but now you're going to dig into the subject deeper. For example, let's say that you wanted to set up an applet that counts integers steadily from 0 up and displays them. That's fine as long as you only have one thread in the applet. But if you have two threads that do the counting, incrementing and displaying the value in the *same* variable, it could be a problem.

For example, it is possible that thread 1 will be interrupted by thread 2 after incrementing your counter from, say, 1000 to 1001. Thread 2 will then increment your counter from 1001 to 1002 and print, and then control might go back to thread 1, which will print out its value, 1001. This means your series of integers would run: 1000, 1002, 1001..., which is obviously a problem. You will see how to protect the variable that holds the current counter value so that only one thread has access to it at a time until the incrementing and displaying operation is completely finished, thus *synchronizing* the threads.

Start by creating the counting applet now. Create a new file called `synchronize` `.java`, adding the standard code and implementing the Runnable interface for your two threads:.

```
import java.awt.*;
import java.applet.Applet;

public class synchronize extends Applet implements Runnable{
        .
        .
        .
}
```

Now add your two new threads, `Thread1` and `Thread2`, and start them as follows:

```
import java.awt.*;
import java.applet.Applet;
```

```
public class synchronize extends Applet implements Runnable{

    Thread Thread1, Thread2;
           .
           .
           .
    public void start() {
        Thread1 = new Thread(this);
        Thread1.start();
        Thread2 = new Thread(this);
        Thread2.start();
    }


           .
           .
```

Let's say that you have a data class named dataClass, with some internal data member named internal_data:

```
class dataClass{
    public int internal_data;
}
```

You can set the internal_data member to 0 in the class's constructor like this:

```
class dataClass{
    public int internal_data;
    public void dataClass(){
        internal_data = 0;
    }
}
```

And we create an object of the dataClass class in our applet, named sensitiveData:

```
import java.awt.*;
import java.applet.Applet;

public class synchronize extends Applet implements Runnable{

    Thread Thread1, Thread2;
    dataClass sensitiveData;

    public void init() {
        sensitiveData = new dataClass();
    }         .
           .
```

Now, in the run() method, which both threads will execute, set up a loop of 1000 iterations:

```
      public void run() {
            int loop_index;
➡         for(loop_index = 1; loop_index < 1000; loop_index++){
                          .
                          .
                          .
➡            }
      }
```

In that loop, each thread will first increment the sensitiveData object's internal_data data member:

```
      public void run() {
            String out_string;
            int loop_index;
            out_string = new String();
            for(loop_index = 1; loop_index < 1000; loop_index++){
➡                sensitiveData.internal_data++;
                          .
                          .
                          .
➡            }
      }
```

Then print out the newly-incremented version of the number in internal_data:

```
      public void run() {
            String out_string;
            int loop_index;
            out_string = new String();
            for(loop_index = 1; loop_index < 1000; loop_index++){
                 sensitiveData.internal_data++;
➡               System.out.println("data value = " + ➡
        out_string.valueOf(sensitiveData.internal_data));
            }
      }
```

This line is just where the problem is. Between the steps of incrementing and printing out the data, the other thread could have slipped in and completed both tasks, which means that the numbers could appear out of order. In fact, if you run this first version of synchronize.java, you'll see that sometimes this indeed happens—the values do sometimes appear out of order. You can fix this problem now by creating a new version of synchronize.java. The first version of the applet, with the synchronization problems, appears in synchronize.java, version 1.

Skill 16

C **synchronize.java, version 1**

```
import java.awt.*;
import java.applet.Applet;

public class synchronize extends Applet implements Runnable{

    Thread Thread1, Thread2;
    dataClass sensitiveData;

    public void init() {
        sensitiveData = new dataClass();
    }

    public void start() {
        Thread1 = new Thread(this);
        Thread1.start();
        Thread2 = new Thread(this);
        Thread2.start();
    }

    public void run() {
        String out_string;
        int loop_index;
        out_string = new String();
        for(loop_index = 1; loop_index < 1000; loop_index++){
            sensitiveData.internal_data++;
            System.out.println("data value = " + ➥
    out_string.valueOf(sensitiveData.internal_data));
        }
    }
}
```

Let's explore how to fix this problem with synchronized functions.

Synchronizing Functions

Since both thread1 and thread2 are working with the same internal_data variable, you're in danger of having one thread being interrupted between the time it increments the counter and the time it reads the value back from the counter to display it. In that case, the other thread could have incremented the counter again by that time, and you could end up displaying the wrong value. This problem can be solved by denying multiple access to the same resource in a program until the currently accessing thread is finished with its work.

One way to deny multiple access to a resource (in our example, the counter variable) is to put all the operations having to do with the counter into a *synchronized* function. To do so, you have to place the sensitive data-handling statements into their own function. Currently, all this code is in the run() method:

```
public void run() {
        String out_string;
        int loop_index;
        out_string = new String();
        for(loop_index = 1; loop_index < 1000; loop_index++){
                sensitiveData.internal_data++;
                System.out.println("data value = " + ➥
out_string.valueOf(sensitiveData.internal_data));
        }
}
```

You can create a new function, called printer() as follows:

```
public void printer(){
        .
        .
        .
}
```

Add the data-handling code here to increment your data and display the new value:

```
    public void printer(){
→       String out_string;
→       out_string = new String();
→       sensitiveData.internal_data++;
→       System.out.println("data value = " + ➥
  out_string.valueOf(sensitiveData.internal_data));
}
```

Now all the sensitive code is in one function; you can restrict access to that function with the synchronized keyword:

```
→   public synchronized void printer(){
        String out_string;
        out_string = new String();
        sensitiveData.internal_data++;
        System.out.println("data value = " + ➥
  out_string.valueOf(sensitiveData.internal_data));
        }
}
```

Now your `printer()` function is synchronized, which means that only one thread can enter it at a time. In the `run()` method, all you have to do is to call your new synchronized function, `printer()`:

```
public void run() {
    int loop_index;
    for(loop_index = 1; loop_index < 500; loop_index++){
        printer();
    }
}
```

And you're finished—if you run the new version of this applet, you'll see the same stream of numbers on the screen, but this time they'll be in order. You've been able to coordinate your threads. The code for this improved applet appears in `synchronize.java, version 2`.

C synchronize.java, version 2

```
import java.awt.*;
import java.applet.Applet;

public class synchronize extends Applet implements Runnable{

    Thread Thread1, Thread2;
    dataClass sensitiveData;

    public void init() {
        sensitiveData = new dataClass();
    }

    public void start() {
        Thread1 = new Thread(this);
        Thread1.start();
        Thread2 = new Thread(this);
        Thread2.start();
    }

    public void run() {
        int loop_index;
        for(loop_index = 1; loop_index < 500; loop_index++){
            printer();
        }
    }

    public synchronized void printer(){
        String out_string;
```

```
              out_string = new String();
              sensitiveData.internal_data++;
              System.out.println("data value = " +
    out_string.valueOf(sensitiveData.internal_data));
        }
    }

    class dataClass{
        public int internal_data;
        public void dataClass(){
            internal_data = 0;
        }
    }
```

Creating a separate class like `dataClass` is a good way to work with multiple threads. However, it's not always convenient to have to place sensitive code into its own function, so Java gives you another way. Let's look into that now.

Synchronizing Code Blocks

The sensitive part of your `synchronize.java` applet is in the `for` loop in the `run()` method:

```
        public void run() {
            String out_string;
            int loop_index;
→           out_string = new String();
→           for(loop_index = 1; loop_index < 500; loop_index++){
→               sensitiveData.internal_data++;
→               System.out.println("data value = " + ➥
      out_string.valueOf(sensitiveData.internal_data));
→           }
        }
```

As it turns out, Java lets you enclose the sensitive part of your code in a synchronized block. You can indicate what data you consider sensitive in parentheses following the `synchronized` keyword. Here, that's the `sensitiveData` object, so you can set up your synchronized code block this way in the applet:

```
        public void run() {
            String out_string;
            int loop_index;
            out_string = new String();
→           synchronized(sensitiveData){
```

```
                    for(loop_index = 1; loop_index < 500; loop_index++){
                        sensitiveData.internal_data++;
                        System.out.println("data value = " + ➡
        out_string.valueOf(sensitiveData.internal_data));
                    }
➡           }
        }
```

Doing so has the same effect as setting up a synchronized function—you restrict access to the sensitive data such that only one thread has access to it at a time. When you run this applet, you'll see the stream of integers scrolling up the screen, in order. The code for the latest version of this applet appears in synchronize.java, version 3.

Ⓒ synchronize.java, version 3

```
import java.awt.*;
import java.applet.Applet;

public class synchronize extends Applet implements Runnable{

    Thread Thread1, Thread2;
    dataClass sensitiveData;

    public void init() {
        sensitiveData = new dataClass();
    }

    public void start() {
        Thread1 = new Thread(this);
        Thread1.start();
        Thread2 = new Thread(this);
        Thread2.start();
    }

    public void run() {
        String out_string;
        int loop_index;
        out_string = new String();
        synchronized(sensitiveData){
            for(loop_index = 1; loop_index < 500; loop_index++){
                sensitiveData.internal_data++;
                System.out.println("data value = " + ➡
        out_string.valueOf(sensitiveData.internal_data));
            }
        }
    }
}
```

```
class dataClass{
    public int internal_data;
    public void dataClass(){
        internal_data = 0;
    }
}
```

That's it for synchronizing your threads and for an overview of multi-threaded programming in Java.

Fast Downloading: JAR Files

You've created a lot of applets in this book, and applets are targeted for the World Wide Web. Java 1.2 includes Java Archive (JAR) files, a new way of speeding the downloading process. Before you finish the book, let's take a look at how to use them.

You can use JAR files to zip and enclose a number of files so they are downloaded all at once in a small package, making the downloading process speedy. To create a JAR file, you use the `jar.exe` tool. For example, the `canvaser.java` applet creates two class files when compiled: `canvaser.class` and `BoxCanvas.class`. You can zip both of those and place them in one JAR file so they are downloaded together. To do that, use `jar.exe` to create `canvaser.jar` as follows:

```
C:\java1-1\canvaser>jar cvf canvaser.jar *
```

The * at the end means that you will compress all the files in the current directory into this JAR file, and the `cvf` string indicates the options you want to use with the `jar.exe`. These options are listed in Table 16.1.

T A B L E 1 6 . 1 : Options available with `jar.exe`

Option	Does This
c	Creates a new or empty archive on the standard output
t	Lists the table of contents from standard output
x [file]	Extracts all files, or just the named files, from standard input. If `file` is omitted, all files are extracted; otherwise, only the specified file or files are extracted
f [jar-file]	The second argument specifies a JAR file to process. In the case of creation, this refers to the name of the JAR file to be created (instead of on stdout). For table or extract, the second argument identifies the JAR file to be listed or extracted
v	Generates verbose output on stderr

Now that you've created a JAR file, you can upload it to your ISP—this is the file users will download, not the applet's `.class` files. But how do you tell a Java 1.2 enabled Web browser to download and unpack this JAR file? That turns out to be easy: just add this `<param>` tag to the `<applet>` tag, naming this parameter `archives` and giving as its value your JAR file, `canvaser.jar`:

```
<html>

<!- Web page written for the Sun Applet Viewer>

<head>
<title>canvaser</title>
</head>

<body>
<hr>

<applet code=canvaser.class
        width=200 height=200>
        <param name=archives value="canvaser.jar">
</applet>

<hr>
</body>
</html>
```

And the Web browser will do the rest. You can run the applet now.

In this book, you have seen many aspects of Java at work, including text fields and text areas, radio buttons and check boxes, a popup adding calculator, printing, the Java `ScrollPane` class, the system clipboard, popup menus, the Delegated event method, scroll bars and scrolling lists, clickable hyperlink-filled images, popup windows, menus, Card layouts, GridBag layouts, dialog boxes, buttons, panels, multi-threading, navigating to URLs, the mouse, a mouse-driven paint program, a mouse-driven image resizer, using the keyboard directly, fonts, animation, the Sun `Animator` class, JAR files, double buffered graphics animation, and Java applications. All that remains is putting all this power to work for yourself. Happy programming!

Are You up to Speed?

Now you can. . .

- ☑ create Java *Thread* objects
- ☑ use Applet methods and multi-threading at the same time
- ☑ coordinate multiple threads using synchronization techniques
- ☑ distinguish which thread is executing in the *run()* method by naming threads
- ☑ prevent threads from accessing sensitive data
- ☑ use JAR files to compress multiple files for easier and faster downloading

Skill 16

GLOSSARY

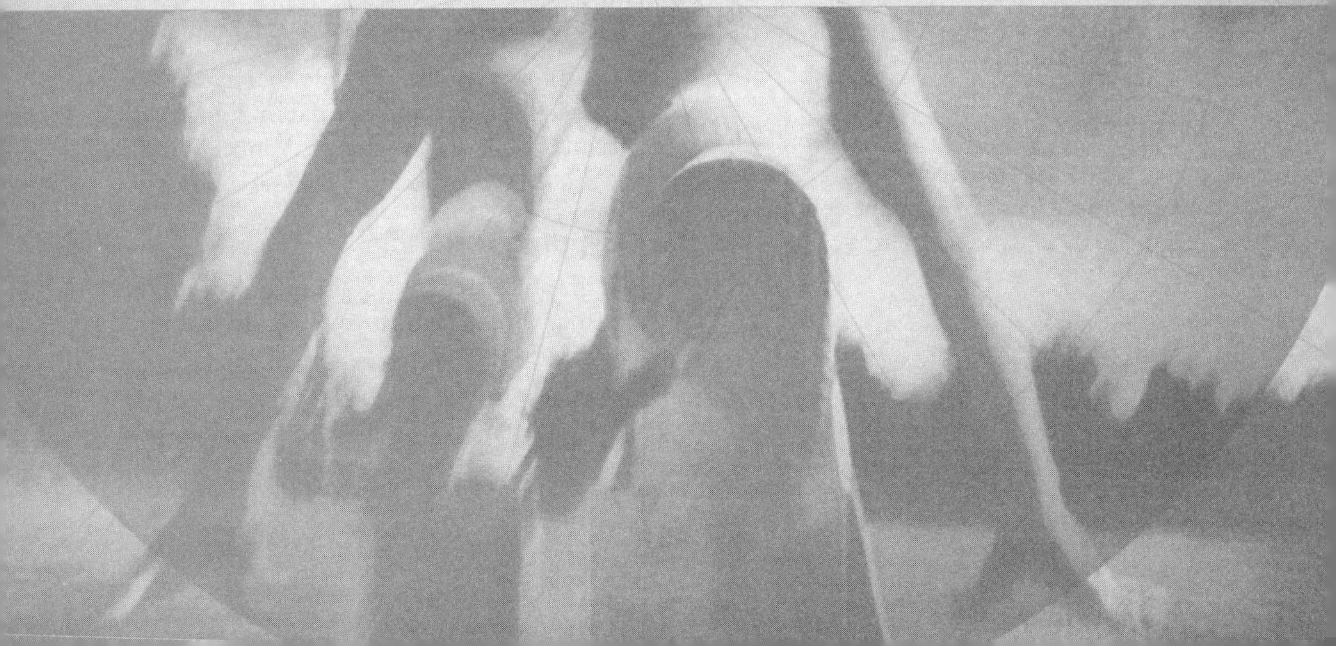

a

API (Application Programming Interface)

A collection of classes, methods, and data members that you can import into Java.

Applet

A compiled Java program that can be embedded in a Web page and downloaded to run in a Web browser.

AWT (Abstract Windowing Toolkit)

The Java package of user interface methods, which handles graphics and windows.

b

base class

Class from which another class is derived.

boolean

A variable type. Boolean variables may be set to only true or false.

bytecodes

Java executable binary codes that make up applets. Bytecodes are what the compiler produces; they make up `.class` files.

c

cast

A means of overriding a variable's type, temporarily changing that type to another type.

check box group

A collection of radio buttons. When check boxes are added to a Java `CheckBoxGroup` object, they become radio buttons.

class

The "template" used to create objects, much like a variable's type (e.g., `integer`). A class is to an object what a cookie cutter is to a cookie.

class library

Libraries that contain various Java classes. These libraries are called packages in Java.

client

One half of a client/server pair. Clients rely on a server to perform some task for them.

client/server model

Splitting an application into two parts, one part in the client and one part in the server, creates a client/server pair. Applications that work this way use the client/server model.

clipping rectangle

A graphics rectangle bounding a part of the display area to which you want to restrict graphics operations.

compiler

A program that translates Java source code into runnable bytecodes. In other words, a compiler translates `.java` files into `.class` files.

constructor

An automatically-run method of a class, used for initialization of an object. A constructor is run whenever an object of the class containing the constructor is created.

container

An object of the Java `Container` class. A container can contain control objects.

control

Any of the various user interface objects, such as text fields, text areas, scroll bars, and buttons.

critical section

A section of code where threads should be allowed to undertake their tasks without interference. In Java, a critical section is enclosed in a `sychronized()` block.

d

debugger

An application that lets you execute a Java program while watching the program's state. The execution of a debugger is often line by line.

double buffering

A graphics method of preparing images off screen in a memory buffer and then displaying the result on screen.

e

encapsulation

The process of wrapping both data and functions into classes.

event

A user-interface–triggered occurrence, such as a mouse click, a button push, or a key strike.

exception

An error message that usually indicates a problem in program flow. For example, when you try to index an array beyond its boundaries, an array-boundary exception occurs.

f

frame

The outline or border of a window or of an individual image in animation.

h

HTML (Hypertext Markup Language)

The programming language used to create Web pages.

i

image map

A "clickable" image with embedded hyperlinks.

inheritance

The process through which derived classes get functionality from their base classes.

ISP (Internet Service Provider)

Usually an external company that provides a machine connected to the Internet, acting as a host machine for individual users.

j

Java 2D

The system that handles the Java high-quality graphics rendering actions.

Java Foundation Classes

See *Swing*.

Java Virtual Machine

The system that loads and executes Java byte-code files.

JDK (Java Development Kit)

Sun's set of tools for Java developers.

l

layout

The arrangement of controls in a Java application or applet, usually handled by one or more Java layout managers.

m

member

A short name for a member of a class, meaning a method, embedded data, or a class constant.

method

Member function of a class.

multi-threading

The basis of multi-tasking in a program. In multi-threading, each thread represents an independent execution stream.

n

null

A value usually set to 0 in Java.

o

object

The instance of a class. A class acts as a "template" for an object. A class is to an object as a cookie cutter is to a cookie.

overloading

In object-oriented language, the process of defining multiple methods with the same name but different parameter lists so that the method may be called with different sets of parameters.

overriding

In object-oriented programming, the process of redefining a method originally inherited from a base class.

p

package

In Java lingo, a class library.

panel

A layout construct that holds controls in a specified arrangement for displaying on the screen.

s

server

A general term for a source of data or an application interface that client programs can interact with.

source file

A text file that holds the Java statements to be compiled into an applet or application.

subclass

A class that descends from a given class.

superclass

The class from which a given class is derived.

Swing

The set of classes that implements enhancements to old Java controls and adds new ones; also know as the Java Foundation Classes (JFC).

t

this keyword

A Java keyword used to refer to the current object. The this keyword is usually passed as a parameter to other methods.

thread

An execution stream in a program. A program may have many threads and therefore be multi-tasking.

throwable object

An object derived from the Java `Exception` class that may be thrown to cause an exception.

thumb

The small box in a scroll bar that the user manipulates, usually with the mouse.

W

Web server

A computer on the Internet that interacts with client programs.

World Wide Web

Large assemblage of documents interconnected through HTTP, FTP, and other protocols over the Internet. Lots of fun and games!

Index

Note to the Reader: Throughout this index **boldfaced** page numbers indicate primary discussions of a topic. *Italicized* page numbers indicate illustrations.

Symbols

& (ampersands) for AND operator, 351

<> (angle brackets) for HTML tags, 22

^ (carets) for XOR operator, 351

- (dashes) for separators, 232

= (equal signs)
  for assigning variables, 32
  in equality operator, 50

! (exclamation points)
  for HTML comments, 22
  for NOT operator, 299, 351, 400

() (parentheses)
  for if statements, 50
  for sensitive data, 521

. (periods) for dot operator, 19, 38

+ (plus signs)
  in increment operator, 324
  for joining strings, 149

; (semicolons) for statements, 20

| (vertical bars) for OR operator, 351

a

Abstract Windowing Toolkit (AWT)
  enhancements to, **6**
  importing, 30

access modifiers
  for data, 33
  for methods, **18–20**

Accessibility API, 8

ActionEvent class, 49

ActionListener interface
  for adder, 80
  for buttons, 46–48, 59–60, 360
  for combo boxes, 367
  for dialog boxes, 252, 257
  for drawing tools, 296
  for menu items, 214
  for menus, 229
  for scrolling lists, 182–183
  for text, 397–398
  for text areas, 67
  for threads, 494–495, 509–510
  for toolbars, **380–382**

actionPerformed() method
  in adder, 80–82, 85
  in adder2, 94
  in buttondialog, 258–260, 263
  in calculatordialog, 270–271, 276
  in canvaser, 429–431, 433
  in clicker, 49, 55
  in clickers, 59–64
  in Command, 381–384
  in dauber, 298–300, 330–331, 478–479
  in dialogframe, 256, 262
  in dialogs, 261
  in employee, 193–196
  in fullmenu, 229, 238
  in JComboBox, 364
  in menudemo, 222–225
  in MenuFrame, 217, 235–236, 239, 267, 274
  in numbers, 510–511, 514
  in popcalc, 265, 273
  in popup, 244, 246
  in scribbler, 399–402, 418–419
  in scrolllist, 182–183
  in spinner, 502–507
  in SwingButton, 362–363
  in SwingCombo, 369, 371
  in threads, 496
  in txtarea, 68, 70
  in windows, 205–206

activating
  buttons, **59–63**
  menu items, **217–220**, **235–237**
  text areas, **67–69**

activeCount() method, 437

add() method
  for buttons, 44
  with card layout manager, 482–483
  in Choice, 171
  in JToolBar, 378
  for labels, 78
  in List, 178, 181
  in Menu, 211, 215–216, 242
  in ScrollPane, 163
  for text fields, 36

addActionListener() method
  in Button, 45, 48, 60
  in JComboBox, 364
  in List, 178
  in MenuItem, 212
  in TextField, 31

addAdjustmentListener() method, 142, 145

addChangeListener() method, 372

adder class, 85

adder.java program, **74–75**, *75*, 86

actions in, **80–82**

GridLayout manager for, **87–94**, *87–89*, *92*

labels for, **76–80**

listing of version 1, **85–86**

listing of version 2, **92–94**

numeric data with text fields in, **82–85**

adder2 class, **89–94**

addImpl() method, 163

adding

menu bars to frame windows, **216–217**

menu items to menus, **212–215**

menus to menu bars, **210**, **215–216**

addItem() method

in Choice, 171, 173

in JComboBox, 364, 367

in List, 178

addItemListener() method

in Checkbox, 96, 99

in JComboBox, 365

in List, 178

addMouseListener() method, 302

addMouseMotionListener() method, 302

addNotify() method

in Button, 45

in Canvas, 428

in Checkbox, 96

in Choice, 171

in Dialog, 255

in Frame, 200

in Label, 76

in List, 178

in Menu, 211

in MenuItem, 212

in PopupMenu, 241

in ScrollBar, 142

in ScrollPane, 163

in TextArea, 66

in TextField, 31

addSeparator() method

in JToolBar, 378

in Menu, 211, 231

adjustable controls, 145

AdjustableEvent class, 146

AdjustmentListener interface, 145

adjustmentValueChanged() method

in scrollborder, 156–161

in scroller, 146–149

advance width of characters, 413

affine transforms, **388–391**

aligning text in labels, 76

allocating memory, **34–35**

allowsMultipleSelections() method, 179

ampersands (&) for AND operator, 351

anchor points

in drawing, 300–301

for images, 342–344

memory for, **304**

for ovals, 311, 314

AND operator, 351

angle brackets (<>) for HTML tags, 22

animation, **426**, *426–427*

Animator class for, **449–451**

card layout manager for, **479–491**, *479–480*

clip regions for, **447**

creating, **427–432**

with dauber, **463–479**, *464*, *474*

double buffering for, **454–463**, *455*

with multi-threading, **433–445**, *434*

with panels, **484–489**

screen flicker in, **445–449**

XOR mode for, **468–473**

Animator class, **449–451**

app.java program, 334–335

append() method, 66

appendText() method, 66

Applet class, 16

<applet> tag, **23–24**

Applet Viewer, 12, *12*

applets, **2–3**, *3*

compiling, **10–11**

contexts for, 352

HTML tags for, **21–25**

parameters for, 24, 169–170, **172**

running, **11–13**

security in, **332–333**

signed, **6**

size of, 23–24

Web pages from, **20–21**, *20*

applications, **334–336**

archive files, **523–524**

arcs, 308

arguments, command-line, 335

arrays

declaring, 322

as return values, 18

ascents for fonts, 408, 413–414

assigning variables, 32

audio, enhancements for, 9

automatic garbage collection, 304

.avi files, 426

AWT (Abstract Windowing Toolkit)

enhancements to, **6**

importing, 30

AWT package, 30

b

b3DRectFlag flag, 297–300

bars (|) for OR operator, 351

base classes, 16–17

baselines in drawing, 19

bBoldFlag flag, 398–400

bCourierFlag flag, 398, 401

bDrawFlag flag, 297–300, 322

BIN directory, 5

binary operators, 351

bItalicFlag flag, 398

bitwise operators, 351

bLargeFlag flag, 398

bLineFlag flag, 297–300

block increments for scroll bars, 142

bMouseDownFlag flag, 297, 304, 343–344

bMouseUpFlag flag, 297, 304, 343–344

.bmp files, 350

<body> tag, 22–24

BOLD constant, 406, 411

boolean data type, 33, 299, 351

boolean flags

creating, **297–300**

in scribbler, 398–399

variables for, 297

BorderLayout manager, **151–161**, *151–152, 154*

BOTH constant, 189

bounding rectangles, 311

bOvalFlag flag, 297–300, 314

Box2D class, 384, 387–388

Box2D.java program

for boxes, **384, 387**

listing for, **392**

for shapes, **387–388**

for transforms, **388–391**

BoxCanvas class, 431–433

break statements, 486

bRectFlag flag, 297–300

bRomanFlag flag, 398–399, 401

bRoundedFlag flag, 297–300, 319

buffering for animation, **454–463**, *455*

Button class, 30, **45–46**

buttondialog class, 257–258, 262–263

buttons

activating, **59–63**

adding, **44–46**, *44*

creating, **42–44**, *42–43*, **58–59**, *59*

events for, **46–51**

listings for, **55, 63–64, 115–116**

multiple, **56–64**, *56–57, 59*

in Swing package, **358–363**, *358–359, 362*

Byte class, 7

byte data type, 32

drawing, 308

wrapped numbers for, 7

bytecodes, **10–11**

bytesWidth() method, 413

c

c option with jar.exe, 523

calculatordialog class, 266–271, 274–276

calculators

adder, **74–94**, *75, 86–89, 92*

popup, **263–276**, *263–264, 268, 271–272*

canDisplay() method, 407

canDisplayUpTo() method, 407

Canvas class, **427–428**

canvaser class, 428–429, 432

canvaser.java program

animation in, **427–432**

listing of, **432–433**

capitalization, 4

captions for buttons, 45

card layout manager, **479–483**, *479–480*

for animating control panels, **484–489**

displaying cards with, **483**

carder class, 480–481, 484–485, 490–491

carder.java program, **480–483**

animating control panels in, **484–489**

displaying cards in, **483**

listing of, **490–491**

cardPanel class, 488–489, 491

carets (^) for XOR operator, 351

case sensitivity, 4

case statements, **485–488**

catch keyword, 352, 443

CENTER constant, 76, 90

center location in BorderLayout, 154

<center> tag, 22

centering text, **414–417**, *417*

ChangeListener interface, 375

char data type, 33

character streams, **7**

characters

  drawing, 308

  width of, 413

charAt() method, 52

charsWidth() method, 413

charWidth() method, 413

check box menu items, 226, **232–233**

check boxes

  connecting to groups, **111–116**

  creating, **94–104**, *94–95*, *103*

  listing for, **104–105**

  and radio buttons, 109–111, **123–137**, *124–125*, *130*

checkAccess() method, 437

Checkbox class, **96–97**

CheckboxGroup class, 108, **110**

CheckboxGroup objects, connecting check boxes to, **111–116**

CheckboxMenuItem class, 232

checkboxpanel class

  constructor for, **119**

  creating, **119**

  for panels, **119–123**

checker class, 95, 104–105

checker.java program

  creating check boxes in, **95–104**

  listing for, **104–105**

checkpanels class, 120–121, 123

checkpanels.java program

  creating panels in, *117–118*, **118–122**

  listing for, **123**

checkStackFrames() method, 437

Choice class, **170–171**

choice controls

  listing for, **176**

  using, **168–175**, *168–169*

choices class, **170–176**

choices.java program

  creating choice controls in, **170–175**

  listing of, **176**

circles, **311–315**, *311*

.class extension, 4

.class files, compiling .java files into, 10

class loaders, 11

class statements, 4, 16

classes

  derived, 16–17

  inner, **7**

  libraries for, **15–16**

  in object-oriented programming, **14–15**

clear() method, 179

clearing display in animation, **445–447**

clearRect() method, 307

clicker class, 43, 47–48, 55

clicker.java program

  adding buttons to, **44–46**, *44*

  creating buttons in, **42–44**, *42–43*

  events in, **46–51**

  listing of, **55**

  strings in, 50–51, 54

clickers class, 57–60, 63–64

clickers.java program

  activating buttons in, **59–63**

  creating buttons in, **57–58**, *59*

  listing of, **63–64**

clip() method, 385

clip regions, **447**

clipboard

  for text fields, 40

  using, **420–423**, *423*

Clipboard class, **420–421**

clipboarder class, 420–421, 423

clipboarder.java program, **420–423**, *423*

ClipboardOwner interface, 421

clipRect() method, 307, 447

closePath() method, 387–388

code blocks, synchronizing, **521–523**

code keyword, 23

CODEBASE keyword, 24

Collections, 8

columns in text areas, 67

combo boxes, **364–371**, *369–370*

Command class, **380–384**

command-line arguments, 335

comments in HTML, 22

compareTo() method

  in String, 52

  in URL, 341

comparisons

  equality operator for, 50

  methods for, 312

  of URLs, 341

compiling applets, **10–11**

compressed files, 6, **523–524**

concat() method, 52

concatenating strings, 149

configureEditor() method, 365

conflicts with variables, 32

connecting

  radio buttons to groups, **111–116**

  scroll bars to code, **145–150**

constants

  in classes, 18

  names for, 189

constraints with GridBagLayout manager, **187–189**, *188*

constructors, **35**, **119**

contentsChanged() method, 365

contexts for Applets, 352

controls, 28

 adjustable, 145

 buttons. *See* buttons

 check boxes. *See* check boxes

 choice controls, **168–175**, *168–169*

 layout for. *See* layout and layout managers

 panels for. *See* panels

 radio buttons. *See* radio buttons

 scrolling lists, **177–184**, *177*

 Swing. *See* Swing package

 text areas, **64–70**, *64*

 text fields. *See* text fields

conversion

 of bytecodes, 11

 of numeric data and strings, **82–85**

coordinate system, 19, *19*

coordinates for points, 301, 303–304

copyArea() method, 307

copying text fields, 40

copyValueOf() method, 52

CORBA, support for, **9**

countItem() method, 171

countItems() method

 in List, 179

 in Menu, 211

create() method, 307–308

createActionChangeListener() method, 378

createChangeListener() method, 372

createDefaultKeySelection-Manager() method, 365

createScaledImage() method, 455

createStandardLabels() method, 372

critical sections, code blocks for, **521–523**

current objects, referring to, **48**

currentThread() method, 437, 512

cursor type for frames, 200

cutting text fields, 40

d

daemons, 437

dashes (-) for separators, 232

data members in classes, 18

data types

 in Java, 32–33

 in overloading methods, 36

dataClass class, 516, 521, 523

dates, localized support for, 6

dauber class

 for animation, 466, 474–479

 for drawing, 295–297, 301, 328–331

dauber.java program, **294–295**, *294*

 animation in, **463–479**, *464*, *474*

 boolean flags in, **297–300**

 circles and ovals in, **311–315**, *311*, *315*

 drawing in, **300–301**

 drawing tools in, **295–297**

 freehand drawing in, **320–327**, *321*, *327*

 lines in, **305–307**, *306–307*

 listing of version 1, **328–331**

listing of version 2, **474–479**

MouseListener support in, **302–304**

mousePressed events in, **301**

mouseReleased events in, **304–305**

paint() in, **468–469**

rectangles in, **316–320**, *316–317*, *319*, *321*

XOR mode setting in, **469–473**

declaring

 arrays, 322

 objects, 34–35

 text fields, **28–33**, *29–30*

 variables, 83

decode() method, 407

delegation-based event model, **47–48**

deleteShortcut() method, 212

delItem() method, 179

delItems() method, 179

demoframe class, 199–206

deprecated methods, 7

derived classes, 16–17

deriveFont() method, 407–408

descents for fonts, 408, 413–414

deselect() method, 179

destroy() method, 437

dialog boxes, **250–256**, *250–251*

 creating, **256–260**, *260*

 for popup calculator, **263–276**, *263–264*, *268*, *271–272*

Dialog class, **254–255**

dialogframe class, 252–256, 261–262

dialogs class, 251–252, 261

dialogs.java program, **251–256**

 creating dialog boxes in, **256–260**, *260*

 listing of, **261–263**

digital signatures, **6**
disable() method, 212
disableEvents() method, 213
displaying
  cards, **483**
  images, **344–346**
  menus, **220–223**
  text fields, 36, *37*
dispose() method
  in Frame, 200
  in Graphics, 308, 333
do loops, 325
dockable toolbars, 377
docs directory, 5
doLayout() method, 163
dot operator (.), 18, 38
double buffering, **454–463**, *455*
double data type, 32
double return type, 18
doublebuffer class, 455–459,
  462–463
doublebuffer.java program
  creating, **454–456**, *455*
  drawing images in memory
    in, **456–458**
  listing of, **462–463**
  run() in, **458–463**
downloading, JAR files for,
  523–524
Drag and Drop feature, 8
draw() method, 385
draw3DRect() method, 308, 318
drawArc() method, 308
drawBytes() method, 308
drawChars() method, 308
drawImage() method
  in Graphics, 308, 345–346,
    461
  in Graphics2D, 385

drawing. *See also* dauber.java
  program
  circles and ovals, **311–315**,
    311, *315*
  freehand, **320–327**, *321*, *327*
  lines, **305–307**, *306–307*
  in memory, **456–458**
  rectangles, **316–320**, *316–317*,
    319, *321*
  strings, **19**, *19*
drawLine() method, 306–308,
  312, 326
drawOval() method, 309,
  312–315
drawPolygon() method, 309
drawPolyline() method, 309
drawRect() method, 309, 311,
  316–317
drawRenderableImage()
  method, 385
drawRenderedImage() method,
  385
drawRoundRect() method, 309,
  320
drawString() method
  in Graphics, **19**, 309, 412, 414,
    416
  in Graphics2D, 385
drawto points, 300–301
  for images, 342–344
  for ovals, 311, 314
drop-down lists
  listing for, **176**
  using, **168–175**, *168–169*
dumpStack() method, 437

e

east location in BorderLayout,
  154
echoCharIsSet() method, 31

edit controls. *See* text fields
editing text fields, 40
editors for JComboBox, 365–366
else statements, 284
employee class, 185, 188–189
employee.java program
  for GridBagLayout manager,
    185–194, *185*, *188*
  listing of, **184–195**
enable() method, 213
enableEvents() method, 213
encapsulation, 15
end() method, 334
endsWith() method, 52
enumerateThread() method, 437
equal signs (=)
  for assigning variables, 32
  in equality operator, 50
equality operator (==), 50
equals() method
  in Font, 408
  in String, 52
  in URL, 341
equalsIgnoreCase() method, 52
error conditions, 352, 443
events, **46–48**
  for buttons, **49–51**
  for choice controls, 171
  for frames, 200
  for JComboBox, 365
  for menu items, 213
  mouseClicked, **285–286**
  mouseEntered, **288–290**
  mouseExited, **290–293**
  mousePressed, **281–284**
  mouseReleased, **286–288**
  for scroll bars, 142
  for scrolling lists, 180

exceptions
  with sleep(), 443
  for URL class, 352
exclamation points (!)
  for HTML comments, 22
  for NOT operator, 299, 351, 400
exclusive OR operation
  for animation, **468–473**
  operator for, 351
extending base classes, 17
extracting archive files, 523

f

f option with jar.exe, 523
files, compressed, 6, **523–524**
fill() method, 385, 389
fill3DRect() method, 309
fillArc() method, 309
fillOval() method, 309
fillPolygon() method, 309
fillRect() method, 309, 460
fillRoundRect() method, 309
finalize() method
  in Font, 408
  in Graphics, 309
fireActionEvent() method, 365
fireItemStateChanged() method, 365
fireStateChanged() method, 372
flags, 297
flicker in animation, **445–449**
float data type, 32
float return type, 18
FlowLayout manager, 74
  for drawing tools, 296
  for labels, 78

flush() method, 340, 455
focus, input, 400
Font class, **406–410**
FontMetrics class, **412–417**
fonts
  installed, 406
  setting up, **405–411**, *405*
  size of, 406, **412–417**
for loops, 325–326
Frame class, **198–200**
frame windows, adding menu bars to, **216–217**
frameWindow class, 251
Framework Extensions, 8
freehand drawing, **320–327**, *321*, *327*
FRENCH constant, 54
fullmenu class, 228–229, 238
fullmenu.java program
  activating menu items in, **235–237**
  check box menu items in, **232–233**
  creating menus in, **228–231**
  exit item in, **234–235**
  listing of, **238–239**
  separators in, **231–232**
  submenus in, **233**
functions. *See also* methods
  in object-oriented programming, 14
  overriding, 17
  synchronizing, **518–521**

g

garbage collection, 304
GeneralPath class, 387–388
GERMAN constant, 54

getAccessibleContext() method
  in JButton, 360
  in JComboBox, 365
  in JSlider, 372
  in JToolBar, 378
getAction() method, 213
getActionCommand() method
  in Button, 45
  in JComboBox, 365
getAdjustable() method, 146
getAdvance() method, 408
getAlignment() method, 76
getAppleContext() method, 352
getAscent() method
  in Font, 408
  in FontMetrics, 413
getAttributes() method, 408
getAvailableAttributes() method, 408
getBackground() method, 385
getBaselineFor() method, 408
getBaselineOffset() method, 408
getBestFontFor() method, 408
GetBlockIncrement() method, 142
getBytes() method, 52
getChars() method, 52
getCheckboxGroup() method, 96
getClip() method, 310
getClipBounds() method, 310
getClipRect() method, 310
getCodeBase() method, 341–342
getColor() method, 310
getColumns() method
  in TextArea, 67
  in TextField, 31
getComponentAtIndex() method, 378

getComposite() method, 385

getContent() method, 341

getContents() method, 422

getContext() method, 437

getCurrent() method, 110

getCursorType() method, 200

getDescent() method
   in Font, 408
   in FontMetrics, 413

getDeviceConfiguration() method, 385

getEchoChar() method, 31

getEditor() method, 365

getExtent() method, 372

getFamily() method, 408

getFile() method, 341

getFont() method
   in Font, 408–409
   in FontMetrics, 413
   in Graphics, 310

getFontMetrics() method, 310

getFontName() method, 409

getGlyphJustification() method, 409

getGlyphMetrics() method, 409

getGlyphOutline() method, 409

getGlyphSet() method, 409

getGraphics() method, 333, 340, 455

getHAdjustable() method, 163

getHeight() method
   in FontMetrics, 413–414
   in Image, 340, 456

getHost() method, 341

getHScrollbarHeight() method, 163

getIconImage() method, 200

getImage() method, 340–341

getInverted() method, 372

getItalicAngle() method, 409

getItem() method
   in Choice, 171
   in List, 179
   in Menu, 211

getItemAt() method, 365

getItemCount() method
   in Choice, 171
   in JComboBox, 365
   in List, 179
   in Menu, 211

getItems() method, 179

getItemSelectable() method
   in Choice, 175
   in ItemEvent, 100–101

getKeyChar() method, 404

getKeySelectionManager() method, 365

getLabel() method
   in Button, 45
   in Checkbox, 96
   in MenuItem, 213

getLabelTable() method, 372

getLeading() method
   in Font, 409
   in FontMetrics, 413

GetLineIncrement() method, 142

getMajorTickSpacing() method, 372

getMargin() method, 378

getMaxAdvance() method
   in Font, 409
   in FontMetrics, 413

getMaxAscent() method, 414

getMaxBounds2D() method, 409

getMaxDescent() method, 414

getMaximum() method
   in JSlider, 372
   in Scrollbar, 142

getMaximumRowCount() method, 365

getMenuBar() method, 200

getMetrics() method, 409

getMinimum() method
   in JSlider, 372
   in Scrollbar, 142

getMinimumSize() method
   in List, 179
   in TextArea, 67
   in TextField, 31

getMinorTickSpacing() method, 372

getModel() method
   in JComboBox, 365
   in JSlider, 372

getModifiers() method, 282

getName() method
   in Clipboard, 422
   in Font, 409
   in Thread, 437, 512

getNumGlyphs() method, 409

getOrientation() method
   in JSlider, 372
   in Scrollbar, 142

getOutline() method, 409

getPageIncrement() method, 142

getPaint() method, 385

getPaintLabels() method, 372

getPaintTicks() method, 372

getParameter() method, 172

getPeer() method, 409

getPort() method, 341

getPreferredSize() method
   in List, 179
   in TextArea, 67
   in TextField, 31

getPriority() method, 437

getProperty() method, 340, 456

getProtocol() method, 341

getPSName() method, 409

getRef() method, 341

getRenderer() method, 365

getRenderingHints() method, 385

getRequestedAttribute() method, 409

getRows() method
in List, 179
in TextArea, 67

getScrollbarDisplayPolicy() method, 163

getScrollbarVisibility() method, 67

getScrollPosition() method, 163

getSelectedCheckbox() method, 110

getSelectedIndex() method
in Choice, 171
in JComboBox, 365
in List, 179

getSelectedIndexes() method, 179

getSelectedItem() method
in Choice, 171, 175
in JComboBox, 365, 369
in List, 179, 183

getSelectedItems() method in, 183

getSelectedObjects() method
in Checkbox, 96
in Choice, 171
in JComboBox, 365
in List, 179

getShortcut() method, 213

getSize() method, 410

getSize2D() method, 410

getSnapToTicks() method, 372

getSource() method
in ActionEvent, 49, 60, 218–219
in Image, 340, 456

getState() method
in Checkbox, 96, 98, 104
for menu items, 236

getStrikethroughOffsetFor() method, 410

getStrikethroughThicknessFor() method, 410

getStroker() method, 386

getStyle() method, 410

getText() method
in Label, 76
in TextField, 32

getThreadGroup() method, 437

getTitle() method
in Dialog, 255
in Frame, 200

getToolkit() method, 332

getTransform() method
in Font, 410
in Graphics2D, 386

getUI() method
in JComboBox, 365
in JToolBar, 378

getUIClassID() method
in JButton, 360
in JComboBox, 365
in JSlider, 372
in JToolBar, 378

getUnderlineOffsetFor() method, 410

getUnderlineThicknessFor() method, 410

getUnitIncrement() method, 142

getVAdjustable() method, 163

getValue() method
in JSlider, 373, 375
in Scrollbar, 142, 147

getValueIsAdjusting() method, 373

getViewportSize() method, 163

getVisible() method, 142

getVisibleAmount() method, 142

getVisibleIndex() method, 179

getVScrollbarWidth() method, 163

getWidth() method, 340, 456

getWidths() method, 414

getX() method
for drawing, 282
for popup menus, 244

getY() method
for drawing, 282
for popup menus, 244

.gif files, 426

global variables, 32

graphics. *See also* images
animated. *See* animation
dauber applet for. *See* dauber.java program
Java 2D. *See* Java 2D package
Java Swing. *See* Swing package
mouse for, **278–280**, *278–280*
mouseClicked() for, **285–286**
mouseEntered() for, **288–290**
mouseExited() for, **290–293**
MouseListener interface for, **281**
mousePressed() for, **281–284**
mouseReleased() for, **286–288**
printing, **332–336**

Graphics class, 16, **307–310**

Graphics User Interface (GUI) programs, 46

Graphics2D class, **384**, **387**
  methods for, **385–386**
  for transforms, **388–391**

GridBagConstraints class, **187–194**, *188*

GridBagLayout manager
  with GridBagConstraints, **187–194**, *188*
  using, **185–187**, *185*

GridLayout manager, **87**, *87*
  adding, **90–92**
  for menus, 229
  for panels, 121, 129, *130*
  using, **88–90**, *88–90*
  for windows, 201

groups
  layout for. *See* layout and layout managers
  panels for. *See* panels
  for radio buttons, **108–116**, *108*

GUI (Graphics User Interface) programs, 46

h

hashCode() method
  in Font, 410
  in String, 52
  in URL, 341
<head> tag, 22
headers in HTML, 22
height
  of applets, 24
  of fonts, 413
  of images, 340
  of text, **414**

height keyword, 24
hello class, 4, 16–17
hello.htm file, 11–13
hello.java program, **2–3**, *3*
  compiling, **10**
  creating, **3–4**
  libraries for, **13**
  running, **11–13**
  Web page from, **20–21**, *20*
hidePopup() method, 365
hiding dialog boxes, 259–260
hit() method, 386
hitString() method, 386
HORIZONTAL constant
  in GridBagConstraints, 189
  in Scrollbar, 143
horizontal rules in HTML, 22–23
horizontal scroll bars
  creating, 140, *140–141*
  installing, **143–145**
host names for URLs, 341
hotspots in image maps, **350–351**
<hr> tag, 22–23
HTML (Hypertext Markup Language), 12, **21–25**
<html> tag, 21

i

I/O enhancements, **7**
icons for frames, 200
IDL, **9**
if statements, 50, 284
Image class, **340**, **455–456**
image maps, **348–351**, *348*
ImageIcon class, 360
ImageObserver objects, 346

images
  for buttons, 360–362, *362*
  displaying, **344–346**
  drawing, 308
  reading, **338–344**, *338–339*
imagesizer class, 339–340, 342–343, 347
imagesizer.java program
  displaying images in, **344–346**
  listing of, **346–347**
  reading images in, **338–344**, *338–339*
imap class, 349–350, 354
imap.java program, **349–350**
  hotspot checking in, **350–351**
  listing of, **354**
  for URLs, **352–353**
implementing interfaces, 47–48
importing
  AWT package, 30
  libraries, **13**
increment operator (++), 324
indexOf() method, 52–53
Ingredients class, **127–135**, *130*
inheritance
  multiple, 47
  in object-oriented programming, **16–17**
init() method
  in adder, 77–79, 85
  in adder2, 90–91, 93–94
  in canvaser, 428–429, 432–433
  in carder, 481–483, 490
  in checker, 96–98, 104
  in checkpanels, 121, 123
  in choices, 171–172, 176
  in clicker, 44, 46, 48–49, 55
  in clickers, 58, 60, 63

in dauber, 295–296, 328–329, 475
in dialogs, 261
in doublebuffer, 456–457, 462
in employee, 186–195
in fullmenu, 228, 238
in imagesizer, 342, 347
in imap, 349, 354
in menudemo, 220–221, 224
in mousedemo, 280, 293
in numbers, 510, 514
in popcalc, 265, 273
in popup, 241–242, 245
in radios, 110–114, 116
in sandwich, 129–131, 136
in scribbler, 397–398, 403–404, 418
in scrollborder, 153–155, 160
in scroller, 143–145, 150
in scrolllist, 181, 184
in scrpane, 162, 164
in spinner, 435, 444, 448, 502, 506
in SwingButton, 361, 363
in SwingCombo, 367–371
in SwingSlider, 371, 374–377
in SwingToolbar, 378–380, 383
in synchronize, 516–517, 520, 522
in text, 33–37, 40
in threads, 495–496
in txtarea, 67–68, 70
in windows, 202–204, 206
initialization
    in constructors, 35
    of labels, **77–78**
    of text fields, **33–34**
inner classes, **7**
input focus, 400

input method framework, 9
insert() method
    in Choice, 171
    in Menu, 211
    in TextArea, 67
insertItem() method, 365
insertSeparator() method, 211
insertText() method, 67
installed fonts, 406
installing Java Development Kit, **5**
int data type, 32
int return type, 18
Integer class, 82
integers, converting text fields to, **82–85**
interface events, **46–48**
intern() method, 53
internationalization
    new features for, **6**
    String class for, 54
interpreter, Java, 335
interrupt() method, 437
interrupted() method, 437
intervalAdded() method, 365
intervalRemoved() method, 366
isAlive() method, 437
isBold() method, 410
isBorderPainted() method, 378
isDaemon() method, 437
isDefaultButton() method, 360
isEditable() method, 366
isEnabled() method, 213
isFloatable() method, 378
isFocusTraversable() method, 366
isIndexSelected() method, 179
isInterrupted() method, 437
isItalic() method, 410

isLightweightPopupEnabled() method, 366
isModal() method, 255
isMultipleMode() method, 179
isOpaque() method, 366
isPlain() method, 410
isResizable() method
    in Dialog, 255
    in Frame, 200
isSelected() method, 180
isTearOff() method, 211
isUniformBaseline() method, 410
isVerticalBaseline() method, 410
ITALIC constant, 406, 412
ItemEvent class, 100–101
ItemListener interface
    for check boxes, 98–99
    for choice controls, 173
    for panel buttons, 130–131
    for radio buttons, 113–114
itemStateChanged() method
    in checker, 100–105
    in choices, 173–176
    in radios, 113–116
    in sandwich, 131–132, 134–135

J

jar.exe tool, 523
JAR files
    enhancements for, 10
    as new feature, 6
    using, **523–524**
Java, packages in, **16**
Java 1.1, new features in, **6–7**
Java 1.2, new features in, **8–10**

Java 2D package, 8, 358
for boxes, **384**, **387**
for shapes, **387–388**
for transforms, **388–391**
Java Archive (JAR) files
as new feature, 6
using, **523–524**
java.awt package, 16
Java Database Connectivity (JDBC), 10
Java Development Kit (JDK), **5**
java directory, 5
.java files
compiling, 10
text files for, 4
Java Foundation Classes (JFC), 358
java.lang package, 312
Java Native Interface (JNI), 10
java.net classes, 7
Java Swing. *See* Swing package
Java Virtual Machine Debugger Interface (JVMDI), 10
Java Virtual Machines (JVMs), bytecode conversion by, 11
JavaBeans, 9
javac compiler, 10
JButton class, **359–360**
JComboBox class, **364–367**
JDBC (Java Database Connectivity), 10
JDK (Java Development Kit), **5**
JFC (Java Foundation Classes), 358
JNI (Java Native Interface), 10
join() method, 437
joining strings, 149
JSlider class, **371–374**
JToolBar class, **377–378**

JVMDI (Java Virtual Machine Debugger Interface), 10
JVMs (Java Virtual Machines), bytecode conversion by, 11

k

keyboard input, **403–405**
keyboard shortcuts, 213, 240
KeyEvent class, 404
KeyListener interface, 403–404
keyPressed() method
in KeyListener, 404, 420
in scribbler, 396
keyReleased() method, 404, 420
keyTyped() method, 403–404, 420

l

labels
adding, **78–80**
for check boxes, 97–98
creating, **76–77**
initializing, **77–78**
for menu items, 213
lastIndexOf() method, 53
layout and layout managers, **74**
BorderLayout, **151–161**, *151–152, 154*
card layout, **479–483**, *479–480*
FlowLayout, 74, 78
GridBagLayout, **185–194**, *185, 188*
GridLayout, **87–94**, *87–89, 92,* 201
for windows, 201–202
leading in fonts, 409, 413

LEFT constant, 76
length() method, 53
LIB directory, 5
libraries
for classes, **15–16**
importing, **13**
line increments for scroll bars, 142
lines, drawing, **305–307**, *306–307*
List class, **178–180**
listing archive file contents, 523
lists, scrolling, **177–184**, *177*
loaders, class, 11
Local Remote Procedure Calls (LRPCs), 6
Locale class, 54
locale-specific applets, 6
logical operators, 351
long data type, 32
long return type, 18
look and feels, pluggable, 358
loops
for threads, 441
types of, 326
lostOwnership() method, 421–422
LRPCs (Local Remote Procedure Calls), 6

m

machine-independent code, 11
main() method
in applications, 334–335
in clipboarder, 420
makeVisible() method, 180
maps, image, **348–351**, *348*
Math class, 312
max() method, 312–313

MAX_PRIORITY constant, 500

MAX_VALUE constant, 82

maximum integer values, 82

maximum settings for scroll bars, 142, 144

members in classes, 18

memory

    allocating, **34–35**

    for anchor points, **304**

    for animation buffering, **454–463**, *455*

    for variables, 32

menu bars

    adding menus to, **210, 215–216**

    for frames, 200, **216–217**

Menu class, **126–127**, 136–137, **211**

menu items

    activating, **217–220, 235–237**

    adding to menus, **212–215**

    check box, 226, *227*, **232–233**

menu panel, **126–127**

MenuBar class, 210

menudemo class, 207–209, *207–208*, **220–225**

menudemo.java program

    activating menu items on menus in, **217–220**

    adding menu items to menus in, **212–215**

    adding menus to menu bars in, **210, 215–216**

    creating menus in, **207–210**, *207–208*

    displaying menus in, **220–223**

    listing of, **224–225**

MenuFrame class

    for activating menu items, **235–237**

    for check box menu items, **232–233**

creating, 208–210, 213–220, **229–230**

    for exit item, **234–235**

    listing of, 225, 238–239, 273–274

    for popup calculator, 265–267, 273–274

    for separators, **231–232**

    for submenus, **233**

MenuItem class, **212–213**

menus

    activating menu items on, **217–220**

    adding menu items to, **212–215**

    adding to menu bars, **210, 215–216**

    check box menu items on, 226, *227*, **232–233**

    creating, **207–210**, *207–208*, **229–230**

    displaying, **220–223**

    popup, **240–246**, *240*

    separators for, 226, *226*, **231–232**

    submenus, 226, *227*, **233**

MenuShortcut class, 240

methods

    access modifiers for, **18–20**

    deprecated, 7

    overloading, **36–40**

    overriding, 17–18, 36

min() method, 312–313

MIN_PRIORITY constant, 500

MIN_VALUE constant, 82

minimum integer values, 82

minimum settings for scroll bars, 142, 144

minimumSize() method

    in List, 180

    in TextArea, 67

    in TextField, 31

modal dialog boxes, 257

modifiers

    for data, 33

    for methods, **18–20**

modifiers member variable, 244, 282–283

mouse

    for graphics, **278–280**, *278–280*

    mouseClicked() for, **285–286**

    mouseEntered() for, **288–290**

    mouseExited() for, **290–293**

    MouseListener interface for, **281**

    mousePressed() for, **281–284**

    mouseReleased() for, **286–288**

mouseClicked() method

    in dauber, 303, 329, 476

    in imagesizer, 347

    in imap, 350, 354

    in mousedemo, **285–286**, 293–294

    in popup, 243, 246

    using, **285–286**

mousedemo class, 280–284

mousedemo.java program, **278–280**

    listing of, **293–294**

    mouseClicked events in, **285–286**

    mouseEntered events in, **288–290**

    mouseExited events in, **290–293**

    mousePressed events in, **281–284**

    mouseReleased events in, **286–288**

mouseDragged() method, 303, 322–324, 329, 467, 476

mouseEntered() method

    in dauber, 303, 329, 476

in imagesizer, 347
in imap, 350, 354
in mousedemo, **288–290**, 294
in popup, 243, 246
using, **288–290**
MouseEvent class, 282
mouseExited() method
in dauber, 303, 329, 476
in imagesizer, 347
in imap, 350, 354
in mousedemo, **290–293**
in popup, 243, 246
using, **290–293**
MouseListener interface, **281**
for drawing, **302–304**
for images, 342
MouseMotionListener interface, **302–304**
mouseMoved() method
in dauber, 303, 329, 476
for URLs, 353
mousePressed() method
in dauber, 303, 329, 466, 475
in drawing, **301**
in imagesizer, 343, 347
in imap, 350–354
in mousedemo, **282–284**, 294
in popup, 243–244, 246
using, **281–282**
mouseReleased() method
in dauber, **303–305**, 312, 329, 467–468, 476
in drawing, 301
in imagesizer, 344, 347
in imap, 350, 354
in mousedemo, **286–288**, 294
in popup, 243, 246
using, **286–288**
moveTo() method, 387–388

moving with transforms, **388–391**
multiple buttons
activating, **59–63**
creating, **57–58**, _59_
multiple inheritance, 47
multiple text lines, text areas for, **64–70**, _64_
multiple threads, **508–513**, _508–509_
for animation, **433–436**, _434_
naming, **511–513**
run() for, 441–443, **511–513**
sleep() for, **443–444**
start() for, **436**, **438–440**
stop() for, **440–441**

n

names
for constants, 189
for threads, **511–513**
native code interface, **7**
negation operator (!), 299, 351, 400
nested menus, 226, _227_, **233**
networking enhancements, **7**
new operator, **34–35**
NORM_PRIORITY constant, 500
north location in BorderLayout, 154
NOT operator (!), 299, 351, 400
numbers
localized support for, 6
in text fields, **82–85**
wrapped, 7
numbers class, 508–510, 514
numbers.java program, **508–510**
listing of, **514**
naming threads in, **511–513**

o

object-oriented programming (OOP), 14
classes in, **14–15**
inheritance in, **16–17**
libraries in, **15–16**
objects in, **14**
objects
constructors for, **35**
declaring and creating, 34–35
initializing, 35
in object-oriented programming, **14**
as return values, 18
serialization of, **6**
obsolete methods, 7
OOP (object-oriented programming), 14
classes in, **14–15**
inheritance in, **16–17**
libraries in, **15–16**
objects in, **14**
OpenConnection() method, 341
OpenStream() method, 341
operators, overloading, 405
option buttons. _See_ radio buttons
OR operation
for font styles, 412
operator for, 351
orientation of scroll bars, 142–143
origin in coordinate system, 19, _19_
ovals, **311–315**, _311_, _315_
overloading
methods, **36–40**
operators, 405

overriding
functions, 17–18
methods, 36

P

packages, **16**
page increments for scroll bars, 142–143
paint() method
in Box2D, 384, 387–392
in BoxCanvas, 432
in Canvas, 428
in dauber, 305–306, 313–320, 322, 324, 329–330, **467–473**, 476–478
in doublebuffer, 459–461, 463
in imagesizer, 344–345, 347
in imap, 349, 351, 354
overriding, 17–18
in scribbler, 398, 405–407, 410–416, 419
in spinner, 442–449, 507
Paint program, 350
paintBorder() method, 378
Panel class, 117
panels, **117**, *117–118*
animating, **484–489**
creating, **118–122**
listing for, **123**
in sandwich shop program, **126–137**, *130*
for scroll bars, 152–153
PARAM keyword, 24
param tags, 170, 523
parameters
for applets, 24, 169–170, **172**
for constructors, 35

in overloading methods, 36
for super classes, 201, 203
paramString() method
in Button, 45
in Checkbox, 96
in Choice, 171
in Dialog, 255
in Frame, 200
in Label, 76
in List, 180
in Menu, 211
in MenuItem, 213
in ScrollBar, 142
in ScrollPane, 163
in TextArea, 67
in TextField, 31
parentheses ()
for if statements, 50
for sensitive data, 521
parseInt() method, 82
parseLong() method, 82
parseNumbers() method, 82
passing parameters
to applets, 24, 169–170
to constructors, 35
pasting text fields, 40
PATH statement for JDK, 5
periods (.) for dot operator, 19, 38
pixels in coordinate system, 19
PLAIN constant, 406, 412
pluggable look and feels, 358
plus signs (+)
in increment operator, 324
for joining strings, 149
Point class, 301
point size of fonts, 406
polygons, 309
polylines, 309
popcalc class, 265, 273

popcalc.java program
creating popup calculator in, **263–272**, *263–264, 268, 271–272*
listing of, **273–276**
popup calculator, **263–276**, *263–264, 268, 271–272*
popup class, 240–242, 245–246
popup.java program
creating popup menus in, **240–245**, *240*
listing of, **245–246**
popup menus, **240–246**, *240*
PopupMenu class, **241**
port numbers for URLs, 341
position
of buttons, 361–362
of mouse events, 282
of points, 301, 303–304
of popup menus, 244
postfix operators, 324
preferredSize() method
in List, 180
in TextArea, 67
in TextField, 31
prefix operators, 324
printComponents() method, 163
printer class, 335–336
printer.java program, 336
printer() method, 519–521
printgraphics class, 332–336
printing graphics, **332–336**
printingThread class, 497
PrintJob class, 332
println() method, 497–498
priority of threads, **500–501**
private access modifier
for data, 33
for methods, 18

processActionEvent() method
in Button, 45
in List, 180
in MenuItem, 213
in TextField, 31
processAdjustmentEvent()
method, 142
processEvent() method
in Button, 45
in Checkbox, 96
in Choice, 171
in List, 180
in MenuItem, 213
in ScrollBar, 142
in TextField, 31
processItemEvent() method
in Checkbox, 97
in Choice, 171
in List, 180
programs, **2–3**, 3
properties of images, 340
protected access modifier
for data, 33
for methods, 18
protocols for URLs, 341
public access modifier
for data, 33
for methods, 18

r

radio buttons, **108**, *108*
with check boxes, **123–137**,
124–125, *130*
connecting to groups,
111–116
creating, **109–111**, *109*
panels for, **117–123**, *117–118*
radios class, 109–116

radios.java program, **115–116**
read-only text fields, 29
rectangles, **316–320**, *316–317*,
319, *321*
reference objects, 9
reflection, 7
REGEDIT tool, 406
regionMatches() method, 53
registry, fonts in, 406
REMAINDER constant, 192
remote methods, 6
remove() method
in Choice, 171
in Frame, 200
in List, 180
in Menu, 211
removeActionListener() method
in Button, 45
in JComboBox, 366
in List, 180
in MenuItem, 213
in TextField, 31
removeAdjustmentListener()
method, 142
removeAll() method
in Choice, 171
in List, 180
in Menu, 211
removeAllItems() method, 366
removeItem() method, 366
removeItemAt() method, 366
removeItemListener() method
in Checkbox, 97
in Choice, 171
in JComboBox, 366
in List, 180
removeNotify() method
in List, 180
in Menu, 211

removeWindowListener()
method, 200
repaint() method
in dauber, 305, 467
in imagesizer, 344
in scribbler, 402, 404
replace() method, 53
replaceItem() method, 180
replaceRange() method, 67
replaceText() method, 67
requestFocus() method, 400
resize() method, 23
resizing
applets, 23
dialog boxes, 258
frames, 200
windows, 203–204
resume() method, 437
resuming threads, 437, **501–505**,
501
return types, 18
RIGHT constant, 76
right mouse clicks, popup
menus for, **240–246**, *240*
RMI, enhancements for, 9
rotate() method, 386
rotating with transforms,
388–391
rounded rectangles, **318–320**,
319, *321*
rows
for JComboBox, 365–366
in scrolling lists, 179
in text areas, 67
ruler lines in HTML, 22–23
run() method
in carder, 484–488, 490–491
in doublebuffer, **458–463**
in numbers, **511–514**

in spinner, **441–443**, 445, 448, 499, 507

in synchronize, 517, 520, 522

in Thread, 438

Runnable interface, 438, **498–500**, 515

running applets, **11–13**

S

sameBaselineUpTo() method, 410

sameFile() method, 341

sandwich class, **128–136**

sandwich.java program, **124–125**, *124–125*

   ingredients panel for, **127–135**, *130*

   listing of, **135–137**

   menu panel for, **126–127**

scale() method, 386

screen flicker in animation, **445–449**

screen pixels in coordinate system, 19

scribbler class, 396–399, 401–405, 412, 415–420

scribbler.java program

   creating, **396–402**, *396*

   font setup in, **405–411**

   font size setting in, **412–417**

   keyboard input in, **403–405**

   listing of, **417–420**

scroll bars

   border layouts for, **151–161**, *151–152, 154*

   connecting to code, **145–150**

   creating, **140–143**, *140–141*

   installing, **143–145**

   listing for, **150–151**

panes for, **161–165**

in text areas, 67

ScrollBar class, **141–143**

scrollborder class, 152–153, 160–161

scrollborder.java program

   listing of, **160–161**

   scroll bar layout in, **152–169**

scroller class, 141, 143–145, 150–151

scroller.java program

   connecting scroll bars to code in, **145–150**

   creating scroll bars in, **141**

   installing scroll bars in, **143–145**

   listing of, **150–151**

scrolling lists

   listing for, **184**

   using, **177–183**, *177*

scrolllist class, **178**, **181–184**

scrolllist.java program

   creating scrolling lists in, **178**, **181–183**

   listing of, **184**

ScrollPane class, 140, **161–164**

scrpane class, 162, 164

scrpane.java program

   creating scroll bar panes in, **161–164**

   listing of, **165**

security

   in applets, **332–333**

   digital signatures for, **6**

   enhancements to, **8**

select() method

   in Choice, 171

   in List, 180

selectItemChanged() method, 366

selectWithKeyChar() method, 366

semicolons (;) for statements, 19

sensitive data, code blocks for, **521–523**

separators for menus, 226, *226*, **231–232**

serialization

   enhancements for, 9

   of objects, **6**

ServerSocket class, 7

set() method, 341

setActionCommand() method

   in Button, 45

   in JComboBox, 366

   in MenuItem, 213

setAlignment() method, 76

setBackground() method, 386

setBlockIncrement() method, 142

setBorderPainted() method, 378

setCheckboxGroup() method, 97

setClip() method, 310

setColor() method, 310, 460

setColumns() method

   in TextArea, 67

   in TextField, 31

setComposite() method, 386

setContents() method, 422

setContext() method, 438

setCurrent() method, 110

setCursor() method, 200, 290

setDaemon() method, 438

setEchoChar() method, 31

setEchoCharacter() method, 31

setEditable() method

   in JComboBox, 366–367

   in TextField, 29

setEditor() method, 366

setEnabled() method
  in JComboBox, 366
  in MenuItem, 213, 235
setExtent() method, 373
setFloatable() method, 378
setFont() method, 310
setHorizontalTextPosition()
  method, 361–362
setIconImage() method, 200
setInverted() method, 373
setKeySelectionManager()
  method, 366
setLabel() method
  in Button, 45
  in Checkbox, 97
  in MenuItem, 213
setLabelTable() method, 373
setLayout() method
  for GridLayout manager, 90
  in ScrollPane, 163
setLightWeightPopupEnabled()
  method, 366
setLineIncrement() method, 142
setLocation() method, 159, 427,
  431
setMajorTickSpacing() method,
  373
setMargin() method, 378
setMaximum() method
  in JSlider, 373
  in ScrollBar, 142
setMaximumRowCount()
  method, 366
setMenuBar() method, 200,
  216–217, 234
setMinimum() method
  in JSlider, 373
  in ScrollBar, 142
setMinorTickSpacing() method,
  373

setModal() method, 255
setModel() method
  in JComboBox, 366
  in JSlider, 373
setMultipleMode() method, 180
setMultipleSelections() method,
  180
setName() method, 438
setOrientation() method, 143
  in JSlider, 373
  in Scrollbar, 142
setPageIncrement() method, 143
setPaint() method, 386
setPaintLabels() method, 373
setPaintMode() method, 310
setPaintTicks() method, 373–374
setPriority() method, 438, 500
setRenderer() method, 366
setRenderingHints() method,
  386
setResizable() method
  in Dialog, 255
  in Frame, 200
setScrollPosition() method, 163
setSelectedCheckbox() method,
  110
setSelectedIndex() method, 367
setSelectedItem() method,
  367–368
setShortcut() method, 213
setSize() method
  in Dialog, 255
  for windows, 203–204
setSnapToTicks() method, 373
setState() method
  for check boxes, 97
  for menu items, 236
  for panel buttons, 133–135
setStroker() method, 386

setText() method
  for check boxes, 101–102
  in Label, 76
  in TextField, 32, 38
setTitle() method
  in Dialog, 255
  in Frame, 200
setToRotation() method, 390
setTransform() method, 386
setUI() method
  in JComboBox, 367
  in JToolBar, 378
setUIClassID() method, 374
setUnitIncrement() method, 143
SetURLStreamHandlerFactory()
  method, 341
setValue() method
  in JSlider, 374
  in Scrollbar, 143–144, 147
setValueIsAdjusting() method,
  374
setValues() method, 143–144
setVerticalTextPosition()
  method, 361–362
setVisible() method
  for dialog boxes, 255–256,
    259–260
  for windows, 204
setVisibleAmount() method, 143
setXORMode() method, 310,
  469–470
shapes, Java 2D package for,
  387–388
shear() method, 386
Short class, 7
short data type, 32
shortcuts for menu items, 213,
  240
show() method

with card layout manager, 483

in PopupMenu, 241, 244

showDocument() method, 352

showPopup() method, 367

signed applets, **6**

size

of applets, 23–24

of dialog boxes, 255, 258

of fonts, 406, **412–417**

of frames, 200

of images, 340

of scroll bar thumbs, 143–144

of scrolling lists, 179

of text areas, 67

of text fields, 31–32

size() method, 414

sleep() method, 438, **443–444**

sliders, **371–377**

Socket class, 7

SocketException class, 7

sources

of events, 49

of images, 340

south location in BorderLayout, 154

spacers with GridLayout manager, 89–90, *89*

spinner class, 434–436, 438, 444–445, 448–449, 499, 502, 506–507

spinner.java program, **434–435**

clearing animation display in, **445–447**

clip regions in, **447**

listing of version 1, **444–445**

listing of version 2, **448–449**

listing of version 3, **506–507**

priority of threads in, **500–501**

run() in, **441–443**

Runnable interface for, **498–500**

sleep() in, **443–444**

start() in, **436, 438–440**

stop() in, **440–441**

suspending and resuming threads in, **501–505**, *501*

start() method

in carder, 484, 490

in doublebuffer, 457, 462

for multi-threading, **436**

in spinner, **438–440**, 444, 448, 499, 507

in synchronize, 516, 518, 520, 522

in Thread, 438, 496

startsWith() method, 53

stateChanged() method, 377

stop() method

in carder, 484, 490

in doublebuffer, 457–458, 462

in spinner, **440–441**, 445, 448, 499, 507

in Thread, 438

streams, **7**

stretching controls, **187–189**, *188*

String class, **50–54**

strings

concatenating, 149

converting with numeric data, **82–85**

drawing, **19**, *19*

width of, **414**

stringWidth() method, 414

submenus, 226, 227, **233**

substring() method, 53

super() method, 201

suspend() method, 438, 503

suspending threads, 438, **501–505**, *501*

Swing package, **8**, 358

buttons in, **358–363**, *358–359, 362*

combo boxes in, **364–371**, *369–370*

sliders in, **371–377**

toolbars in, **377–384**, *382*

SwingButton class, **360–363**

SwingButton.Java program

for creating buttons, **359–362**, *362*

listing for, **363**

SwingCombo class, 364, **367–371**

SwingCombo.java program

for combo boxes, **364–370**, *369–370*

listing for, **370–371**

SwingSlider class, 371, **374–377**

SwingSlider.java program

listing for, **376–377**

for sliders, **371–376**

SwingToolbar class, 377–380, 382–383

SwingToolbar.java program

listing for, **382–384**

for toolbars, **377–382**, *382*

switch statements, **485–488**

synchronize class, 515, 518

synchronize.java program

listing of version 1, **518**

listing of version 2, **520–521**

listing of version 3, **522–523**

setting up thread synchronization in, **515–517**

synchronized keyword, 521

synchronized methods, 504

synchronizing threads

setting up for, **515–518**

synchronizing code blocks for, **521–523**
synchronizing functions for, **518–521**

t

t option with jar.exe, 523
tags in HTML, **21–25**
tear-off menus, 211
templates, classes as, 14–15
text
    with <applet> tags, 24
    centering, **414–417**, *417*
    clipboard for, **420–423**, *423*
    fonts for, **405–411**, *405*
    keyboard input for, **403–405**
    in labels, aligning, 76
    scribbler applet for, **396–402**, *396*
    width of, **414**
text areas, **64**, *64*
    activating, **67–69**
    creating, **65–67**
    listing for, **70**
text boxes. *See* text fields
text class, 30–31, 33–35, 40
text fields, 28, *28*
    adding, **36–40**, *37*
    clipboard for, 40
    constructors for, **35**
    declaring, **28–33**, *29–30*
    displaying, 36, *37*
    initializing, **33–34**
    listing for, **40**
    memory for, **34–35**
    numeric data in, **82–85**
text files for .java files, 4
text.java program, 30, **40**

TextArea class, **68–69**
TextField class, **30–32**
textPanel class, 152–153, 161
this keyword, **48**, 380–381
Thread class, **436–438**, 495–496
threads
    creating, **494–498**, *494*
    multiple. *See* multiple threads
    priority of, **500–501**
    Runnable interface for, **498–500**, 515
    suspending and resuming, **501–505**, *501*
    synchronizing. *See* synchronizing threads
threads class, 495–496
threads.java program, **494–498**, *494*
3D rectangles, **318**
thumbs in scroll bars, 143–144
time, localized support for, 6
<title> tag, 22
titles
    for dialog boxes, 255
    for frames, 200
toCharArray() method, 53
toExternalForm() method, 341
toggling settings, 399–400
toLowerCase() method, 53
toolbars, **377–384**, *382*
toString() method
    in CheckboxGroup, 110
    in Font, 410
    in FontMetrics, 414
    in Graphics, 310
    in JSlider, 374
    in String, 53
    in Thread, 438
    in URL, 341

toUpperCase() method, 53–54
transform() method, 388–389
transforms, **388–391**
translate() method
    in Graphics, 310
    in Graphics2D, 386
trim() method, 54
try keyword, 352, 443
two-dimensional arrays, 323
txtarea class, 65–66, 70
txtarea.java program
    activating text areas in, **67–69**
    creating text areas in, **65–66**
    listing of, **70**

u

unit increments for scroll bars, 142–143
update() method, 445–447, 449, 507
updateLabelUIs() method, 374
updateUI() method
    in JButton, 360
    in JComboBox, 367
    in JSlider, 374
    in JToolBar, 378
URL class, 340–341, 352–353
URLs of applets, 24

v

v option with jar.exe, 523
valueOf() method, 54, 83–84
values
    comparing, 312
    of scroll bars, 142–143, 147

variables
  assigning, 32
  for boolean flags, 297
  declaring, 83
  global, 32
  in object-oriented program-
    ming, 15
vertical bars (|) for OR opera-
  tor, 351
VERTICAL constant
  in GridBagConstraints, 189
  in Scrollbar, 143
vertical scroll bars, 140, *140–141*
visibility of scrolling lists, 180
visible amount of scroll bars,
  142–143
Void class, 7
void return type, 18, 34

W

wait states, 503
Web pages, **20–21**, *20*
weight of controls, **187–189**, *188*
weightx member variable, 187
weighty member variable, 187
west location in BorderLayout,
  154
while loops, 326
width
  of applets, 24
  of characters, **414**
  of images, 340
  of strings, **414**
width keyword, 24
windows
  adding menu bars to,
    216–217
  creating, **198–206**, *198–199*

for dialog boxes, 250, *250*
for menus, 207, 229
windows class, 198–200, 202
windows.java program
  handling windows in,
    198–205, *198–199*
  listing of, **206**
wrapped numbers, 7
writetext class, 421–423

X

x coordinates for points, 301,
  304
x direction weight for controls,
  187–189, *188*
x option with jar.exe, 523
XOR operation
  for animation, **468–473**
  operator for, 351

y

y coordinates for points, 301,
  304
y direction weight for controls,
  187–189, *188*
yield() method, 438

z

zipped files, **523–524**

SYBEX BOOKS ON THE WEB

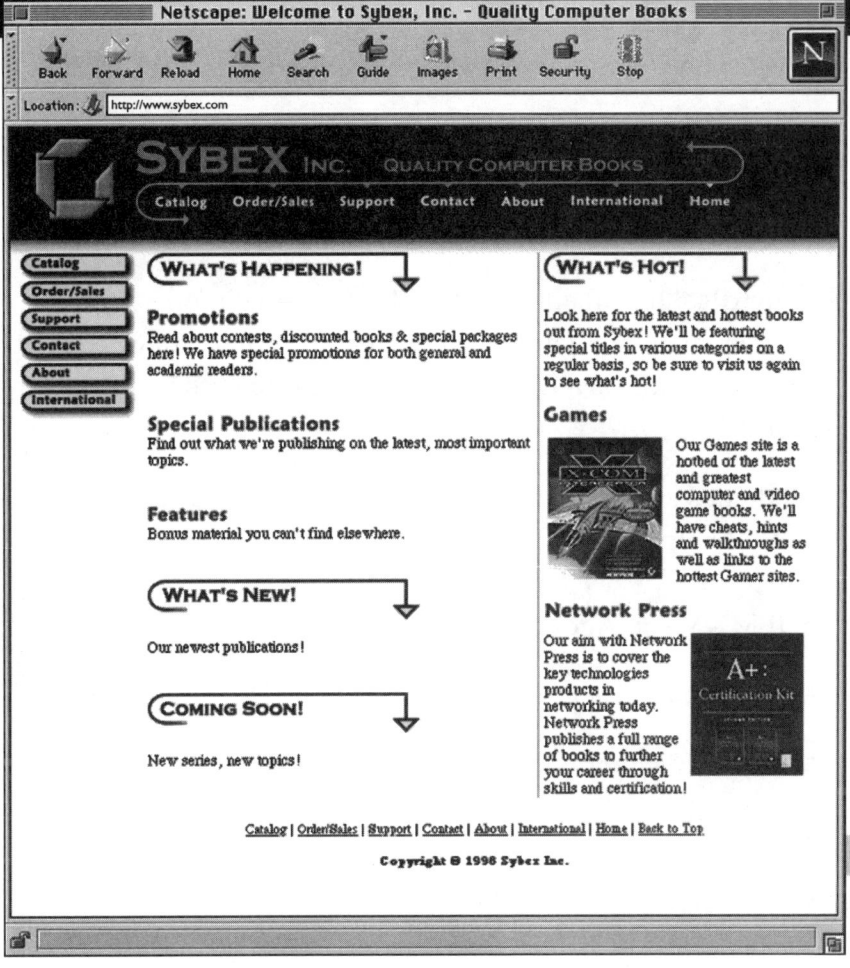

A t the dynamic and informative Sybex Web site, you can:

- · view our complete online catalog
- · preview a book you're interested in
- · access special book content

- · order books online at special discount prices
- · learn about Sybex

www.sybex.com

SYBEX Inc. • 1151 Marina Village Parkway, Alameda, CA 94501 • 510-523-8233

What's on the CD-ROM...

*J*ava 1.2 In Record Time's companion CD-ROM contains all the source code and executable files from the book, plus links to third-party tools to use with Java. Here's what you'll find:

- **Source code files:** Install all the examples from Skills 1 through 16 to your own machine. These files will enable you to follow along in the text and learn Java, without having to type in all the examples.

- **Links:** To demos and more information on these third-party tools that will help you get the most out of Java.

    - IBM's VisualAge

    - Marimba's Castanet

    - Interleaf's Jamba

    - InPrise's JBuilder

    - Penumbra's SuperMojo

    - Supercede's Supercede